the complete

A-Z
ECONOMICS

handbook

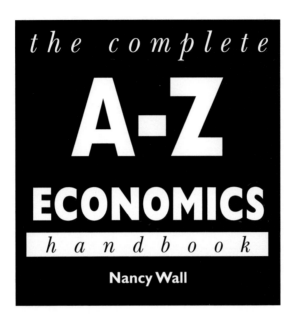

the complete
A-Z
ECONOMICS
handbook

Nancy Wall

Hodder & Stoughton

A MEMBER OF THE HODDER HEADLINE GROUP

British Library Cataloguing in Publication Data
A catalogue record for this title is available from The British Library

ISBN 0 340 789549

First published 2001
Impression number   10 9 8 7 6 5 4 3 2 1
Year   2005 2004 2003 2002 2001

Typeset by GreenGate Publishing Services, Tonbridge, Kent
Printed in Great Britain for Hodder & Stoughton Educational, a division of Hodder Headline Plc, 338 Euston Road, London NW1 3BH, by The Bath Press Ltd

HOW TO USE THIS BOOK

The *A–Z Economics Handbook* is an alphabetical textbook designed for ease of use. Each entry begins with a one-sentence definition. This helps the user to add precision to the completion of reports or case studies.

Entries are developed in line with the relative importance of the concept covered. *Monopsony* is covered in a few lines, whereas a central economics issue such as the *Phillips curve* or *economic growth* receives half a page. The latter would provide sufficient material to enrich an essay. Numerate topics are developed through the use of worked examples. All formulae are set out explicitly.

The study of economics can be developed further by making use of the cross-referenced entries. For example the entry for *unemployment* refers the reader to *demand deficiency* and *structural unemployment*. Cross-referenced entries are identified through the use of italics. Therefore essay or project writing should benefit from following the logical pathway indicated by italicised entries.

Economics students have always had difficulties with the language of the subject. This stems from several factors:

- economics has its own jargon
- the media and politicians use or invent new terms (such as 'private finance initiative'), some of which prove temporary, while others need assimilating into course content
- textbooks recommended by the exam boards use technical terms in different ways.

The *A–Z Economics Handbook* is a glossary providing a single solution to these problems. Where terms have more than one meaning, both are explained. In addition, the entries have enough detail to make the book a valuable reference/revision companion. It provides full coverage of the new GCE A level specifications.

To aid the revision process, carefully selected lists are provided at the back of the book. Those facing examinations can use the lists to make the best use of the *Handbook* during their revision time. The revision recommendations are split into modules, for ease of use. The section on examiners' terms provides an explanation of the trigger words used on exam papers, such as 'analyse', 'discuss' and 'evaluate'.

This *Handbook* will help anyone who wants to understand current events in the economy. Many terms that are used in the financial media are fully explained so that their significance will become clearer. We hope that, as well as providing an invaluable resource for A level Economics, this *Handbook* will be used more widely by people with an interest in the general field.

Nancy Wall

Newcastle-under-Lyme College
Staffordshire

ACKNOWLEDGEMENTS

In compiling this dictionary, I had help from a huge range of sources. Particular thanks are due to Peter Maunder, who advised on matters relating to the Edexcel specifications. Colin Bamford provided valuable clarification of OCR requirements. David Wall gave advice on issues relating to trade and developing countries, as well as being generally very patient with the whole process of writing.

I am much indebted to Ian Marcousé and to Tim Gregson Williams, who created the series and gave much help.

Researching, writing and editing a book of this size requires the occasional willingness to sacrifice technical accuracy in favour of clarity. A considerable amount of time went into checking the entries, but if any mistakes have slipped through, the author apologises and accepts full responsibility.

Nancy Wall

A

ability to pay: the principle by which people should be taxed according to the level of their incomes. People need a minimum income to cover the basic costs of food, clothing and shelter. So people on very low incomes are usually not taxed directly, i.e. by income tax. This principle is reflected in the *personal allowance*, which is not taxed. In another context, ability to pay is used as a basis for deciding whether people have access to benefits in kind, such as free school meals or certain social services.

abnormal profit: see *supernormal profit*.

absolute advantage: a country has an absolute advantage in trade in a particular good with another country if it can produce that good using fewer real resources. This means that its costs will usually be lower in money terms. For example, Jamaica has an absolute advantage over the UK in the production of bananas because its climate is suited to banana production.

absolute poverty: a standard of living which fails to provide basic necessities of life. Poverty may also be relative, in the sense that some people have very much less income than others, and may therefore be unable to buy the things which are regarded as necessary in that society. Poverty can therefore be defined in different ways in different societies: a poor person in the UK will usually have a higher standard of living than a poor person in India.

Some international organisations have defined poverty as having to live on less than $1 per day. Low income countries are defined by the *World Bank* as those with annual income of less than US$755 per head.

Selected low income countries

	Income per head, 1999, US$	% of population with less than $1 a day
Bangladesh	370	29
Ethiopia	100	31
Honduras	760	41
India	450	44
Indonesia	580	15
Kenya	360	27
Mongolia	350	14
Nigeria	310	70
Rwanda	250	36

Source: World Bank, World Development Report, 2000

NB The percentage living on less than $1 a day is calculated using purchasing power parity figures; income per head uses current exchange rates.

ACAS: see *Advisory, Conciliation and Arbitration Service*.

accelerator: the relationship between *investment* and the rate of change of output. The theory is that investment will be determined not by the level of output but by the rate at which it changes. If output grows faster than before, the rate at which new productive capacity is created will need to increase. In contrast, if output stabilises, no additional investment will be needed, other than that needed to replace worn-out machines. So investment will actually fall. In short, the accelerator relationship causes investment to fluctuate much more than output.

accelerator/multiplier model: the theory that the *accelerator* and the *multiplier* interact to bring about cyclical changes in the economy. An increase in investment during the upswing of the business cycle will have a multiplier effect, generating a larger increase in income. As the economy approaches full capacity and real growth slows, the accelerator theory predicts that investment needs will fall, leading to a downturn. The fall in injections will have a downward multiplier effect, until such time as the need for replacement investment again causes investment to grow. At that point the cycle repeats itself.

accountability refers to the way in which people may be required to explain their decisions in both the *private sector* and the *public sector*. An organisation in which responsibilities have been clearly defined will identify the people who are accountable for the various actions of that organisation. If mistakes have been made, individuals may be held responsible. In the public sector, particular organisations or people may be answerable to a higher authority such as a minister or the House of Commons. The government is accountable to Parliament and ultimately to the electorate.

accounts: a statement of any financial activity, most usually a summary in money terms of all the activities of a business. This will be produced for a certain period, most often one year, but also quarterly or half-yearly. *Public limited companies* are required by law to produce a *balance sheet*, a *profit and loss account* and a *cash-flow statement*.

accumulated profit is the total of profits which have been kept in reserve from previous years and ploughed back into the company rather than being distributed to shareholders. These profits are important to the business as a source of funds for investment in new production capacity.

acid rain occurs when emissions of pollution from industrial activities are blown away but then absorbed into rain. This may fall in areas far removed from the original source of the pollution, so that acid rain becomes an international problem. Lakes have been badly affected in parts of Scandinavia because they are downwind from industrial areas in the UK and other parts of Europe.

ACP states are the African, Caribbean and Pacific states which had colonial links with member countries of the European Union. To some extent they have been able to negotiate favourable trading arrangements with the EU. India is not included despite its ex-colonial status.

acquisitions: a term used to refer to firms which have been or are being taken over. (See also *mergers, take-overs* and *Competition Commission*.)

activism refers to the process of macro-economic intervention using fiscal and monetary policies to control the economy. It implies willingness to increase spending at times when there is high unemployment, with a view to raising the rate of economic growth. It is particularly associated with the Keynesian policies of the 1950s and 1960s. The relevant policies are sometimes described as *interventionist policies*.

activity rates: see *participation rates*.

adaptive expectations: the idea that people's expectations about the future will be affected by their observations about the present. For example, if the rate of *inflation* is increasing, then expectations about future inflation will also tend to increase over a period of time. This could apply to other variables such as *unemployment*.

added value refers to the value added to an input by a business, as it creates its final output. (See also *value added*.) It can be calculated by subtracting the cost of all the material inputs from the value of output. It reflects the value of the services of land, labour, capital and entrepreneurship which have been used in the process of production.

adjustable peg: a type of exchange rate system in which the value of the exchange rate is kept at or close to a fixed parity, but the government can change that parity if the exchange rate appears to be permanently over- or under-valued. Broadly, this was the system in use all over the world from 1948 until 1971, the *Bretton Woods* system. Normally fixed parities were changed after consultation with trading partners.

administration: when a business is unable to pay its debts, the courts may bring in an administrator who will try to restructure the company in order to enable it to carry on trading. Sometimes a part of the business may be sold or closed down. If these measures do not bring the business back to profitability, it may go into *liquidation*.

administrative costs are part of *fixed costs*.

ad-valorem tax: a tax which is charged as a proportion of the price. The tax will be set as a percentage of the price charged by the retailer, and then included in the final price to the customer. A good example is VAT (*Value Added Tax*).

advances: banks use the term 'advances to customers' to describe their loans and overdrafts. These are usually the most profitable part of the bank's activities but they are also likely to be the most risky. The bank may require some kind of collateral as security for the loan. For example, land or buildings can be collateral for a business loan or a house for a personal loan. *Shares* can also be used in this way.

advertising involves paying for activities which will help to sell products. Many different media may be used including radio and TV, newspapers and magazines, billboards, catalogues and websites, to name just a few. The objective is to shift the *demand curve* to the right, so that at any given price more will be sold than before the advertising campaign. The effect is to engineer a change in consumer tastes or fashions.

Though many different types of firms advertise, advertising spending is most likely to be high when there is intense *non-price competition*, as often happens under *oligopoly*.

advertising costs: the high cost of national advertising can shift the average total cost curve for the firm upwards. However, if the advertising is successful, the firm may be able to reap *economies of scale* such that the amount of average total cost is actually less.

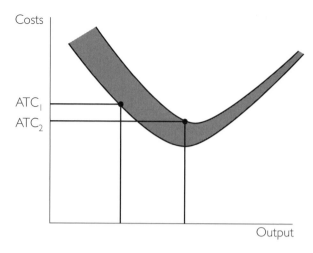

Advertising increases sales; economies of scale lead to lower average cost

Advisory, Conciliation and Arbitration Service (ACAS) was set up in 1975 to settle or help to prevent industrial disputes. Help may be sought by individuals, businesses or trade unions in both small and large cases.

after-sales service is often an important part of the product itself and can be seen as a *complement* to the item actually sold. The most obvious example occurs with a new car or machine, which will usually be guaranteed for a certain period, with spares, repairs and advice made available through a local agent. After-sales service may be an important part of the package which makes the product competitive and attractive to potential consumers.

age-earnings profile: on average, there is a process by which earnings start relatively low at the beginning of the working life, peak in middle age and then decline. In many occupations, young people start out with very little experience and become progressively more useful to their employers as they become trained and experienced. Their earnings reflect this. As they become older, the benefits of increasing experience become less marked and are usually outweighed by the disadvantages of becoming older. So their earnings gradually fall somewhat.

ageing population occurs where people are living longer and therefore the average age of the population is rising. Japan and a number of European countries have rapidly ageing populations. The UK population is ageing more slowly. The economic implications include the necessity of providing more health care and pensions. Also, there may be problems arising as the ratio of the working population to the *dependent population* becomes lower. A larger transfer from the *working population* to the retired population may become necessary. The pressures created by this trend can lead to rethinking of pension policies.

ageism is discrimination in the labour market against people who are older. It is legal in the UK but not in the US. It is less likely to be a problem where labour is scarce or there are skill shortages.

aggregate demand refers to the total demand for goods and services from all sources in the economy. It includes:

- consumer spending
- *investment* by firms in plant, machinery and stocks
- government spending
- the net effect of *international trade*, i.e. exports minus imports.

An increase in aggregate demand may lead to an increase in output provided there is underutilised productive capacity in the economy. If there is no spare capacity, and the economy is producing its maximum potential output, rising demand is likely to lead to inflation. (See also *circular flow of national income*.)

The level of aggregate demand will to a large extent therefore determine the level of activity in the economy. A low level of aggregate demand is likely to be associated with high levels of unemployment. This situation is usually described as *cyclical unemployment* or *demand deficiency unemployment*. It is usually accompanied by a high level of business failures and sometimes also by declining real incomes. Rising levels of aggregate demand will increase profitability, encouraging firms to increase output and take on more labour. This will tend to have a *multiplier* effect on the economy.

Aggregate demand is affected by changes in all its constituent components.

- A fall in savings can lead to an increase in consumption and vice versa.
- Changes in interest rates affect levels of investment.
- Tax changes affect disposable incomes and therefore both consumption and investment. Government expenditure changes feed directly into the level of aggregate demand.
- Rising imports reduce demand for domestically produced goods and services. Export levels have a direct effect.

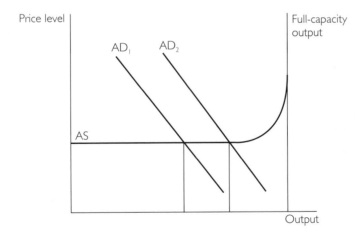

An increase in aggregate demand leads to increased output if there is underutilised productive capacity in the economy.

aggregate demand curve: *aggregate demand* can be graphed by plotting output on the horizontal axis and the price level on the vertical axis. It will be downward sloping because lower prices will allow higher levels of output demanded for any given income level. In combination with the *aggregate supply curve*, it can be used to analyse macro-economic events.

aggregate demand shock: any sudden change in a component of aggregate demand which has a noticeable effect on the economy. For example, a change in interest rates may rapidly affect both consumer and investment demand, so that there is a shift in the aggregate demand curve.

aggregate supply: the total of all goods and services produced in the economy. In the short run, aggregate supply may increase in response to rising *aggregate demand*. In the long run, it can increase only if more resources become available (e.g. oil) or if there are improvements in technology or if efficiency is increased in some other way. (See also *full-capacity output*.)

In the long run, aggregate supply has increased in the UK by a little over 2% per year. This is the long-run trend rate of growth, made possible by investment and improved technologies. Better, more efficient management can also help. These are sometimes associated with increases in *human capital* – the expertise available in the economy.

Long-run aggregate supply is shown diagrammatically as a vertical line which shifts to the right as the capacity of the economy to supply goods and services increases. At any one time the total amount which can be supplied is fixed, being determined by the quantity of resources available to produce. As the stock of capital increases and people acquire more knowledge and skills, the line shifts outwards, increasing full capacity output. The result will be a process of economic growth, provided demand is increasing to absorb all the goods and services which can now be produced. The increased quantity of resources will make it easier to achieve rising standards of living and to avoid inflationary pressures.

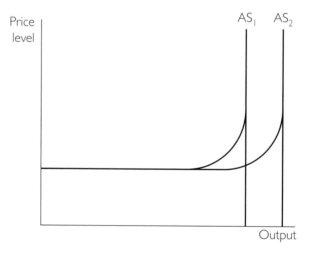

Rising aggregate supply

aggregate supply curves show aggregate supply diagrammatically. Short and long-run *aggregate supply* can be distinguished. In the short run, the aggregate supply curve slopes upwards because an increase in *aggregate demand* will raise profits and encourage producers to expand. However, unless there are ample supplies of under-utilised labour and capital, prices will tend to rise in the process. (See diagram above.) In the long run, aggregate supply is determined by the stock of resources, land, labour and capital. So the long-run aggregate supply curve is a vertical line. This can only be shifted outwards by an increase in the stock of resources, e.g. through investment in plant, machinery, development of new technologies or education and training. These kinds of changes take time.

aggregate supply shock: a sharp change in the capacity of the economy to supply goods and services. This may occur if there is a natural disaster, a war, or a sudden change in the price of an important commodity such as oil. These kinds of events will cause the *aggregate supply curve* to shift.

agricultural policies: many governments intervene in some way in agricultural markets. In developed countries, the objective is to raise farm incomes, usually by keeping prices above the world market price, and perhaps to keep out cheap imports. This tends to raise food prices to consumers. Within the EU, most policy decisions are embodied in the *Common Agricultural Policy.*

Developing countries sometimes intervene more directly, sometimes trying to keep prices down so that food will be cheap. These interventions tend to distort markets and can lead to both shortages and surpluses.

AGM: see *annual general meeting.*

aid is provided by wealthier developed countries to countries with low per capita incomes. It includes payments made by charities. However, the political aspects of foreign aid can be extremely complex. It may be given as a grant or a loan, and loans may be at market or at concessional rates of interest. Some kinds of aid are more effective in meeting poor countries' needs than others. Much depends on how the money is spent. Spending on some major construction projects such as dams has attracted criticism because it has been unsuited to the long-term needs of the country concerned. There are serious controversies surrounding much aid spending. Some of the money which is classed as aid is spent on defence.

Many developing countries have tried to negotiate larger aid donations. Their efforts have not been successful: over the years, aid payments have tended to fall as a percentage of the donor countries' GDPs. Some developing country governments have instead tried to improve access to developed country markets through trade negotiations.

Aid remains an important source of finance, particularly for spending which does not have an easily measured rate of return, such as education, and disaster relief. Current debates include proposals to withhold aid where governments are known to be particularly corrupt. (See also *foreign aid.*)

air pollution is the discharge of waste products into the air. The main sources are vehicle exhausts, power stations and industrial processes.

allocation of resources: economic decisions about the uses which should be made of land, labour and capital leading to an overall allocation of resources, which generally matches the pattern of consumer demand. Consumer demand creates profitable opportunities for *entrepreneurs* to organise inputs of *factors of production* so as to meet that demand. In this way the allocation of resources responds to the pattern of demand exhibited by consumers. This is known as *consumer sovereignty*. However, the idea of the allocation of resources can be applied much more widely to a range of decisions which may be taken by individuals or by governments. People decide how to allocate their own resources when they choose between work and leisure or whether to save more or consume more. Governments make resource allocation decisions when they consider making changes to different categories of spending: they may consider whether to allocate more towards defence or education or towards health care or unemployment benefit.

It is not always the case that the allocation of resources conforms to the pattern of consumer demand. Firms and governments can sometimes control certain aspects of the allocation of resources through monopoly power or through administrative decisions. Where this happens, there is said to be a distortion of the allocation of resources so that it does not accurately reflect consumer preferences.

allocative efficiency describes the extent to which the *allocation of resources* matches consumer preferences. The most efficient allocation of resources will be the one which fits the genuine needs and wants of consumers most closely. An economy can move closer to allocative efficiency when ways are found to help firms to respond effectively to consumer demand. For example, in a *centrally planned economy* such as China's, some producers may be bound by administrative decisions and will not necessarily be able to produce the type of goods which consumers want most. The transitional economies, such as Hungary and Poland which have moved a long way towards being market economies, have become more allocatively efficient because enterprises producing items which consumers do not want will eventually go out of business. Government controls of any kind are liable to reduce the responsiveness of markets to consumer demand. However, they may be able to protect consumers from the market power of large firms.

alpha stocks are the most frequently traded shares on the *Stock Exchange Automated Quotations system (SEAQ)*.

animal spirits is the term used by J M Keynes to describe the way in which many investment decisions are taken. Often the crucial deciding factor will be expectations about the future performance of the economy. This can be governed by careful reasoning, but can also be affected by a kind of herd instinct. When in general business expectations are optimistic, many investors take risks which they would not take if expectations were gloomy. Once they see others doing this they become more likely themselves to take risks. (See also *self-fulfilling prophecy*.)

Annual Abstract of Statistics is an annual publication containing a wide variety of useful statistics. It comes from the Office of National Statistics and includes population, social, legal, employment, production, income and price data as well as some industry-specific figures.

annual general meeting (AGM): a meeting held each year by public and sometimes also private limited companies to which all shareholders are invited. They are expected to:

- approve the year's accounts
- elect directors
- question the company chairman.

However, some AGMs can be acrimonious affairs as shareholders hold directors accountable for company policies.

annualised hours agreements are used when the firm wants to employ people on a flexible basis. They will be hired for a certain number of hours' work each year and then employed when they are needed. This can help firms which experience seasonal fluctuations as longer hours can be worked without the use of overtime payments. This type of agreement has become more common as competition in both product and labour markets has led to contracts which allow *flexible working*.

annual report and accounts: the report which all companies must send to their shareholders and to Companies House each year. They include: a *balance sheet*, a *profit and loss account*, a *cash-flow statement*, a *directors' report* and an *auditor's report*.

anticipated inflation: expected *inflation*, which has rather different consequences from unanticipated inflation. People will build their inflation expectations into their wage demands. In this way anticipated inflation may become self-perpetuating.

anti-competitive activities: firms which have a degree of *monopoly* power in their markets may be able to take steps which give them some control over the prices they charge and the quantity sold. They may also be able to damage the chances of competing producers. For example, two dominant producers may agree to share the market, one selling in the North, say, and one in the South. In this way they avoid competing with each other. Or a firm may insist on an exclusive dealership arrangement with its distributors.

The main categories of anti-competitive activities include:

- *cartels*, where a group of businesses agree a marketing strategy which avoids strong competition
- *market sharing agreements*, in which competing firms agree not to sell in each other's territory
- *price fixing* agreements which avoid competing on price.

Anti-competitive activities are usually illegal under competition legislation. However, the *Office of Fair Trading* and the *Competition Commission* sometimes allow them if there are compelling reasons.

anti-dumping measures are designed to prevent other countries from selling their products at a price lower than their costs of production. Despite *trade liberalisation*, it is still legal under certain circumstances for governments to use import controls to exclude dumped imports. Although these will be very cheap and competitive, they may disrupt the market for domestic producers. The *WTO* has strict rules about the use of anti-dumping measures but it is still difficult to decide exactly when dumping has taken place because it is hard to isolate genuine costs of production. So some economists suspect that dumping is used by governments as an excuse to exclude cheap imports.

antitrust laws are the laws in the USA which control the growth of large businesses in order to prevent monopoly power from developing.

applied economics involves the use of economic theories to analyse real world situations.

appraisal is used as a management tool to ensure that employees are reaching the standards required of them. It provides an opportunity for discussion of the employee's situation as well as a review of targets and performance.

appreciation occurs when the value of something rises. *Capital appreciation* means a rise in the value of an asset such as a factory building or land. *Currency appreciation* means a rise in the exchange rate such that the same amount of one currency will buy more than before of another. This means that import prices will be lower and exports will lose some competitiveness.

apprenticeship: this used to be the main way to acquire craft skills and a full understanding of a particular job. Typically apprentices were based in the work-place, with day release to the local college. As employment in manufacturing dropped during the 1980s, apprenticeships became very few in number. Training became much less uniform in approach, with new technologies and *multi-skilling* affecting the outcome. Modern apprenticeships have developed and to some extent fill the gap.

appropriate technology is a term applied to the production method which has the lowest costs in the particular situation under discussion. Where capital is rela-tively cheap and labour costs are high, a *capital intensive* technology will be the most appropriate. This would apply to agricultural activities in developed countries. Where labour is cheap, it is inappropriate to use capital intensive methods, but small-scale equipment may still increase *productivity* and incomes. For example, a wheelbarrow may have an advantage over a basket carried on the head. (See also *intermediate technology*.)

a priori is a Latin term meaning from first principles. It will usually be used in rela-tion to a theoretical argument which cannot be derived directly from observation of the real world but relies on logical connections.

arbitrage involves buying in one market and selling at a higher price in another. It prevents prices from diverging in different markets by more than the *transaction costs*.

For example, for many years dealers bought antiques in the UK and shipped them to the Netherlands, where prices were higher. Similarly, when a *currency* is losing value in one country as the *exchange rate* falls, dealers will buy it and sell it again in a coun-try where the exchange rate is higher. This tends to even out exchange rates so that they are normally very similar in different countries.

arbitration: where there is a dispute which cannot easily be settled by the parties concerned, they may choose a process of arbitration in preference to legal or indus-trial action which would have high costs to both sides. Arbitration means that both sides accept a mediator who will listen to the arguments and make a decision. This decision can be legally binding if both sides have agreed. (See also *conciliation, Advisory, Conciliation and Arbitration Service*.)

arithmetic mean: a measure of average value. It is calculated by adding the values of all the observations in the series and dividing by the total number of observations.

$$\text{FORMULA:} \quad \frac{\text{Sum of all observations}}{\text{Number of observations}}$$

The mean is a useful measure provided there are few extreme observations. In this situation the *median* may be more useful. For example, average income data may be misleading if it is distorted by some very high incomes.

ARR: see *average rate of return*.

Asian Development Bank exists to provide development finance for developing countries in Asia and the Pacific. Its affiliate, the Asian Development Fund, provides loans at concessional rates of interest to poorer countries in the region.

Asian financial crisis: in 1997, Thailand and Korea encountered serious problems with loss of confidence in their banking systems. There followed very rapid selling of their *currencies* and sharp falls on their *stock exchanges*. This led quickly to depressed trading conditions and similar problems in other countries including Japan and Indonesia. The fall in Asian exchange rates generally made UK exports uncompetitive and the loss of a large part of their export markets affected some UK businesses quite seriously. Confidence was gradually restored and by 1999 the problems were much reduced, but the crisis interrupted the usually high *economic growth* rates in the affected countries.

During the crisis, it was suggested that the countries concerned should undertake various structural reforms in order to prevent a re-occurrence. Time will tell whether these have been made effectively.

Asian tigers: see *tiger economies*.

assembly line: manufacture of complex products may be designed as a sequence of work stations, connected by conveyor systems, which take the product along a line of employees, each having a different part to play in the production process. Originally, assembly lines took advantage of the opportunities created by a *division of labour*, so that each person on the line had a single task to accomplish. Assembly lines have been much modified in recent years to get around two problems: difficulty in achieving good quality control and the boredom associated with repetitive tasks.

asset: anything of value which can be made to yield benefits. Financial assets include cash, shares, savings, insurance policies, etc. Real assets include property and machinery.

In accounting terms, assets are balanced against liabilities in the *balance sheet*. Liabilities are all the payments that the business is liable to have to make in the future. (See also *intangible assets*.)

asset markets are the markets where various different types of *assets* are traded. The stock exchange is a physical location where shares can be traded. The foreign exchange market, on the other hand, has no physical location but is just as much a market, as is the property market.

asset prices: most assets can be bought and sold in the market place. Prices can vary very sharply because they are influenced by expectations about what will happen to them in the future. For example, if people expect property prices to rise, they may rush to buy, thus driving up prices. (This is known as a *self-fulfilling prophecy*.) Similarly, share prices are affected by business optimism or the lack of it and the prospect of gains and losses can cause rapid buying and selling with price fluctuations.

asset stripping occurs when the value of the individual parts of the firm are greater in total than the value of the business as a whole. It may happen after a *merger* or *take-over*, when the new owners want to rationalise production and avoid duplication of some of their facilities. It may occur if a part of the business has been run rather inefficiently and could be more profitable under different ownership. The polite term for asset stripping is corporate restructuring, which has fewer overtones of destruction.

assisted areas are part of the government's *regional policy*. Firms considering locating or expanding there become eligible for various grants and other benefits. These incentives apply to both the manufacturing and the service sectors. Certain areas are designated as Tier 1 which qualifies for the highest levels of help. Others come into Tier 2, which will get some help but not as much.

The objective of this policy is to reduce the *unemployment* which has been caused by the decline of many traditional industries such as coal and steel. In recent years the extent of the assisted areas has been reduced, as has the real value of the concessions and grants made available. At times, the policy has been crucial in attracting *foreign direct investment*, e.g. the Nissan plant in Sunderland. There is often competition between assisted areas here and abroad to attract particular companies.

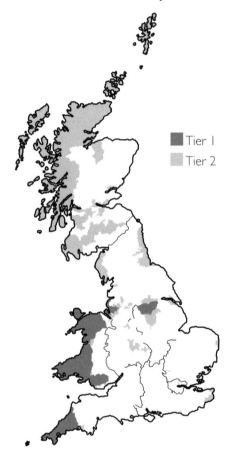

Tier 1
Tier 2

assumptions are important in economic theory because they make it possible to simplify the basis for the economic analysis. *Economic models* are based on assumptions about behaviour. For example, the theory of the firm is to a large extent based on the assumption that the firm's objective is to maximise profits. This may be regarded as a useful approximation even though in reality business objectives are often somewhat more complex.

asymmetric information refers to the fact that decision takers usually do not all have the same information. People who are taking business decisions cannot know what other businesses are planning in the same market. Some kinds of information are private. Everyone is aware that the information they have is different from the information others have, but they cannot know what others know or do not know.

auction is a situation in which potential buyers bid against one another openly until the highest bidder gets the sale. It is used to organise a sale when the *market clearing* price of the item concerned is uncertain. Common examples include properties with unique features, antiques and live farm animals.

audit: company law requires that accounts be checked by independent auditors who will uncover any inconsistencies or irregularities. Internal bookkeeping will be checked to ensure that all transactions have been accurately recorded. An audit should ensure that accounting conventions have been followed and that there has been no fraud. However, auditors are paid by the company and may not always be entirely independent in their view.

Austrian School: Austrian economists have been associated since the 19th century with a strong commitment to a free market determined allocation of resources. In this century these ideas have been associated particularly with the work of Friedrich von Hayek, who left Austria in the 1930s to work at the London School of Economics and later at the University of Chicago. His view was that governments could not make decisions which would lead to an efficient allocation of resources because they would always lack the necessary information. Further, in a planned economy, people would lack the incentive to take risks. It is the prospect of large personal gains that stimulates entrepreneurs to make decisions which lead to efficient use of scarce resources.

automatic fiscal policy: see *automatic stabilisers.*

automatic stabilisers: *fiscal policies* which work to reduce fluctuations in income over the course of the *trade cycle* without needing adjustment at the time. For example, spending on unemployment benefits automatically rises with the level of unemployment. So during *recession*, government spending will rise as firms contract employment. The extra spending helps to compensate for the reduction in earned income. Consumption spending will fall more slowly than it otherwise would have done if the unemployed had lost all their income at once.

The other important automatic stabiliser is *income tax.* As incomes rise in the *boom* phase of the trade cycle, income tax receipts rise more than proportionately because income tax is progressive. Similarly, if incomes are falling during a recession, tax receipts will fall more than proportionately. In this way the tax system takes more spending power out of the economy in a boom than it does in a recession, so helping to counteract the fluctuations in aggregate demand and to diminish their impact.

automation means using machines to produce, rather than people. Increasingly, machinery is computer controlled although people are still needed to design, organise and monitor the production process.

average cost is the total cost divided by the number of units produced. It is also known as *unit cost.*

FORMULA: average costs = $\dfrac{\text{total cost}}{\text{units of output}}$

Worked example:

A firm buys materials at 50p per unit and spends £1 000 on weekly fixed costs and labour; the production rate is 4 000 per week.

So average costs are: $\dfrac{(£0.5 \times 4\,000) + £1\,000}{4\,000} = 75p$

Average costs vary according to the level of output. In general they fall at first as output is increased, because the fixed costs are being spread across a larger quantity of output. This can be seen in the diagram below.

Average costs may also fall because there are *economies of scale* to be reaped. At higher levels of output it may be more efficient to use larger machines and invest in different technologies. This can cause costs to fall considerably at higher levels of output.

If levels of output continue to increase, then it is possible that there will be *diseconomies of scale*. These will cause average costs to rise with output. These may possibly be caused by the difficulties of communication in a large organisation.

These two contrasting trends give the textbook average total cost curve its characteristic U-shape. However, in practice there may be a large range of possible outputs at which average costs are more or less constant. This gives the curve a long flat bottom.

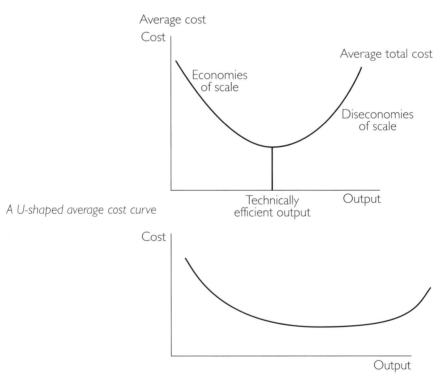

A U-shaped average cost curve

Long-run average cost curve with a range of efficient outputs

The minimum average cost is associated with *technical efficiency*. When all resources are being used as efficiently as possible, it follows that average costs will be at a minimum.

average cost pricing: setting a price so that it just covers the average cost, which allows the organisation to break-even. This may not be the most profitable price, so firms in the private sector are rather unlikely to use this strategy. However, it can make sense for non-profit making organisations or for government agencies.

average fixed costs are the costs of all inputs which cannot be changed in the short run, per unit of output. Land and capital will be important fixed costs, but they may also include the cost of key employees. Fixed costs fall as output increases in the short run because the costs are spread between more units of output.

FORMULA: $\quad$ average fixed costs $= \dfrac{\text{total fixed costs}}{\text{units of output}}$

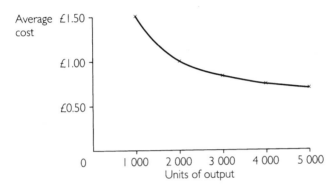

Average fixed costs falling as output rises

In the long run average fixed costs can change as machines are replaced and new technologies are adopted. They may rise if more capital intensive production methods are used. They may rise or fall under the impact of new technologies.

average propensity to consume: that proportion of income which people choose to allocate towards consumption spending.

average propensity to import: the average proportion of total income which is spent on imports. In an open economy, the average propensity to import is quite high, perhaps 30% or 40%.

average propensity to save: the average proportion of total income which is saved. This will tend to be higher in rich developed countries than it is in very poor countries.

average rate of return (ARR): a measure of profitability which can be used to assess the relative merits of alternative investment projects. It relates the average annual profit to the amount spent on the investment. This can then be compared with current interest rates.

FORMULA: $\quad \dfrac{\text{total profit over project life} \div \text{number of years}}{\text{capital outlay on project}} \times 100$

It is not enough to be able to cover the interest rate alone. The investment decision should depend on whether the intended project is the most profitable available given the risks involved.

average revenue: total revenue derived from sales divided by the number of units sold.

average tax rates: the average percentage of total income which is paid in taxes. If the tax system is progressive, i.e. the proportion paid rises as income rises, the average rate of tax will be lower than the marginal rate of tax.

average variable costs are the costs of variable factors of production such as labour, raw materials and components. In the short run they may rise as output rises, because efforts to produce more without increasing the amount of capital (a fixed factor) may make production less efficient.

$$\text{FORMULA:} \quad \text{average variable costs} = \frac{\text{total variable costs}}{\text{units of output}}$$

B

backward integration is the extension of the firm's activities to include production of inputs which were previously bought in from outside. If Birds Eye bought farms on which to grow peas, instead of buying the peas from independent farmers, that would be backward integration. The objective could be to ensure regular supplies of a crucial input.

backward sloping supply curve of labour: initially, increases in pay encourage people to work longer hours. However, beyond a certain level, people will not necessarily be induced to work more and may prefer to work less. Effectively, they are choosing to use their increased incomes to consume more leisure. This means that the curve showing how much labour they are willing to supply will bend backwards.

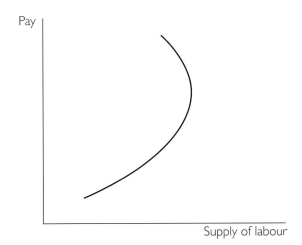

This analysis works for individuals. It does not work for the firm. The supply of labour to an individual firm is unlikely to slope backwards because increases in pay will attract recruits from other firms which are paying less.

bad debt: a debt which is unlikely to be paid. Banks realise that they have bad debts when customers to which they have made loans are unable to make the scheduled interest payments. Firms encounter bad debts when businesses to which they have sold their product become insolvent or go into liquidation. In this way unsuccessful firms can drag others down with them.

balance of invisibles: the balance between invisible exports and invisible imports. Invisibles are the traded output of the service sector, as opposed to visible exports and imports which are all goods, i.e. output from the primary or secondary sector. Invisibles include tourism, financial services, shipping and consultancy services. This invisibles balance is one component of the *balance of payments*.

balance of payments: a record of all transactions associated with imports and exports, together with all international capital movements. It consists of the *current* *account*, the *capital account* and the financial account. The current account shows trade in goods and services, income from employment and investments abroad, and transfers which may be made by governments or individuals. As can be seen from the figures, in 1998 payments were broadly in balance.

	Credits	Debits	Balance
Current account			
Total goods	165.7	192.4	−26.7
Total services	64.0	52.4	11.6
Income			
employment abroad	1.0	0.8	0.2
investment income	108.1	100.0	8.1
Current transfers	18.3	22.4	−4.1
Total current account	357.0	368.0	−11.0
Capital account			
Totals	1.6	0.8	0.8
Financial account			
UK investment overseas	–	180.1	–
Overseas investment in UK	186.0	–	–
Net errors and omissions	4.4	–	–

UK balance of payments, 1999, £billion.
Source: ONS, Annual Abstract of Statistics, 2001

It is not always possible to identify all payments: unrecorded transactions are shown as 'errors and omissions'. The capital account is of little significance, accounting for changes associated with immigration and emigration.

The financial account shows the capital outflow from the UK caused by investments overseas and the capital inflow resulting from foreign investment in the UK. These investments may consist of factories or offices built by foreign companies in the UK or they may be money flowing into or out of UK bank accounts (known as *portfolio investment*).

balance of payments crisis: if imports persistently exceed exports and if holders of the currency begin to lose confidence in the capacity of the economy to pay for those imports, there is said to be a balance of payments crisis. The usual consequence would be a fall in the exchange rate which might create a problem for the government in power. The key factor in the situation will be the confidence of holders of the currency.

balance of trade: the record of all trade in visible exports and imports, i.e. goods from the primary sector or manufactures. It is a component of the balance of payments. The UK balance of trade has for many years tended to be in deficit. This deficit is usually balanced by a surplus on the invisibles account or it may be covered by a capital inflow.

balance on current account: this is the total of visible and invisible exports and imports.

balance sheet: all companies are required by law to produce a balance sheet as part of their annual report. This shows a breakdown of its *assets* and its *liabilities*. The objective is to indicate where the firm's capital has come from and how it has been used.

balanced budget: if the government exactly balances tax revenue and expenditure it is said to have a balanced budget. In fact, on an annual basis this happens rather rarely. Most often there is a budget deficit, sometimes a budget surplus, and very occasionally the budget nearly balances. Over a period of time the annual budget deficits and surpluses may balance each other out. The current 'golden rule' is that expenditure should not exceed tax revenues by more than the level of public investment. Borrowing to invest can be justified because of the expected future income which the investment will create.

balanced growth is a term which has been used in three different ways.

- It can mean *economic growth* which occurs at roughly the same rate in all regions. This is actually rather hard to achieve.
- Alternatively, balanced growth may be used to mean growth which does not produce *environmental degradation* or permanently reduce the resource base of the economy. This means that there must be measures which prevent businesses from causing environmental damage, and the use of depletable resources must be controlled. The emphasis will be on using resources in a sustainable way.
- Thirdly, balanced growth may refer to the argument set out in the 1950s and 1960s that in *developing countries*, a wide range of industries, together with the *infrastructure* needed to support them, should all be developed at once. This means that the infrastructure is properly utilised from the start of its life, and the other industries supply the consumer goods wanted by all the employees in the newer industries who are on higher incomes than before. The disadvantage of this approach was that most developing countries would lack the resources for the massive *investment* needed. Also, agricultural development might be neglected while the investment took place. It was generally assumed that to mobilise resources in this way, government involvement would be required and much of the investment would have to come from the public sector. This approach has gone rather out of fashion.

balances with the Bank of England: the balances kept by the banks with the Bank, which they use to settle accounts with each other. These accounts provide an important liquid reserve asset for the banks, which can be used if they need cash to meet the demand from customers who are withdrawing funds.

balancing item: in the past, the balancing item was used as a way to show the difference between the current balance and total net capital movements in the balance of payments. It reflected payments about which the Bank of England had no details and ensured that the balance of payments always balanced. Since 1999 the accounts have been constructed in a different way and the balancing item is no longer included as such.

ballots: during industrial action, there may be a ballot in which employees or trade union members can vote for or against a particular outcome. Under the terms of the Trade Unions Act 1984 and the Employment Act 1988, ballots to decide for or against a strike are held under strict rules and must be secret.

bank: a bank is a *financial intermediary* which takes deposits from people or businesses which wish to save, and lends money to people or businesses which wish to borrow. By doing this on a large scale, and by exploiting the fact that not all of its deposits will be withdrawn at any one time, a bank can expand its lending over and above the total of deposits which it receives from savers. This process is known as *credit creation*. Normally, banks are supposed to be carefully regulated to ensure that they do not over lend.

Traditionally, banks make their money by 'borrowing long and lending short'. Borrowing long means taking deposits which are unlikely to be withdrawn and which are available at relatively low *rates of interest*. Lending short, i.e. making loans for short periods, will be profitable because a higher interest rate can be charged. The margin between the two rates gives the bank its income.

Banks supply a wide range of financial services. Some also specialise. *Merchant banks* exist to meet the needs of large businesses. Retail banks take deposits from all kinds of small and large customers. Investment banks specialise in funding large investment projects and in advising on finance. In recent years a number of building societies have become banks.

bank advances are the loans which banks make to individual or business customers. They may be made in the form of an *overdraft* or a fixed term loan. Overdrafts provide permission to borrow up to an agreed total level, as and when the funds are required. Interest is paid only on the amounts outstanding. They suit businesses which have difficulty in predicting their need for finance and experience variations in their income and outgoings. Fixed term loans are more appropriate where the loan is for a specific purpose, e.g. the purchase of new machinery. The *interest* payments and repayments will be fixed in advance.

bank bills are very short-term loans, usually for three months only. They can be bought and sold on the *money market*. There is no interest to pay on them but the maturity value will be larger than the loan, so giving a rate of return to the lender. This means that until maturity they are traded at a *discount*. They are sometimes known as bills of exchange.

bank deposits are the amounts deposited by customers with their banks. They may be current accounts or deposit accounts. (In the US these are known respectively as sight deposits and time deposits.) With a current account there may be no interest payable but the depositor can withdraw the money at any time. With a deposit account interest will be paid but there will be a period of notice before withdrawals can be made.

Bank for International Settlements: an international bank which co-ordinates banking activities for many countries. It was originally set up in 1930 to organise payments of reparations after World War I. Over the years its functions have evolved. It has at times been important in arranging currency swaps between central banks when countries had surpluses or deficits on the *balance of payments*. It now sets *capital adequacy ratios* for European banks and has been active in seeking ways to avoid another Asian financial crisis.

bank note: a note issued by a bank which makes a 'promise to pay on demand the bearer…'. Originally the promise was to pay in gold but this is long since discontinued, merely guaranteeing that the note is legal tender.

Bank of England: the central bank of the UK. It is responsible for the note issue and for the determination of *monetary policy* including interest rate and exchange rate policy. It is also responsible for ensuring that the *public sector net cash requirement* is funded through the sale of bills and bonds. Until 1997 the Bank of England acted as a watchdog for all banking activities in the economy. This *bank supervision* is now carried out by the *Financial Services Authority*, an independent body whose other main objectives are to ensure that financial services such as insurance, accounting, stockbroking and investment advice operate honestly and competently.

There have been calls to make the Bank of England independent, to make monetary policy less political. There used to be close collaboration between the *Chancellor of the Exchequer* and the Governor of the Bank of England. This has changed since the *Monetary Policy Committee* was set up in 1997. This has given the Bank considerable independence in setting interest rates.

The role of the Bank of England will change dramatically if the UK adopts the *euro*. The determination of monetary policy will shift to the *European Central Bank* (ECB).

bank rate: this is the original name for the interest rate set by the *Bank of England*. It is still sometimes used (as is *base rate*) by the press when referring to the interest rate set monthly by the *Monetary Policy Committee*. The real name for this is the *repo rate*.

This rate is a basis for determining the interest rates throughout the banking world, and influences rates on loans taken out by individuals and firms. It is therefore an important weapon in monetary policy, which attempts to influence the level of economic activity.

bank supervision: the process by which the *Financial Services Authority* aims to ensure that banks do not lend more than they ought to, also known as bank regulation. If they do they will eventually be unable to meet the demands of their customers to withdraw their cash. This is known as bank failure. Supervision means making sure that the banks are holding a sufficient quantity of liquid assets, enough to balance the growth of their lending, so that they do not run out of cash.

bankers' balances are the accounts held by banks with the *Bank of England*, which they use to settle their accounts with each other, and which are a very liquid asset.

banking system: this includes the banks, the central bank and the bodies which regulate the banking system. In the UK this would mean the retail banks which deal with the general public, the merchant and investment banks which advise and lend to major businesses, the *Bank of England* and the *Financial Services Authority*. A well-developed banking system is essential to the smooth running of a *developed economy* because it provides a safe income for savers and channels the funds towards borrowers who can use the money to generate incomes.

bankruptcy: individuals who cannot pay their debts become bankrupt, which means that their creditors are starting legal proceedings against them in order to recover their funds. Their assets will be taken over by an official receiver who will sell them to repay the creditors if possible. The term bankruptcy does not apply to limited liability companies (see also *insolvency* and *liquidation*).

bargaining power refers to the capacity of any party to negotiate to achieve their objectives. In the market place, the bargaining power of any seller who is desperate to sell and raise some cash may be quite limited. The bargaining power of a *trade union*, which can by striking cause the employer serious losses, may be great.

barriers to entry occur when it is difficult for new firms to enter an industry. This most commonly arises because there are substantial *technical economies of scale* being reaped by existing firms, and a new entrant to the industry, starting up in a small way, would have higher costs. Many manufacturing industries have barriers to entry because the production process is very *capital intensive*. Other economies of scale, marketing and financial, may be important too.

A second source of barriers to entry is legal and arises from *patents*. When an invention is patented, only the holder of the patent is allowed to produce it for a specified number of years. This means that no other company can copy the product until the patent expires. Other barriers include exclusive dealership arrangements and any kind of collusive agreement between existing firms in the industry.

barriers to trade: see *import controls*.

barter occurs when people trade without using money by exchanging one good or service for another. It is used when people want to avoid paying expenditure taxes or sometimes when nations have *bilateral trade* deals which allow them to save on scarce *foreign exchange*.

base rate: a commonly used term for the interest rate at which the Bank of England lends to the banks whenever they are short of cash. (The real name for this is the *repo rate*.) This rate is the subject of the monthly meetings of the *Monetary Policy Committee* and is the basis for the setting of interest rates throughout the banking system.

base year: *index numbers* are calculated with a base year value of 100. It is important to select a base year which has a reasonably representative value. The purpose of index numbers is to allow easy comparisons when using *time series* data. For example, an index number of 150 will show clearly that the value has increased by 50%.

basis point: literally, 1% of 1%. It is a term used in the financial markets to measure very small changes over the very short run. So if a particular interest rate rises by ten basis points, it has gone up by 0.1%.

basket of currencies: when exchange rate changes are measured, an *index number* is created which shows the extent of the change for one currency against those of its main trading partners. The currencies selected for this are known collectively as a basket of currencies. (See also *exchange rate index*.)

bear market: a time when expectations are that share prices and the returns on *shares* are likely to fall. This will encourage people to sell shares in order to avoid losses. The result will be falling share prices so that bearish expectations can become a *self-fulfilling prophecy*. A *bull market* has the opposite effect. Expectations of rising prices will make the market buoyant with steadily increasing prices.

beggar my neighbour policies are measures which restrict trade with the intention of protecting domestic industries, but have the effect of reducing trade overall. The term is used to describe the events of the 1930s when many governments brought in *import controls* to protect their domestic producers from competition from cheap imports. This had the effect of reducing the exports of many countries, so reducing aggregate demand and worsening the plight of the many countries caught up in the depression.

benefits: payments from the government in cash and in kind which ensure that individual incomes cannot fall below a floor level which provides a minimum standard of living. Examples include *unemployment benefit* and *income support*. Benefits may be means tested or universal. The latter avoids the unpopularity of enquiring into individual sources of income but are expensive because they are paid to all.

benefits in kind: people receive many benefits from the welfare state which are not given in the form of money. Health care, education and other services provide benefits in kind which add to people's well-being but do not increase their money income in the short run.

benefits system: a full system of benefits aims to ensure that people are provided with a minimum income whatever the reason for their inability to work. Their benefits may be in cash or in kind. They may be universal, i.e. given as of right, or means tested according to income. The objective is to protect the young and the old, the sick, the disabled and those who cannot find work.

Beveridge Report: in 1942 Lord Beveridge produced his report, Social Insurance and Allied Services, which provided much of the thinking which underpinned the creation after 1945 of the *welfare state*. Some of the benefits of the welfare state have remained to the present, others were gradually eroded by the changes brought in by the Conservative governments in power from 1979 to 1997.

bias occurs in any investigation where the findings tend to be different from the reality. For example, if a sample for survey is for some reason not representative of the population as a whole, it will give biased results. It might have too many or too few of a particular age group. Bias can also occur when the investigator allows a personal view to influence the conclusions.

bilateral monopoly occurs where there is a single seller and a single buyer. A *trade union* which represents all the workers in an industry and a dominant employer can create a bilateral monopoly, as in the case of the British Medical Association which negotiates doctors' pay, and the National Health Service which employs most of them.

bilateral negotiations involve two parties. Bilateral trade negotiations might involve two governments.

bilateral trade occurs when two countries swap equal quantities of exports and imports. More often trade is multilateral, characterised by surpluses and deficits between pairs of countries, so that the UK might export engineers' services to Saudi Arabia, which might in turn export oil to Japan, which in turn exports cars to the UK.

bill: see *bank bills*.

biotechnology involves applying understanding of biological processes to the development of new products and production methods. It has the potential to lead to big cuts in production costs as well as to improved products and *productivity*.

birth rate: the average number of live births occurring in a year per 1000 population. Information derived from the birth rate can be an important basis for production decisions, for the planning of the education system and for understanding a number of long-term trends. Low birth rates in developed countries are leading to *ageing populations*. High birth rates, for example in Africa, are making it difficult to increase per capita incomes. There is strong evidence that rising incomes in the long run lead to falling birth rates.

black economy is the term used to describe all those transactions which do not appear in the *national income statistics*. Some of these are legal, others are not. The black economy includes the wages of people who are on means-tested benefits while actually working more than the few hours allowed. It also includes payments, e.g. to babysitters, which do not need to be recorded for tax purposes. It is estimated that 3–5% of tax revenue is lost through illegal activities taking place on the black economy.

black market: when a market is controlled, e.g. by rationing, a black market develops, where people who have things to sell and people who want to buy them evade the controls. A black market developed during World War II in the UK and more recently countries with strict foreign exchange controls have experienced black markets in *currencies*.

Blue Book: a publication of the Office of National Statistics which contains the UK National Income Accounts.

blue chip: a company the shares of which are regarded as being a very safe investment.

blue collar union: a *trade union* that represents manual workers.

board of directors: the people who have ultimate responsibility for the affairs of a business. They represent *shareholders* and are elected by them at the *AGM*. Day-to-day and strategic decisions will usually be in the hands of executive directors who work for the firm full-time. *Non-executive directors* may be elected to provide additional expertise or to give an impression of independence.

bonds: a borrower may issue a bond, which is a promise to repay a certain sum of money at a date some time in the future (from one to 20 years or so). In return for the loan which is the price of the bond, interest will be paid, usually at a fixed rate. Bonds may be traded on the *Stock Exchange*, and the price will reflect the attractiveness of the interest rate relative to current market rates. Bonds issued by the *Bank of England* to finance government spending are known as Treasury Bonds, also as gilts, because the government will always be able to repay on maturity, since it has the right to tax. (Hence, they are said to be 'as good as gold'.) Bonds issued by companies are known as corporate bonds. Because the rate of interest and the maturity value is fixed, bonds are much less risky than shares, but are likely also to have a lower rate of return.

bonus: an amount over and above normal salary paid to employees who are considered to have done their job particularly well. They can be used to try to ensure loyalty or to act as an incentive. Sometimes they are used to pay very large amounts, the wisdom of which has been questioned by some shareholders and members of the public.

boom: the phase of the *trade cycle* in which economic growth is at its most rapid. As recovery gathers pace, economic growth becomes faster until in a boom it is growing at a rate which cannot be sustained in the long run. The economy will be characterised by relatively low levels of *unemployment* and little underutilised capacity.

In the later stages of a boom, bottlenecks or *supply constraints* develop. Employers find it hard to recruit some scarce types of skilled labour. Firms producing *investment* goods develop long order books, so that buyers have to wait. Wages will tend to be bid up in an attempt to recruit more people. This increases costs and may lead to increasing prices so that *inflation* accelerates. In any case, the ease with which firms can sell their output in a growing market encourages them to raise prices. In these ways inflation may accelerate.

If governments implement counter-inflation policies, the heat will be taken out of the economy and the downswing of the cycle will begin. Even without such policies the economy is likely to slow down because expectations that growth is likely to slow will reduce the rate of investment, which in turn reduces *aggregate demand*.

bottlenecks in the economy occur when it is impossible to increase supply to match an unexpected surge in demand. In *boom* years, for example, there have been shortages of microchips, forcing producers of a huge range of products to slow down their rate of output. There may also be shortages of skilled labour which make it difficult for firms to hire the kind of people they need in order to expand. Bottlenecks can lead to prices of scarce resources being bid up as buyers compete for them. This can be the start of an acceleration in *inflation* during a boom.

boycott: a movement to stop buying certain products because of consumer concern, usually about ethical issues. Over the long run, the boycott of South African products was a factor in the ending of the apartheid regime and the holding of free elections with votes for all. On a much smaller scale, the boycott of Nestlé products by consumers worried about sales of baby milk in developing countries has given the company some cause for concern.

Brady Plan: an early attempt in 1989 to reduce the weight of the debt burden on some *developing countries*. It was named after the then US Treasury Secretary. It involved some reduction in the debt and some new money.

brand: a way of differentiating the product to make it recognisably distinguishable from competing products. This may be done with logos and packaging and there may be quality factors which can give the brand a genuine edge. In the long run, some products can acquire *brand loyalty* because they are seen as a reliable choice. For some firms, their brands are important *intangible assets* which attract other firms which are interested in taking them over. Rowntree brands were a great attraction for Nestlé when they launched their hostile takeover bid. This is a factor in the increasing concentration of some industries.

brand loyalty refers to the way in which certain brands become associated with particular qualities so that consumers will buy them again and again in preference to competing products. Brand loyalty can allow the producer to raise prices above those of similar products because people come to rely on them. It can give the firm some degree of *market power.*

breach of contract: contracts specify the conditions under which a transaction takes place. Breach of contract means that one or more of these conditions has not been adhered to by one of the contracting parties.

The law of contract is an essential basis for an efficient economy. Both buyers and sellers need to be sure that they can rely on the terms of an agreement in order to deal with one another. If they cannot, business becomes extremely risky. The lack of a reliable legal system is a major factor in the risks which dog firms expanding in developing countries. This applies to domestic firms as well as international ones. For example, China is an attractive market but a risky one because its legal system is slow and unpredictable, and commercial law is limited in its scope.

break-even level of output is that at which neither losses nor profits are made. In the early stages of its existence, breaking even is an important objective for a business. It will be able to survive losses for a while but in time it will need to become profitable. For non-profit making organisations, breaking even may be a long-term objective.

Bretton Woods: the name given to the post-Second World War economic system that sought freely convertible currencies within a worldwide *fixed exchange rate* system. Between 1945 and 1971 this was remarkably successful, helping world economic growth achieve its highest ever levels. The name Bretton Woods stems from the location of the wartime conference that set up this system.

broad money: a measure of the stock of money which attempts to capture total potential purchasing power. In the UK this is *M4*, which is defined as notes and coin and all bank and building society sterling deposits. It does not include foreign currency deposits, although these can very easily be converted into sterling.

broker: a person or firm which creates a link between buyers and sellers. The broker often has more information than the buyer or the seller, so can make a living out of acting as an intermediary.

brownfield site: an urban location which has already been built upon once, which could now be redeveloped. There is pressure to build on brownfield sites rather than on greenfield sites (which have never been built on before) for environmental reasons.

bubble: a situation in which the price of an *asset*, such as a *share*, rises fast because of buyer enthusiasm which is speculative in nature. Expectations of higher prices in the future cause people to buy, driving up the price. Eventually, the market loses confidence that the price will rise further. Demand dries up, the price collapses and the bubble bursts.

Budget (the): the occasion on which the *Chancellor of the Exchequer* sets out taxation and expenditure plans for the year. Detailed changes will be made to both *direct and indirect tax* rates as they affect firms and individuals. There may also be changes in certain areas of expenditure such as health and *social security*. Because it has a direct effect on almost everyone, which can be measured in money terms, the Budget attracts a great deal of attention.

The Budget occurs in March each year. Each November the Chancellor of the Exchequer sets out the government's spending plans. Both occasions provide all-embracing statements of economic policy, including detailed forecasts of expected levels of economic activity.

The Budget performs a macro-economic management function, as well as involving detailed adjustments to policies which affect the allocation of resources. An example of the latter occurs when there are changes in expenditure taxes on fuel, which have environmental objectives.

A significant part of the Budget speech will review *macro-economic policy*. Tax and expenditure changes will lead to changes in the overall budget deficit or surplus (*PSNCR* or *PSDR*). This will have an effect in turn on the level of *aggregate demand* and the prosperity of the economy.

budget balance: a situation in which tax revenues are equal to government expenditure. A precise match is rather unlikely; more often than not there is a *public sector deficit*. From time to time there is a surplus.

budget constraint: the maximum amount of spending possible within a given sum of money, which may come from income or from accumulated wealth or borrowing. The budget constraint prevents anyone from spending above that amount. Within the budget, choices may be made and people can have more of one product so long as they have less of another.

budget deficit: the amount by which government expenditure exceeds tax revenue. The deficit can be financed by borrowing. The *Bank of England* will sell Treasury *bonds* and *bills* in sufficient quantities to raise the funds. Useful amounts may also come from *National Savings*. In general the government can borrow at low rates of interest because it can guarantee to be able to pay back the money, because of its right to tax. However, if it needs to borrow a great deal more to finance the deficit, it may be necessary to raise *interest rates*. This may have the effect of discouraging investment and therefore future economic activity.

Normally the budget deficit varies over the course of the *trade cycle*. During a boom, tax revenues rise, usually even faster than incomes. Unemployment is fairly low and benefits will cost less. There may be a surplus. During the downturn, increased unemployment leads to increased spending on benefits and tax revenues may be static or falling. There will be a public sector deficit. This will help to stimulate the economy into growing again. In recent years governments have generally aimed to balance the budget over the course of the trade cycle, but not in the short run.

Borrowing for *investment* makes sense when the income generated by the investment is likely to be sufficient to pay the interest on the debt. The annual budget deficit is known as the *public sector net cash requirement*. The combined deficits from the past are called the *National Debt*.

The *convergence criteria* for entry to the *euro* requires that the budget deficit be no more than 3% of GDP. A number of countries including the UK have worked towards and met this target in order to be ready. (See also *automatic stabilisers*.)

budget surplus: the amount by which tax revenue exceeds government expenditure. (See also *budget* and *budget deficit*.) The surplus in any one year is called the *public sector debt repayment*.

buffer stock: stocks of *commodities*, such as wheat, which are held in many countries and can be used in the event of shortages at some time in the future. Some are held by government bodies and some in the private sector. For many commodities, both demand and supply can vary. The demand for oil is affected by the level of economic activity, worldwide; the supply can be affected by wars. So prices do fluctuate from time to time. Releasing buffer stocks onto the market – or buying up a glut – helps to keep prices stable. The supply of agricultural products varies because of weather and other problems. So keeping a buffer stock can help to prevent very low prices during a glut or very high prices at times of shortage.

building society: a *financial intermediary* which specialises in lending for house purchase, i.e. very long-term loans. In recent years building societies have diversified into offering retail banking services to customers and several have changed their status to become banks.

built-in stabilisers: during different phases of the *trade cycle*, the government will automatically be changing the level of spending on benefits and will receive varying levels of tax revenue. These changes offset the changes in *aggregate demand* in the economy as a whole. As more people become unemployed, their benefit entitlement rises and they are able to continue spending, albeit on a lower level, even though they are no longer earning. Similarly they will pay little or no tax. The reverse happens as the economy recovers. So as demand falls in *recession*, it is offset by a rise in government expenditure and a fall in taxation, which reduces leakages from the circular flow of money. This reduces the severity of the slump. The opposite happens as the economy recovers and so the boom is slowed.

bulk–value ratio: the relationship between bulk or weight and the value of the product. When the ratio is very high, transport costs will be high in relation to the final price and this may affect the location of production. Firms located close to the market may have a cost advantage.

bull market: one in which expectations of price rises generate a rush to buy immediately. On the *Stock Exchange*, a bull market may last for some time as prices rise and confidence becomes infectious. If the higher prices are justified by reasonable expectations of profit there may be no problem. This seems to have happened in the US during the 1990s. However, the boom in new technology shares during 1999-2000 led to very high prices for shares in firms which had never actually made a profit. This was followed by a correction during which some prices fell very sharply as confidence diminished. Something similar but on a much larger scale happened in the *Wall Street Crash* of 1929, when a bull market was followed by loss of confidence and collapsing prices.

Bundesbank: the central bank of Germany. During the 1970s, 1980s and 1990s the Bundesbank acquired a reputation for sound financial management and successful control of *inflation*. It is fully independent of the German government, so that it is not influenced by impending elections. With the advent of the *euro*, its position was greatly altered and it became much less important.

business confidence is an important element in the formation of *expectations*. These in turn affect firms' decisions, particularly in relation to investment. The *CBI* Industrial Trends Survey monitors business optimism, export optimism and perceptions of limiting factors, i.e. the availability of skilled labour and the cost of finance. These are all known to be important indicators of willingness to invest in the immediate or near future. (See also *animal spirits.*)

business cycle: the sequence of slump, recovery, boom and recession which has been a feature of economic life for many years. (See also *trade cycle.*)

business objectives: the range of targets which a firm may have. For some these will be related to profit. In economics it is often assumed that firms will in fact seek to maximise profits. However, there are other objectives, some of which are related to profit and some of which are not. These include achieving a significant *market share*, such that the firm has some control over prices, having a reputation for excellence in design or quality, taking ethically responsible decisions or sometimes just breaking even over the long run.

business rate: the payments to local authorities which are levied on businesses and determined on the basis of the value of the premises. For some firms these are an important cost.

business responsibility: the idea that businesses should take their decisions in a way which considers the needs and interests of all their *stakeholders*. As well as *shareholders* and employees, these include customers, suppliers, creditors and the community. Some managers see business responsibility as being part of effective management and believe that it can be achieved without reducing profits because it is in the long-term interests of all. Most firms say that they abide by the laws of the countries in which they are operating but some go beyond that and actively try to improve employment conditions or look for production methods which minimise environmental impact.

buyers' market: if there are large numbers of sellers trying to sell to a relatively small number of buyers, then the buyers will be able to force a drop in price. This is sometimes used to describe the housing market when the number of houses for sale exceeds the number of potential buyers.

buyout: see *management buyout.*

bygones: there is an old saying in economics, bygones are bygones. These are events which happened in the past and should have no impact on current decision taking. For example, after the Millennium Dome was built, it became clear that it was unlikely ever to make enough money from entrance fees to cover its costs. The correct decision at this point would have been to close it down and dispose of it in the most economical manner, since it could never be profitable. However, people sometimes have great difficulty with the concept of bygones, believing that if much money has been poured into a venture, it should therefore be kept open. What do you think?

by-product: when a production process leads to the production of other goods which are not the main objective for the producer, these are known as by-products. The term is often used in relation to the chemical industry. Straw, however, is a by-product of wheat.

CAP: see *Common Agricultural Policy.*

capacity: the maximum amount which can be produced with given amounts of fixed capital. For example, a chemical plant may have a maximum output which is technically possible with the equipment it has. Capacity can be increased by building another plant or by extending the existing one. However, it is sometimes possible to increase capacity by improving the efficiency with which resources are used.

capacity utilisation means the extent to which existing capital equipment is in use. An individual business might be operating at 50% of capacity if it normally operates two shifts a day but there is actually only one shift a day or if a single shift is normal and half the machines are idle.

$$\text{FORMULA:} \quad \frac{\text{actual output per period}}{\text{full capacity output per period}} \times 100$$

Underutilised capital raises costs because the fixed costs are spread over fewer units of output. It can be a serious problem during *recession* because cuts in output inevitably lead to underutilised capacity. Eventually, if demand for the product does not recover, the capital equipment will be taken out of use permanently in order to cut losses.

Capacity utilisation for the economy as a whole is an important indicator. It shows how close the economy is to *full-capacity output* and will help to show when the pressure of *aggregate demand* is likely to lead to accelerating *inflation*, because the amount of unused resources in the economy is diminishing. The CBI measures capacity utilisation for a representative sample of firms; the data will reflect the position of the economy within the *trade cycle*. In a recession there will normally be substantial underutilised capacity.

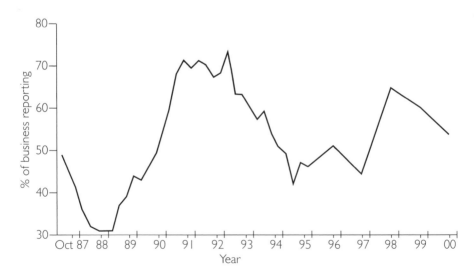

Percentage of respondents working below capacity (in manufacturing). Source: CBI

capital has several different meanings but all of them imply that capital can be used to generate an income stream over a period of time.

1 Capital is a *factor of production* consisting of buildings, plant and machinery which can be used in the production process. With the other factors of production, land and labour, it can be combined to produce goods or services which can be sold.

2 Capital can also mean *financial assets*. The funds available to a firm include shareholders' capital and loan capital. This can be used to invest in property, capital equipment, plant and machinery. Alternatively it provides *working capital* which finances the production process until sales revenue comes in.

3 *Human capital* means the skills and experience which individuals accumulate and which are a valuable asset which can be used to make the production process more efficient.

The return to capital may be *interest*, *profits* or *rent*. These provide compensation to the owner of the capital for not having the use of it at the present time for consumption purposes.

capital account: that part of the *balance of payments* accounts which records capital movements. It is shown as a series of changes to the level of assets and liabilities held outside the UK, and by overseas residents inside the UK.

capital accumulation: the process by which investment adds to the stock of capital and the capacity of the economy to produce. Much investment in capital equipment simply replaces worn-out plant and machinery. However, when there is *net investment*, i.e. spending on capital which is greater than the amount needed to replace worn-out equipment, the stock of capital increases. This is one element in the process of economic growth (the others being *population growth* and *technical change*).

capital adequacy ratio defines the amount of capital needed by banks to ensure that they do not run out of funds when customers ask to withdraw their deposits. The amount is fixed in relation to the amount and types of loans which the bank is providing to customers.

capital appreciation: an increase in the value of assets. This could be an increase in the market value of a house or other property, of land or buildings owned by a firm or of the prices of a particular share. If the capital assets are going to be used for the same purposes as before the appreciation, then the increase is in the book value of the assets. However, if they are to be sold, the owner will make a *capital gain*.

capital consumption measures the amount of capital needed to replace equipment which has worn out during the course of one year. The term is used in the national accounts to show how much of total (gross) investment can be attributed to normal wear and tear or depreciation and how much reflects a net addition to the nation's stock of capital or productive capacity.

capital deepening occurs when more capital equipment is provided for each person employed. It will normally lead to an increase in *productivity* or output per person employed.

capital deficiency: many developing countries experience slow growth, or sometimes no growth at all, because there is a low level of investment in capital equipment and infrastructure. This is particularly prevalent in sub-Saharan Africa where the capital stock has in most countries remained small in relation to the population.

capital expenditure is spending on investments which will yield an income in the future. This may apply in the public or the private sector. In the public sector it might apply to new motorways or hospitals.

capital flight: when there is a serious loss of confidence in the performance of a particular economy, many owners of capital assets may try to sell them very quickly. For example, they will try to sell the currency, exchanging it for another currency which feels safer. They may also try to sell shares. Usually a capital flight will lead to a sharp drop in asset prices. A recent example occurred when confidence in a number of Asian economies was greatly reduced during the *Asian financial crisis*, 1997-1999. Countries such as Korea and Indonesia saw their exchange rates and the price of shares on their stock exchanges falling very rapidly.

capital gain: the increase in the value of an asset between its purchase and a subsequent sale or revaluation. The term applies mostly to shares or to homes and other property.

capital gains tax: a tax on gains made when an asset which has appreciated in value is sold. This is a way of taxing the gains made by *shareholders* or property owners when they sell at a much higher price than they originally paid. Only the increase in value which exceeds the increase in the *retail price index* is taxed. No tax is payable on a person's main residence and the first £7000 of any gain in any one year is tax free.

capital gearing shows the extent to which a firm uses loan finance rather than equity (share) finance to pay for its capital investments. Capital gearing is, as a percentage:

$$\text{FORMULA:} \quad \frac{\text{total loans}}{\text{total capital employed}} \times 100$$

High gearing means that the business is heavily reliant on loans. This may matter if the business finds itself in difficult trading conditions. It will still have to pay interest on its loans. If it had relied more on equity finance (an issue of shares), dividends could have been reduced during that year to reduce the overall financial pressures. This is one of the risks that *shareholders* expect to have to carry. A gearing level above 50% is seen as being high, for this reason. High gearing can be risky for the lender.

capital goods means equipment of any kind which can be used as an input to the production process. Some capital goods can only be used as such; for example, a power station or a railway line. Others can be used as consumer items or as capital goods; for example, a car or a sewing machine.

capital inflows are the movements of large amounts of money into the country from abroad. These can be bank balances which are coming in search of high interest rates or they can represent investment in productive capacity – plant and machinery. For example, many US and Japanese companies have invested in factories in the UK, such as Ford and Toyota. These inflows will be recorded in the *capital account* of the *balance of payments*.

capital-intensive production uses a high proportion of capital equipment and a relatively low proportion of labour. Most manufacturing is now capital-intensive in the UK. The introduction of computerised production systems and robots makes processes more capital-intensive.

The decision as to how capital-intensive production should be, will be determined by the relative prices of capital and labour. In countries with relatively low wage rates, *labour-intensive* production will be more appropriate. As wage rates rise during the process of economic development, firms increasingly substitute capital for labour. This raises productivity and often also wage rates, leading to further investment in labour-saving capital.

capitalism: the system in which the price mechanism is used to determine how resources are allocated. Land and capital are owned by individuals who will decide how they are used on the basis of the profit that can be obtained. Similarly, they will pay employees according to the amount needed to attract them to undertake the required work.

The extreme alternative to capitalism is a *centrally planned economy*. Most economies, however, fall between those extremes, being mixed economies, with market systems and some government involvement in economic activity. The advantage of capitalism is that the allocation of resources is determined primarily by the demand for final products.

capital-labour ratio: the proportion of capital used in production relative to the proportion of labour. Where wages are relatively high, the capital-labour ratio will tend to be high also and production will be *capital-intensive*. The ratio may vary over the course of the trade cycle: during recession, redundancies may reduce the labour input. The capital used will be a fixed factor of production in the short run.

capital markets are the markets in which borrowers can obtain funds and lenders can find suitable borrowers who will pay a rate of interest. For example, in the short-term money market, banks and other businesses with a surplus of funds for a few days can lend to banks and other businesses who need extra funds for a similar period, sometimes just overnight. Also part of the capital market is the *Stock Exchange*, which brings together buyers and sellers of shares and *bonds*. In between these two there are markets for a range of different kinds of assets.

Efficient capital markets make it easy for lenders to make a return on their assets and for borrowers to obtain funds to finance production. They therefore have an important role in the process of income and wealth creation. Developing countries often experience difficulty in financing entrepreneurs because they do not have well-organised capital markets.

capital mobility: the extent to which capital can be switched to alternative uses. Generally speaking, capital invested in plant and machinery is not very mobile in the short run because it has a particular use, e.g. a car assembly line. The capital is only mobile insofar as it need not be replaced in the long-run if there is no longer sufficient demand for the product. The capital invested then becomes available for use in producing a more profitable product.

Capital mobility can be important in international terms. The EU provides for the free movement of capital between member countries. Owners of capital can invest it in the EU location considered most likely to be profitable. Many governments have reduced controls on capital movements in recent years.

capital movements are flows of capital from one currency to another. The location of the money may or may not change: it could be moved from a dollar account in New York to a sterling account in London, but it might equally be moved from a dollar account in London to a sterling account in London. Money which is 'footloose' in this way and moves from one currency to another in search of the best rate of interest is sometimes called *hot money*.

capital outflow: a movement of large sums of money to destinations abroad. This could be for any of three reasons:

- a *capital flight*
- the money may be being moved into a currency with higher interest rates
- the capital may be being invested in factories and other productive capacities in other countries.

Globalisation has brought rising flows of capital from one country to another as the world economy becomes more integrated.

capital output ratio measures the amount of capital employed in producing a given amount of output. A high capital:output ratio will indicate *capital-intensive* production because wage rates are relatively high and some labour-saving investment has taken place.

capital stock: the amount of capital currently available for use in the economy. Changes in the capital stock provide a guide as to the productive potential of the economy.

capital transfer tax (CTT): a tax on capital transfers from one person to another as a gift or inheritance. The first £242,000 inherited is free of tax (2001 figures). Above this amount the transfer is taxed at 40%. Gifts given seven years before death are not included in the estate.

capital widening occurs if employment is increasing and there is investment in new plant and machinery to give them the capacity to produce. This contrasts with *capital deepening*, which enlarges the amount of capital available to a given number of people.

carbon tax: a proposed tax which would be levied on the use of fossil fuels. Because it is believed that an excess of carbon dioxide is accumulating in the atmosphere and that this will lead to climate change, it is important to consider ways of reducing the use of fossil fuels. The outlook for such taxes is not promising unless international agreement can be reached; this is slow in coming.

cartel: a group of firms which agree to limit output in order to keep prices higher than they would be if there were free competition. The best known cartel is OPEC (the *Organisation of Petroleum Exporting Countries*) which at times in the past has restricted output so that world oil prices would rise. This is different from the standard cartel in that governments are involved.

Firms which collaborate in this way may have market sharing agreements in which they each have a geographical area where they can operate without fear of competition. Or they may agree a minimum price or limit their range of products or non-price competition.

Cartels are now relatively infrequent for two reasons:

- in most developed countries, *competition policy* makes cartels illegal. By restricting competition, they lead to lower levels of output and higher prices for consumers.
- cartels are quite hard to create and maintain, because the high prices act as an incentive for other firms to enter the market. Also, participating firms may try to cheat by offering secret discounts or not sticking to their output quotas. The parties to the agreement have to have a large share of the market in order to achieve the desired effect.

In the past the cement makers have been accused of forming a cartel. The process by which cartels achieve their objectives is called *collusion*. Evidence of this will encourage the Office of Fair Trading and the *Competition Commission* to investigate.

cash means literally notes and coin. However, it is usually used now to mean very liquid assets, as in 'cash in the bank', i.e. money held in instant access accounts.

cash flow statement: a component of a firm's *annual report and accounts*. It records all the revenues and payments made by the business. A cash flow forecast indicates possible times when money may not be available to cover necessary payments. Firms in this situation can run into difficulties even though they are likely to be profitable over the long run. Having adequate liquidity available to deal with cash flow problems can be important to the survival of the firm.

CBI: see *Confederation of British Industry.*

ceiling price: a maximum price which may be set by a government or a regulatory body. If this is below the *equilibrium price*, there will be excess demand and shortages, unless the government holds *buffer stocks* which can be sold. Ceiling prices set by regulators, e.g. *OFGEM*, usually affect the producers' profits rather than the supply of the product.

cell production: a way of splitting up an assembly line process into separate areas where teams can be responsible for a particular part of the overall process. It has been used as a way of increasing *productivity*. Its advantages are:

- the team can be jointly responsible for quality
- in time, members of the team become expert at solving production problems without having to call in outside help
- motivation may improve as the work may be less repetitive and more challenging
- the team may be able to improve the working arrangements in ways that cut costs.

census: the government's enquiry into population trends which takes place every 10 years. Information covers age, sex, family status and occupation. Other information can be collected at the same time, e.g. on housing or ethnic groups.

central bank: the bank which is responsible for overseeing the banking system as a whole and operating *monetary policy*. In the UK it is the Bank of England and in the US, the Federal Reserve Bank (the Fed). The central bank acts as banker to the other banks and to the government, issues notes and coin and acts as lender of last resort; this means it ensures that the banking system is kept as stable as possible by lending to banks which find themselves temporarily short of cash to meet their depositors' needs. Within the *euro* zone, the central bank function has been taken over by the *European Central Bank*, the ECB. Whether central banks should be independent or controlled by the central government is an open question at the present time.

central bank independence: in recent years there has been a trend towards making the central bank independent of the government. Where governments control monetary policies, they may be tempted to allow monetary expansion at a time of slow growth or high unemployment. This may in the long run lead to accelerating inflation. Where the central bank is independent, monetary policy can be decided on the basis of the need to maintain stability and control inflation. Short-term political considerations will not be a major factor in decisions. The *Federal Reserve System* in the US and the *Bundesbank* in Germany have always been independent. Other central banks have moved in this direction in order to strengthen the commitment to control of inflation, as in the UK.

central bank intervention most often describes the process by which central banks buy the domestic currency in order to keep up its value. This would happen if the central bank wanted to maintain the existing *exchange rate* at a time when market forces were causing a *depreciation*. The bank can use its foreign exchange reserves to buy currency so that the increased demand counteracts the market forces which are pushing it down.

central government refers to the highest level of government which controls the affairs of the nation as a whole. In contrast, *local government* deals with the provision of local services such as housing and environmental services. The situation is complicated in the UK by the process of devolution. Wales, Scotland and Northern Ireland have their own representative bodies and areas of particular responsibility. Even so, the scope of central government in the UK is greater than in federal systems such as the US and Germany, where state governments have wider responsibilities.

centrally planned economies are those in which the allocation of resources is determined by the planning process rather than by market forces. Many previously centrally planned economies (such as Russia and Poland) began the process of becoming market economies in 1989. China, Cuba and Vietnam remain substantially centrally planned, although market forces are operating in some sectors of their economies. Some economies have retained a measure of central planning within what is mainly a market economy. India falls into this category. Most developed countries have privatised most of their state enterprises, thus reducing the amount of central planning within individual economies.

certificate of deposit is a way of turning a *bank deposit* into a negotiable asset. A business may turn a bank balance into a certificate of deposit (CD) which it can then sell if it needs to get the cash. In the meantime it will yield a higher rate of interest than an ordinary bank account. It thus gives a good rate of return while retaining liquidity.

ceteris paribus: a Latin term meaning 'other things being equal'. When using economic theory, it helps to be able to isolate a single change and think of all other conditions as being unchanged, so as to simplify the analysis. For example, we can say that ceteris paribus, an increase in the price will act as an incentive for firms to produce more. In practice, things are often not equal: an increase in costs might reduce the price incentive to nothing. Nevertheless, the *assumption* of ceteris paribus allows us to analyse one change at a time.

CFCs: see *chlorofluorocarbons*.

CGT: see *capital gains tax*.

Chancellor of the Exchequer: the chief finance minister in the UK. He determines fiscal policy, i.e. the levels of taxation and expenditure across the whole economy. Plans are set out in the Budget each year, usually in March. The Chancellor, with the Treasury, must decide important aspects of stabilisation policy which can have a considerable impact on individuals and on business. The Chancellor's decisions may also have a substantial effect on income distribution. Until 1997 the Chancellor would decide monetary policy in consultation with the Bank of England but that role has now been passed to the Bank's *Monetary Policy Committee*.

In addition to the *Budget*, the Chancellor reviews all aspects of taxation and spending in November each year. This creates an opportunity to prepare for the Budget, which then defines the precise changes required.

change requires that decision takers constantly review their policies. Constant change in the economy requires a flexible response. For example, rapid shifts in the pattern of demand mean that production has to be changed to match. This is much easier if the workforce is flexible enough to adapt fairly quickly. *Retraining* may be necessary and *multi-skilling* helps. Both can promote *occupational mobility*. Governments can help this process through their education and training policies. Firms have responded by requiring employees to have more flexible *employment contracts*.

Chicago School: a group of economists who have either worked at or been associated with the University of Chicago, who have promoted the importance of market forces in creating efficient, growing economies. They have tended to criticise government interventions in the economy as being likely not to produce the desired effect. Their work on the consumption function, on regulation and on monetary theory has been important. In particular, *Milton Friedman's* thinking underpinned much of the Conservative government's monetary policy in the early 1980s.

Chinese walls: within financial firms, employees are forbidden to pass on information about events which may lead to big changes in share prices. For example, a department of a merchant bank which is advising a business on a possible takeover bid must not allow the information about it to reach the bank's stockbroking department. If they had the information early enough, dealers could make big profits by buying shares which will rise in value once the information is made public. They may then be guilty of *insider dealing*, which is illegal.

chlorofluorocarbons CFCs: the substance which has been used in refrigerators and air conditioners but which is now known to deplete the ozone layer, with potentially large health risks. By international agreement they were phased out by 2000. However, there are rumours of their continued illegal use.

choice: underlying much basic economic analysis is the idea that resources are scarce and therefore everyone has to make choices. The three fundamental areas of choice are:

- <u>what</u> goods and services will be produced. There are not enough resources to produce everything people want. So choices must be made which will reflect personal preferences.
- <u>how</u> goods and services should be produced. There will usually be several different ways of production. The choice of production method will depend on the relative prices of the inputs and the technologies available. Firms will decide which strategy is likely to be the most cost effective.
- <u>for whom</u> goods and services will be produced. In other words, how income will be distributed. Incomes depend partly on the level of wages needed to attract particular types of labour and partly on how much wealth individuals have accumulated through saving, inheritance or luck. However, the distribution of income which results from market forces can be altered by *fiscal policy* and the benefits system.

cif stands for cost-insurance-freight. Exports and imports may be calculated cif, thus including transport costs, or fob (freight on board), thus excluding transport costs.

circular flow of national income: the way in which income flows around the economy, from firms to households and back to firms in a continuous process. Payments to employees are income, as are profits and rent. Income from all these sources is spent on goods and services. This spending becomes the revenue received by firms. Hence, the flow of money is circular. The model can be extended to take in savings and investment, taxes and government expenditure and imports and exports. These *withdrawals* and *injections* respectively reduce or increase the circular flow.

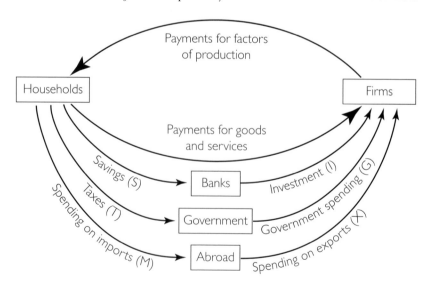

The circular flow of income

CITES: see *Convention on International Trade in Endangered Species.*

The City: the network of organisations based in the City of London which includes the banking system, the money markets, insurance companies, commodity exchanges, the *Stock Exchange* and other firms concerned with financial affairs.

civil law: legislation which allows individuals to take their disputes with one another to the courts. (See also *commercial law.*)

claimant: a person who is claiming benefits, e.g. unemployment benefit.

claimant count: the number of people who are claiming unemployment benefit. This is a rather rough and ready way of measuring unemployment which is still used but is recognised as unsatisfactory. The problem is that it does not count people who want to work and do not have a job but are not eligible for unemployment benefit. *Labour Force Survey* data includes this group and therefore gives a fuller picture.

classical economics was developed by, among others, Adam Smith, David Ricardo and J S Mill, between 1776 when Adam Smith's WEALTH OF NATIONS was published, and 1848 when J S Mill's PRINCIPLES OF POLITICAL ECONOMY was published. These economists laid down the general principles of the market economy, perfect competition and the theory of comparative advantage. They were concerned mainly with the principles of micro-economics and the assumption of *perfect competition* was crucial to their analysis. They held that government intervention was mainly unhelpful and that the operation of self-interest would bring about efficient production in the long run. The classical economists continue to influence thinking right up to the present day, being the forerunners of what is now known as *neoclassical economics.*

clearing banks are the main high street banks. The name comes from the fact that these banks belong to the London Clearing House. This body organises the payments between banks which result from the massive number of cheques exchanged each day. (See also *commercial banks.*)

closed economy: one which does not trade with the rest of the world. The idea of a closed economy is used in economic theory simply so that the effects of certain changes on the macro-economy can be studied in isolation. In contrast, an *open economy* is one in which trade is important. However, some economies are more open than others. Larger countries such as the US tend to be less open because they can be relatively self-sufficient. Some governments try to keep their economies somewhat isolated by restricting imports and capital movements in the hope that this will protect them from unwanted changes.

closed shop: the requirement that all employees in a particular workplace belong to a specific trade union. Enforcing this is illegal under the Employment Act of 1988, which reduced union bargaining power considerably. Where it does occur, which must be with the consent of both employer and workforce, it gives the union some monopoly bargaining power.

Club of Rome: an international group of academics and civil servants who collectively advocated a greater degree of environmental awareness in the formation of government policies. They showed that current rates of resource depletion may not be sustainable in the long run and have researched ways in which environmentally desirable changes might be implemented.

clusters: groups of competing producers who locate in the same area. For example, there are four prestigious restaurants in the small Shropshire town of Ludlow. They attract large numbers of customers from outside the surrounding area because of their reputation. High technology clusters also develop in specific locations such as Cambridge. Sometimes but not always, clusters develop where there are *external economies of scale.*

coalition: a group of individuals, firms, pressure groups or political parties which each have their own objectives but co-operate in order to achieve shared goals. Coalitions can be unstable; individual coalition members may over time perceive advantages in seeking new allies or simply returning to solo operation.

cobweb theorem: a theory which analyses the changes which occur in markets over time when there are time lags between the decision to produce and the arrival of the output in the marketplace. For example, farmers may decide to produce less lamb because the price is currently low (point A on the diagram). If they all make the same decision, there will in time be much less lamb on the market (B) and this will cause the price to rise sharply (C). This in turn will make farmers want to expand their flocks (D). The situation is thus inherently unstable, although it may eventually settle down (E).

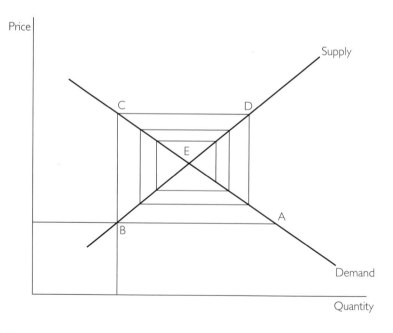

Cobweb theorem

Whether or not the resulting diagram makes a nice-looking spidery cobweb like the one above depends upon what is assumed about the price elasticity of the supply and demand curves. It is possible to show that the situation may be unstable and characterised by wide fluctuations in price over time. Sugar is one commodity with a tendency towards regular periods of unstable prices on world markets.

coefficient: the numbers in an equation which provide the structure. For example, in the equation y = 2x + 3, 2 is the coefficient of x and 3 is the constant term. Coefficients represent some of the assumptions about the relationships depicted in the equations which underlie an economic model.

collateral: when taking out a bank loan, it is usually necessary to provide some kind of security, known as collateral. For new businesses, this will often be the owner's own home. The bank will get the property in the event of the business failing and it being impossible to pay back the loan in any other way.

collective bargaining involves direct negotiations between the trade union representing the employees and the employers or the employers' organisation. Some employers welcome collective bargaining as it allows them to make a single agreement covering all employees. Others prefer to negotiate directly with individuals who may have less bargaining power than the union. Research has shown that on average, unionised workforces' pay will be about 10% above that of non-unionised workforces.

Since the legislation of the 1980s which reduced trade union power, unions have got into the habit of offering members a range of benefits in addition to that of collective negotiation.

collective farm: under communism, individual farms were often amalgamated to form large, community wide organisations. The farmers became employees of the collective. On the whole, this gave farmers little incentive to try to increase production so that over time, food shortages developed. When the Chinese government abandoned collectives in the late 1970s and gave individual farmers much more responsibility, output went up very fast.

collusion occurs when firms act together in an informal way to avoid strong competition with each other. They may agree on a minimum price or share the market on a geographical basis. Firms will take great care to conceal their agreements from the *Competition Commission*, which has the power to investigate them. Collusion is most likely to occur where there is an *oligopoly*, with relatively few producers and *barriers to entry*.

collusive oligopoly: where producers in an oligopoly situation collude, they can collectively behave like a monopolist. By operating jointly, they can maximise profit in the same way that a *monopoly* would. This means that output will be reduced and prices will be higher than they would be in a competitive market.

colonialism: the process by which European countries took possession of large parts of the rest of the world during the 17th to the 19th centuries. Although few colonies remain as possessions of other countries, the aftermath of the colonial period has entailed a large number of very uneven trading relationships. Some developed countries still try to exclude imports from competitive producers in developing countries, just as they did in the colonial period. Although the EU has concessional trading arrangements with its ex-colonies, these are not nearly as generous as they could be.

command economy: an economic system in which decisions about how resources are to be allocated are made by the government or its agencies. The underlying philosophy was contained in the works of *Karl Marx*, as interpreted by the Communist parties of the countries concerned. The East European countries, Russia and the other component countries of the old USSR all abandoned communism in 1989 when it became apparent that the USSR government was no longer prepared to maintain the system by armed force. China, Cuba, Vietnam and North Korea still have large parts of their economies operating under a command system, although all except North Korea are moving closer to a market system.

The major problem for command economies is that decisions are administrative in nature and not linked to levels of demand for the final product. All the command economies tended to concentrate on heavy industry at the expense of consumer goods production. Many products were of poor quality because producers had no incentive to improve them. So in the end the system failed to provide the rising standard of living experienced in the West. See also *centrally planned economy*.

commercial banks accept deposits from the general public and make loans to individuals and small and medium-sized businesses. They are also known as high street or retail banks. They provide a variety of financial services such as credit cards, mortgages, foreign exchange transactions and stockbroking. They are different from central banks, with their official functions, and from merchant banks, which deal only with larger businesses.

commercial law means the system of laws with which all businesses must comply. The law requires them to pay their debts and honour contracts. This is important because it creates a level playing field for all business activity and removes some of the risks associated with buying selling, borrowing and lending.

commercial policy means the set of measures which determine how trade takes place both within the country and internationally. It includes policies on import controls and export promotion.

Commission for Racial Equality: the government organisation which aims to reduce racial discrimination in the labour market. Unemployment statistics and earnings data show quite clearly that discrimination is still going on, even after differences in qualifications are allowed for. Members of ethnic minorities are paid less than their market rate or are simply passed over during the recruitment process.

commodity: literally, any good which can be bought and sold. However, the term is usually taken to mean raw material or semi-manufactured goods which are traded in bulk. Examples include tea, sugar, iron ore, wheat, wool and so on. These are widely traded on world markets. In London there are specific commodity markets which deal in these goods, sometimes in a speculative fashion by effectively betting on their future prices. The term commodity is usually used when the good in question is homogeneous, so that no one producer's output is distinguishable from another's. For example, one load of iron ore is much the same as another of the same grade, irrespective of which firm mined it.

Commodity markets have some particular features:

- Commodity prices can be very volatile. Most of them can be stored and demand and supply are not always in equilibrium. Demand for metal ores varies with the *trade cycle* and the supply of agricultural products depends on weather conditions. Markets may be slow to respond to changes.

- Many commodities have rather inelastic supply. Relatively small changes in demand and supply can lead to large changes in price. For example, when the demand for metal ores rises during a boom, little can be done in the short run to increase supply and the price may rise sharply, rationing existing supplies amongst the buyers prepared to pay the highest prices.

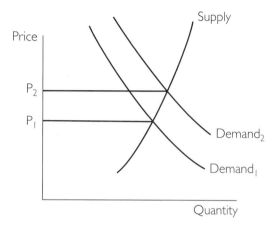

Rising demand leads to a sharp rise in price if supply is inelastic

commodity agreement: for some commodities which have experienced fluctuating prices, the exporting countries have agreed on measures which might stabilise the world price. The main method of doing this is to create a *buffer stock*, adding to it when prices are low and so helping to prevent them from falling further. Stocks can be sold when the price rises, limiting the increase. In this way it was hoped to stabilise producer incomes. The most important example was the International Coffee Agreement.

It is very hard to make commodity agreements work because it is so difficult to control the market effectively. Currently none are in operation although the coffee-exporting countries investigated the possibilities again in 1999-2000.

commodity markets: the means by which commodities are bought and sold. In the past, commodity markets would be in a specific location, such as the London Metal Exchange. This is no longer necessary to the existence of a market, which consists of buyers and sellers who keep in touch with one another electronically. Provided the commodity is classified and graded in a way which minimises disputes over quality, the market may consist simply of a network of dealers.

Common Agricultural Policy (CAP) embodies all of the agricultural policies of the EU. The original objectives were to support and stabilise farm incomes and to provide food at a reasonable price. It was set up at a time when agriculture was declining in economic importance and many European farmers were operating on a small scale and rather inefficiently. Consequently farm incomes were low and growing more slowly than incomes on average.

Shortly before entry to the EU in 1973, the UK adopted similar policies to the CAP. The basic framework involves:

- guaranteed prices for farm products and an arrangement by which farmers can sell their output at that price
- a variable levy on imported foods, which brings their prices up to the EU
  level
- export subsidies for surpluses
- grants to encourage efficient operation
- a set-aside scheme designed to prevent overproduction, by which farmers
  are paid to leave a part of their land fallow.

EU prices have mostly been above the level of world prices. Keeping the prices high,
and not allowing competition from imports, gave farmers an incentive to increase
output. The increase has made the EU including the UK largely self-sufficient in food
but it has also lead to the accumulation of large surpluses. Subsidies were used to
enable the CAP authorities to sell the surpluses on world markets. These cheap food
exports have caused some disruption on world markets and are very unpopular with
major food exporters such as the US and Australia. They have at times depressed
world prices for some products. They may also have depressed food prices in Africa
and so reduced local production. The diagram shows how high prices lead to excess
supply, commonly known by names such as 'the butter mountain' and 'the wine lake'.

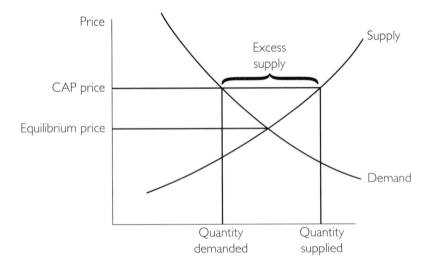

If prices are above the equilibrium level, a surplus will develop

Since 1992 the CAP has been much reformed and the guaranteed prices are now
considerably lower than they were. This policy was aimed partly at reducing the huge
cost of the CAP. At various times the CAP has absorbed between one half and two
thirds of the EU budget. In addition, it was estimated in 1994 that the CAP was cost-
ing £134 per person per year in higher food prices. Further reforms are under way
and there was a considerable fall in farm incomes during 1999 and 2000. There are
increased grants available to farmers but at present they do not fully compensate for
the lower guaranteed prices.

High food prices hurt poorer people directly. In addition, the cost of the CAP has inflated the EU budget. This comes partly from tax revenues (such as the 1% levy drawn from national VAT revenues). The EU has come under heavy pressure to reduce *protection* of agriculture in *WTO* negotiations. Meantime, EU farmers have become very much more efficient. It should be remembered that new technologies have had a big impact on farming as well and have been partly responsible for the surplus production.

common external tariff: the import duties which are set by the European Union to cover certain imported goods for all member countries. The common external tariff favours producers within the EU and discriminates against producers outside the EU. In recent years the *tariffs* on many manufactured products have been reduced as a result of international trade negotiations under the auspices of the World Trade Organisation. The common external tariff remains an important element in EU trade policy.

common market: a commonly used term meaning an area within which there is free trade and free movement of people and capital.

commons: resources which can be used freely by anyone. No one has property rights over these resources. The simplest examples are common grazing land and sea fishing. The resources have no price so everyone has an incentive to make as much use of the commons as is profitable for them. If the resources are abundant this causes no problems but if they become scarce, e.g. through over fishing, the resources are destroyed. Some way has to be found to assign property rights, e.g. through quotas or charges. 'The tragedy of the commons' refers to the dangers of overuse.

communism: the political system which underpins *centrally planned economies*. Until 1989 communist governments maintained power across Eastern Europe, Russia and the Central Asian republics. At that time the President of the USSR, Gorbachev, discontinued the long-standing policy of supporting communist governments by force. Quite rapidly all these countries moved towards a more democratic approach. China, Vietnam, North Korea and Cuba remain communist inspired though with varying degrees of liberalisation in their economic organisation. Communist countries are characterised by the repression of political opposition, limitations on human rights and a considerable degree of economic control on the part of the government, even where some decisions are market determined.

Communist ideology was inspired by the work of *Karl Marx*. It was originally intended to improve the standard of living of ordinary people by restricting the power of private sector businesses.

company: the basic organisational structure for a firm. The company is legally separate from the people who own or run it and can own assets and enter into contracts. The formation of companies is controlled by law. An important objective of company law is to encourage entrepreneurs to take risks in ways which are likely to be productive. The important element in this process is *limited liability*, which means that the owners of the business (i.e. the *shareholders*) cannot lose more than the money put into the business. Personal possessions cannot be seized in order to pay the firm's debts. This encourages a flow of finance for investment in productive capacity.

company taxation: the taxes levied on firms' profits. The main tax is *corporation tax*. However, companies may be liable for other taxes such as *capital gains tax*.

comparability: a yardstick for determining wage levels in negotiations between employers and trade unions. Unions may use wage rates in other comparable occupations as part of their argument for a pay increase. There is economic logic in this as a comparable wage could be seen as the *opportunity cost* of continuing to work for the current employer.

comparative advantage: the economic theory which holds that countries can produce more if they trade with one another. This theory has been immensely influential. Although the theory is very much a simplification, the impact which international trade has had on economic growth in a number of countries is very striking. The theory does help to explain the connection.

The theory of comparative advantage was first set out by David Ricardo in his book THE PRINCIPLES OF POLITICAL ECONOMY, published in 1817. He argued that all countries would be able to increase output if they specialised and traded with each other. This would hold even if one country was more efficient at producing everything than the other, i.e. it had an *absolute advantage*. Specialisation works to increase output whenever the *opportunity costs* of particular products are different between countries. If one country is not the best at producing anything, it can still gain by specialising in the product it is least bad at producing.

It works like this. The theory assumes that there are two countries and two products. Think of a country like the US, producing computers and wine. It is highly efficient at producing both. Still, it trades with Chile, which also produces computers and wine, but is less efficient at producing both. It will still pay to specialise because Chile's comparative disadvantage is less in wine.

Think of each country having 1000 workers. Before trade, half produce computers and half produce wine. The table shows how much each can produce.

	Output of computers	Output of wine (cases)
US	100	250
Chile	20	200
Total output	120	450

For Chile it takes 25 people to produce a computer. These 25 people could produce 10 cases of wine. So the opportunity cost of a computer is 10 cases of wine. Similarly, it takes 2.5 people to produce a case of wine and these people (i.e. this amount of labour) could produce one tenth of a computer, so this is the opportunity cost of the wine.

By contrast, in the US, it takes five people to produce a computer. Those five people could produce 2.5 cases of wine. The opportunity costs are shown in full in the table.

	Opportunity cost of computer	Opportunity cost of a case of wine
US	2.5 cases of wine	2/5 of a computer
Chile	10 cases of wine	1/10 of a computer

Now it is possible to see that the opportunity cost of wine in Chile is lower than it is in the US. It will pay Chile to specialise in the production of wine and give up producing computers. If each country concentrates on the product with the lowest opportunity cost, total output will increase. If the US moves people into computer production so that there are 800 altogether, it will be able to produce 160 computers, while still producing 100 cases of wine. Chile, specialising entirely in wine, will produce 400 cases of wine. The table shows the totals.

	Output of computers	Output of wine
US	160	100
Chile	0	400
Total output after specialisation	160	500

It is not possible to say which country will benefit most from the increase in output. In the real world, trade is greatly affected by all kinds of import restrictions and also by exchange rates. The theory of comparative advantage explains why trade and growth are linked and draws attention to the damage caused by trade restrictions. It does not make precise predictions possible.

compensation principle shows that society gains from a certain change if the gainers gain more than the losers lose. In other words, the gainers could compensate the losers and still be better off. It is actually rather difficult to use the compensation principle in practical situations, because it is often hard to quantify gains and losses in money terms.

competition: the process by which businesses strive against one another to capture a larger market. In price competition they may try undercutting each other's prices. This is known as competitive pricing. The impact of competition on prices is plain to see. For example, since BT's monopoly of telephone calls came to an end, the cost of phone calls has fallen sharply. This is partly because of new technologies but also because of competition.

Competition is immensely important in ensuring that consumers get the products they want at the lowest possible cost. Only through competition do firms have the incentive to minimise their costs and produce as efficiently as possible. So technical efficiency is sometimes improved through the action of competition.

Perfect competition defines a theoretical scenario in which it is impossible for any producer to gain any kind of control over the market. It has the following features:

- there are many sellers
- all firms make homogeneous products, which means that it is impossible to distinguish one firm's product from that of a competing firm
- firms can enter and exit the market freely – there are no *barriers to entry*
- everyone has full information about the market
- all producers use the same technology.

Imperfect competition may still be very strong competition but involves fewer sellers. Through non-price competition they may seek to improve product quality or increase demand through advertising and other marketing strategies. Three types of imperfect competition can be identified:

- *monopolistic competition* refers to a market with easy entry and many sellers, each of whom has a slightly differentiated product
- *oligopoly* refers to a market with a few large producers who compete but devise complex strategies for gaining ground in the marketplace
- *duopoly*, in which there are just two big producers.

With both oligopoly and duopoly there may be long periods when there is little sign of price competition, but plenty of evidence of non-price competition.

Competition Act 1980: this legislation extended the existing competition policy to cover the public sector as well as the private sector. It also defined *anti-competitive activities* as activities which might have the effect of restricting, distorting or preventing competition. The *Director General of Fair Trading* was made responsible for investigating such activities.

Competition Act 1998: by 1998 all political parties in the UK wanted to see consumers getting stronger protection from monopoly power. The act had two important features, both based on EU law:

- all anti-competitive agreements, such as *cartels*, were prohibited
- firms were prohibited from abusing a dominant market position.

This meant that agreements between firms on prices and any process designed to restrict supply became illegal. The *Director General of Fair Trading* was given new powers to investigate price fixing and to fine companies found guilty up to 10% of their UK turnover.

The *Monopolies and Mergers Commission* was renamed the *Competition Commission*. The act came into force on March 1st 2000. Early indications suggest that its extra powers will actually be used to act against monopoly power more strongly than before.

Competition Commission: the organisation responsible for investigating markets in the UK to ensure that they are kept in line with *competition policy*. It has two main functions:

- to investigate planned mergers and to determine whether they will lead to excessive monopoly power
- to act as a court of appeal for firms which have been found by the Director General of Fair Trading to be engaging in *anti-competitive activities* such as a *cartel*.

An early forerunner of the commission was set up in 1948 by the then Labour government. Successive acts of Parliament gradually increased its powers and changed its way of working. Its name was changed by the 1998 Competition Act from the *Monopolies and Mergers Commission* to the Competition Commission.

The *Director General of Fair Trading* can recommend to the President of the Board of Trade that a particular market situation or possible merger should be investigated. It is then up to the Minister to decide whether the Competition Commission should go ahead with the investigation.

As a general rule, any merger which is likely to lead to a 25% or greater share of the market will be investigated by the Commission. The Commission itself cannot take legal action; it can only advise the *Office of Fair Trading* that action is necessary.

Increasingly, UK merger policy is influenced by EU directives.

At the time of writing it is too soon to decide what the effect of the 1998 legislation may be over the next decade. The measures came into force early in 2000. The evidence suggests that action against anti-competitive activities will be strengthened.

competition policy: monopolies are generally considered to be against the interests of consumers and the public and governments legislate to restrict them. In the UK, the *Office of Fair Trading* (OFT) has the job of policing monopolies, supported by the *Competition Commission*. Any merger which creates a market share of 25% or more is likely to be referred by the OFT to the President of the Board of Trade and to the Competition Commission, which will investigate whether the merger is thought to be in the public interest.

Increasingly the power of the EU has come into play in this area.

- Article 86 of the Treaty of Rome works to control the development of monopolies.
- Article 85 of the Treaty of Rome works to reduce restrictive practices. These include market sharing agreements and any other restriction on supply.

Monopoly theory shows that a firm with market power may restrict output and raise prices. This can be shown to reduce consumers' real incomes. Firms which use their market power may require an unnecessarily large quantity of real resources to produce their output, which is quite simply wasteful. Hence the perceived need to control market power in the interests of the consumer.

competitive advantage describes the quality needed by a business which can flourish when there are many other businesses with competing products. It may be that the business has lower costs and prices, better quality or design skills or it may enjoy superior marketing skills. Investment in new technologies may sometimes yield a competitive advantage. In general, competitive advantage usually rests on the extent to which the business emphasises innovation, the way it exploits relationships with other businesses and its reputation with customers.

competitive behaviour involves striving to sell the product without collaboration of any kind with other firms. It may include price competition or non-price competition, which means competing on quality, design, special promotions or after-sales service.

competitive devaluation involves a government trying to devalue by more than a trading partner so as to achieve a price advantage for exports. It was seen in the 1930s when many countries tried to devalue to counter the effects of depression. If all trading partners do the same, the only effect is to destabilise all their economies. Something similar was seen during the *Asian financial crisis*, 1997–1999, though it was probably not intentional, when confidence in a number of Asian currencies hit successive new lows.

competitive markets are those markets where a number of firms compete strongly with one another. In these markets prices are likely to be kept close to the minimum *average cost*; they will therefore tend to be technically efficient.

competitiveness: the degree to which a firm succeeds in selling its product when there is competition in the marketplace. Its competitiveness may rest on a price advantage, which may reflect lower costs than those of competitors, or a willingness to accept lower profits. Alternatively, competitiveness may rest on an advantage in design, quality, reliability or customer service or some other important product feature. Either way, it is likely to be related to consumers' perceived value for money.

International competitiveness is important to economies and to governments because it enables both domestic producers and exporters to expand, leading ultimately to economic growth. It is usually associated with strong *productivity* growth or a commitment to innovation. It can be measured by examining unit costs in comparison with those of other economies. Without competitiveness, both domestic producers and exporters face strong competition from foreign producers. Imports will rise and exports fall, leading generally to falling aggregate demand and to depressed trading conditions.

competitive tendering occurs when several firms bid for the opportunity to provide a particular service. It has been used by local authorities in the UK in order to increase efficiency through competition. It provides an incentive to the competing firms and can mean that the quality of the service improves. It can also mean that wage rates and employment conditions deteriorate if there is labour available at a low wage.

complementary goods are consumed together so that a change in demand for one will lead to a change in demand for the other. A fall in the price of a CD player occurring after some technological change could mean increased demand for CDs. Similarly a rise in petrol prices could lead to a fall in demand for cars, particularly large ones. *Cross-price elasticity* is used to measure the closeness of the relationship between complementary goods.

In practice, price and quantity changes for complementary goods may be quite hard to detect. However, economic theory allows us to decide the direction of change, even when the overall effect is quite small. (See Figure on page 51.)

complex monopoly means a situation in which a small number of oligopoly producers are not really competing effectively although there is no *collusion* or *cartel*. Often, they will all be charging very similar prices. This could be a result of *tacit agreement*. Early in 2001, the *Competition Commission* announced its findings that the big

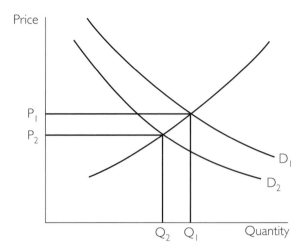

Complementary goods (see page 50)

A fall in demand for cars after a rise in the price of petrol. Both equilibrium price and equilibrium quantity may fall

four banks, HSBC, Lloyds TSB, Barclays and the Royal Bank of Scotland, were operating a complex monopoly in services to small businesses. Between them they had 89% of all small business current accounts. It had been suggested that the banks were making 'excess profits' out of this side of their business by abusing their dominant position.

compliance costs are costs associated with legal requirements. Products which are subject to tight regulations, such as electrical goods, will have compliance costs. Some compliance costs apply to all firms, e.g. health and safety regulations.

components are inputs to the production process which have already undergone a manufacturing process. They can be made in the same factory but more often nowadays they will be bought from a specialist supplier. Car batteries and computer chips are components – on their own they have little value, but combined with other components they become a valuable final product.

Many manufacturers support large numbers of component suppliers, which depend on them for their markets.

composite demand applies to products which are used for more than one purpose. An increase in demand for quarried stone for building purposes could increase the price and have an impact on the availability of stone for road building.

compound interest: over time, if interest is paid on the sum outstanding plus previously paid interest which has been reinvested, the value of the original sum can be greatly enhanced. This is important for contributors to pension funds, who will not normally take out the interest they earn until they retire.

computer-aided design (CAD) involves programs which allow the designer to visualise the design in many different ways. It thus speeds up the design process and can reduce costs or improve the product.

computer-aided manufacture (CAM) means that manufacturing processes are computer controlled. This can reduce costs of production, through improved stock control, or save labour, e.g. with the use of robots.

computerised trading: the use of computers in the marketplace, for example to track share prices. Computers can be programmed to sell shares automatically if their price falls by a certain amount.

concentration means the extent to which a particular market is dominated by a few firms. A high degree of concentration implies that there are relatively few firms in the market and conditions are similar to *oligopoly*. A low level of concentration implies that there are many sellers, with a market system such as monopolistic competition or near-perfect competition.

concentration ratio expresses the percentage of the market accounted for by a given number of firms, for example, by five firms. Within the EU, in 1996, it was estimated that the five largest firms had 73% of the total market in optical instruments. This is a very high concentration ratio. The five largest clothing manufacturers had only 4% of the market.

conciliation occurs when a person or a body intervenes to try to get both parties in a dispute to agree to an appropriate compromise. Conciliation can be important in the resolution of industrial disputes between unions and management. ACAS, the Advisory, Conciliation and Arbitration Service, exists to provide conciliation services for such situations.

conditionality refers to the practice of the IMF of offering loans on condition that the government complies with various requirements as to its economic policies.

conduct refers to the behaviour of firms in relation to their competitors. A study of the conduct of some bus companies during the period immediately following de-regulation would have revealed some 'dirty tricks' such as running a very frequent, cheap service for just long enough to drive a competitor out of business. More often, conduct will be anti-competitive in a much more subtle way.

Confederation of British Industry (CBI): the UK's foremost employers' association, which acts as a mouthpiece for businesses generally. It represents their interests to the government when necessary. It has the resources to collect important information which it publishes in its Quarterly Survey of Economic Trends.

conflicting objectives: governments often face a situation in which they can only achieve one of their policy objectives at the expense of another. The most obvious example is the short-term *trade-off* between inflation and unemployment. There were many occasions during the 1970s, 1980s and early 1990s when it would have been possible to reduce unemployment by increasing *aggregate demand* in the economy, but the consequence would have been increasing inflation due to *excess demand* in the economy.

conglomerate: a firm which includes many unrelated businesses. It used to be thought that a firm which had strong management skills could apply these to any type of business. So taking over a wide variety of potentially successful firms and improving their management made some sense. However, conglomerates have been less successful in recent years and some have been broken up by selling off components.

conservation concerns the way in which depletable resources are used. When production involves the use of real resources which cannot be replaced, there will be a case for conserving those resources in such a way that they do not become excessively scarce too quickly. In this way conservation measures may apply to petrol, on which taxes have been raised so as to discourage consumption. Alternatively conservation may apply to a resource which is damaged by consumption; when new roads are built, countryside which could have been conserved will be destroyed.

consortium: a group of organisations which undertake to carry out a project in collaboration. For example, the Channel Tunnel was built by a consortium of contractors.

conspicuous consumption: the process of buying goods and services not for their actual usefulness but in order to impress other people. Normally economists assume that people make independent choices about the products they buy, basing their decisions on their own personal preferences. With conspicuous consumption the decision will be based on what products are most likely to impress others.

constant prices are used when it is important to be able to measure a certain variable in a way that avoids distortion by inflation. For example, real income is measured in constant prices. This will involve the selection of a base year, so that the variable is expressed in, for example, 1995 prices.

constant returns to scale: when output can be increased in such a way that exactly the same quantities of inputs are required for each unit of output, there are said to be constant returns to scale. This situation contrasts with increasing returns to scale, which means that output increases with proportionately fewer inputs. This would correspond roughly to reaping economies of scale. Similarly, decreasing returns to scale might be associated with diseconomies of scale.

constraint refers to the way in which a firm or the economy may be prevented from expanding. An obvious constraint which may affect either is a shortage of skilled labour. Legal constraints, in the shape of various employment laws, may affect firms. Governments are usually constrained by a wide range of factors, including the need to retain some popularity. *Supply constraints* are those which hinder the growth of output and can reflect any kind of shortage of resources.

consumer: a buyer of goods and services for their own use or for others. In economics, consumers are sometimes perceived as individuals or they may be seen as households, in which many purchasing decisions are collective. Most of us do consume more than just the products we buy for ourselves.

The consumer is an important player in the market because a decision to buy creates a potentially profitable situation for the supplier. There is then an incentive to ensure that the products desired are made available at a price which generates some profit. Equally, decisions not to buy may end in a producer going out of business or cutting back production. This is the basis of *consumer sovereignty*.

consumer confidence: decisions to buy may be curtailed if consumers are expecting hard times ahead and prefer to save for the time being. Expectations of rising unemployment or an imminent fall in income will usually depress consumer confidence. Similarly, a high level of consumer confidence will usually lead to buoyant sales and a high level of consumption spending. This may be financed by rising consumer credit, i.e. borrowing.

consumer durables are goods which provide a continuous flow of services over an extended period of time. For example, a washing machine, a car or a TV can be used over a period of 10 years or more. This means that the demand for them is more variable than it is for, say, food items. If incomes are stagnant or falling, the purchase of new durable goods can be postponed. The existing ones can be repaired or made to last longer. Demand for durables can fluctuate with the *trade cycle*. During the optimistic period of a boom people may take advantage of their rising incomes and replace their durable goods and vice versa. Demand for durables may also be affected by changes in interest rates because they are often financed by borrowing.

consumer expenditure is the sum total of all spending by consumers in the whole economy over a period of time. It is a component of *aggregate demand*. The level of consumer expenditure and its likely future growth are sometimes important variables for a business which is considering whether to expand.

consumer goods are the tangible products bought by consumers for imminent use. They contrast with investment or intermediate goods which are bought by firms as inputs for the production process.

consumer preferences: the pattern of personal likes and dislikes that determine decisions to buy. Consumer preferences change over time, creating a changing market to which firms must respond. Of course, firms may try to influence consumer preferences by advertising and other means of promotion.

consumer price index: the index which measures changes in the prices of consumer goods and services. In the UK this is the *Retail Price Index*.

consumer protection: a set of laws designed to prevent firms from doing things which are not in the best interests of consumers. Health and safety standards and labelling requirements are obvious consumer protection measures, as are many of the requirements of *competition policy*. Some aspects of consumer protection are resented by some firms because they raise costs.

consumer sovereignty is the name for the process by which consumer demand determines the *allocation of resources*. An increase in demand will tend to make it more profitable to produce the item in question. This encourages firms to produce more. Similarly, if demand falls, losses may be made and these create an incentive for producers to move resources into some other line of production. In this way the *profit-signalling mechanism* transmits the information given by consumer demand to producers so that the allocation of resources is kept in line with the pattern of demand. This theory underlies the competitive market model upon which much of micro-economics is based.

In practice, *market imperfections* can greatly reduce consumer sovereignty. Market power and advertising can push consumers into choices that for them are less than optimal. (See also *supernormal profit* and *invisible hand*.)

consumer surplus: a consumer good will be valued more highly by some consumers than by others, yet they will all pay the same price for it. Some consumers would be willing to pay a price higher than the actual market price. The term consumer surplus refers to the value of the extra satisfaction which these consumers get from the item, over and above what they have had to pay for it. The consumer surplus is shown on a supply and demand diagram by the triangle enclosed by the demand curve and the price line. The demand curve shows how consumers value the product and all those who are prepared to pay a higher price get some extra satisfaction.

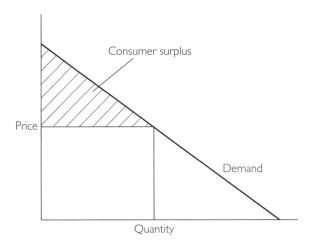

consumption means total consumption in the economy as a whole. It is an important component of *aggregate demand*. (See also *consumer expenditure*.)

consumption function: the relationship between income and consumption is known as the consumption function. The proportion of income consumed can be measured in two ways, using the *average propensity to consume* or the *marginal propensity to consume*.

consumption bundle: a collection of consumer goods which a consumer might choose to purchase.

contestability: the extent to which the market is contestable. This means whether it is easy or not for a competing firm to enter the market and operate successfully. Contestable markets are likely to be more competitive.

contestable markets: it may be comparatively easy for newcomers to the industry to break into a contestable market. This means that existing businesses, already in the field, face a constant threat of increasing competition. In the reverse case, where there are *barriers to entry*, existing businesses are protected from competition. We might expect that prices will be generally lower in contestable markets, merely because of the possibility of competition. If they announce very large profits, firms already in the industry may be advertising the possibility of large profits for others and this may encourage new entrants.

continuous improvement: see *kaizen*.

contract: a legal agreement between two parties which defines the relationship in terms of what is expected on both sides. It will detail the actions to be taken and the payments to be made. An employment contract is between the employer and the employee and states the work to be done, the payment to be made and the conditions of employment which the employer must provide.

Contracts are of great importance for the efficient working of a market economy. They:

- allow firms to be reasonably confident that they will be paid for work completed or orders fulfilled
- give individuals some assurance that they will not be cheated
- encourage lending and borrowing which provides finance for investment.

The absence of a system of commercial law which governs the enforcement of contracts makes business transactions risky and therefore raises the cost of doing any kind of business. This can severely hamper the process of economic development in poorer developing countries and in countries in transition from central planning to a market system.

contracting out means buying in inputs from an independent supplier rather than sourcing all inputs from inside the organisation. It may apply in the private or the public sector. In the private sector it may involve buying *components* or services from another firm. This might include canteen, cleaning or accounting services, for example. This is now often known as *outsourcing*.

In the public sector, local authorities have contracted out services such as refuse collection or street cleaning. The objectives of this are:

- to promote greater efficiency by getting access to new management strategies
- to save money by encouraging competition between potential suppliers.

Sometimes contracting out has been very unpopular because it can mean that the people who actually do the work may be paid less if the labour is available at the lower wage.

contraction: the process by which the economy actually becomes smaller when output falls. It starts with a fall in *aggregate demand*. Sales fall and firms find they have rising stocks. They cut back their output and quite soon make some employees redundant. This leads to a reduction in real incomes which may lead to a further fall in aggregate demand.

contractionary policy is used when the economy appears to be growing unsustainably fast or when *inflation* is becoming a problem. The policies are of two kinds:

- *monetary policy*, which would require high interest rates, is decided by the Bank of England
- *fiscal policy*, in the form of either tax increases or government expenditure cuts, or both, is decided by the government.

In both cases, the objective is to reduce the rate of growth of aggregate demand so that inflationary pressures are reduced. Reducing demand will slow down firms' attempts to recruit more labour, thus reducing the demand for scarce skills and making it harder for people to negotiate higher pay.

Convention on International Trade in Endangered Species (CITES): an international treaty agreed in 1972 to regulate international trade in species which could become extinct. The objective is to reduce the demand for these species. Unfortunately this does not encourage potential exporters of endangered species to help with conservation measures. Quite often the species is threatened by economic development which reduces the amount of space for its habitat. Some have argued that it would be better to allow trade provided the exporting country organises a conservation programme.

convergence: refers to the process of bringing the *European Union's* economies and currencies into line with each other. This was an essential prerequisite for *Economic and Monetary Union* (EMU) and the single currency. Unless all the member countries have similar levels of economic activity, rates of inflation and interest rates, joining the currencies together could cause major economic upheavals. The main focus for convergence is upon public sector borrowing and inflation rates. Convergence could present problems for some of the countries which will apply to join the EMU in the future. (See also *convergence criteria*.)

convergence criteria: the specific conditions for entry into the EMU which must be met by all participants, as set out in the *Maastricht Treaty* of 1993. These are:

- consumer price inflation not higher than 1.5% above that of the three best performing countries in the Union
- interest rates on long-term government bonds not more that 2% higher than those in the same three member states
- the government deficit to be at or below 3% of GDP
- total government debt to be at or below 60% of GDP
- the exchange rate to have been fairly stable for the past two years.

These criteria have been fudged somewhat for some countries but substantial progress has been made towards them. At the time of writing, the UK would have no difficulty in satisfying all except the last.

convertible currency: a currency which can be freely converted into other currencies. The advantage of a convertible currency is that it encourages *foreign direct* *investment* and leads to the integration of capital markets. The disadvantage of convertibility is that it can mean that there are sudden runs on the currency which lead to instability and a sharp drop in its value. This happened to Malaysia during the *Asian financial crisis* in 1998. The government responded by suspending convertibility. In the same situation most other countries did not.

co-operative: a business owned by its employees or its customers. Retail co-operatives, like the Co-op, are owned by the customers. Some co-operatives are owned by their employees, all of whom will have some say in major decisions. Sometimes co-operative selling organisations are set up by farmers to distribute their products.

Copenhagen criteria: in 1993 the EU set out three conditions for countries wishing to join. These are:

- stability and democracy, with protection for the rights of minorities
- a market economy capable of competing within the EU
- the capability to meet all the requirements of membership including a functioning competition policy, compliance with harmonisation regulations and, eventually, joining the EMU.

Five countries are thought to be close to meeting these criteria: the Czech Republic, Estonia, Hungary, Poland and Slovenia.

copyright protects the work of authors, composers and artists and includes film and television. It is illegal to copy work which is copyright without the permission of the originator or the owner of the copyright. Copyrights confer *intellectual property rights*. Without these, there would be little incentive to produce original work.

There are open issues relating to music which is downloaded over the Internet and also to so-called pirate copies of CDs. Making a copy of any commercially produced musical recording, without the permission of the copyright owner, is illegal and can be regarded as stealing intellectual property rights.

core: the central part of an economy where infrastructure and communications are easy to access and economic growth is most buoyant. At the *periphery*, there are likely to be lower standards of living and lack of the facilities which could encourage growth. In the UK the South East is generally regarded as the core, although other regions have also prospered. Parts of Scotland and Wales and Northern England would be seen as the periphery. It is a matter for debate whether government policies can tackle the problems of the periphery effectively.

corporate bonds are loans to companies which carry a fixed rate of interest and have a fixed maturity value. They may be held by individuals, by banks or other financial intermediaries. They may be traded on the *Stock Exchange*, should the holder require *liquidity*. The price at which they are traded will vary according to interest rates and the comparative profitability of other investments.

corporate governance refers to the way in which decisions are taken within a *public company*. It has become an issue because there has been some evidence of company directors acting in their own best interests rather than the interests of *shareholders* or of the wider community. In theory, shareholders can vote to remove directors at the *annual general meeting* but in practice this almost never happens.

Shareholder power may be limited to the influence of the big institutional share-holders such as the pension funds but they do not always act in the public interest if the share price and dividends are not at risk.

corporate objectives: see *business objectives.*

corporate responsibility reflects the extent to which a firm accepts obligations to any group of people other than the *shareholders* or owners of the business. A firm which takes corporate responsibility seriously will recognise the rights of employees, customers, suppliers and the community at large. This will mean taking into account the environmental and ethical impact of the firm's activities. Some businesses now produce an environmental report in addition to the conventional *annual report and accounts*; for example, Sainsbury's does this. Others have explicit ethical policies which change the nature of their *business objectives.*

corporate saving occurs when firms retain some of their profits, keeping them in reserve for the future. Often they will use their savings to replace capital equipment, or expand the business, in the future.

corporation: a limited company. Most often the term is used for a *public limited company.*

Corporation tax is the tax paid on profits. Every business is assessed and required to pay a percentage of its profit after all costs have been deducted. The rate is set each year in the Budget; the level has usually been around 30%. Smaller firms pay a lower percentage, currently 20%.

Worked example: Company A pays 30% tax on profits while the smaller Company B pays 20%

	Company A	Company B
	£000	£000
Revenue	9500	1200
Total costs	7300	840
Pretax profit	2200	360
Corporation tax	660	72
Profit after tax	1540	288

---

correlation measures the extent to which two variables move together. It might be found that changes in spending on luxury cruises are closely related to changes in income, while changes in interest rates are related, but less closely, to the level of con-sumer spending generally.

corruption: using bribes to influence politicians or officials to secure a favourable decision. Corruption has a very bad effect on the *allocation of resources* because deci-sions are made on the basis of the bribe rather than the well-being of the community concerned or the market forces which reflect consumer preferences. It undermines the effectiveness of democratic systems which are designed to reflect the wishes of the electorate. It greatly reduces the efficiency with which market economies work.

Corruption probably takes place in all economies, although the US government has very strict laws against it. The problems it causes loom largest in developing economies and those making the transition from a centrally planned to a market economy. It is almost certainly a major causal factor in the unequal distribution of incomes which often persist in these countries. Powerful businesses and individuals use it to ensure that they are not too exposed to the rigours of competition. This often means that they can go on charging high prices which bring great benefit to themselves.

cost: the value of all the inputs to the production process. These will include the factors of production, land, labour and capital, raw material inputs, energy, transport and component inputs. (See also *average cost, marginal cost, total cost, fixed cost* and *variable cost.*)

cost–benefit analysis examines all the costs of a particular project or decision, be they *external costs* or *internal costs*. The internal costs are private costs which are experienced by the producer, sometimes called the financial costs. For example, the chemical plant will count the financial cost to itself of all the inputs to the production process. In addition to these costs, there will be external costs which are paid by a third party who is not a producer or a consumer. These usually reflect the pollution created in the neighbourhood of the plant, which affects the people who live there. These are social costs and may be hard to quantify.

Including both private and social costs can give a better idea of the true cost to society of some projects. The Victoria Line in the London Underground, the Channel Tunnel and numerous motorway projects have been subjected to cost–benefit analysis. The difficulty is that although some social costs and benefits can be quantified, others cannot. The benefits of faster moving traffic can be estimated for the people who will spend less time in traffic jams during working hours. The benefits of improved health through reduced pollution are more difficult to define. This means that cost–benefit analysis has to be based partly on value judgments about the relative importance of different factors in the decision. However, looking at all costs and benefits does mean that decisions are not made solely on financial evidence.

cost curves relate the cost of the product to the quantity produced. (See also *average cost* and *marginal cost.*)

cost effectiveness means achieving a given objective in the cheapest possible way. This usually means that the cheapest solution must be checked to see that it is not causing unexpected disadvantages which are themselves costly.

cost inflation is a general rise in prices caused by rising costs of production. It can occur if *commodity* prices are rising because these will be important inputs for a number of manufactured goods. Rising wages can contribute as can rising property values. Another cause is a fall in the exchange rate, because this will make imports dearer. Many products have imported inputs and the cost of these will rise. Cost inflation is just one element in the overall inflation process and demand factors are likely to also be present in any inflationary situation.

Expectations of future price increases may affect cost inflation because they feed into employees' efforts to secure pay increases.

cost of living: the cost of a selection of goods and services considered necessary to a normal life. This is measured by the *Retail Price Index*, which is based on price data for a wide range of products and retail outlets. The term 'cost of living' tends to be used rather vaguely because it is itself a very imprecise idea. The problem is that it varies from one household to another and specific price changes have a different impact in different types of household.

cost of production: see *cost*.

cost plus pricing means that the seller simply calculates costs and adds a mark-up for profit. This will work quite well for the seller, provided other firms are not able to compete with lower prices. It may or may not be the price which maximises profits.

The seller will have no incentive to control costs. However, even with a large contract, e.g. for military equipment using new technologies, it may be the best option for the buyer because costs will be very uncertain. Any fixed price would include a large allowance incase costs turned out to be higher than expected.

cost structure: the way in which costs of production are spread between different inputs. Some products will have high capital costs (e.g. electricity) while others will have high labour costs (e.g. medical care).

costs of growth: the negative aspects of the growth process, such as pollution and congestion and the depletion of resources generally. As negative *externalities* increase in number the benefits of *economic growth* are reduced.

council housing: housing for rent provided by local authorities on the basis of need. Rents are usually slightly below the market level and there are often waiting lists indicating *excess demand*. Priority is given to families which are homeless or living in overcrowded conditions. Those who cannot pay the rent may be given housing benefit. Once they have a council house, tenants are allowed to stay there indefinitely but will not usually be able to move to a council house in another local authority area. This may mean that they become *geographically immobile* and have difficulty in finding work close to their homes.

Council of Ministers: the group which takes the biggest decisions in the EU. There will be one Minister from each member state, chosen according to the type of decision to be made. For economic decisions that will usually be the Chancellor of the Exchequer or the President of the Board of Trade. The composition of the Council of Ministers and the way in which it works may well be changed as the EU approaches the changes needed to accommodate new members during the enlargement process.

council tax is a tax raised on the value of houses by local authorities. If it is assumed that larger houses are owned by people who are better off, it is broadly related to ability to pay. People on benefits are generally exempt. Council tax funds a part of local expenditure, the rest coming from central government.

counter-cyclical policy is used by governments to try to reduce the severity of fluctuations in economic activity associated with the *trade cycle*. They will use *fiscal policy* and *monetary policy* either to reduce or to increase *aggregate demand*. A good deal of careful judgment is required to ensure that the actions taken are timely and appropriate to the precise situation in the economy.

- Fiscal policy may be automatic or discretionary. *Automatic stabilisers* work without further decisions, by reducing tax payments during recession and increasing benefits paid to unemployed people. In addition, the Chancellor may choose to alter tax rates at the time of the Budget. A tax cut during a recession or an increase in government spending, financed by borrowing, may be appropriate. If the economy is booming and approaching an acceleration in inflation, tax increases and expenditure cuts might be sensible but may be difficult politically.

- Monetary policy can be implemented without political difficulty because it is in the hands of the *Monetary Policy Committee* of the Bank of England. If inflation is rising due to unsustainably fast growth and excess demand, the committee will raise interest rates at its monthly meeting. This will make spending financed by borrowing dearer. It is likely to discourage investment and spending on consumer durables. However, it will work with rather a long time lag, perhaps up to two years. Similarly, low interest rates in a time of recession will make sense as they may encourage firms to invest. Again, timing is critical because action too late may not help to stabilise the economy.

counter-inflation policy: if inflation is accelerating, the Bank of England may adopt contractionary monetary policies, by raising interest rates. This will have the effect of reducing *aggregate demand* and pressure on resources. (See also *monetary policy.*)

countervailing duty: an import duty which compensates for the effect of a subsidy on another country's exports.

credit enables firms and individuals to buy products immediately and pay for them later. In the case of firms, the credit is often provided by the supplier and is known as *trade credit.* This can be important for some firms because it enables them to pay for the goods when they have received some sales revenue. Alternatively, firms and individuals may borrow, using an overdraft or a loan to finance their purchases. This will involve a rate of interest which increases the amount which has to be paid.

credit creation: the process by which banks expand their lending by a multiple of any new deposits they receive. Not all their customers will want to withdraw their deposits at any one time. This allows the banks to keep just a percentage of their assets in the form of *liquid reserves* and to use the rest to make loans. As borrowers spend the money, it is deposited once more in the bank, allowing a further expansion of credit.

credit creation multiplier: an initial increase in bank deposits leads to a multiple expansion in the amount of credit available. The credit multiplier defines the precise amount by which credit increases, in relation to the initial increase in deposits.

credit rating: an assessment of the likelihood of a business or an individual being able to repay debts. For individuals, credit ratings are based on the promptness with which they have paid their debts in the past. For businesses, credit ratings will be arrived at after careful perusal of their accounts. In general, a good credit rating is likely to mean that interest rates charged will be lower. Governments are also given credit ratings, which relate to their sales of *bonds.* Those with rather weak and fragile economies are likely to have to offer higher interest rates in order to make the bonds attractive to potential buyers.

creditors are those to whom the organisation owes money, perhaps through having purchased goods or services on credit so that payment is still outstanding.

cross-price elasticity measures the responsiveness of demand for one good to a change in the price of another. The demand for a particular product will be affected by a change in the price of a substitute or a complement. For example, a significant increase in the price of petrol will lead to a decrease in demand for cars.

Cross-price elasticity is measured using the formula:

$$\text{FORMULA:} \quad \frac{\text{percentage change in quantity demanded of good X}}{\text{percentage change in price of good Y}}$$

Cross-price elasticity is significant when the relationship between the two products is a close one. Where two close *substitutes* are involved, an increase in the price of one will lead to a significant rise in the demand for the other. Competing *brands* may be in this position or competing foodstuffs, e.g. cauliflowers and leeks. Notice that the elasticity will be positive – both the numerator and denominator will rise.

With complements, cross-price elasticity will generally be negative. The cross-price elasticity of demand for cars with respect to the price of petrol involves an inverse relationship. If the price of petrol increases, demand for cars decreases. Of course, you can consider the different effects of petrol prices on larger and smaller cars in which case you will get a more complex result.

cross-section data allow comparisons across different groups. For example, a cross-section of a number of countries could be compared by examining investment and growth rates in a single year. This compares with time series data, which might, for example, examine trends over a period of years in a single country.

cross-subsidy: if there is an unprofitable activity taking place within an organisation, the losses can be offset by a profitable activity elsewhere in the same organisation. This is called a cross-subsidy. When publishers bring out unsuccessful books the losses will be covered by the enormous profits made from bestsellers.

crowding out: the idea that an increase in government investment leads to a decrease in private investment. If the government borrows to finance investment, it is likely that it will have to pay higher interest rates than before. The increased demand for funds will mean higher interest rates generally and this may deter private borrowers. It makes any planned investment somewhat less profitable than before. Crowding out figured in economic analyses of the 1970s, when public spending as a percentage of GDP was higher than it is now.

culture: the general ethos of a particular business, which determines the ways in which people work together. Corporate culture can be important in influencing competitiveness and profitability because it affects managers' and employees' willingness to adopt new strategies when the market is changing.

currency: the notes and coins which are used as a medium of exchange in the country concerned.

currency appreciation occurs when the exchange rate rises and the purchasing power of the currency increases. This might reflect an increase in demand for the country's export products or a capital inflow. Either of these would increase demand for the currency and drive up the exchange rate. (See also *appreciation* and *capital movements.*)

currency crisis: if dealers on the foreign exchange market expect the value of a currency to fall, they may start selling large quantities of it. This may make it impossible for the central bank to buy enough of the currency to keep up its value, because its foreign exchange reserves are limited. This would be termed a currency crisis. (See also *fixed exchange rate.*)

currency stabilisation is attempted when there is a sense that fluctuating exchange rates are making life more difficult than it need be for people who have to take economic decisions. If the value of the currency fluctuates less, the future profitability of exports becomes more predictable. This can help potential exporters to make production decisions with more confidence. The *euro* is in part a response to the desire of some European businesses for a more stable *exchange rate regime.*

current account: see *balance of payments.* The term also refers to bank accounts kept mainly for the purpose of making transactions.

current prices: a term used in relation to data which is expressed in the prices of the year concerned, i.e. not corrected for inflation. In contrast, *constant price* data gives values in real terms, using the prices of a base year. It is very important to know whether data are given in current or constant prices. In the presence of inflation, current price data, on GDP for example, could be very misleading.

customer service is often an element in the product, involving as it does the direct contact between producer and consumer. It could involve sales advice, *after-sales service* or simply a pleasant service. For some firms, it is an important aspect of competitiveness or of product differentiation.

Customs and Excise: the body responsible for collecting indirect taxes in the UK. These include VAT, tobacco and alcohol taxes and import duties.

customs duties: the taxes levied on imports as they are brought into the country, also known as *tariffs.*

customs union: a group of countries which agrees to trade freely within their borders and imposes a *common external tariff* on imports from outside the area. The European Union is a customs union. This may lead to *trade creation* and *trade diversion.* Overall it will usually promote the growth of trade and specialisation, thus allowing member countries to become better off.

cyclical instability: the fluctuations in GDP associated with the *trade cycle.* A boom may be followed quite quickly by recession, during which expectations about the future become very gloomy. This instability is usually very detrimental to the long-term growth process. It reduces investment and incomes. *Macro-economic policy* is usually directed towards reducing cyclical instability by limiting unsustainable growth and stimulating recovery during recession.

cyclical unemployment occurs when *aggregate demand* in the economy is slowing and is not enough to buy the output which can be produced when all resources are fully employed (*full-capacity output*). In these circumstances, cyclical unemployment could be reduced if *aggregate demand* increased.

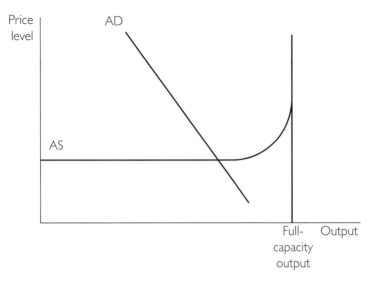

Aggregate demand will buy a level of output which leaves many people unemployed

Cyclical unemployment is sometimes lagged to the *trade cycle*, perhaps by as much as a year. As demand falls, employers may postpone making people redundant as long as possible. Similarly, during the upturn, employers will wait to be sure that the increased demand is permanent before recruiting more staff.

Government policies to reduce cyclical unemployment could:

- reduce taxation and increase government expenditure
- try to reduce labour costs, for example by reducing the employer's National Insurance charges.

In recent years, governments have often not been willing to use counter-cyclical measures because of the perceived risk of increased aggregate demand causing excess demand and accelerating inflation. This has meant that cyclical unemployment has persisted for a number of years, e.g. during much of the 1980s and during and after the recession of 1990–1992.

cyclically adjusted budget deficit: what the *budget deficit* would be if the economy were neither booming nor in recession. Normally, a budget deficit will increase during recession, because unemployment benefit payments rise and tax revenues fall. This process is automatic and occurs as employees are laid off. Similarly, in a boom, tax revenues rise and unemployment benefit payments fall, reducing the government's deficit or taking it into surplus. A modest cyclically adjusted deficit may be used to justify a much larger actual deficit during recession.

D

data: information with some basis in fact. Data can be used to support conclusions. The information can be verbal or numerical. Great care must be taken in evaluating and selecting data. For example, is it the most suitable data for the purpose in hand? Was it collected in a reliable and impartial way?

database: a set of data which has been collected for a particular purpose. For example, Companies House keeps data on all businesses which have *limited liability*.

dawn raid: an unexpected sudden attempt to buy enough shares in a particular company to eventually obtain a controlling interest. The buyer has a chance to get hold of some of the shares cheaply before news of the raid pushes their price up. The term can also mean an unexpected visit from the tax authorities or others with a legal interest to examine the company's accounts or records.

DCF: see *discounted cash flow*.

deadweight loss: the welfare loss to the consumer which occurs when an industry becomes a *monopoly*. The market power of the firms in the industry is such that they can push up prices and reduce the quantity supplied. This effectively reduces consumers' real incomes by diminishing the *consumer surplus* which they might have had. An example of deadweight loss would be where a drug company limits the supply of a new and effective drug for which it holds the patent. High prices could be charged but that would mean that some sufferers who could benefit from the drug will not be able to afford it (as with AIDS drugs in developing countries). Against this, there is always the possibility that a monopoly can rationalise production and achieve cost savings which will be at least partially passed on to consumers.

dear money: if interest rates are high, borrowing will be costly and the money borrowed may be said to be dear.

death duties: see *estate duty*.

death rate: the number of people dying per thousand of population. This is an important component of the rate of population increase, particularly in developing countries where life expectancy has increased dramatically.

debenture: a loan to a company with a fixed interest rate. Unlike *shareholders*, debenture holders have no control over the business, but they may get their money back if the company goes into *liquidation*. Debentures are thus less risky than shares but are likely to have a lower rate of return and there can be no *capital gains* when share prices rise.

debt: money owed by one individual or organisation to another. Debts are usually created with an agreement as to the interest payable and date of repayment. There may be a contract which can be enforced through the courts.

debt crisis: this could apply to any borrower unable to make interest payments or debt repayments on the due date. Recently the term Debt Crisis has referred to the difficulties which some *developing countries* have had in servicing their debts to foreign banks, governments and international organisations. The movement Jubilee 2000, which became Jublilee Plus, a coalition of charities and aid agencies, has pressed hard for the debt to be written off. Some progress has been made but debt remains a problem. (See also *Debt Problem.*)

debt finance means using loans to pay for investments, rather than share capital. Most firms rely on a combination of debt and *equity* (share) finance. If there is heavy reliance on loan or debt finance and the business takes time to become profitable, interest payments may become a problem. This happened with the Channel Tunnel. Initially, finance came from share issues but as time went by there were cost overruns which were financed by borrowing from the banks. Eventually the company was unable to cover its interest payments out of current income and had to restructure its debts, giving the banks shares in exchange for their loans. This reduced the interest payable.

debt forgiveness means writing off all or part of an outstanding debt in recognition of the fact that the borrower will not actually be able make repayment in full. It is relevant to those *developing countries* which have become overburdened with debt.

debt management is needed when a firm or a government has borrowed from a range of sources and needs to make sure that there will always be funds available for interest and repayments. There must be forecasts of when more borrowing is needed; the cost of borrowing must be kept down and *maturity dates* on existing debt must be phased so that they are spread over an appropriate period.

Debt Problem: during the 1970s, many *developing country* governments borrowed large sums from banks in the developed countries. When interest rates rose in the early 1980s, the borrower countries became unable to service the debt (i.e. pay the interest). The amounts of foreign currency they could generate by exporting were insufficient to cover their commitments, even after they had cut back their imports substantially. In time they were also unable to repay their debts. This became known as the Debt Problem.

Many countries have had to negotiate *debt rescheduling* with the help of the IMF. Some banks have written off part of the debt. Those most seriously affected include many countries in Africa south of the Sahara, as well as Mexico, Brazil and some other Latin American countries. The problem continues and is particularly acute for the poorest countries. Governments have been urged by many people and organisations to clear these debts as soon as possible through the international organisations but so far it seems unlikely that the problem will be completely solved. Two bodies, Drop the Debt, a lobbying group, and Jubilee Plus, a long-term strategy group, are continuing the campaign.

debt ratio: the amount of a country's debt in relation to the level of its exports.

debt relief involves agreement by a lender to accept delayed interest payments or capital repayments. This will happen if the lender thinks that the borrower will eventually be able to pay but will have difficulties with agreed payments in the short run. Delayed payments may be considered preferable to *default.*

debt rescheduling may occur when a firm or a government with large loans cannot meet the repayments. The lenders can extend the term of the loans and postpone the repayment dates. They can also give an interest holiday, so that interest payments can be temporarily suspended to give time for the borrower to recover. On the international level, debt rescheduling means lengthening the periods over which governments can repay their debts, in order to reduce the problem. Rescheduling is often preferable to *default*.

debt service: the payment of interest on loans.

debt service ratio: the relationship between total interest payments and total export earnings. The ratio gives an indication as to whether a government can realistically cover interest payments out of export revenue, i.e. whether it has enough foreign exchange flowing in to cover the interest outflow.

debtors owe money whereas *creditors* are owed money. There is an age-related cycle of debt: young people are usually in debt for some time before they eventually pay off mortgages and other loans and become net creditors as a result of saving.

decentralised wage bargaining occurs when negotiations are between individual employers and their employees, rather than between an *employers' association* and a *trade union*, operating at a national level. Decentralised bargaining allows local variations in labour market conditions to be reflected in local wage rates. It may help to generate jobs in areas of high unemployment if locally agreed wage rates are lower than national rates.

decile: the boundary line between one tenth of a population and the next tenth. If the population is ranked according to income, the lowest decile marks the income level at which 10% of the population are poorer while 90% of the population are better off.

declining industry: an industry for the products of which demand is falling. There are several causes:

- a shift in *comparative advantage*, such that competing imports are becoming available at prices below those which the domestic industry can achieve (as happens with textile products in developed countries)
- *technical change* leading to the development of new products which are superior to the old one (as when air travel reduced demand for ocean liners).

The major declining industries in the UK have been coal, iron and steel, shipbuilding, textiles and footwear and, to some extent, vehicles. Unfortunately all of these have been localised industries so the effects of decline have been particularly hard on some communities.

decreasing cost industry: an industry in which expansion leads to a fall in average costs of production. This would occur if there were *economies of scale* to be reaped as output rose. The situation is sometimes described as increasing returns to scale.

default occurs when a borrower is unable to make interest payments or repay the loan itself. The lender may take steps to get the money through the courts. Alternatively, if court action may end in *liquidation*, the borrower may negotiate easier terms, allowing the borrower more time to pay.

deficit: occurs when expenditure is greater than income.

- A *budget deficit* means that the government is spending more than it receives in tax revenue and will need to borrow to cover the difference.

- A *balance of payments* deficit means that import costs are greater than export revenue. This is likely to be covered by a capital inflow or a change in the level of foreign exchange reserves held by the central bank.
- A deficit in the accounts of a charity or non-profit making organisation means that it has made a loss over the year: payments are greater than receipts.

deficit spending occurs if a government spends more than it receives in tax revenue. It will then have to borrow to make up the difference.

deflation is a term which is used in two different ways. It can be:

- a fall in the general price level. This is different from a fall in prices in a particular sector of industry (e.g. telecommunications) or a fall in the rate of *inflation* (which means that prices are rising more slowly than before). Up to and including the 1930s, prices generally fell from time to time and were as likely to fall as to rise.
- a period of reduced economic activity, when *aggregate demand* is falling, output and employment are cut and incomes fall. These, the conditions of a *slump*, can be accompanied by falling prices.

deflationary gap: a situation in which the level of expenditure is less than the capacity of the economy to produce. It will be characterised by a significant amount of unemployment and idle capital equipment. It may be eliminated by *injections* into the circular flow of money, i.e. by increasing investment, government expenditure or exports or by reducing withdrawals (saving, taxation or imports).

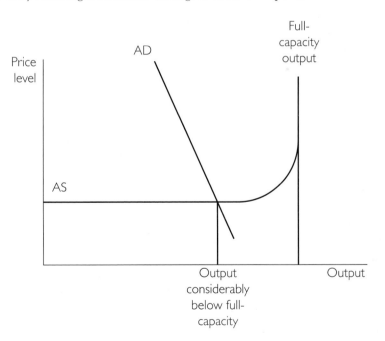

Aggregate demand is well below the level needed to buy all that the economy can produce

deflationary policies or *contractionary policies* are those which are designed to reduce demand by the use of *fiscal* or *monetary policies.*

deindustrialisation refers to the way in which the UK economy has tended to shift resources out of the manufacturing sector and into the service sector. The causes of deindustrialisation have been identified as:

- loss of competitiveness in manufacturing. This can be due to rising wage costs or to failure to improve productivity or quality
- a shift in the pattern of consumer demand. As incomes rise, spending on manufactures may grow more slowly if people prefer to spend the extra money on services, e.g. leisure and tourism.

All mature economies (i.e. those which have had a substantial manufacturing sector for a long time) experience a tendency for resources to shift out of manufacturing and into the service sector. This is most marked in the USA and the UK. It is not necessarily a bad thing, although many commentators have regretted the process. The crucial question is whether the economy remains competitive enough in the sectors where it has a *comparative advantage* to export successfully and generate income to pay for imported manufactures.

demand means the quantity of a good or a service that people want to buy at a range of different prices. Market demand refers to the level of demand which comes from everyone in a particular market. *Effective demand* means demand backed by the ability to pay for the product. *Aggregate demand* means demand for all goods and services available in the economy as a whole.

The level of demand for individual products may be influenced by:

- incomes
- tastes or fashions
- changes in the prices of other goods, be they *substitutes* or *complementary goods.*

Individual demand will be particularly influenced by incomes and family circumstances. (See also *demand curve.*)

demand curve: a line graph which relates the quantity demanded to a range of possible prices. The curve almost always slopes downwards to the right because as prices fall, people tend to buy a larger quantity. This is known as a movement along the demand curve.

A shift in the demand curve will occur if tastes or incomes change or if there is a change in the price of a related good, either a *substitute* or a *complement.*

As telephone calls have become cheaper, people are using the telephone more often. Similarly, the falling price of mobile phones has increased the quantity demanded. These are movements along the demand curve.

Equally, rising incomes could mean that more people want to own mobile phones at all price levels. This means that the demand curve for mobile phones will shift to the right. It is often important to use the *ceteris paribus* assumption when analysing market changes. It allows us to deal with one change at a time and analyse its effect in isolation.

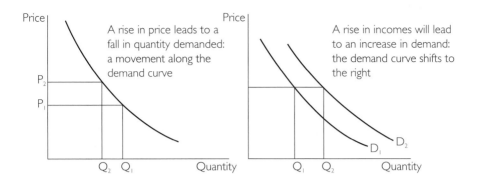

Demand curve

demand deficiency unemployment occurs when people are unemployed because the level of *aggregate demand* is well below that required to purchase *full-capacity output*. This is unemployment which could be reduced if the level of expenditure in the economy were to be increased. This might be achieved by means of *expansionary policies*. Unemployment of this kind may also be described as *cyclical unemployment* because it is likely to increase during the recession phase of the *trade cycle*. Sharp increases in unemployment occurred in 1980–1981 and in 1990–1992 when the UK economy experienced falling demand for many products. (See also *depression*.)

demand for labour: the number of employees required by firms at a range of different wage rates. This will be a *derived demand*, based on the demand for the final product. The number of employees required by each individual firm will depend on the *marginal revenue product* of labour, i.e. how much each employee is able to produce and the price at which the output can be sold. (See also *wage determination*.)

demand for money means the amount of money which people will want to hold. This will be determined by the purposes for which they want to hold the money. Active balances are kept to finance current spending. Idle balances are kept as a way of having extra money available for emergencies or as part of an investment strategy. An increase in the demand for money, other things being equal, will increase interest rates as people compete to obtain the funds available. The interest rate is effectively a price for money which rations funds among potential holders.

demand function: an equation which expresses the relationship between price and quantity demanded. It will show how quantity demanded depends on incomes, tastes and the prices of other goods (complements or substitutes).

demand inflation occurs when *aggregate demand* is greater than the capacity of the economy to meet it with an equal supply of goods and services. This excess demand occurs when aggregate demand is growing fast and almost all the real resources in the economy are fully employed. Shortages, i.e. *supply constraints*, will appear, typically of skilled labour, and this will make it easy for people to negotiate pay rises. This in turn raises firms' costs and they will be quick to raise their prices to cover the increase. As the economy approaches its *full-capacity output*, it is impossible to increase output to meet the growing demand and any further increase in aggregate demand will quickly push up prices. Inflation will then tend to accelerate. In the diagram, aggregate demand grows from AD_1 to AD_2 to AD_3, but with the economy close to full capacity, the resources to increase output are scarce and their prices are bid up by the rising demand.

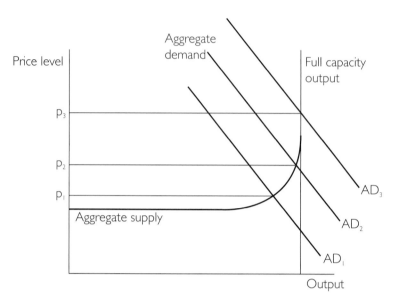

Excess demand leading to rising prices

demand management refers to government policies which aim to control the level of *aggregate demand* in such a way that there is neither excessive inflation nor high unemployment. *Fiscal and monetary policies* can be used in such a way as to control demand and prevent it either from growing faster than the capacity of the economy to produce or from slowing to well below that level. Demand management policies have been associated with the work of *J M Keynes*, and are sometimes called Keynesian policies. They were highly fashionable in the 1960s and 1970s; unfortunately they proved less easy to operate than many politicians suggested, mainly because they found it difficult to predict exactly how much of a change in demand would be needed to secure their objectives. Although demand management is seldom referred to by politicians nowadays, it is still used all the time. Interest rates (monetary policy) are adjusted by the *Monetary Policy Committee* of the Bank of England in order to influence both investment and consumer spending. Governments use fiscal policy in this way too but rather less frequently.

demand schedule gives the quantities sold of a product at a set of different prices. It gives the data from which a *demand curve* may be drawn.

demarcation defines the differences between each job, so that each employee is assigned only those jobs for which they are formally qualified. Quite often this was used as a way to protect the employment rights of particular groups. Up to the 1970s demarcation disputes between trade unions created management difficulties. Since then, increasingly flexible working practices and *multi-skilling* have gradually led to there being much less dispute over these issues. Often, people with a variety of skills become part of a team which has to find the most effective way of completing the job. People are expected to do a range of tasks, moving between them as needed.

demerger means dividing up a firm into separate companies. Usually the objective is to assign to each business the core activities in which it has the most expertise. In this way, it is thought, both businesses will be run more efficiently. Alternatively, the parent company may be selling off the less profitable parts of the business.

Demergers are sometimes referred to as *divestment.*

demerit good: a good which has been found through the political process to be socially undesirable. Illegal drugs provide the simplest example.

demographic projections: estimates of likely population changes. These can forecast changes in the size and age structure of the population which may have an impact on the resource needs of the economy.

demographic transition: as developing economies grow, their populations are at first likely to rise rapidly as *life expectancy* rises and *death rates* fall. Population growth slows later as birth rates fall. This has happened in all parts of the world where incomes are rising rapidly. Falling infant mortality and better welfare provision gradually persuade people of the wisdom of having smaller families.

denationalisation means returning to the private sector a business that was previously operated by the public sector. (See also *privatisation.*)

Department for International Development (DfID): the government department which handles UK relations with developing countries.

Department of Trade and Industry (DTI) is the ministry which creates trade and industrial policies which are the basis for the operation of firms. These include *competition* and *regional policy* as well as trading regulations and *import controls.*

dependency culture: the set of attitudes which may lead to unemployed people giving up the search for employment and depending permanently on benefits. To combat this, everyone who can work is required to be available, and sometimes to attend for training and help in making applications.

dependent population: all those people who are either in education or are too young or too old to take paid employment or who are unable to work because of disabilities. The proportion of the population in this position varies from one country to another.

dependent variable: a variable which is determined by changes elsewhere in the system and therefore depends on another variable. For example, we usually view the level of tax revenue as depending on the level of income, for a given set of tax rates. Income is thus the independent variable and tax revenue is the dependent variable.

depletable resources are things which are fixed in quantity and, once consumed, cannot be replaced. The term is used particularly in relation to energy: gas and oil are fossil fuels and once used, cannot be replaced, although it is possible to search for new sources. Similarly, tropical hardwoods are depletable in that they cannot be replaced at the rate at which they are currently being used.

deposits: amounts of money which are held in bank accounts. Deposits intended to finance current spending are held in current accounts while savings deposits are held in deposit accounts. (In the US, these are referred to respectively as sight deposits and time deposits.)

deposit insurance: a system whereby bank deposits can be insured against the possibility of the bank becoming *insolvent* and running out of funds so that the depositors cannot withdraw their money. This reduces the risks for depositors but also makes it easier for banks to take risks in their lending.

depreciation has two different meanings:

- capital equipment depreciates over time, as wear and tear take their toll and new technologies make the equipment less useful. Its value diminishes. Prudent owners of capital equipment set aside depreciation allowances which can be used to replace the capital at the end of its useful life.
- an exchange rate, the value of which is falling on the foreign exchange markets, is said to be depreciating. It is losing value and purchasing power. It is also making exports cheaper and therefore easier to sell. (See also *exchange rate depreciation*.)

depressed area: a geographical area which is growing more slowly than the rest of the economy or not growing at all. As a result, incomes, output and employment will be lower. There are likely to be a number of declining industries which face diminishing demand in the marketplace. These may be localised heavy industries such as iron and steel and shipbuilding which have both declined through competition from imports. The workforce may have problems with *occupational immobility*.

depression: the phase of the *trade cycle* when economic growth is low or negative, when *recession* becomes prolonged and business confidence is very low. This phase will be characterised by:

- falling *aggregate demand* and output
- redundancies and high unemployment
- falling incomes and consumer spending
- very low levels of *investment*; as output falls productive capacity is reduced
- falling rates of inflation.

Depression may be countered by expansionary policies. Reduced interest rates (*monetary policy*) may induce both consumers and firms to borrow and spend. Investment may increase in some sectors. Tax cuts and increases in government expenditure will help to increase aggregate demand further. *Automatic stabilisers* such as the rise in unemployment benefits will help to protect incomes and contribute to more spending in the economy.

The unemployment which occurs will be *demand deficiency unemployment* (alternatively known as cyclical unemployment), caused by insufficient levels of aggregate demand. In the diagram, the level of aggregate demand is well below that needed to buy all the output which could be produced if the economy was working at *full-capacity output*.

The worst depression was that of the 1930s, when output fell by 30% and unemployment and loss of income was a serious problem all over the world.

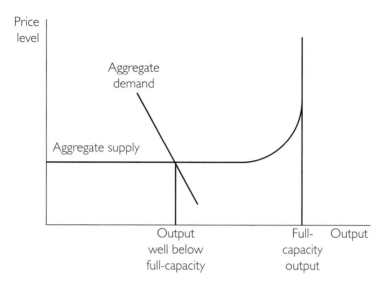

deregulation: the removal of legal restrictions on businesses. Usually the objective is to increase competition. Deregulation has proceeded alongside *privatisation*. Both were designed to reduce the role of the government in the economy. Deregulation has applied to different industries in different ways.

- In the 1960s and 1970s, banks were deregulated. Competition was greatly encouraged and probably did lead to lower prices and more varied financial products which benefited consumers.
- In the late 1980s buses were deregulated. Independent bus companies were allowed to compete with local authority-run bus companies. Competition has certainly increased but the effects on bus travellers are rather hard to determine.
- Airline deregulation over a long period has undoubtedly reduced air fares considerably, especially on some routes, e.g. the North Atlantic.

Meanwhile, increasing concern about the environmental, employment and health and safety issues is tending to increase rather than reduce regulation.

derivatives involve a contract, the value of which is based on the value of another asset or on an index which measures changes in values. Derivatives are used as a way of reducing risks. They may be based on interest rates, currencies, *equities* or *commodities*. They include *futures* and *options*. Futures involve an agreement to buy an amount of a commodity, or a financial asset, on a date in the future, at an agreed price. They are a way of protecting the buyer from the uncertain nature of commodity prices. If you know that you will need a certain quantity of iron ore in three months time, it may make sense to buy futures at an agreed price now, thus reducing the risk. *Financial futures* are another important derivative.

derived demand: employers' demand for labour is said to be derived demand, because they do not want labour for its own sake but for what it may be able to produce. The demand is thus derived from the demand for the final product.

deskilling: some jobs which were highly skilled in the past are now mechanised and only semi-skilled. People who stay in the same line of production may find that their skills are no longer valued and their pay may fall. Job satisfaction may be reduced.

destocking: at the start of a *recession*, some firms find they have unused stocks of inputs because demand for their product is falling. Stocks are costly to hold so they may reduce orders for inputs to well below the replacement level in order to get stocks back to a level which reflects the new lower level of demand and production. This will cut demand for the suppliers' products and deepen the recession. Destocking may be intensified if interest rates rise because stocks are often financed by borrowing.

devaluation: where the government has fixed the exchange rate in relation to that of other countries, it may decide to reduce the value of the currency and fix it at a new lower level. This may be because it has a persistent *balance of payments* deficit, indicating that the currency is overvalued. There may also have been a loss of international confidence in the currency. This would lead to heavy selling on the foreign exchange markets and downward pressure on prices coming from market forces. So the devaluation would really be a simple recognition that the rate could not be held at its old high value.

This sort of process was fairly commonplace up to 1972 when most exchange rates were fixed. It can still be relevant in those developing countries which tie their currency, e.g. to the US dollar.

Devaluation has a number of consequences:

- Export prices will fall and import prices will rise. This improves competitiveness and will reduce the *balance of payments deficit*, after a time lag.
- Higher import prices may mean a rise in the rate of inflation which will require *contractionary policies* later.

developed countries: the countries with high per capita incomes and high levels of investment which have become prosperous during the 20th century. This group used to consist of Western Europe, USA, Canada, Japan, Australia and New Zealand. Recently, Hong Kong, Singapore and South Korea have raised their incomes to the point where they are generally regarded as developed countries. A number of others are not far behind them.

developing countries are characterised by low incomes, low levels of *investment* and *infrastructure* and some difficulty in achieving improvements in standards of living. They are often heavily dependent on *primary products* for their export earnings and suffer if *commodity* prices fall. They tend to have small manufacturing sectors, though this is changing fast in Asia. Access to training is often a problem.

In the past many developing countries shared their distinguishing features. They are now a very diverse group. Some developing countries have moved on altogether, such as Singapore and the other so-called 'Asian tigers', Taiwan, Korea and Hong Kong. Incomes are at or approaching European levels. Many other Asian countries such as China and Thailand are developing fast. Meanwhile many African countries remain desperately poor. Some of the countries which are growing fast still have sectors of the economy where many people remain very poor. (See also *aid, debt problem*.)

development areas: geographical regions which have tended not to share the growing prosperity of the country as a whole. They include isolated areas and areas which have a legacy of localised heavy industries which have for some time been experiencing declining demand. In the UK, they correspond to the *assisted areas*. These qualify for varying levels of support for firms which locate in the area. The EU determines how some regional policies will operate and funding can be obtained from its regeneration budget. The *Regional Development Agencies* have become an important vehicle for regional support.

differentials are the differences in pay between employees who have different skills and responsibilities. A differential can act as an *incentive* to acquire additional skills or accept responsibility. When differentials are reduced, some people may become less occupationally mobile because they have less incentive to change jobs.

differentiated products are usually substitutes for one another, but are nevertheless subtly different. Though they may perform the same function, their design features distinguish them from each other. They contrast with *homogeneous products*; with these it is impossible for the buyer to distinguish one supplier's product from another's. Differentiated products are a feature of *imperfect competition*. By differentiating their product a particular firm may be able to exert some degree of control over the market. Some firms may use branding or qualitative differences which make their product distinctive. (See also *product differentiation*.)

diminishing returns occur when, as a producer adds more of one factor of production to a fixed quantity of other factors of production, the output increases but less than proportionately. For example, if 10 people have 10 spades and are digging a trench, the addition of one extra person digging and allowing each person to take a break will allow the team to dig a longer trench in a given time. But if more people are added to the team, each extra one will add less and less to the distance dug, because the rest of the team will gain little benefit from further breaks.

direct controls: a way for the government to affect firms' decisions through regulation. Most governments say they will reduce government intervention in the economy. Generally, markets are regarded as being effective in promoting economic activity and direct controls are found to introduce *distortions*. In practice, employee and consumer protection law creates large numbers of direct controls, many of which have been effective in improving standards.

direct investment: see *foreign direct investment*.

direct relationship: where two variables move together, they are said to have a direct relationship. For example, output and employment tend to rise and fall together, though with a time lag.

direct taxes are levied on the incomes of individuals and firms. They include income tax, corporation tax and council tax. They also include taxes on wealth, principally *inheritance tax*. Direct taxes are usually *proportional* or *progressive*. They also include *national insurance charges*. In contrast, *indirect taxes* are levied on expenditure and collected from the sellers of goods and services (e.g. VAT). (See also *taxation*.)

director: all *limited companies* have a *board of directors* who are responsible for major decisions. In a large company, directors will be elected by shareholders and are supposed to represent their interests. Executive directors are employees of the company. *Non-executive directors* are part-time, usually experienced managers from other companies, who are expected to give independent advice.

Director General of Fair Trading: working from the *Office of Fair Trading*, the DGFT supervises the investigation of *cartels* and other *anti-competitive practices* with powers greatly strengthened by the 1998 Competition Act. If he/she finds that there has been an anti-competitive agreement, the firm concerned can be fined up to 10% of its UK sales revenue. Firms can appeal against the finding to the *Competition Commission*. It will be several years before the full impact of this legislation is clear, as it came into force early in 2000.

dirty float means that the exchange rate floats in response to market forces, but may be subject to central bank intervention from time to time. Intervention may be designed to iron out day-to-day fluctuations. Alternatively, intervention may prevent the exchange rate from moving beyond certain limits. The central bank may avoid publicising its intervention policy in advance, in order to prevent speculation. Intervention takes the form of buying the currency to prevent its weakening, using the bank's foreign exchange reserves, or selling it to prevent it from strengthening.

disclosure of information requires firms to give detailed information about the way they operate so that the various stakeholders can form a judgement on the outcome. Many firms do not want to do this, preferring to treat as confidential information on the nature of their profits, their accident rates and environmental issues. However, this is becoming more difficult as the need for business responsibility is promoted. Some firms have taken a lead and produced environmental reports (Sainsbury's have done this) or social audits. One possibility would be to compel firms by law to disclose more information in their *annual report and accounts*.

discount: a price reduction designed to bring about a sale. It may be an incentive to pay quickly. In the financial markets, *bank bills* (short-term loans) may be sold at a discount which reflects the current interest rate. The discount compensates the lender for doing without the money for a short time, in the same way as an interest payment would.

discount houses were *financial intermediaries* which specialised in lending on a very short-term basis. The last ones left in business ceased to operate as such in 1998. Their functions were taken over by the relevant departments within the banks. This occurred as a result of the change in the Bank of England's rules. Previously it lent directly only to the discount houses. Now it lends directly to all recognised banks.

discount rate: this term is sometimes used to describe the rate at which the Bank of England lends to banks which are temporarily short of funds with which to meet their obligations. If the Bank of England wishes interest rates to rise generally, it can raise the discount rate. (See also *bank rate* and *repo rate*.)

discounted cash flow (DCF): a way of investigating a planned investment to see whether it will be worthwhile. It compares the expected future income stream from the investment with the opportunity cost of the funds involved. Estimated future income is discounted at a rate which reflects the interest lost while the funds are tied up. The discounted income stream is compared with the costs of the project to see if it is worthwhile.

discouraged workers: people who have been unemployed for some time, despite making an effort to find work, sometimes give up the search for a job. Effectively, they drop out of the labour market in the sense that they are no longer making themselves available for work.

discretionary policy refers to deliberate changes in tax rates or government expenditure which will affect the level of *aggregate demand*. In contrast, some changes in the level of taxation and spending are referred to as *automatic stabilisers*, because they will increase or reduce aggregate demand automatically as incomes and unemployment change over the course of the business cycle. (See also *fiscal policy*.)

discrimination: the practice of preferring an applicant for a job because of the person's race, gender or religion. Although discrimination is illegal there is a good deal of evidence of its continuation. Preferred groups generally are able to earn higher rates of pay and may have lower unemployment rates.

discriminatory pricing: see *price discrimination*.

diseconomies of scale: as firms grow, they may encounter certain cost increases which make the larger scale of production less efficient.

- Communication costs: with more layers of management, communication may become harder.
- Loss of flexibility: larger organisations sometimes find it harder to react effectively to changing market conditions. In markets where nimble reactions are important, smaller firms may be able to take advantage of opportunities.

Diseconomies of scale seldom appear to trouble manufacturers. They can be more of a problem when certain kinds of customer service are an important part of the product.

Some firms which expand very quickly encounter congestion costs but these can usually be put right with time.

disequilibrium occurs when there is *excess supply* or *excess demand*, either in a particular market or in the economy as a whole. For example, if there are large stocks of unsold butter, we can say that the market is in disequilibrium. The likely explanation will be that the price is too high for *market clearing* to take place. The diagram shows how a high price may cause excess demand. Reducing the price will bring the market back into equilibrium.(See Figure on page 80.)

On the macro-economic level, high levels of *aggregate demand*, in excess of the economy's capacity to supply goods and services, would indicate disequilibrium. The likely outcome would be accelerating inflation and the government might want to use *fiscal* and *monetary policies* to reduce the level of demand.

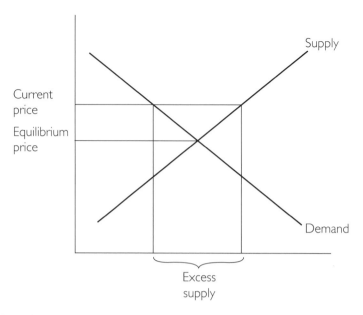

A price above the equilibrium level will lead to excess supply (see page 79)

disguised unemployment occurs when people who would like to work do not register, usually because they are not entitled to unemployment benefit, and therefore have no incentive to do so. The *claimant count* measure of unemployment fails to count these people. The Labour Force Survey usually produces a higher figure for unemployment because it can take account of people who do not register.

disinflation means a fall in the rate of inflation. In other words, prices would still be rising but more slowly than before. This happened in the early 1990s when inflation peaked at 11% in 1990 and then fell to around 4% the next year.

disposable income is the income left over after tax and *national insurance charges* have been deducted. Benefits such as income support and child benefits will increase disposable income, enabling people to spend more than they can earn. Because of taxes and benefits, disposable income is more equitably distributed than gross income.

dissaving: in the macro-economic model of the circular flow of money, dissaving occurs when consumption exceeds income and is financed by drawing on past savings. During a recession, dissaving can help to increase spending, but that is when people are apt to be nervous and want to keep their savings intact.

distortions: when prices are distorted, they fail to reflect the true costs of production. This means that either more or less will be consumed than would be if prices covered all the costs. For example, the apparent cost of motoring is less than the true cost because the road system is free to users. If road users paid the full cost of the roads they travelled (i.e. if roads were priced) they would probably choose to make fewer journeys. People who do not own cars would probably have to pay less tax for road building as the costs would be covered by road users. To the extent that road users were deterred by the pricing system from making journeys, there would be less congestion.

distribution: the system by which goods and services are actually sold in the places where consumers can conveniently buy them.

distribution of income refers to the way in which total income is shared among the different groups in society. A very equitable distribution of income might involve the richest tenth of the population having no more than three times the income of the poorest tenth. In the UK, the distribution of income became considerably less equitable between 1977 and 1991. Since then there have been some attempts to reverse this process but the UK distribution of income remains one of the least equitable in Europe. It has been shown that in 1990, the poorest tenth of the UK population received 2.5% of the total income, while the richest tenth received 22.9% of the total. This contrasts with Finland, where the corresponding figures are 4.5% and 17.8%.

The intention of taxation and social security benefits is usually to redistribute income from the richer towards the poorer members of society. The more *progressive* the tax system, the more effective this process will be.

A relatively unequal distribution of income may increase incentives to work but may also increase tensions between employers and employees. Some *developing countries* have a much more unequal distribution of income than developed countries.

distribution of wealth refers to the ownership of assets and how it is spread amongst different groups of people. Wealth can consist of bank balances, shares, property, businesses and anything else which provides a continuing income or can be sold. Wealth is a *stock*, in contrast to income, which is a *flow*. Income is paid continuously whereas wealth is held over a long period. A relatively equal distribution of wealth would imply that most people had some and few had either none or a great deal. The distribution of wealth may be affected by *inheritance taxes* and by changes in property prices or ownership.

diversification means moving into the production or sale of different products. These could have similarities with the original product or be completely different. The objectives of doing this are:

- to spread risks. If the original product comes up against a sharp fall in demand, the new products may still be selling well and will reduce the risk of business failure
- to exploit additional profit-making opportunities.

Diversification is easily visible in the *conglomerate* companies like Unilever, which produces numerous cleaning and food products as well as cosmetics. At the other end of the scale, many farmers have found additional activities to supplement income when the prices of farm products fell. Yoghurt and cheese making, bed and breakfast, golf courses and farms turned into visitor attractions are all easy to find. Sometimes the management skills developed with one product turn out to be useful in producing the diversified product.

Some firms have diversified too far. They have found that they did not have the expertise needed to produce in the new field or did not fully understand the market. Sometimes they have found that combining completely different lines of production in one company was not cost effective and encountered diseconomies of scale. In some cases the solution to this is *demerger* or *divestment*, when the firm splits up into separate businesses for each product or product range.

divestment means disposing of part of the business by setting it up on an independent basis or selling it to another firm. The assumption is usually that the new management will be better able to run it profitably. This allows the original parent company to concentrate on the core products in which it has proven expertise. ICI did this with its pharmaceuticals division which became Zeneca in 1993 (later called Astra Zeneca). Subsequent experience seems to have confirmed the wisdom of divestment in this case.

Sometimes, firms which are developing some market power are required by the competition authorities to sell part of the business in order to ensure that they do not get too large a market share. At one stage several large UK breweries were required to sell some of their tied pubs to prevent their having too much market power.

dividend policy: profitable firms can choose to pay large dividends to shareholders. Alternatively they may want to keep some of their profit for future investment projects. This is particularly likely if profitable opportunities are apparent, be they new markets or improvements in technologies which will cut costs. Higher *retained profits* in the short run may make it possible to pay bigger dividends in the future. Shareholders can express their views on this at the annual general meeting. It is sometimes said that UK firms have tended to retain too little profit; there have been suggestions of *short termism*. There is concern at the power of big institutional shareholders such as pension funds and insurance companies in this area.

division of labour means the way in which people specialise in particular types of job. There are two elements in the division of labour:

1 A manufacturing process is usually split into a sequence of individual tasks. This is easily seen in an assembly line. Each person has a small task which is repeated for each product which comes past. This is usually faster and cheaper than having one person or a team assembling the entire product on their own. Costs are cut and prices can come down, bringing the product within the reach of a mass market. This was the type of process observed in the pin factory by *Adam Smith* and described in his book, *The Wealth of Nations*, published in 1776.

2 All jobs are specialised in a modern economy and people move into the type of occupation in which they have a *comparative advantage*. This allows them to exploit their natural advantages and also to acquire specialist skills which will increase their productivity. Experience adds further to their advantages as they learn to avoid mistakes.

The breaking down of manufacturing processes into individual component tasks has made it possible over the past 200 years to mechanise most areas of production. This has led to huge increases in productivity, and similarly large price cuts, but it has also *deskilled* many people. This means that many manufacturing processes have become very dull and it can be hard to motivate employees to maintain quality. In recent years ways have been found to reduce this problem through teamwork and *multi-skilling*, so that the division of labour has actually diminished in some workplaces.

divorce of ownership and control refers to the way in which public companies are owned by shareholders but controlled by managers. These two groups are likely to have rather different objectives and managers may not act in shareholders' best interests. In theory, shareholders can control overall policy by being active at *AGMs* but in practice this is not likely if there are large numbers of small shareholders.

dollar ($): the currency of the United States of America. Other countries such as Canada, Australia, Hong Kong and Singapore also refer to their currencies as dollars but they are separate currencies with their own exchange rates. Many products are priced in US dollars because this avoids complications arising from exchange rate changes. Oil is the most obvious example. The euro may well become a similarly important world currency sometime in the future.

dollarisation: the process by which a currency gradually goes out of use as people in the country concerned lose confidence in the local currency and switch to using dollars whenever they can. This may or may not be part of government policy. For a few Latin American countries it has provided a means of achieving greater financial stability.

dominant firm: one which has a position of *market leadership* within the industry. The firm would have to have a significant market share and would be able to influence prices considerably. Microsoft is the obvious example. However, dominant firms can lose some of their power through the application of competition policy or competition from smaller rivals. For example, Boeing is the biggest aircraft manufacturer but is now threatened by Airbus Industrie, its European competitor.

dominant price leader: a firm which is first to raise prices and is then followed by the rest of the industry. Ford has sometimes been considered to be a dominant price leader in the UK car market. This type of situation may be accompanied by *tacit agreement*. No actual agreement is made – this would be illegal – but the industry simply follows the lead of the dominant firm and avoids competing on price.

Dow Jones Industrial Average is the main measure of changing share prices used on the New York Stock Exchange. It is a price index of the 30 most widely traded stocks.

downsizing: contracting the size of the firm to meet a lower level of demand. The term is sometimes used when redundancies are going to be needed.

down time is when machinery is idle because of breakdowns or the need to reset controls. Reducing down time can help to increase productivity and cut *average fixed costs*.

downward multiplier: when *injections* fall or *withdrawals* rise, the level of spending in the *circular flow of income* falls. Some firms find that demand for their products has fallen. They cut back output and eventually employment. Incomes fall and *aggregate demand* falls again. Because of the cumulative nature of the decline in demand, the eventual fall in income will be larger than the fall in spending which brought it about.

DTI: see *Department of Trade and Industry*.

dual economy: an economy in which there is a highly developed sector coexisting alongside a traditional sector with very little capital and few benefits from advanced technology. All economies have some sectors which use more high technology production methods than others. However, in some developing countries there is a huge gap between those areas where there are modern manufacturing operations and the largely traditional agricultural sector. China is a case in point: there has been much foreign investment in the manufacturing capacity along the eastern coast but the interior is dominated by agriculture, much of which uses very traditional methods.

dumping means selling exports at less than their cost of production. Dumping occurs when:

- the producing country is very short of foreign exchange and will sell its exports at a loss in order to pay for necessary imports. This was the underlying reason why up to 1989 centrally planned economies dumped some manufactured goods. China may still be doing this: there are a number of difficult trade disputes in which Western producers are accusing Chinese producers
- the industry is in decline and has spare capacity. This has been a particular problem in the steel industry. EU producers have in the past tried to delay closure of some plants by dumping surplus production.

The *World Trade Organisation* holds dumping to be illegal and has mechanisms for resolving disputes about it. Competing producers who are damaged by cheap imports have been known to use the accusation of dumping to protect themselves even when prices equate to production costs.

duopoly: a market with two sellers. There may be strong rivalry as each firm watches the other and devises strategies which look ahead to the likely reaction from the other. *Game theory* offers a range of predicted outcomes based on different assumptions about likely reactions.

Non-price competition is very likely as a price war might damage profitability for both firms. Advertising and various means of promotion may be strong features of a duopoly. There may be some *tacit agreement* or even *collusion* but this must fall short of exciting the interest of the competition authorities. Unilever and Procter and Gamble are a virtual duopoly in the production of washing products. Non-price competition is very visible in this market.

durable: see *consumer durable.*

earned income comes from wages, salaries and freelance or self-employed earnings. It contrasts with unearned income, which comes from interest, dividends, rent or profit from a business. At times in the past unearned income has been more heavily taxed than earned income.

earnings means total pay and includes overtime and bonuses. In examining the labour market, changes in earnings give a rather different picture from changes in wage rates, which may grow more slowly than earnings.

easy fiscal policy means tax and government expenditure policies which increase *injections* into the economy. This may be an objective when the economy is growing slowly or not at all during a *recession*. Tax cuts will lead to rising consumption expenditure which will add to *aggregate demand*. Similarly, increased government expenditure will add directly to spending. These are *expansionary policies* which should help to increase output and, after a time lag, employment. Such policies were brought in in the 1991 Budget because the economy was in recession at the time. The result was a big increase in government borrowing (the *Public Sector Net Cash Requirement*) but this diminished again as the economy recovered in subsequent years.

easy money means low interest rates which encourage individuals and firms to borrow. Investment will rise provided firms are confident about the future. Consumers will be able to borrow more cheaply and will usually increase spending on consumer durables such as cars. This is an *expansionary policy* which will be useful during *recession*.

EBRD: see *European Bank for Reconstruction and Development.*

EC: see *European Community.*

ECB: see *European Central Bank.*

ECGD: see *Export Credit Guarantee Department*

e-commerce means electronic commerce and has two components.

- Consumers may shop on line rather than in shopping centres. This may have the potential to cut prices in some instances. Or it may simply increase convenience. There is some evidence that on line sellers are finding their costs higher than anticipated and their profits correspondingly disappointing. By the time you read this the situation may be clearer.
- Firms may buy from other firms on line. This is known as the B2B market, business to business. This seems likely to be a highly significant development. In 1999 this market was estimated to be worth US$100 billion. By 2002 it is expected to be worth $1300 billion. (Find out: did it grow as expected, faster or more slowly?)

Estimates concerning the car industry vary but show that there are likely to be substantial cost savings. A cautious view in a study by Deutsche Bank/Roland Berger suggests that North American car companies may save about $1200 per car. This would be about 3% of the average vehicle cost and could make a noticeable difference to prices.

If these cost savings were replicated in other areas of manufacturing, there could be a significant impact on real incomes.

E-commerce makes it easier to identify the cheapest supplier so it may lead to stiffer competition in some areas. This could have painful consequences for some firms including many traditional shops.

econometrics means, literally, the measurement of economic relationships. It involves generating hypotheses from economic models and testing them against the data, to determine what statistical support there is for the existence of particular relationships.

economic activity means any effort made in producing or distributing something which is scarce and can therefore be sold for some kind of reward. The NHS surgeon sells his or her services. So does the security guard. Other people actually produce tangible goods or transport them to where they will be sold. These activities create a *circular flow of money*. The money paid for the goods and services sold goes to producers who spend it on *factors of production*. The owners of the factors of production in turn spend it on another round of goods and services.

economic analysis: the use of economic theory to achieve an active understanding of real world events and relationships. The analysis seeks to break down complex phenomena into simpler sequences of cause and effect. When related to the *empirical evidence*, the analysis clarifies relationships and allows us to predict what may happen next.

Economic and Monetary Union (EMU): the adoption by many EU members of a single currency, the *euro*. The process began in January 1999 and will be complete by mid-2002. By then all the members' own currencies will be out of use and the euro will be used for all transactions.

The founder member countries are Austria, Belgium, Finland, France, Germany, Ireland, Italy, Luxembourg, the Netherlands, Portugal and Spain. Greece joined at the start of 2001. It is quite likely that Sweden will join soon, leaving only Denmark and the UK outside.

This will have a number of far-reaching implications.

- Firms in the euro zone will find it very easy to trade with one another. There will be none of the uncertainties arising from having different exchange rates. Transactions costs will be reduced.
- Prices across the euro zone will become much more transparent. It will be easy for buyers to see who is charging the least and to buy from them. This may increase competition and lead to lower prices for consumers.
- With a single currency, there must be a single *monetary policy*, determined by the European Central Bank (ECB). It will be difficult to determine an *interest rate* which is appropriate for most members and those whose economies are not moving in parallel with the majority are likely to find that the interest rate is either too high or too low. In time, member countries will be forced to try to keep their economies running at a similar level of activity, but this may not be easy to achieve.

So far, the ECB has had some difficulty in gaining the confidence of the financial markets. The euro depreciated by about 30% against the US dollar in the first two years of its existence. There have been doubts that the ECB would maintain a monetary policy stance as prudent as that of the Bundesbank, the German central bank, which had previously enjoyed a great deal of international confidence. The governor of the ECB, Wim Duisenberg, has had many problems in trying to build a reputation for the Bank. During late 2000, the ECB attempted, with some help from other central banks, to support the euro, with only partial success. Find out what has happened since.

economic convergence is the situation when countries adopt similar economic policies and so have similar rates of inflation and public sector deficits. It is an important prerequisite for *Economic and Monetary Union*. Without it, some countries would, within a monetary union, become increasingly uncompetitive and therefore economically depressed relative to other member countries.

The *convergence criteria* for membership of the EMU are as follows:

- The inflation rate must not exceed that of the three best-performing member countries by more than 1.5%
- Interest rates on government bonds must not be more than 2% above those in the same three countries
- The government deficit must be no more than 3% of GDP
- The total government debt must be no more than 60% of GDP
- The exchange rate must have been reasonably stable for the past two years.

Although some of the EMU member countries had not achieved the convergence criteria by the beginning of 1999, they were deemed to be close enough for membership to be realistic. With the possible exception of the exchange rate criterion, they do not appear to pose any problem for the UK, should the government seek membership in the near future.

economic cost: an *opportunity cost* resulting from the production process. Economic costs are not the same as commercial costs. The latter include only those which the producer actually has to pay. Economic costs can include those *external costs* which can be quantified in economic terms. These increase the cost to society of the activity concerned. For example, when new factories are built, their transport needs may lead to nearby roads becoming more congested. This increases the transport costs of other local firms. Some local authorities require investors to finance road improvements as a condition of their receiving planning permission.

economic development is the process by which a country may experience economic growth and a *reallocation of resources* away from primary production and towards manufacturing. The term is usually used to describe what is happening in relatively poor countries which are referred to as *developing countries*. Rapid economic development is usually associated with high levels of investment and improvements in education and training opportunities and sometimes with a policy of allowing relatively *free trade* and an increasingly *open economy*.

economic efficiency implies that output is being produced at the lowest possible cost in terms of resources and in the types and quantities which most closely reflect patterns of consumer demand. Minimising costs in turn implies that there is *technical* *efficiency* (sometimes known as productive efficiency). This means that the production process uses the best available technology and is organised so as to eliminate wasted resources. When the structure of production reflects consumers' wants there is *allocative efficiency*, arising from *consumer sovereignty*. Another frequently used way of describing economic efficiency is to say that no one can be made better off without making someone else worse off. This is sometimes referred to as *Pareto efficiency*.

economic expectations reflect the level of confidence in the economy. People will base their expectations on their experience of past events. So if they have experienced *inflation* in the past, they will tend to expect prices to rise in the future. However, the level of confidence can change quite quickly and have a big impact on investment and spending plans generally. A sense of optimism will be likely to make many managers go ahead with investment plans. The resulting increase in *aggregate demand* will itself increase expectations of future prosperity. The converse is also true, that pessimism about future levels of demand may cause many firms to abandon investment plans. Consumer spending plans tend to fluctuate rather less.

economic forecasting is the process by which economists use *economic models* to predict future trends in the main economic variables. The accuracy of forecasts depends on the extent to which the assumptions on which they are based actually correspond to reality. Forecasting is made difficult by the fact that shocks may occur which are quite unexpected and have far-reaching effects which are by their nature unpredictable. The oil price rise of 1973–1974 and the reunification of Germany in 1989 are examples of shocks which had a major effect on a number of countries.

economic goods are all those items which have a cost in terms of real resources and are therefore scarce in nature. A price must be paid in order to obtain them. The opposite of an economic good is a *free good* and it is actually difficult to identify examples of these. Sometimes wild blackberries are said to be a free good.

economic growth means an increase in output and real incomes. It is usually measured using *gross domestic product* (GDP).

The important elements in the growth process are as follows:

- *Investment*, which increases the amount of capital per person employed and increases productivity. This may be generated domestically or may come from abroad.
- Education and training which enhance *human capital*, again making people more productive.
- *Technological change* which leads to the availability of bigger and better machines, and also helps to create better ways of managing people.
- Exports to new markets which increase demand for the country's products.

These four factors in combination have a big impact on growth rates. All have a healthy effect on the way resources are used to increase production. However, GDP figures must be interpreted with caution. A developing country may have strong growth in GDP and also a high birth rate. This means that per capita income growth is less than the growth of GDP. Also, increases in GDP do not always improve welfare because some of the external effects of growth are not always positive. Pollution, deforestation and climate change can all reduce the positive effects of growth and this will not show in the GDP figures.

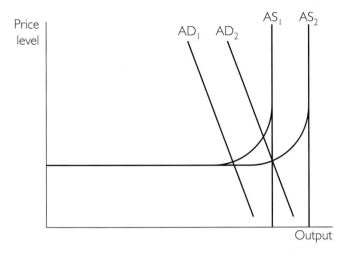

Price level / Output

Rising capacity in the economy, as aggregate supply increases, means that output can grow without inflation accelerating

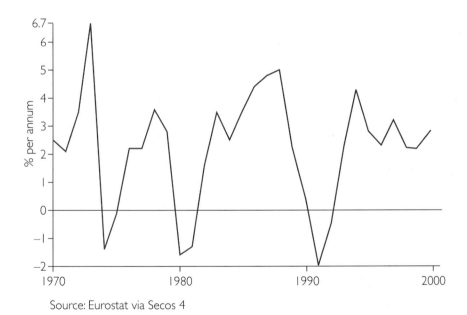

Source: Eurostat via Secos 4

Economic growth rates fluctuate over the course of the trade cycle

economic indicators are data series that help to show what is happening to economic performance. *Leading indicators* can be particularly useful as they help to forecast the immediate future. For example, difficulty in recruiting people with scarce skills can indicate future labour market tightness and the likelihood of inflation tending to accelerate. However, where the data is very recent, it is subject to error and great caution is required.

economic incentives are price differences which encourage people to change their course of action. For example, if the price of apples rises, people have an incentive to buy bananas instead (provided their price has stayed the same). Similarly, rising prices may indicate that the product is likely to be more profitable and may provide firms with an incentive to increase supply. A wage *differential* may provide an incentive to acquire more skills.

Tax changes are often made to create incentives. Higher tobacco taxes create an incentive to give up smoking. Fuel taxes are varied to create incentives to use cleaner fuels.

economic integration refers to the increasing interdependence of modern economies. Integration grows through increased international trade and increases further within economic unions such as the EU. *Harmonisation* of regulations makes it easier to produce for all markets within the EU, because there is no need to design a slightly different product for each market. Good transport facilities enlarge markets for many producers. The objective of the *single market* is increased integration. For energetic producers, integration creates many opportunities to sell to a larger market.

economic man is a term which reflects the assumptions of neoclassical economics that people act in their own self-interest. *Adam Smith* argued that if everyone acts in their own interest, society as a whole is made better off. Self-interest leads people to choose the product they most want. This means that the price of those products will tend to rise. Self-interest also leads firms to identify products with rising prices as profitable. So resources are allocated in accordance with consumer preferences. This is the so-called *invisible hand*, which Adam Smith wrote about.

economic models are constructed from the relationships between different variables which enable economists to examine the connections between changes. A model may use only those variables which are most important within the situation being studied and thus can reduce the level of complication which must be considered. In this way they may enable us to gain important insights into the way the economy works.

A model may be constructed in terms of a number of simultaneous equations or the relationships may be represented graphically or verbally. Models can be judged by their effectiveness in predicting what will happen under particular circumstances. They will not give accurate predictions if they are based on unrealistic assumptions. A model may be very simple, as in the basic supply and demand diagram, or very complex, as for example in the Treasury model of the whole economy which has over 500 equations and variables.

economic performance can be examined using a number of different criteria:

- The rate of *economic growth* is measured using GDP data, suitably deflated to remove the effects of inflation and provide a measure of the real increase in income.
- *Inflation and unemployment* rates provide information on the scale of economic problems.
- *Productivity* data indicates whether progress is being made in terms of increasing output per person employed. This can be achieved by investing

more in both physical and human capital and by increasing technical progress through research and development.
- *Competitiveness* can be measured using data on unit costs of production in different countries.
- The level of spending on investment and research and development indicates whether efforts are being made to produce in more efficient ways.

This list could be extended indefinitely but the above would give a great deal of information about economic performance in comparison with either past experience or other economies.

economic planning: the creation by a government of a plan for a period of years which gives a series of targets for output, investment, training and other means by which its objectives may be met. In the UK this approach to economic policy was used in the 1960s. In France it has been in continuous use for many years.

economic policy encompasses a large range of different types of policy which have some impact on the economy. These are the broad categories of policy:

- Macro-economic policy involves taxation, government expenditure and interest rates, all of which can be used to influence the level of aggregate demand and output in the economy.
- Micro-economic policies are used to foster competition, encourage particular types of industrial development and influence the allocation of resources.
- Trade policies can be used to adjust import controls and sometimes to influence the level of exports.
- Exchange rate policies determine the extent to which the exchange rate floats or is managed and will determine whether the UK joins the EMU.

Governments may be more or less interventionist in their economic policies. In the past governments used to think they could 'pick winners', i.e. decide which were likely to be the most successful industries and intervene to provide assistance. Equally, they saw themselves as having a role in helping *declining industries*. Very little of this happens nowadays, partly because the policies were found to be very expensive and not effective.

economic principles are the fundamental ideas of the subject. They are based on hypotheses that have been extensively tested and found to correspond to real world observations. Once a hypothesis has been tested in this way, it becomes a theory which has value in helping to explain events. Theories can be used to predict possible future developments. They can also help us to understand important economic relationships. Some theories seem rather unrealistic, e.g. perfect competition, but are useful for their explanatory power as teaching tools.

economic problem: the *scarcity of resources* and the gap between what most people want and what they actually have together capture the nature of the economic problem. Real resources are in fixed supply at any one time and are always less than the sum total of human needs and wants. So *choices* must be made. Each individual decides what to buy, given their personal preferences. This creates a pattern of demand which makes some products more profitable than others. Firms will try to produce profitable products, thus channelling resources into the production of items which consumers want to buy more of. Firms will also try to minimise the resource cost of production so as to get as much output as possible from a given quantity of resources.

economic profit is the difference between total revenue from the sale of the product and the opportunity costs of all the resources used in production. It is a reward for the taking of unquantifiable risks by the entrepreneur. Profit in excess of the full opportunity cost of the resources encourages entrepreneurs to divert more resources to production because it shows that there is a high level of demand for the product. (This is the *profit-signalling mechanism.*)

economic rent is the amount which someone can earn which is in excess of their *transfer earnings*, i.e. what they could earn elsewhere. It is a demand-determined reward to labour and will be earned when labour is to some degree in inelastic supply. For example, doctors are in perfectly inelastic supply because the number of places available to study medicine is determined by the government and the profession. To the extent that the demand for doctors exceeds the supply, they will be able to negotiate higher salaries than most could earn as research scientists or in other occupations.

economic resources are all the goods which are already available, together with all the *factors of production* which can be used to create finished products, either goods or services. They include everything which can be used to satisfy demand.

economic sanctions prohibit or discourage trade in certain items with a particular country, usually with a political motive. Sanctions against South Africa were partly responsible for the government of the country eventually abandoning its policy of racial discrimination.

economic system refers to the way in which resources are allocated in the economy concerned. *Centrally planned economies* allocate resources according to the bureaucratic decisions of a government department. *Market economies* allocate resources using the *profit-signalling mechanism* which creates incentives for producers to meet consumer demand.

Economic Trends: a monthly publication from the Office for National Statistics that provides some of the most important data series needed to examine *economic performance*, including national income statistics and the inflation and unemployment rates.

economic union involves the creation of an area composed of several different economies which all agree to use the same economic policies and regulations. Successful economies almost all have large markets, in which there are major opportunities for competent producers. This may be because the economy itself is large (as in the case of the US) or it may be because they are very *open economies* (as with Singapore) and trade extensively with the outside world. One way to create a large market is to form an economic union. The *European Union* has roughly 350 million people. All member countries operate according to harmonised economic rules laid down by the European Commission, so producers can design their products according to the same requirements wherever they sell within the EU.

economic welfare refers to the extent to which people have the resources needed in order to lead a satisfying life. The welfare state aims to ensure that everyone has the minimum requirements for living in reasonable comfort, without providing any real luxuries. In practice it does not always provide all the basic necessities. The study of economic welfare involves deciding how particular changes affect people's sense of physical well-being. Some of the judgements required depend on how well-being is defined.

economics is a social science that studies how society allocates its scarce resources in order to satisfy its unlimited human needs and wants. Thomas Carlyle, the 19th century writer, described it as 'the dismal science' because at that time some economic theories appeared very pessimistic. Because of technological change, economic theories have become rather more optimistic.

The interesting feature of economic theory is that it is constantly catching up with events; the conventional wisdom seldom stays the same for long. This makes it much more exciting to study than a subject full of established truths.

In fact, economics is not so much a set of theories as a way of thinking about economic relationships.

economies of scale: as some firms grow, they are able to produce at a lower *average cost* than before. These economies of larger scale production can cut costs to the point where prices can be cut and larger markets can be reached. The car industry in the early to mid 20th century demonstrates the sequence of events. At first, cars were handbuilt in very small numbers and were very expensive. Gradually the production process was mechanised and in the late 1920s Henry Ford pioneered the first assembly line in Detroit. Costs of production fell dramatically, so that far more people could afford a car and further economies of scale were reaped. From the 1950s onwards to the present time, the car industry has been the scene of numerous mergers, as car companies combine to reap further economies of scale in design and development, in the production of standardised components and in marketing campaigns.

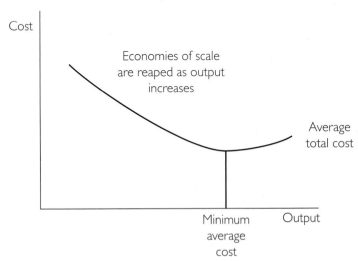

Economies of scale and average costs

The diagram on page 93 shows how costs fall as output increases. There can come a point where the level of output has increased so much that *diseconomies of scale occur.* If this happens average costs will start to rise again.

(See also *internal economies of scale, external economies of scale* and *diseconomies of scale,* for more detail.)

economy: as a whole, the people who make consumption decisions, the firms which make production decisions and the government bodies which oversee the process within a particular area. Normally we refer to the economy of a particular state, but we can refer to the local economy or the world economy. The term encompasses all the people who have a hand in making decisions which affect the *allocation of resources.*

ECSC: see *European Coal and Steel Community.*

ECU: see *European Currency Unit.*

EEC: see *European Union.*

effective demand: in order to actually buy a product, consumers must not just want it but also be able to afford to pay for it. If they cannot, then they are really just dreaming; we say they are not in the market. Effective demand means demand backed by the ability to pay.

effective exchange rate: the exchange rate as measured by the *exchange rate index,* which values the currency as a weighted average of the currencies of the nation's major trading partners. The weights are proportional to the amount of trade involved.

efficiency generally means using resources in the most economical way possible. This means that *average costs* will be at a minimum. Output from a given quantity of resources will be maximised. The jargon term for this is *technical efficiency.* It can be measured by examining *productivity* in one of its forms:

- labour productivity means output per person employed
- capital productivity means output per unit of capital invested.

The higher the level of productivity, the more efficiently the resources are being used. Waste is kept to a minimum.

The term efficiency can also mean *allocative efficiency,* which refers to the extent to which the allocation of resources tallies with the real preferences of consumers. An economy is said to be allocatively efficient when the goods and services produced are on sale at prices which reflect true costs of production and in quantities that accurately reflect levels of consumer demand.

Allocative efficiency is sometimes also known as *economic efficiency.*

efficiency/equity trade-off: see *equity/efficiency trade-off.*

EFTA: see *European Free Trade Association.*

elasticities measure responsiveness to change. *Price elasticity of demand* measures the responsiveness of quantity demanded to a change in price. Other important elasticities include *income elasticity of demand, cross-elasticity of demand* and *supply elasticity.* All of these refer to product prices. Elasticity of demand is also important in the analysis of the labour market.

elasticity of demand for labour: the responsiveness of demand for labour to a change in the wage rate. In some occupations, this is very low. A new, higher wage rate may be negotiated and there will be little effect on the number of people hired by employers. The important determining factors are:

- whether there is a substitute for the type of labour in question. An increase in teachers' pay is unlikely to lead to a fall in the quantity of teaching services demanded, because substitutes are not very realistic
- whether labour is a significant part of total costs. In a power station the bulk of the cost comes from the capital invested and the cost of fuel; labour is a very small part of the total, so a pay increase will make little difference to the demand for labour
- whether the demand for the product is price elastic. If demand is inelastic, the increase in wage costs can be passed on to the customer with little change in the quantity sold, so there will be little change in the quantity of labour demanded.

elasticity of supply of labour means the responsiveness of the supply of labour to a change in price. An inelastic supply of labour means that an increase in the going wage will produce only a limited increase in the number of people available to do that particular job. This can happen when particular skills are scarce. During a boom, the wages of skilled construction workers typically rise sharply. The extreme case occurs when the supply of a particular type of labour is more or less fixed, i.e. there is perfectly inelastic supply. In this case, *economic rent* will be earned.

electronic mail (e-mail) involves sending written messages to and from computers, via a telephone line. It is making communications within a firm very much cheaper and quicker. It is also creating opportunities in retailing direct to the customer from a website. (See also *e-commerce*.)

e-mail: see *electronic mail*.

embargo: complete prohibition of trade with a particular country or prohibition applying to particular products (e.g. anything useful for military purposes). An embargo can be agreed amongst trading partners as a way to discourage terrorist activity or aggression. In the case of South Africa, the embargo was designed to stop the government from ignoring the human rights of the majority of the population.

The term can also be applied where information is being given out but is not to be published until after a certain time or date.

emerging markets: countries which in recent years have increased manufacturing output very rapidly, while also adopting a more market-oriented pattern of production. They include China, Hong Kong, India and a number of other Asian countries; Eastern European countries such as Poland and Hungary and some Latin American countries such as Mexico and Brazil. The term is used very loosely. Sometimes it refers to the ex-communist countries, Russia and Eastern Europe; at other times it includes countries which were until recently relatively poor and now have flourishing manufacturing sectors.

emissions are substances which pollute air or water, coming from the activities of individuals or firms. Liquids and solids may be discharged into rivers or the sea. Solid particles and gases may be discharged into the atmosphere.

emissions trading programmes provide for companies in certain parts of the USA to trade the right to allow a certain quantity of polluting gases to escape into the atmosphere. This ensures that those companies which create air pollution actually pay for the right to do so. Companies which do not do so will have to control emissions of polluting gases. The price of the right to pollute creates an incentive to pollute less.

empirical evidence means data or information collected from the real world and reflecting the factual basis of the issue being investigated.

empirical testing is the use of data to test economic theories or the predictions of *economic models*.

employee involvement: the extent to which employees are made a part of the decision-making process. At one end of the spectrum, managers might have a suggestion box, into which employees may put their ideas for improving production methods. At the other end of the spectrum, employees may have opportunities to participate directly in the management process, through consultation and representation on the Board of Directors. In between there may be various methods of communication which ensure that employees are regularly consulted.

employee stock ownership: the process by which employees acquire shares in the company as part of their reward package.

employer: someone or some body which pays people to work for them.

employers' association: a body which represents all the employers in a particular industry or product group. Those that wish will join by paying a subscription. In return they may get:

- collective representation at government level or with local authorities, through which they may be able to increase their influence on policy
- collective bargaining with trade unions, which may make it easier for them to resist large wage demands
- joint advertising designed to increase the total market (e.g. by the Meat and Livestock Commission, which encourages people to buy more meat)
- joint market research efforts.

Where an employers' association negotiates directly with a single industry-wide trade union, there is said to be *bilateral monopoly* in the labour market.

employment: the process by which people provide their labour in a production process for which they are rewarded with a wage or salary.

Employment Acts: between 1980 and 1990, in a series of Acts of Parliament, employment legislation was overhauled by the Conservative government of Margaret Thatcher. The overall effect of the legislation was to weaken the power of trade unions to take action against employers. The important features of the legislation were:

- industrial action could be taken only in relation to the individual's own employer
- before a strike could take place, there had to be a secret ballot of members
- individuals could be dismissed for taking part in an unofficial strike (i.e. one not approved by the relevant trade union)

- closed shops were made difficult to enforce, meaning that employees could not be compelled to join a particular union
- many employment restrictions were removed, e.g. restrictions on hours worked by young people
- trade unions were made liable for damage caused by industrial action taken by their members.

The legislation was generally credited with making the UK labour market much more flexible. However, it probably also increased the opportunities for employers to employ some people on very low wages.

employment contract: a legal document that defines the employee's responsibilities as well as the rate of pay and conditions of employment. In recent years, employment contracts have become much more flexible, so that employers can vary the number of hours worked and their timing much more easily. This has made the labour market in the UK much more flexible but has also removed some of the employee's security.

The Employment Relations Act 1999 gave employees somewhat enhanced rights. It:

- allowed employees to claim unfair dismissal after one instead of two years' employment
- allowed employees to insist that a trade union be recognised in the workplace under certain circumstances
- improved maternity and paternity leave requirements.

To a degree, this adjusted the balance between employee and employer powers which had been set in the *Employment Acts* of the 1980s.

employment protection: the laws which protect the position of the employee at work. Employees are protected from unfair dismissal and are entitled to statutory redundancy payments, according to the length of time they have been with the employer. There is some concern that there is a *trade-off* between protecting the employee and encouraging employers to create more jobs. Employment protection is stronger in some EU countries than in the UK and this may help to explain why these countries have higher unemployment rates. Equally, there is less employment protection in the US than in the UK and a lower unemployment rate.

employment zones: small areas of the country which qualify for extra government help by virtue of their high unemployment levels. They are areas where regeneration is particularly hard to achieve because of past dependence on industries which were very localised and then declined, such as shipbuilding, coal and iron and steel.

EMS: see *European Monetary System.*

EMU: see *Economic and Monetary Union.*

endangered species: normal economic activity can lead to certain species being hunted or suffering the destruction of their environment or the encroachment of alien species. When total numbers fall so that successful breeding becomes difficult, there may be economic consequences. Measures to reduce the threat may also have economic consequences.

endogenous variable: one which is determined by changes within an *economic model*. For example, the level of consumption is determined largely by income. It is said that consumption is dependent on income. In contrast, *exogenous variables* are determined outside the model, i.e. they have causes which are independent of what happens within the model. Investment, for example, is determined largely by expectations of future profit and these cannot be given a specific value.

energy tax: a tax on energy purchases which would be designed to discourage consumption of *depletable resources*. At present energy taxes are the subject of much debate. Differences in energy taxes create difficulties for international road haulage businesses which have to compete with foreign businesses which pay less tax on their fuel. The international agreement which could remove this problem is currently elusive because high energy taxes are politically unpopular with a wide range of people.

enterprise is a term which is used in two ways:

- an enterprise is a business which takes risks and sells a product
- enterprise is the quality which involves initiative and willingness to take risks in order to create and sell a product.

enterprise allowance: a payment made to unemployed people to raise their incomes during the first year if they go into business on their own.

enterprise culture: the state of mind commonly found in a market economy, where decisions are made on the basis of future profit and people are generally willing to work hard and to take risks in ways which will generate income and wealth.

enterprise policies are all those measures which are designed to help encourage businesses to set up and expand.

enterprise zone: small areas which have suffered severe unemployment, in which businesses have been encouraged to set up and create jobs. Incentives included 10 years free of business rates. The cost of the extra jobs created turned out to be rather high and the zones are being phased out.

entrepreneur: an individual who is willing to take risks and who makes the decision to go into production. The entrepreneur develops a product and decides how it will be produced using *factors of production*. He or she carries the risks associated with bringing the product to the marketplace. Sometimes the entrepreneur is described as the fourth factor of production.

entry refers to the process by which a firm may set up in business and become part of the industry. Easy entry implies that the industry will be at least fairly competitive because profits will attract additional producers who will then compete with each other. An individual or an existing business can start off a new line of production and find ways to sell the product at a profit. Exit is the reverse process. Entry and exit are an important part of the process of *structural change*. *Barriers to entry* make it difficult for new businesses to get started.

environment: the surroundings in which people live and firms operate. The natural environment includes all the natural resources which affect and are affected by a particular activity. The built environment includes all the man-made resources which surround the activity.

environmental accounts attempt to put a value on the impact of a business on the surroundings which it affects. These may or may not be part of an annual report.

environmental audit: an attempt to measure pollution levels, recycling activities and any other activity which is likely to affect the environment of a firm. Some businesses which make *business responsibility* a high priority voluntarily carry out an audit as a way of monitoring progress towards environmental objectives. Sainsbury's undertakes an annual audit, the outcomes of which appear in a public report. This approach is still the exception rather than the rule.

environmental degradation: the process by which economic activity leads to the destruction of real resources. For example, overgrazing in developing countries leads to the destruction of plant life, which makes erosion of the soil more likely when there is rain. In turn, erosion makes it harder for plant life to recover and grazing lands lose their value as such. Equally, environmental degradation can occur when there are spills from a chemical plant which lead to long-term contamination of the soil around it and from many other causes.

environmental economics is the study of environmental problems and lays particular emphasis on evaluating the costs and benefits of different kinds of solutions to the problems posed by pollution, congestion and the general destruction of resources. Most environmental problems are associated with some kind of *market failure* and *externalities* which enable producers to avoid paying the full resource costs of production.

Traditionally, economics regards national income figures as a fair measure of the standard of living. However, these are constructed on the basis of recorded accounts and to the extent that there are external costs and benefits arising from economic activity, these accounts may not reflect the true improvement in welfare. Environmental economics tries to measure the standard of living in ways which allow for the costs of economic growth.

environmental policy: the plans of the government in relation to protection of the environment. Individual firms may also have an environmental policy.

environmental pollution: contamination of air and water by production processes. Where climate and weather conditions make it possible for atmospheric pollution to travel long distances, it may materialise as *acid rain* far away from the original sources.

equality means that people do not experience large differentials in income within a society. Total equality has seldom been achieved in any society, but some countries have for long periods had a much greater degree of equality than others. Sweden has been most notable in this respect while the USA has tended to have very little equality in its *income distribution*, though rather more equality of opportunity through its education system. (See also *equity/efficiency trade-off*.)

equal opportunities: the provision of fair consideration for all applicants, regardless of gender, ethnic group, religion or disability, so that there will be no discrimination between employees or job applicants or those seeking educational opportunities. There is ample evidence that although some progress has been made in fostering equal opportunities, much discrimination remains. For example:

- variations in unemployment rates between ethnic groups cannot be explained by variations in their qualifications
- lower rates of pay in jobs traditionally taken by women are also very persistent.

In theory discrimination deprives employers of the best candidate for the job and employers who do not discriminate will have a *competitive advantage*. In practice, many organisations seem not to recognise that hiring the best candidate for the job can cut costs.

Equal Opportunities Commission: an organisation which aims to prevent discrimination on grounds of gender.

equation: a statement in symbols that relates one variable to another. An *economic model* is normally built up from a number of equations, each of which links two or more variables. Together the equations form a system in which each variable is identified by its connections to other variables.

equation of exchange: connects the *quantity of money* (M), the *velocity of circulation* (V), the price level (P) and the number of transactions (T).

FORMULA: $MV = PT$

Sometimes known as the Fisher equation, this is an identity rather than a relationship: it is true by definition. PT is the total value of all output, which is equivalent to national income. MV is the amount of money needed to pay for it, since the velocity of circulation is simply the number of times each unit of currency circulates within a given time period. It can, however, be used to predict the rate of inflation under certain circumstances. If the velocity of circulation is constant and the number of transactions only grows slowly, then it follows that inflation will be directly related to the quantity of money in circulation.

Some economists have taken the view that velocity is constant and that the equation of exchange illustrates simply a fundamental and direct link between money and inflation. But the data on velocity in recent years rather suggests that it is not constant, at least in the short to medium term. The reality is certainly more complicated than the equation of exchange suggests.

equilibrium in the marketplace means that the quantity supplied is exactly the same as the quantity demanded. This means that there is an equilibrium price at which the market clears. No one is left with unwanted stocks of unsold goods and consumers get all they want at the going price. There will be neither *excess supply*, nor *excess demand*. This process of *market clearing* comes about because the price is free to change and settles at the equilibrium level.

equilibrium prices apply in labour and capital markets as well as the market for goods and services. A wage rate which is above the equilibrium level can lead to unemployment and an excess supply of labour, and vice versa. A very high interest rate may lead to an excess supply of funds in the capital markets, with banks willing to lend but a shortage of viable investment opportunities.

The primary importance of the concept of equilibrium is as a tool of analysis, rather than an exact description of the real world. It allows us to identify the problems in markets which plainly do not clear, such as the housing market when many potential sellers are unable to find buyers at the price they would like to get. Price theory predicts that the houses will sell if prices fall to the equilibrium level, a prediction which sellers who must sell frequently discover to be accurate, even if the exact level of the equilibrium price is not at first obvious.

In macro-economics, equilibrium is a situation in which *aggregate demand* is exactly equal to the level of planned output. Thus buyers wish to buy all that firms intend to produce. There is no change in the level of stocks. If aggregate demand is greater than or less than output (i.e. there is disequilibrium), stocks will fall or rise to accommodate the difference. It is important to remember that a macro-economic equilibrium does not imply that the level of output will be sufficient to employ everyone who wants to work. It may well be associated with a high level of unemployment.

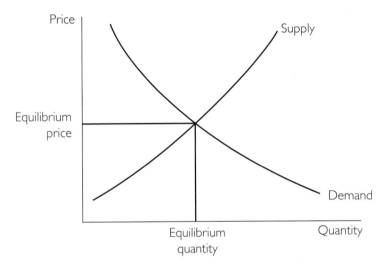

Equilibrium in the market for goods

equities are shares in a company. Shareholders are the owners of the company and have the right to review the directors' decisions.

equity: a term associated with the notion of fairness. Equity requires that incomes be reasonably close, without large variations between the highest and the lowest incomes. It requires also that the benefits of economic growth be reasonably equally distributed. (*See also equity/efficiency trade-off.*)

equity/efficiency trade-off: decisions which are taken in the interests of promoting efficiency may have the effect of increasing inequality. For example, incentives which encourage people to increase *productivity* may lead to an increasingly unequal distribution of income. In a different sphere, when a product is very scarce, the price will usually rise to ration the product among those most able to pay the higher price. This will hurt poorer people much more than richer people.

For governments, there may be a choice between *equity*, i.e. creating a relatively equal distribution of income, and *efficiency*, which may require some incentives. Incentives to work and take risks imply that some people receive rewards in the form of earnings or profits which make them much better off than most other people. Yet without incentives, economic growth may be slow and therefore fail to deliver the improvement in standards of living which people expect.

This area is very controversial. It is fairly clear that the limited incentives which exist in a *centrally planned economy* do not encourage people to improve productivity in the way that they usually will in a market economy. However, in the context of a market economy, it is not clear that measures to reduce inequality, such as progressive taxes and spending on social services, actually reduce economic growth and the quest for efficiency. Scandinavian countries have on the whole a fair degree of equality and acceptable or better growth rates.

equity finance means funds generated by selling shares. There is an important distinction between equity finance and *loan finance*. Shareholders expect a dividend, but in fact they may be prepared to wait some time for it if they believe that in the long run the business will be profitable. Lenders expect, and must be paid, a rate of interest which will fall due on a regular basis. Equity finance may therefore be cheaper for the company during the important early phase of a new project. When the Eurotunnel's costs overran and profits were slow to materialise, it was for a time unable to cover interest payments to the banks. The solution was to convert some of the bank loans into equity.

ERM: see *Exchange Rate Mechanism*.

estate duty was a tax on inherited wealth. It has been replaced by *inheritance tax*.

ethical investment is the use of finance for capital investment in projects which avoid certain kinds of unethical activity. It applies mainly to investment funds such as *unit trusts*. Businesses which might be excluded from funding could be those producing defence equipment or tobacco products or those which have a weak record on pollution control. Others might be excluded because they deal with governments which have a poor record for respecting human rights.

ethical policy: some firms have now developed an ethical policy which sets out their objectives in relation to what they see as their *social responsibilities*. The emphasis will vary from one firm to another. Likely areas for the policy coverage would include environmental targets, community programmes and the integrity of the business in its dealings with its *stakeholders* such as consumers and suppliers.

ethical pricing is an attempt by some organisations to pay higher prices to poor producers in developing countries in order to give them a fairer return for their labour. Café Direct is perhaps the best known example. The Fair Trade Foundation exists to give approval to businesses which satisfy their criteria for ethical pricing.

ethical responsibility: see *business responsibility* and *corporate responsibility*.

ethics are the moral principles which may or may not be used as a basis for decision taking. Some firms are genuinely ethical in their intent, giving a high priority to the value they can provide for the customer and treating employees and other businesses fairly at all times. Others may take decisions primarily on the basis of the profit to be made. Sometimes, firms will take into account the impact of their decisions on public opinion and make an ethical decision for purely practical reasons.

EU: see *European Union*.

EU enlargement: there is a long queue of countries interested in joining the EU. The Czech Republic, Estonia, Hungary, Poland and Slovenia are to be in the first wave, which will join sometime between 2003 and 2005. However, first, the existing member countries must agree how to adapt their system to accommodate more members. This may require majority voting and an end to the right to veto. This involves some very vexed questions.

Next come Cyprus, Slovakia and, possibly, Turkey. Applicants have to be able to adopt the economic policies of the EU, must have effective competition policies and must be capable of protecting the rights of minority peoples; this means that negotiations could be very protracted.

euro: the single European currency which will be used for all transactions from June 2002. The euro was introduced at the start of 1999 by 11 member countries: Austria, Belgium, Finland, France, Germany, Luxembourg, Ireland, Italy, the Netherlands, Portugal and Spain. Greece joined in early 2001. There are three European Union countries outside the so-called *euro zone*: the UK, Denmark and Sweden, and Sweden is quite likely to join soon. The currency could also be adopted by East European countries if they join the EU and can satisfy the *convergence criteria*. (See also *European Central Bank* and *Economic and Monetary Union*.)

euro zone: a journalistic phrase for the 12 countries linked by their single currency, the euro. The zone represents nearly 80% of the population of the European Union.

eurocurrency: bank balances held in currencies which are not the normal local one. For example, pounds held in a Frankfurt bank are called eurocurrency. Dollar balances held in a London bank are termed eurodollar deposits.

European Bank for Reconstruction and Development (EBRD) was set up to provide development finance for the of Eastern Europe in 1990. It is based in London.

European Central Bank (ECB): the central bank of the *euro zone*. The bank itself is based in Frankfurt with Wim Duisenberg as governor. Decisions are taken by a committee composed of representatives from all member countries. Each month the committee decides on the appropriate monetary policy and sets the interest rate for the whole euro zone. The Bank is charged with keeping inflation within the 2.2% limit. However, the steady fall of the euro since its introduction has caused the ECB to be much exercised as to how to create some confidence in the euro as a currency.

European Coal and Steel Community (ECSC): an early forerunner of the European Union. Set up in 1952 by Belgium, France, Germany, Italy, Luxembourg and the Netherlands, it reduced trade barriers on coal and steel products. Later, in 1958 it became part of the then European Economic Community and extended trade concessions to manufactures and agricultural products.

European Commission: the central body which administers the affairs of the *European Union*. Very importantly, it also initiates policy by establishing policy guidelines and giving opinions. Proposals are discussed with member country governments and with employers' organisations and trade unions.

The President of the Commission is currently Romano Prodi. There are 19 other commissioners, two each from the larger countries and one from each of the rest.

The commissioners, once appointed, act independently of the national interest and defend the EU as a whole.

There is a procedure for initiating legislation within the EU:

- the Commission's proposals are sent to the European Parliament, which may amend them
- the proposals then go to the Council of Ministers for further discussion
- there will be a continuing dialogue between the Commission and the Council of Ministers. The latter provides for national interests to be considered while the former pursues the interest of the EU as a whole.

European Community (EC): the name for the *European Union* until November 1993.

European Court of Justice in Luxembourg is the highest court of the European Union. Where the interpretation of European law and of the EU treaties is in dispute, it can decide the outcome. It can fine firms and challenge national laws.

European Currency Unit (ECU): a form of international money used by a number of EU bodies in their accounts, before the introduction of the *euro* in 1999. It was a weighted average of several EU currencies. It provided the basis for the *euro*.

European Development Fund: a fund created by the EU to provide finance for investment in less developed countries.

European Economic Area was created by the agreement signed in 1991 between the members of the European Union and the *European Free Trade Association*. It allows for free trade between EU countries and Norway, Iceland and Liechtenstein.

European economic integration: the process by which EU member economies are becoming more and more like a single economy. The *single market*, with its harmonised regulations and elimination of border controls, has contributed to this.

European Free Trade Area (EFTA): was originally set up in 1960 by the European countries outside the European Union. At the time, the UK was a member, along with Austria, Denmark, Norway, Portugal, Sweden and Switzerland. Since then, all but Norway and Switzerland have left to join the EU; these two, together with Iceland and Liechtenstein, are the only members. It allows free trade between members, but is not a *customs union* as the EU is.

European Monetary System (EMS) was an attempt beginning in 1979 to bring EU member currencies more closely into line with one another. It had two components:

- the ECU or *European Currency Unit*
- the Exchange Rate Mechanism.

The objective was to increase stability by making sure that member currencies were kept close to each other through *central bank intervention*. Each currency was given an exchange rate band within which it might fluctuate to a limited extent.

The UK joined in 1990 but left again when the value of the pound collapsed in 1992. It was simply impossible for the Bank of England to defend the exchange rate against the fierce speculation which developed. In general, the strategy of locking member currencies more closely together worked and made it possible to develop full monetary union from 1999.

European Monetary Union: many people think that this is what EMU stands for. Not so! It stands for *Economic and Monetary Union.*

European Parliament is democratically elected and exists to debate and amend the proposals which are made by the European Commission. At the time of the first direct elections in 1979, it had few powers but these have gradually been extended. In 1999 it used its power to sack all of the EU commissioners on grounds of corruption. This has made its relationship with the Commission rather delicate. Despite this and the fact that the last elections proceeded with a very low turnout, its influence is gradually increasing.

European Regional Development Fund was set up by the European Union in recognition of the fact that increased trade would cause adjustment problems in some regions. Southern Italy, parts of North East France and Merseyside are examples of areas which have been chronically depressed and have qualified for development assistance from the fund.

European single market: see *single European market.*

European Social Fund was set up by the European Union to improve employment opportunities for people in parts of the EU which have suffered from *structural unemployment.* It provides funds for training schemes and job creation.

European Union (EU): formerly the European Community (EC) and before that the European Economic Community (EEC), is a *customs union.* However, many influential people have always seen it as much more, with the possibility of integration proceeding to the point where it becomes, essentially, like a single economy.

The EEC was set up with the Treaty of Rome in 1957. At that time the members were Belgium, France, Germany, Italy, the Netherlands and Luxembourg. They were joined by:

- the UK, Denmark and Ireland in 1973
- Greece in 1981
- Portugal and Spain in 1986
- Austria, Finland and Sweden in 1995.

It is likely that some of the emerging East European countries will join soon, perhaps by 2005.

The Single European Act in 1987 moved the EU towards much closer harmonisation of regulations and reduced the costs associated with border controls. Effectively, most businesses can rely on being able to sell the same product throughout the EU. This has helped to cut costs and increase competition.

With *free trade* between EU members and a *common external tariff,* the EU provides a market of some 380 million people. There is immense scope for reaping *economies of scale* in such a market. Some foreign direct investment within the EU has been attracted by this large market; locating within the EU reduces the impact of the common external tariff. If EMU works as planned, there will be further benefits from the fact that prices will be very easy to compare and competition may be strengthened.

The *European Commission* in Brussels initiates all new legislation. Its proposals are sent to the *European Parliament* and then to the *Council of Ministers. The European Court of*

Justice will determine how the treaties and regulations should be implemented, whenever disputes arise. This sequence is shown in the diagram. Despite the creation of this structure, national governments retain strong influence, visible in the crucial role played by the Council of Ministers.

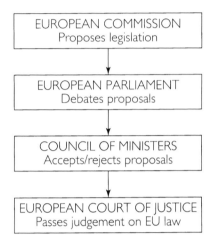

Although the EU has had many positive effects on member countries, its impact on the rest of the world has brought some problems. Subsidised exports of farm surpluses have upset major exporters of agricultural products such as the US and Australia. They may also have depressed food prices in parts of Africa and diminished the incentives for African farmers to increase production. The bargaining power of the EU within the *World Trade Organisation* is strong. Concessions which might enable developing countries to export more easily have been very modest.

The EU still lacks the democratic controls which are desirable as its scope increases. The *European Parliament* is hampered by the fact that the political parties are still national in scope rather than international. (See also *Common Agricultural Policy, EU enlargement, Economic and Monetary Union*.)

ex ante is a Latin term, used in economic theory, meaning before the event. It is used mainly to refer to what we might know in advance. It contrasts with *ex post*, after the event, when hindsight adds an extra dimension to what we know and understand.

excess aggregate demand means that the quantity of goods and services demanded in the economy as a whole is greater than the amount which can be produced, given the available resources (*full-capacity output*). The consequence is likely to be accelerating *inflation*. It will be possible to raise prices and still sell the product. Firms will bid up the price of labour as they compete for the few available employees, especially if they have scarce skills. This will raise costs and prices will rise further. Expectations of inflation may set in and influence pay negotiations. The diagram overleaf shows that if the economy is producing at or near full-capacity output, rising aggregate demand will lead to excess demand and a rising price level. The solution will be to reduce aggregate demand using *fiscal* and *monetary policies*.'

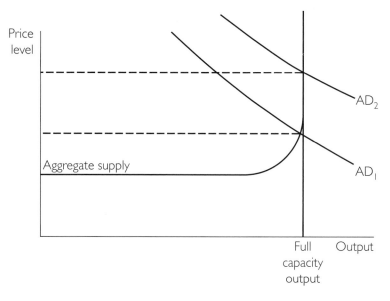

Excess aggregate demand

Excess aggregate demand will usually be associated with the boom phase of the *trade cycle*. Prospects of economic growth will make firms optimistic about investing and consumers will have increasing incomes, leading to higher consumption. *Aggregate demand* will grow faster than the capacity of the economy to produce. This situation is unsustainable because it will lead to inflation and probably to *contractionary policies*.

excess capacity: a situation in which resources are being underutilised. There is likely to be unemployment and many firms may contract or close down because of low levels of aggregate demand. The economy is therefore producing less than it could and some resources are being wasted.

The idea of *capacity utilisation* can be applied to the whole economy or it can be used in relation to an individual firm. Any firm which has enough capital equipment to produce more than it is doing is said to have excess capacity. Reasons for this could include falling demand for the product, lack of appropriately skilled labour or investment in anticipation of growing demand later.

excess demand occurs when the quantity demanded outstrips the quantity supplied, as in the diagram below. This shows disequilibrium in the market, which fails to clear. Excess demand can be seen when there are large numbers of people wishing to buy an item which has just become fashionable and shops have difficulty in obtaining adequate stocks. This situation will not usually last long as either prices will rise or supplies will increase.

One market in which excess demand can persist for quite a while is the housing market. If incomes are rising, demand for housing will rise in many areas. However, in the short run the supply of housing is fixed (i.e. perfectly inelastic). It will take time to acquire land with planning permissions and add to the stock of housing by building more. In this situation, houses will sell very quickly, reflecting their scarcity on the market. Prices will usually rise, perhaps very sharply.

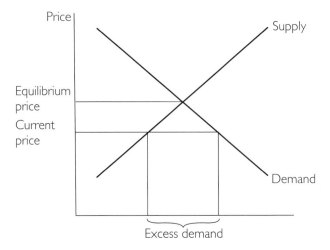

Excess demand

excess supply occurs when the quantity supplied is greater than the quantity demanded. On the micro-economic level, it means that the price is higher than its equilibrium level and gives producers an incentive to supply more of the product. At the same time the high price discourages buyers and the result is seen in stocks of unsold goods.

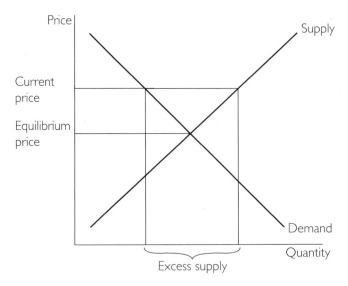

Excess supply

Excess supply will usually come to an end if sellers cut prices. However, in some markets this may take quite a while. You can see excess supply in the housing market if there are a great many 'for sale' signs, relatively few buyers looking around and people making offers well below the advertised price.

On the macro-economic level, excess supply would imply that firms were producing more than consumers wanted to buy, there would be stocks of unsold goods and in time firms would adjust production downwards. This could happen at the onset of a *recession* when there would be falling aggregate demand.

exchange is the process by which people trade with each other, offering goods and services they have produced for goods and services they need or want. Exchange is crucial to economic life, making it possible for people to specialise in the type of production in which they have an advantage. This *specialisation* allows people to produce much more than they can if they have to be self-sufficient. In a primitive system, exchange takes place through *barter* but the use of money makes the process of exchange much more efficient. Instead of having to find someone who has the products required, one's own products can be exchanged for money which is used to buy other products.

exchange controls prevent people from selling their own currency in exchange for another. The objective is to protect the *exchange rate* from market forces. They were used temporarily by the Malaysian government during the Asian financial crisis in 1998 to prevent a dramatic fall in the exchange rate such as had happened in neighbouring countries. In this they were quite successful. Normally, governments in countries where international trade is an important engine of growth will remove exchange controls in order to make trade easier. The UK abandoned their use in 1979.

Exchange Equalisation Account: the account in which the Bank of England keeps the *foreign exchange reserves*. These may be used to influence the value of the currency as and when the need arises.

exchange rate: the rate at which one currency can be exchanged for another. Effectively, it is a price for the currency, expressed in terms of other currencies. If it is said that the pound fell against the US dollar, it means that the pound is now worth fewer dollars.

The exchange rate influences the prices of imports and exports and the ease with which producers in different countries can compete with each other. A rise in the exchange rate (*appreciation*) means that export prices will be higher and import prices will be lower. All producers who compete with overseas producers will lose competitiveness. (See also *exchange rate depreciation*.)

exchange rate bands: where the exchange rate is managed, i.e. floating but with some central bank intervention, a band may be set indicating the upper and lower limits within which the exchange rate will float. The best example of this relates to the European *Exchange Rate Mechanism* (ERM). If the currency threatens to float down below the limit of its band, the central bank will buy the currency using its *foreign exchange reserves*. This will support the exchange rate and, provided the operation can be kept up for long enough, maintain some stability.

exchange rate depreciation: occurs if market forces cause the exchange rate to fall, so that exports become cheaper and imports dearer in terms of the domestic currency. This may happen because the demand for exports has fallen over a period of time or because *capital inflows* have diminished. Either way, demand for the currency will fall and with it the equilibrium exchange rate, as shown in the first diagram.

The same outcome will occur if there has been an increase in demand for imports or a *capital outflow*. There will be an increase in the supply of the currency (see the second diagram) by people who want to buy foreign currency on the foreign exchange markets, leading to a fall in the exchange rate.

Appreciation leads to the reverse situation in which the exchange rate rises, imports become cheaper and exports become dearer.

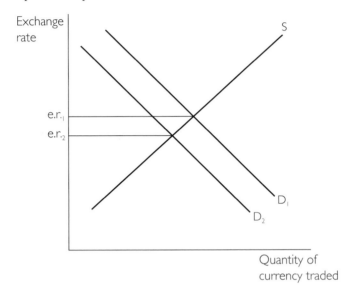

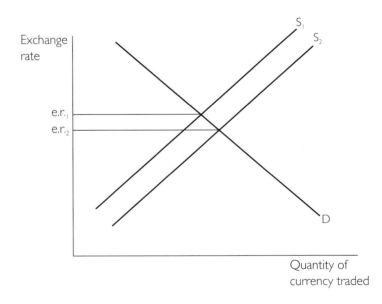

Exchange rate depreciation can have a very favourable effect on the level of economic activity. It makes potential exporters more competitive. Equally it helps firms which compete with imports on the domestic market. Both are likely to find their products bringing in more profit. The potential benefits of depreciation are an important advantage of a *floating exchange rate.*

exchange rate determination: normally, exchange rates will be determined by market forces. With a *floating exchange rate*, there is no central bank intervention in the foreign exchange markets and the rate will be entirely market determined. With a *fixed exchange rate*, there will be a very narrow exchange rate band and central bank intervention will keep the exchange rate very close to its *parity.* This system was abandoned by the UK in 1972, since then there has been a *managed exchange rate*, determined largely by market forces except in exceptional circumstances.

exchange rate fluctuations: when an exchange rate is floating freely, its value in terms of other countries' currencies may fluctuate markedly. This can be destabilising. Firms find it hard to predict what revenue they will get from export sales. Importers do not know what they will have to pay. Planning is made more difficult and the prices of traded goods may rise to cover the extra risk. Day-to-day changes in exchange rates are usually ironed out by central bank intervention. (The process works in just the same way as intervention to maintain a *fixed exchange rate.*) However, fluctuations which reflect changing levels of international confidence in the currency may be hard to prevent and generally speaking central banks will usually not try to defend the exchange rate against market forces.

exchange rate index: a measure of change in the exchange rate which takes a weighted average of the changes across a number of currencies. Currencies are selected according to their importance in the trade pattern of the country concerned. For the UK, these will be first the euro, then the US dollar and the yen. These will be given the largest weights, with other currencies having smaller weightings. The resulting index number is sometimes called the *effective exchange rate.* It provides a useful measure of changes in competitiveness due to exchange rate variations.

UK effective exchange rate, 1994 = 100

1993	99.7
1994	100.0
1995	95.1
1996	96.7
1997	112.7
1998	116.5
1999	116.3
2000	109.0
2001 est.	105

Source: National Institute Economic Review

Exchange Rate Mechanism (ERM): a forerunner of the *Economic and Monetary Union* (EMU) which linked EU currencies within the *European Monetary System.* Member currencies were kept within fairly narrow *exchange rate bands* so that their exchange rates with each other could vary only to a small extent. If market forces pushed a currency down to its limit, the central bank used its reserves to buy the currency, thus defending its value. (See also *central bank intervention* and *fixed exchange rates*.) This increased stability for the member countries and so encouraged trade.

The ERM was set up in 1979 and included most of the EU countries. The UK entered in 1990 but left again in 1992 when it became apparent that the pound was set at a parity too high to be sustainable. The ERM was superseded by EMU in January 1999.

exchange rate policy: a government may allow its exchange rate to float freely or, in consultation with its trading partners, may seek to fix the rate or it may seek to manage the exchange rate so that fluctuations are reduced. Since 1972, most currencies have floated most of the time, with central banks intervening to eliminate day-to-day fluctuations. The drawback to a *floating exchange rate* is that it may be unstable. EMU will remove this instability within the *euro zone* but the euro will fluctuate against all other floating currencies.

exchange rate regime: the system chosen by the government for determining its exchange rate or the system generally in operation for most of the world at the time. (See also *exchange rate determination*.)

exchange rate target: governments may choose to maintain a target for the exchange rate, as a means of controlling inflation. Then, in the event that prices rise, domestic producers become less competitive and demand for their products will fall on both export and domestic markets. This will discourage them from raising prices and reduce aggregate demand generally, reducing inflationary pressures. The UK government adopted this policy in the late 1980s.

excise duty is an *expenditure tax* levied by HM Customs and Excise. Unlike VAT which generally applies to most products, excise taxes apply to specific products and the rate varies depending on the product. The main products concerned are alcohol, tobacco and petrol. An important objective in all three cases is to reduce consumption, but these taxes are also significant revenue raisers.

excludability relates to *private goods* (as opposed to *public goods*). An important distinguishing factor of private goods is that people who do not pay for them can be excluded from using them. It is easy to see that you will not be able to consume something which has not been paid for. In contrast, no one can be excluded from consuming *public goods* such as street lighting in a public place or using the services of the police. If people cannot be excluded from benefiting from a particular good or service, then it cannot be sold. It is a public good and must be paid for by government. (See also *rivalry*.)

exhaustible resources are being consumed at a rate faster than that at which they can be replaced. For example, some forest products are being consumed at a rate beyond that at which new trees can be planted and grow to maturity.

exit: the way in which businesses may leave the market, or close down altogether, if the product in question has begun to make losses or just become less profitable than alternative uses of the resources. Easy exit is very important in ensuring efficiency, because without it the allocation of resources cannot adjust to changes in the pattern of consumer demand. Exit can be difficult in state-owned enterprises and may be affected by employment protection legislation. The absence of easy exit was one of the reasons why centrally planned economies failed to adapt to changing patterns of demand and led to rather slow growth in standards of living.

expansion: the process by which the economy grows through increasing *aggregate demand.*

expansionary gap: the difference between the level of *aggregate demand* and the *full-capacity output* of the economy. This is also known as an *inflationary gap* because excess demand is likely to be causing inflationary pressures. This is a macro-economic disequilibrium situation in which the level of aggregate demand is too high and cannot be satisfied even if all the resources in the economy are working flat out.

expansionary policies may be used by governments which wish to reduce *unemployment* and achieve higher rates of *economic growth. Fiscal policies*, e.g. tax cuts and increases in expenditure, and a *monetary policy* of reduced interest rates will all tend to increase aggregate demand and encourage firms to take on more labour and expand output. Care must be taken not to overdo expansionary policies, lest growth leads to pressure on resources and accelerating inflation. Expansionary policies will not help in the long run to reduce *structural unemployment.*

expectations: a term which refers to what people expect to happen. Expectations are based on past experience. They have an important influence on what actually happens because expectations of change will in turn change people's behaviour.

Expectations can be very important in a macro-economic context. Investment plans are often based on expectations about future demand. Optimistic expectations may provide the business world with a self-fulfilling prophecy as the increase in investment does actually stimulate the economy. Inflationary expectations will tend to make people want to negotiate pay increases to cover whatever they expect inflation to be. So control of inflation requires that inflation expectations be reduced.

expectations-augmented Phillips curve provides a way of looking at the relationship between inflation and unemployment which helps to explain why both variables may either rise or fall together.

Normally, it is possible to see a trade-off between inflation and unemployment. When unemployment is high there is a relatively low level of aggregate demand in the economy and there will be few inflationary pressures. The reverse holds too: low unemployment indicates that labour resources are scarce, prices will be bid up by competing employers and inflation will follow. This is the relationship found in the *Phillips curve.*

Strong expectations of inflation cause people to expect large pay increases in compensation. This means that at any given level of unemployment, inflation accelerates. This pushes the Phillips curve upwards and to the right as shown in the diagram. The trade-off remains but at a new, higher rate of inflation.

(See also *non-accelerating inflation rate of unemployment* and Figure on page 114.)

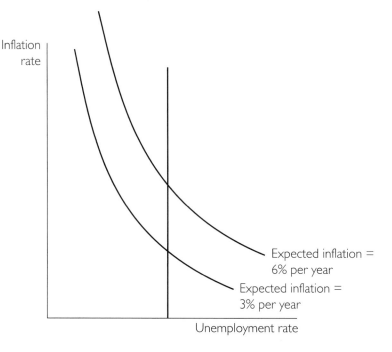

Inflation rate

Expected inflation = 6% per year

Expected inflation = 3% per year

Unemployment rate

The expectations-augmented Phillips curve (see page 113)

expenditure simply means spending. Consumer expenditure and government expenditure are commonly used terms.

expenditure method refers to one of the ways in which *national income* may be counted. The three methods are the expenditure method, the income method and the output method. In certain respects the expenditure method is the most reliable because sales revenue is hard to hide.

expenditure-reducing policies entail reducing the level of *aggregate demand* using *fiscal* and *monetary policies*. The term is used in relation that policies to deal with a trade deficit.

expenditure-switching policies reduce expenditure on foreign produced goods and services and increase it on domestic products. They include *import controls* and exchange rate *depreciation.*

expenditure taxes tax spending rather than income. They include VAT and the *excise taxes*, but the term may also refer to a system by which people are assessed according to their expenditure rather than their income. This might give people an incentive to save more.

Expenditure taxes are important as sources of government revenue but are sometimes considered *regressive* in their effect, i.e. they have more impact on poorer people than on richer people.

exploitation means paying people less than the value of what they produce. Employers who pay less than the amount of extra revenue generated by an employee are exploiting that person. To the extent that the employer has some monopoly power in either the labour market or the product market, prices may be kept up and costs kept down so that some of the extra revenue becomes profit.

export credit: because of time lags in reaching the market, many exports are sold on *credit*. This is particularly important for capital equipment because it will be a long time before it generates income.

Export Credit Guarantee Department (ECGD) provides a guarantee that if foreign buyers of UK goods do not pay for them, this government department will. The objective is to encourage exports, which are made much less risky by the guarantee. A fee is charged for this service.

export incentives include all kinds of inducements which are designed to encourage exporters:

- subsidies (as with surplus agricultural products in the EU)
- tax incentives which require less tax to be paid on exports than on domestic sales
- low-cost loans.

Differences in the incentive structures of competing economies can lead to some unfair competition in international markets.

export-led growth occurs when there is rapid growth of exports which then has a *multiplier* effect on the rest of the economy. In the past Japan and South Korea have both experienced this type of rapid growth leading to improvements in the standard of living there. An *undervalued exchange rate* may be helpful in achieving this.

export marketing means making an effort to sell in overseas markets. Some of this activity may be similar to marketing in the domestic setting. However, there are some important decisions to be made when considering new markets.

- Will a standardised product be appropriate for this market or would it be better to tailor the product precisely to the requirements of the market concerned?
- How will the product be distributed effectively?

Both questions have an important impact on costs and therefore on potential competitiveness.

export promotion means any kind of activity which can lead to an increase in exports. Governments often promote exports by trying to increase the flow of information about available products to people in countries which offer a promising market. Embassies have a role in this.

export subsidy: a payment by the government to an exporter made so that the price of the exported product can be reduced. These subsidies are illegal under the terms of the World Trade Organisation, but many governments find ways around this. They may refund import duties paid on imported inputs or provide cheap loans. Subsidies can end in exports which are really *dumping*. The EU still subsidises exports of surplus agricultural products, though less than it used to due to fierce opposition from major agricultural exporters such as the US and Australia.

exports: goods and services sold for foreign currency. Goods from the *primary* or the *secondary sector* are *visible exports* while services such as tourism or insurance are *invisible exports.* (See also *pattern of trade.*)

ex post refers to the view of a situation after the event. It is possible to look back and with luck the data will give an accurate message as to what happened. This is in contrast to the *ex ante* view, essentially a forecast of the expected event.

external balance: a situation in which exports and imports are roughly the same in value. If they are not, then we might say that the external balance is in either surplus or deficit, depending on whether exports are higher or lower than imports.

external benefits: see *externalities.*

external costs occur when some of the costs of production are paid by third parties, rather than the producer. For example, a new factory will usually create extra traffic on the nearby roads. If this increases congestion, other road users will pay the costs because their journeys will be delayed. Pollution also creates a wide range of external costs. The polluting firm will not normally stop polluting without some kind of action because to do so would require extra spending, raising costs and reducing profit. Government action can limit pollution by direct controls. Some firms now set their own targets for polluting emissions from their processes because they wish to be seen to be acting responsibly. A *cost–benefit analysis* of an investment project can be used to compare external costs and benefits as well as the internal ones.

There are some serious external costs associated with night flights into Heathrow airport. The government may decide to change the regulations and ban night flights. However, BA want night flights and say that they will lose money if they cannot have them.

external economies of scale: cost savings which occur as the industry grows. These will reduce costs for the whole industry and not just the individual firms. This can happen through:

- government-funded research efforts or research funded collaboratively by firms in the industry, which create new cost-reducing technologies available to all the firms in the industry
- the development of a pool of specialised skilled labour in the area, to which all firms have access – as with Sheffield in the 19th century when the cutlery industry developed, giving the area a general advantage in the production of special steels and in metalwork skills. This may be the result of some collaboration between firms in the industry or it may result from government training provision
- the growth of a network of suppliers with specialist skills and experience, from whom all firms can buy their inputs.

The economic development of Cambridge provides a recent example. Developments in electronics and biotechnology came from research conducted in the university. Firms set up in the area in order to have easy access to knowledge of relevance to the new technologies. The area developed a whole network of suppliers and specialists with very scarce skills, which in turn attracted more firms and further development. This is sometimes known as the Cambridge Phenomenon.

The diagram shows how external economies of scale shift the average total cost curve downwards for all firms in the industry.

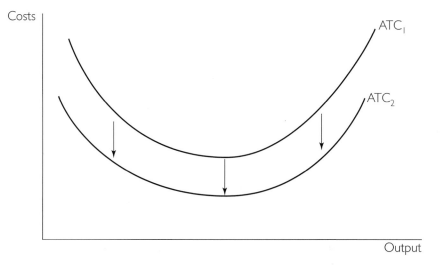

External economies of scale cut the firm's average costs as the industry grows

external financing means that the funds for investment are being obtained outside the business. In contrast, *internal finance* is generated from past *retained profits* which the firm has been able to save. External finance could come from:

- bank loans, which might be overdrafts, for day-to-day finance or fixed term loans for longer term purposes
- share capital, which could come from a new issue or a rights issue
- grants which for some purposes in some areas may be obtainable from the government or the EU. These are unlikely to provide more than a small part of the funds required and that only in areas which the government is trying to regenerate.

external growth occurs when a firm is taking over other firms or merging with them. It contrasts with internal growth, when firms develop new markets for themselves and increase output using their own resources. It provides an easy way for firms to increase their productive capacity quickly but may lead to management problems as they try to integrate different systems.

external shocks: see *shocks*.

externalities are the costs and benefits which result from a firm's operations but which are paid for by (or give benefit to) third parties. They are economic side effects. They include external costs such as pollution and congestion and external benefits such as the improvement in the general appearance of a shopping area when new shops open up in previously derelict premises.

Externalities indicate the presence of *market failure*. Output will either be greater than or less than the level consistent with an optimal resource allocation, one which meets consumer needs most effectively.

- If all the external costs of a product were included in the decision to produce, total costs would be higher and so would the price. This would help to reduce the quantity demanded. The true costs of production would be included in the price. As it is, prices are less than the true cost and there is a higher level of consumption than is really efficient. It is quite likely that consumers would have used electricity more economically if the price had reflected the cost of cleaning up emissions sufficiently to eliminate *acid rain*.

- Similarly, external benefits can cause underconsumption. If all the benefits are counted in to the decision to produce, output might be higher. It might pay the local authority to consider subsidising new shops in areas which require regeneration, in order to get more external benefits.

One way to improve the *allocation of resources* is to ensure that the polluter pays all the costs of production. Polluters may be required to clean up their emissions; this internalises the cost of dealing with waste products. Or they may be required to pay for a pollution permit, which will give them an incentive to clean up. (See also *tradeable permits.*)

factor cost describes a way of measuring national income. Output will be valued at the cost of the *factors of production* which contributed to production. So we might examine figures for *Gross Domestic Product* at factor cost. In contrast, GDP at market prices would include the same data as GDP at factor cost but would also include the effect of expenditure taxes such as VAT and also any subsidies. So factor cost provides data which reflects the actual resource cost of production.

factor endowment: the collection of real resources which are available within an economy. The nature of the factor endowment will depend on the *factors of production* available and will differ from one economy to another. For example, China has very abundant labour and much less abundant capital. Japan has relatively scarce labour but abundant capital and technical knowledge. Both countries are rather short of good flat land, useful for agriculture or manufacturing, compared to the US or Australia. Factor endowments are important in determining which products have a *comparative advantage* in each economy.

factor immobility occurs when factors of production cannot easily be moved to different uses if demand for the product declines. For example, when the demand for UK-built ships declined in the 1970s and 1980s, the shipyards (the capital) could not in general be used for other purposes. Similarly the people who had worked in the shipyards had skills which were not generally transferable to other industries, so the labour was immobile too.

Capital is only immobile in the short run: it need not be replaced at the end of its life. Similarly, labour will cease to be immobile if a move to suitable alternative employment is possible. (See also *occupational immobility* and *geographical immobility*.)

factor incomes are the returns to each *factor of production*. For labour, factor incomes are wages and salaries. For capital, factor incomes come from interest, profit and rent.

factor inputs are the *factors of production* needed as inputs in order to create output.

factor markets include the markets for labour and capital. Capital markets provide a source of finance for businesses and individuals. The price of capital is the interest rate. Labour markets are made up of the people who would like to be employed and the employers who want to hire people. The price of labour is the going wage or salary.

factor mobility: if factors of production are mobile they are able to move into alternative lines of production relatively easily. Much capital equipment is too specific for this, but sewing machines, computers and lorries are examples of exceptions. For labour, retraining facilities will increase mobility. Education generally increases mobility because it makes people more flexible.

factors of production include land, labour and capital. They can be combined together in a great variety of ways which lead to the creation of output and hence of incomes and wealth. Each factor of production receives a return:

- the returns to labour are wages and salaries
- the returns to capital are interest and profit
- the returns to land are rent.

Sometimes a fourth factor of production is introduced as enterprise. The logic for this is that the entrepreneur has a special role in organising the other factors of production and taking the risks associated with the decision to produce. It is these decisions which, in a *market system*, allow profit to be made and bring about improvements in the standard of living.

factor prices: the prices of factors of production. These will be determined by the usefulness of the factor in the production process, which will generate a demand for the factor, and the supply of the factor, which will depend on availability and cost. There are markets for factors of production just as there are for goods and services. The labour market can be analysed using supply and demand theory, as can capital markets – the markets where funds for investment are borrowed and lent.

Differences in factor prices have a big impact on the choice of production methods. If labour is relatively cheap, *labour-intensive* production methods will normally be appropriate. Where capital is relatively cheap and abundant, capital will be substituted for labour as wages rise.

factory gate prices are the prices charged by producers for output sold to wholesalers. They provide a helpful *leading indicator* of possible future consumer price changes.

fair trade means buying imported products from developing countries at prices which give a fair return to the producers. It is an attempt to avoid buying products which depend upon very cheap labour, implying that the producers get a very poor return for their efforts. The Fair Trade Foundation certifies firms which are engaged in fair trade so that consumers have some guarantee that producer incomes will benefit if they buy the product.

Fair Trading Act 1973 provided for the setting up of the *Office of Fair Trading* (OFT), which investigates complaints about anti-competitive practices.

Family Expenditure Survey: carried out by the Office for National Statistics, this provides the information needed to construct the *Retail Price Index*, which measures the rate of inflation.

FAO: see *Food and Agriculture Organisation.*

Federal Reserve System (the 'Fed') is the central bank of the United States. It includes the Federal Reserve Board and 12 regional reserve banks. The governor is appointed by the President with Senate approval and presides over the Federal Open Market Committee which decides all matters of *monetary policy*. The Fed is independent of the US government.

Alan Greenspan, current Governor of the Fed, has a formidable reputation for skilful management of monetary policy. The evidence lies in the strong economic growth that the US has enjoyed since 1990. Should this period of growth come to an end there may be some loss of confidence which will itself have a major impact. Watch this space. Have things changed since this was written?

fertility rate: the number of births per thousand women between the ages of 15 and 45. It provides a useful way of predicting population changes.

final goods: goods which are complete as a product and ready for immediate sale and use, e.g. cars. In contrast, *intermediate goods* will undergo further processing or be built into a final product, e.g. car batteries.

finance: a term covering sources of funds which may be borrowed to pay for investment or consumption.

financial assets include, cash, bank and building society balances, *bills, bonds, shares* and pension entitlements.

financial conglomerates: firms which offer a wide range of financial services. For example, a bank might provide banking services to firms and individuals, mortgages, business loans, investment advice, pension plans, insurance policies, a share-dealing service and even act as an estate agent. In the past, financial institutions were rather more specialised but a long period of take overs and mergers has led to the formation of a number of financial conglomerates.

financial deregulation: the removal of restrictions on *financial intermediaries*. In the past many governments placed restrictions on the way banks operated and many of these have now been removed. The objective was to increase efficiency and encourage competition. Regulations which have been removed included controls on the level of interest rates, restrictions on the activities of foreign banks and restrictions on the type of business which could be done.

financial economies: see *internal economies of scale*.

financial futures: agreements to buy *financial assets* such as bonds at some date in the future.

financial intermediaries include *merchant* and *retail banks, building societies, pension funds* and *insurance companies* and some other financial institutions. They exist mainly to channel funds from savers who want to lend to borrowers who want to spend. Borrowers can be consumers or firms which are investing.

financial markets fall into two categories:

- capital markets, which allow people to buy and sell bonds and shares. Governments and firms use them to raise the long-term finance they need. Holders of bonds and shares rely on them in order to be able to turn their financial assets into cash when the need arises.
- markets which provide opportunities to lend and borrow funds for a few months or at the other extreme, just overnight. They are used by firms, banks and the government which are constantly in need of short-term funds to finance their operations on a day-to-day basis.

financial sector reform may be needed when the financial sector is failing to deliver an efficient system which allocates scarce capital towards those borrowers who can make the best use of the funds. Most developed countries have a reasonably well-developed financial sector capable of providing finance for *entrepreneurs*. Many developing and transition economies have people with potentially good business ideas who cannot get the finance they need and this hinders the process of economic development. The development of an efficient banking sector can help in this respect.

Financial Services Act 1986: the legal basis for the system of self-regulation which is used in City institutions. The intention is to protect the customer by giving full information. There have been continuing doubts about whether it does this.

Financial Services Authority: the organisation which supervises the operations of the financial system. It was set up in 1997 to create a new, overarching system which supervises banks as well as other financial intermediaries, such as insurance companies. It works in close collaboration with the *Treasury* and the *Bank of England*. Supervision is important; properly carried out it can, for instance, prevent banks from making imprudent loans and financial advisers from misleading the public.

fine tuning: the notion that governments can adjust *fiscal* and *monetary policy* to create just the right amount of aggregate demand, keeping unemployment and inflation low and encouraging growth. The idea was fashionable in the 1960s and 1970s. The results of attempts to fine-tune the economy were disappointing because it proved very difficult to decide the exact amount of change needed. Governments tended to overshoot or act too late, partly because of weaknesses in current data and uncertainty about future events.

finite resources are resources which are fixed in supply and cannot be renewed. They are also referred to as *depletable resources*. Oil is one example, along with many other mineral products. Others include tropical timber and fish stocks which are not being exploited in a sustainable way.

firm: a collection of factors of production brought together by an entrepreneur for the purpose of producing goods or services. The term is often used when theory is being employed to analyse a particular situation, in contrast to the term business, which is used in a more practical context.

firm-specific skills are those skills which are acquired on the job and relate to that particular employer. A business will try hard not to make redundant a person with firm-specific skills because a replacement will have to be trained all over again. Their wages may be viewed as a fixed cost for this reason.

first world: the developed countries of Western Europe, the US, Canada, Japan Australia and New Zealand. The other groups in this terminology were the second world, which was the communist bloc, and the third world, the developing countries. These terms are used much less than they used to be because increasing incomes in some parts of the third world have rendered this simple classification inappropriate. Similarly, the second world has shrunk dramatically. New categories, the transition economies and emerging economies, have been created.

fiscal drag occurs if there is *inflation* and *tax allowances* are left unchanged. The value of the allowance falls as inflation reduces its purchasing power. So the tax paid rises without any change in tax rates. Similarly, if benefits are not raised in line with inflation, their real value will fall. Fiscal drag will also occur if there is economic growth. Tax revenue will rise as the increases in income are taxed at the marginal rate.

fiscal policy includes all measures relating to taxation and other revenue-raising activities and government expenditure. It is set out each year in the Budget by the

Chancellor of the Exchequer, when all new measures are announced. There is also an annual review of fiscal policy which is set out in the Pre-Budget Report which comes out each November.

Fiscal policy has certain important objectives:

- Raising revenue to pay for the provision of *public* and *merit goods* and the day-to-day operation of government. Governments have long shopping lists and even with careful consideration of priorities, all recent governments have found it difficult to reduce expenditure. There is a significant consensus amongst voters that the NHS must be preserved and improved and the *ageing population* places heavy demands on health funding. Public spending in 2001 was roughly 37% of GDP.
- Influencing the *allocation of resources* by encouraging some activities and discouraging others. For example, all governments want to discourage smoking and encourage small businesses to get started. Smoking has important *external costs* in the shape of related illnesses which require health spending. So tobacco is taxed. Small businesses are an important source of new jobs so there are various measures designed to help self-employed people in the early years. *Fuel taxes* raise revenue but they are also thought to reduce demand for fuel and so reduce emissions of greenhouse gases. Every year there are changes to the tax system designed to reduce some incentives and increase others.
- Influencing the distribution of income. The tax and *benefit* system can be used to reduce *disposable income* for richer people and increase it for poorer people. The extent to which redistribution takes place is very much a political matter and there is now rather less of it than there was 20 years ago. However, the 40% higher marginal rate of income tax combined with the various benefits paid still have a very significant effect.
- Stabilising the economy so that the fluctuations associated with the trade cycle do not become a problem. During a recession, it makes sense to increase aggregate demand by cutting taxes and raising government expenditure. This will tend to reduce the rate at which people are made redundant and encourage firms to invest. However, it will mean that there will be a *budget deficit* – perhaps quite a large one. Similarly, when the economy begins to grow unsustainably fast and there is a risk of inflation accelerating, governments can raise tax rates or introduce new taxes and cut back expenditure. There may then be a budget surplus which can be used to reduce the total debt outstanding.

Fiscal policy to stabilise the economy needs to be co-ordinated with *monetary policy*. The present UK government adheres to its 'golden rule', by which the budget will balance over the course of the trade cycle. Monetary policy is determined by the *Monetary Policy Committee* of the Bank of England which acts independently of the Treasury, though in close consultation with it. Fiscal policy can be adapted to fit in with the monetary policy stance at the time, though there are often time lags involved.

Fisher Equation: see *equation of exchange.*

fixed capital formation: see *gross domestic fixed capital formation.*

fixed costs are all those costs which stay the same regardless of the quantity produced. They include the cost of capital equipment and buildings, interest charges,
management and administrative costs. Part of the wage and salary bill may be a fixed
cost when the people concerned are not directly involved in the production process.
Fixed costs are only fixed in the short run: in the long run, alterations can be made
to the quantity of capital equipment and the way the firm is run. (See also *average
fixed costs.*)

fixed exchange rates are rates which have been set at a particular level in terms
of other currencies. This means that they are not determined by the forces of supply
and demand. If market forces are pushing the currency outside the band within
which it is allowed to fluctuate, the central bank will intervene, buying or selling the
currency to keep it very close to its fixed *parity.* If the currency is threatening to
depreciate, the central bank will support it by using sufficient foreign exchange
reserves to buy the currency and maintain the exchange rate. In other words it would
make up for the shortfall in demand. (See diagram.)

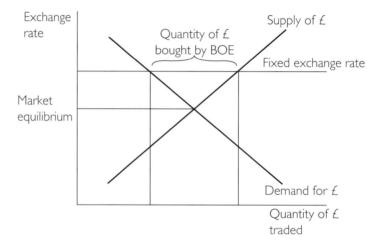

Fixed exchange rate

There are two major disadvantages with fixed exchange rates:

- If the exchange rate reflects market forces over the long term, there may
  be no difficulty in keeping it fixed. But if the exchange rate is overvalued,
  large foreign exchange reserves will be needed in order to defend the rate.
  The existence of large amounts of money which can be moved into different currencies very easily can lead to very large capital movements and a
  rather unstable exchange rate, if holders of the currency do not have confidence in the ability of the government to maintain the fixed rate.
  Speculators, hoping that the rate will fall, may then be able to make large
  sums by selling currency at the fixed rate and later, after a devaluation or
  depreciation, buying it back at the new lower rate.

- An overvalued exchange rate can cause firms to have great difficulty in competing in export markets, and with imports in the domestic market.

After World War II the Bretton Woods System provided for all currencies to be fixed in terms of the US dollar. From time to time, a currency would be devalued if it had become overvalued in terms of long-term trade and capital flows. The UK devalued in 1948 and 1967. The system broke down in 1972 because it was incompatible with the inflation which was developing at that time. Since then most currencies have floated most of the time although arguments in favour of fixed rates are still heard.

Stability is the main advantage of fixed rates: firms can plan ahead with some degree of certainty about the prices of imports and exports. This was the logic of the Bretton Woods system, as well as for the *Exchange Rate Mechanism* which fixed EU member currencies loosely against one another. Ultimately, of course, these currencies were fixed irrevocably by the introduction of *Economic and Monetary Union* (EMU).

fixed factors of production are the resource inputs to a production process, the quantity of which cannot be altered in the short run. In other words, the quantity of the factor employed does not change with the level of output. For example, capital equipment is a fixed factor because it takes time to arrange to have more or less of it. Labour will be a fixed factor if there are difficulties about increasing or decreasing the quantity of it as output changes, as in the case of managers.

fixed investment is spending on capital equipment, buildings and so on, which can be expected to yield an income over a long period. In contrast, investment in stocks and work in progress will be used in the production process, or sold, very quickly.

fixed rate loan: a loan, the terms of which are agree in advance with a specified interest rate. This can be useful to a firm which needs to be certain about what its interest rate commitments will be and works well if interest rates are tending to rise. On the other hand, it will be inflexible if interest rates fall or the circumstances of the firm change.

flexibility can be important in two ways:

- A firm which is flexible can review its decisions and make changes in its products or pricing strategies in the light of changes in the marketplace. Firms which manufacture clothing benefit from being flexible because demand can change at any time and they can keep up with the changes.
- *Flexible labour markets* can adjust to changing technologies and changing markets easily because there are people who have transferable skills and are willing to do a range of different types of work or acquire new skills.

flexible exchange rate: see *floating exchange rate*. The way in which lost competitiveness can be regained through depreciation of a floating exchange rate has been mentioned by many people who oppose UK entry to EMU. Competitiveness is most commonly lost through an inflation rate which is higher than those of other countries. If the UK joins EMU and then experiences accelerating inflation, it will lose competitiveness within the euro zone.

flexible labour markets occur where employers are able to take on new employees on a full-time or a part-time basis, temporarily or permanently, at wage rates which are not set by union agreements or government controls, and are able to make employees redundant without great expense. Labour market flexibility can be further enhanced if employees are willing to do a range of different tasks and acquire new skills, i.e. *multi-skilling*. It is generally thought that there is less unemployment in a flexible labour market. The US labour market is believed to be more flexible than the UK labour market. Within the EU, the UK and the Netherlands are thought to have more flexible labour markets than most other member countries.

flexible prices: prices which adjust so that the market clears quickly. For example, in *commodity markets*, an increase in the quantity supplied of, say, iron ore will produce a swift fall in price which will eliminate any unsold stocks. Similarly, tomatoes in a street market on Saturday afternoon will have their price reduced if they are soft. Manufactures usually have rather less flexible prices and house prices change even less readily, particularly when prices are falling. Inflexible prices usually lead to a *disequilibrium* situation.

flexible specialisation: the idea that manufacturers should be able to produce small quantities of goods aimed at particular markets, in such a way that the level of production can be varied at short notice to match changes in demand. This contrasts with the idea of mass production, where vast quantities of standardised products are produced in ways which maximise *economies of scale*. Computer-controlled processes and flexible labour forces are making flexible specialisation much easier than it would have been in the past.

flexible wages can change quickly to reflect labour market conditions and in particular, wage rates for a particular type of labour will fall if demand for those people's services decreases. In practice, wages are usually not like this because there is an agreed rate for the job and a fall in wages may cause serious disaffection in the workforce. Some economists have argued that flexible wages will reduce unemployment because there will be a wage rate for everyone at which some employer will take them on. This could be debated.

floating exchange rate: one which is determined by market forces. Changes in demand and supply are brought about by changes in imports and exports or by capital movements or by speculation. A floating exchange rate will undergo an *exchange rate depreciation* if demand for the currency falls or if supply rises and an *appreciation* if demand for the currency rises or supply falls. (See also *exchange rate*.) A floating exchange rate may be managed by the central bank so as to reduce day-to-day fluctuations.

The diagram shows how an increase in demand for exports might lead to an exchange rate appreciation. The demand for exports generates a demand for the currency needed to pay for them. The demand curve shifts to the right and the exchange rate rises.

Floating exchange rates do have advantages.

- A balance of trade deficit, occurring when imports exceed exports by a significant margin, will lead to automatic adjustment. The high level of imports will create a large and growing supply of pounds (in the UK). This will lead to exchange rate depreciation. This will in turn make exports more competitive and imports dearer, increasing exports and reducing imports (after a time lag). The deficit will diminish. So a floating exchange rate will, in time, bring about an automatic adjustment in the balance of trade.

- There is no need for potentially expensive central bank intervention to maintain the exchange rate at a fixed parity. Defending an unrealistic exchange rate can require the use of foreign exchange reserves and can be very costly.

The difficulty with a floating exchange rate is that it can be quite unstable. Firms may be unable to predict future profitability because they do not know what prices they can charge or how competitive they will be, if the exchange rate appreciates or depreciates. Furthermore, the exchange rate which results from market forces may be influenced more by *capital movements* than by trade. Economic and Monetary Union can eliminate this uncertainty within the euro zone but not outside it.

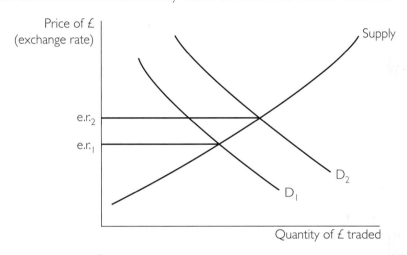

An increase in demand for pounds leads to appreciation

flotation: when a firm changes from being a *private limited company* to a *public limited company*, it is said to be floated on the Stock Exchange. Its shares are offered to the public.

flow: some variables are described as flows, others as *stocks*. Income is a flow: it comes in steadily, year by year. Wealth is a stock: it includes all sorts of assets (houses, bank deposits, shares and so on) which you hold, sometimes over a long period. Similarly, investment is a flow, while the stock of capital, the accumulated investments of past years, is a stock.

fob means free on board, a way of valuing exports at the point at which they are loaded for transport abroad. It is of no significance for the student but appears in balance of payments data.

focus is the opposite of *diversification*. It means concentrating on core products, usually the ones in which the firm has the greatest competitive advantage. The firm will stick to its main line of business which is the one which it understands the best. Subsidiaries producing other products may be sold.

Food and Agriculture Organisation (FAO): a constituent body of the United Nations. It undertakes research into agricultural methods and disseminates knowledge which can help to increase output of food products and improve nutrition.

footloose industries are able to locate in a wide range of places because their costs do not vary much between one place and another. Traditional industries are often tied to a location for historical reasons, such as past raw material or energy availability. Recently developed industries such as electronics are likely to be footloose.

Footsie (FT–SE 100): a measure of changes in the average level of share prices. It stands for Financial Times–Stock Exchange 100, because it is based on the share prices of the leading 100 firms. Price changes are weighted and an index is constructed on a continuous basis. A rise in the index suggests some optimism about future profitability generally, so the index is useful as a *leading indicator*.

forecasting: predicting future changes. Firms forecast likely future demand and other variables. Macro-economic forecasting uses sophisticated models to predict changes in the economy as a whole. Output, investment, inflation, employment and unemployment might all be the subject of forecasts. The models consist of a large number of equations which are used to represent the relationships between different variables in the economy.

foreign aid may be offered to developing countries with a low per capita income in order to help them invest. It may also be available to countries with serious famine problems. It may be bilateral aid, given by one government to another. Or it may be multilateral, given through an international organisation, often the World Bank or the European Development Fund. There have been strenuous efforts over the years to persuade the developed countries to give more foreign aid, almost always unsuccessful. A target of the 1960s and 1970s, that 1% of GDP should be given by each developed country, never came near to being reached and since then aid has tended to diminish rather than to grow.

Not all aid has been well used; some has been spent on prestige projects and military objectives which have not benefited poor people. There has been some evidence of corruption in the disbursement of aid and its usefulness has been further compromised by the tying of aid payments to a commitment to buy goods from the donor country. In some cases aid has been tied to the purchase of military goods.

foreign debt: the debts owed to foreign country lenders. These are most significant in the case of a number of developing countries which are heavily indebted. The lenders may be governments, banks, firms or international organisations. (See also *debt problem.*)

foreign debt management refers to the problems of heavily indebted developing countries. Sometimes the *debt–service ratio* is so high that after interest and repayments have been covered, there is little foreign exchange left to cover other needs. In these circumstances *debt rescheduling* may be considered. (See also *debt problem.*)

foreign direct investment (FDI) refers to investment by companies with their head office in another country, which are setting up factories or distribution outlets. In other words, it implies that the investment is in actual productive capacity which will generate output, rather than in financial assets such as shares or bonds. Many governments have been keen to encourage FDI. Within the UK, Wales has been particularly successful in attracting foreign investors. FDI has been important in helping some developing countries that have experienced rapid growth, e.g. Thailand.

foreign exchange may mean foreign currency, the medium of exchange of another country.

foreign exchange markets consist of the buyers and sellers of foreign exchange and the dealers who offer to buy and sell. Deals may be made in either the spot or the forward market. The spot market deals in currencies available immediately, while in the forward market deals are made which fix a price today for currency which will be available in the future, say in three months' time. Currencies are exchanged for trade reasons but also when there are capital movements. Money will be moved from one currency to another in order to get the best interest rate or for investment in production capacity overseas or perhaps to speculate on exchange rate changes.

foreign exchange reserves are the stocks of foreign currency held by the central bank and available if the exchange rate needs to be maintained at its existing level at a time when market forces are tending to push it downwards, i.e. to bring about a depreciation. The level of the reserves becomes important if there is either a *fixed exchange rate* or a *managed float*.

foreign investment may take place in two ways:

- *foreign direct investment* means spending in another country which will create production facilities
- *portfolio investment* means buying shares in companies based abroad or bonds issued by other countries' governments or moving money to bank accounts abroad.

formal economy: that part of the economy which is recorded in official statistics. So it includes all legally organised business and all government activity but excludes the use of resources which are not paid for such as voluntary and domestic work and work done for cash which is not declared for tax purposes. Some of the latter will be legal but some will not.

forward integration means creating a business which takes care of further processing and/or distribution and marketing of the final product, as well as its manufacture. It means that producers of intermediate goods may expand their business by taking the production process a stage further. Makers of computer chips might actually start to manufacture computers. The more likely route would be to buy or merge with an established business which has some expertise in the next stage of the process.

forward markets are the markets in which it is possible to buy a certain quantity of goods or foreign currency at a price agreed today, for delivery at a specific future date. This can act as insurance against unforeseen problems that may damage the profitability of an export order, such as a sudden jump in oil prices due to war breaking out in the Middle East. Contracts made in the forward market are known as *futures*.

franchise: a system by which independent businesses acquire the right to sell a branded product. The franchisee makes a payment to the owner of the brand, the franchisor. The franchisee is then entitled to sell the product and use the franchisor's marketing devices. These might include logos or the design of the premises or advertising material. In addition to the initial fee, the franchisee will also pay a percentage of sales revenue to the franchisor.

The advantage of a franchise is that the independent business can benefit from having a well-known branded product. Some of the advertising will be carried out by the franchisor. It may be much easier and less risky to go into business this way than to create and market a new product. The drawback is that the franchisor may strictly control the activities of the franchisee. From the franchisor's point of view, this may be one way to expand across a very wide area, maybe internationally, without having to acquire or finance all the outlets. Many retail outlets are franchised, such as Body Shop, Pizza Hut and McDonalds.

franchise monopoly: a franchise may be so arranged that the franchisee has a part of the market to itself. If the number of franchises is strictly limited and they are kept away from one another's natural territory, e.g. by making sure that they are a certain distance apart, the individual franchise will face less competition.

fraud means the use of misrepresentation in order to make money. It can include selling goods which are not what they appear to be, continuing to trade knowing that the business cannot pay its debts and generally taking money under false pretences.

free enterprise: a system by which individuals are allowed to set up in business without interference from governments, whether local or national. Free enterprise is commonly regarded as a good thing and it often is where there is strong *competition*. It can lead to there being lively and innovative producers who strive to meet real consumer needs and wants. If on the other hand producers acquire market power through monopolies or cartels they may be able to charge unnecessarily high prices. Or they may sell poor-quality goods against which the consumer has little protection. Regulation may be needed to protect consumers.

free entry refers to the situation in which entry is very easy for firms which seek to break into a new market. Where the market has a large number of small businesses, e.g. hairdressers, antique shops, accountants and so on, entry is usually fairly free. Manufacturing industries in which large potential economies of scale create barriers to entry illustrate the reverse situation. Free entry is used as a theoretical concept which helps to define *perfect competition*. Easy entry will always make for a more competitive market.

Free entry is important in that it is necessary in order to ensure that resources can be reallocated to adapt to changes in the pattern of consumer demand. Easy *exit* is also important in this respect, because it frees the resources needed by growing industries.

free goods are goods which have no price and no property rights associated with them and require no factors of production for their enjoyment. It is rather hard to find satisfactory examples because, increasingly, it has become apparent that the traditional examples such as fresh air and sunshine are not free at all. Hence the saying, there is no such thing as a *free lunch*.

free lunch: it is usually said that 'there is no such thing as a free lunch'. However, occasionally a policy will be found to benefit gainers while actually having no losers. This may be the result of deliberate efforts to compensate any losers. This situation is exceptional though: most decisions have an *opportunity cost*. The 'passports for pets' scheme *might* be a free lunch if none of them actually bring diseases home with them.

free market: a market in which there is no government interference. The concept of a free market underlies the *laissez faire* principle, *capitalism* and the *market system*. In practice, a market with literally no government intervention would be totally chaotic, as there would be no legal system to ensure fair play. The term is used to describe markets where the government does not actually control decision making.

free market economy: one in which the government plays a limited role. All governments place some legal restrictions on firms, but if the government aims to avoid interfering in business decisions, the market may be reasonably free.

free market policies are designed to reduce government intervention in the economy and ensure that decisions are made on the basis of market forces. Privatisation was a move in this direction and has led to closer attention being given to consumer preferences. However, many of the privatised industries – telephones, water, electricity and so on – are subject to regulation to ensure that they do not take advantage of their market power by overcharging.

free movement of people: an important element in the underlying framework of the *European Union*. (The other two pillars of the system are free movement of goods and services and free movement of capital.) All EU citizens have the right to live and work anywhere in the EU and moves have been made to recognise qualifications across all member countries.

free rider problem: where there is a *public good*, no one can be excluded from benefiting from it and so no one has an incentive to pay for its installation or upkeep. Streetlighting is a standard example; because of the free rider problem no individual will pay for it. All will wait for someone else to provide it, knowing that they will have the use of it without paying. This is why public goods must be provided by governments which have the legal right to tax people to pay for them.

free trade means trade which is not restricted by import controls such as *tariffs*, *quotas* or other methods. The theory of *comparative advantage* states that output can be increased when each country specialises in producing the goods and services with the lowest opportunity cost. The growth of free trade has in fact been associated with unprecedented economic growth and greatly improved standards of living.

The World Trade Organisation exists to encourage free trade. Trade negotiations under its auspices have done much to reduce trade barriers, most recently in the Uruguay Round of negotiations. Many trade barriers still exist, however, and some of these are detrimental to the welfare of some of the world's poorest countries.

free trade area: a group of countries which allow free trade amongst themselves but retain a separate set of trade barriers against other countries. The most important free trade area is NAFTA, the *North American Free Trade Area*, which comprises Canada, the US and Mexico.

freight transport: facilities to move goods from one location to another.

frictional unemployment is the unemployment caused by the time taken to find a new job after one has come to an end. In many ways it is not serious in that time spent seeking an appropriate job, rather than taking the first which is offered, should improve the fit between the individual's personal qualities and the requirements of the job. Improved information can reduce frictional unemployment so the various contributions of Job Centres may be helpful. (See also *unemployment*.)

Friedman, Milton (b. 1912) is an American economist with an unusual devotion to the free market. He is closely associated with the view that governments should not involve themselves in business decisions.

His most important work concerned the relationship between the growth of the money stock and the rate of inflation. For this he was awarded the Nobel Prize for economics in 1976, after a lifetime of research and teaching at the University of Chicago. He was very influential in the *Chicago School* of economists. His view of monetary policy as the essential antidote to inflation was adopted by the Conservative government of 1979, though not very rigidly enforced. His followers, who advocated strict monetary policy, became known as *monetarists*. Their views were opposed by the *Keynesians*, who perceived a much stronger role for governments in preventing unemployment. Friedman's concept of the *non-accelerating inflation rate of unemployment* (NAIRU) and the *expectations-augmented Phillips curve* provided a helpful explanation for the tendency of economies in the 1970s to experience growing unemployment and accelerating inflation at the same time (*stagflation*).

fringe benefits: extra benefits over and above normal wages and salaries which increase the real income of employees. Company cars are the most common but there are many others.

fuel tax: excise taxes which raise the market price of petrol, diesel and heating oil. Initially the purpose of the taxes was to raise revenue. In the case of petrol and diesel, this was partly intended to cover the cost of building and maintaining roads. In recent years fuel taxes have been raised to discourage consumption of fuels which generate greenhouse gases. The Department of Transport has estimated that a 10% increase in the real price of fuel will reduce quantity demanded by 3%.

fuel tax escalator: the system by which fuel taxes were raised by more than the rate of inflation at each budget, so that the proportion of the price which was tax rose steadily. This was abandoned in the 2000 Budget due to its unpopularity with road users. This may have some impact on greenhouse gas emissions.

full-capacity output is the highest level of output which can be achieved in the economy as a whole, given the type of resources available and their existing location. *Aggregate demand* for goods and services in excess of this level of output will lead to accelerating inflation. However, there may at this level of output still be some *structural unemployment*. This will occur if the unemployed people do not have the skills which are required by employers or if they are located in areas other than the ones in which employers are recruiting. In other words, if they are *occupationally immobile* or *geographically immobile*, they may be unable to contribute to production.

full employment is the level of employment at which all those who wish to work have found jobs, with the exception of those who are *frictionally unemployed*. What level of unemployment in the UK now represents full employment is a matter of some debate. Structural change, which includes an increasing rate of technological advance, has created a high level of unemployment which is slow to go away even when the economy is booming. During 1999 and 2000, unemployment fell further than it had for 20 years, so the problem of structural unemployment may be diminishing.

full employment national income: the level of national income which would be possible if all resources were fully employed. It is a measure of what the economy is capable of producing.

function: a relationship between two variables, one of which depends on the other. The dependent variable is said to be a function of the independent variable. For example, consumption is said to be a function of income.

functional distribution of income: the shares of national income which go to labour, capital and land.

fundamentals: the underlying forces which determine how the economy performs. Many of the changes which take place are transitory and will be reversed later. Fundamentals determine the real long-term trends. The fundamental consideration in deciding how the level of exports is determined is the level of competitiveness, which is in turn determined by the exchange rate, incomes in other countries, the quality of the product and the costs of production.

futures trading is when commodities or financial assets are bought or sold at some time in the future at an agreed price. In London such trading in financial assets occurs on the floor of the LIFFE (London International Financial Futures Exchange). Commodities such as wheat, oil, wool and many other products can also be bought or sold 'forward' on the commodity exchanges. This can be purely speculative, but it can also be vital for a business to protect itself against possible exchange rate or commodity price fluctuations. (See also *hedging*, *derivatives* and *options*.)

G

G7: see *Group of Seven.*

gains from trade: the benefits arising from trade which result in increased output from a given quantity of real resources. The theory of comparative advantage shows that trade allows countries to specialise in the goods and services which they produce most efficiently. By increasing efficiency, gains are made overall.

Galbraith J K (b. 1908): a Canadian-born economist who taught at Harvard University. He holds views which contrast with conventional *neoclassical economics.* In his writings he has emphasised the dominating influence of big businesses. He sees them less as satisfying consumer preferences and more as moulding preferences for their own ends, primarily through advertising. He argues that large firms should be tightly regulated by governments to prevent abuse of their market power. He also emphasises the role of the public sector in providing goods and services which could prevent gross inequalities. He contrasted 'private affluence' with 'public squalor', which can be a result of the operation of a free market.

galloping inflation: see *hyperinflation.*

game theory applies when the bodies which are competing in the marketplace exhibit *interdependent behaviour.* This means that for each one, the actions of the other will have an impact on the decisions taken. For example, if one business decides to cut prices, its competitor may follow suit. Game theory can be applied in a range of situations, whether the businesses are competing or colluding with each other. There may be gainers and losers or all may gain together.

Gates, Bill: the founder and head of Microsoft. Having started the business in 1975 he is now the world's richest man. Microsoft provides an excellent example of a market leader and *dominant firm.* Cases under US competition law seem likely to run on indefinitely and the debate about whether Microsoft abuses its market power will absorb many newspaper columns.

GATT: see *General Agreement on Tariffs and Trade.*

GDFCF: see *gross domestic fixed capital formation.*

GDP: see *gross domestic product.*

GDP deflator: a price index which includes the prices of all the goods and services produced in the economy. It is thus more comprehensive than the *retail price index,* which measures the prices of commonly bought products. It is used to find the real value of output.

gearing measures the relative importance of *loan finance* in relation to share finance (*equity*). The gearing ratio is:

FORMULA: $$\frac{\text{debt}}{\text{debt} + \text{equity}}$$

Gearing is important because a firm with a lot of debt will have to pay interest on it in good times and bad. If the firm relies more on share finance and if profits are poor, it can pay a lower *dividend* to shareholders or none at all.

A gearing ratio above 50% would usually be regarded as high. A highly geared firm is running some risks because it is more vulnerable to a fall in profitability.

General Agreement on Tariffs and Trade (GATT) was set up after World War II. At the time, it was expected that it would function as an international organisation on a par with the IMF and the World Bank. In practice it remained very small until it became the *World Trade Organisation* in 1995. Its objective was to encourage the growth of international trade by removing or reducing *tariff* and *non-tariff barriers.*

Agreements under the GATT were reached after what were known as 'rounds' of negotiations, which often lasted many years. The latest was the Uruguay round which was started in 1986 and was concluded after very protracted negotiations over agricultural subsidies at the end of 1994. It has had an impact on trade in many products, including services.

GATT was instrumental in making the world trading environment very much freer than it was before World War II. Not all its members always adhered to the general principles which it laid down; for example, the *Common Agricultural Policy* of the EU is contrary to GATT principles. Nevertheless, as a forum for negotiation it led to very large reductions in tariffs which in turn led to large increases in trade in manufactures. This increase in trade has been a major factor in worldwide economic growth. However, GATT's main contributions affected the developed countries the most and neglected the trade interests of developing countries.

general equilibrium refers to the type of economic analysis which examines the consequences of changes in all the markets which they might affect. In this way it takes account of the interrelationships between different markets. So partial equilibrium analysis would consider the impact of a change in demand for restaurant meals on their price and quantity sold, whereas general equilibrium analysis would go on to include consideration of the effect on demand for chefs and other labour market consequences, the impact on other producers in food processing and leisure activities and so on.

genetically modified (GM) foods: foods which have been grown or produced from new varieties based on changes in the genes which determine their attributes. These foods have enormous potential to cut costs and increase output but the wisdom of developing them is still hotly debated because of possible unknown effects on health and the environment.

In the long run, GM foods could eliminate food shortages in *developing countries.* New varieties could be created which will tolerate poor growing conditions in areas with low rainfall which are currently the scene of serious poverty. However, in order to make the new varieties available to people with low incomes, international organisations and governments will have to negotiate with the *multinationals* which are developing them.

geographical immobility occurs when people who have been made redundant are unable to move to areas in which jobs are available and thus remain unemployed. It is made worse when there is a lack of housing for rent at reasonable prices in the areas where jobs exist. Also differences in house prices, such that areas with high unemployment have low prices, make it hard for people without jobs to move to areas with jobs. Improved transport facilities can reduce geographical immobility.

Giffen good: a product for which quantity demanded rises when the price rises. This is so rare as to be almost a matter of theory, the single useful example being potatoes during the Irish potato famine in the 1840s. When potato crops failed, the price rose so spending on potatoes rose, leaving many people unable to afford anything other than potatoes and thus demanding more of them to satisfy their food needs.

gift tax: a tax on large gifts between living individuals. The objective is to prevent people from avoiding inheritance tax by giving the money to their heirs before they die. *Capital transfer tax* in the UK combines the features of an inheritance tax with a gift tax. The overall objective is to redistribute wealth.

gilt-edged security: a loan to the government for the purpose of covering a budget deficit.

The term gilt-edged reflects the fact that the government can guarantee to pay the money back because of its legal right to tax. The shortened form, gilts, often used in the press, refers to the *bonds* which are the actual securities, i.e. pieces of paper stating the amount of the loan, the rate of interest and the maturity date (i.e. when it will be repaid).

Gini coefficient: a measurement of inequality in the distribution of income. It is the ratio of the area between the diagonal and the *Lorenz curve* to the total area under the diagonal. It measures the extent to which the distribution of income diverges from precise equality. Latin America has the greatest inequality with a Gini coefficient around 0.5. Developed countries typically have a Gini coefficient of around 0.3.

global brands are products with a brand name which is recognised all over the world. Some are tailored to local tastes but generally, such products are standardised. Coca Cola is the archetypal example.

global warming is the rise in temperatures that is occurring as a result of the emission of '*greenhouse*' *gases* from industrial processes and vehicle exhausts. The likely consequences, climate change and rising sea levels, will probably have profound economic effects. Meantime, economic analysis can help us to understand the policies which might be used to combat the emission of greenhouse gases. (See also *fuel tax*.)

globalisation of the international economy refers to the process by which there is both an increasing world market in goods and services and increasing integration in world capital markets. This means that governments need to consult with their trading partners in order to co-ordinate their *macro-economic policies* and to avoid destabilising capital movements. Otherwise the success of their policies is likely to be compromised.

Globalisation has been associated with the rapid growth in world trade and has encouraged *economic growth*. It has improved standards of living for many people. It may also have increased the power of the multinationals. Some of the growth in trade has evolved as a result of efforts to make trade easier through the trade negotiations of the *World Trade Organisation*.

glut: a quantity supplied which is well above the amount needed to satisfy demand at current prices. For example, an unusually large crop of tomatoes will lead to increased supplies in the marketplace and to fast-falling prices as producers try to get rid of the crop before it spoils. (See diagram.) There can also be a glut of a mineral product (e.g. oil) if more has been produced than is being demanded. Depending on the extent to which the product has *inelastic demand*, the fall in prices will be higher.

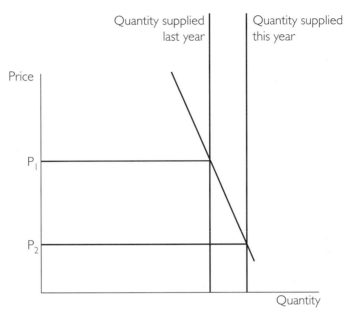

Inelastic demand will mean a sharp fall in price if quantity increases significantly

GM foods: see *genetically modified foods.*

GNP: see *gross national product.*

going rate: the current level of pay increases being negotiated.

gold: the precious metal now used in the financial system only as part of central banks' *foreign exchange reserves.* However, since it pays no interest, its role is diminishing further and central banks are selling it slowly. Gold is still used by some individuals as a *store of value.* They believe it can protect them from the effects of inflation, even though its value in the marketplace has not kept pace with inflation.

gold standard: a system for fixing exchange rates. Each currency had a fixed value in terms of gold. Until 1914 this was helpful in creating stability. Then the strains of World War I followed by the Great Depression made it impossible for most currencies to maintain the gold standard. The UK left the gold standard for good in 1931.

After World War II, the *Bretton Woods system* fixed the US dollar in terms of gold; all other currencies were fixed in terms of the dollar but could devalue when absolutely necessary to correct a balance of payments deficit. This last link to gold was finally abandoned in 1971. Gold reserves could not be expanded fast enough to finance the rapidly increasing levels of world trade.

golden rule: the idea that government budgets should balance over the course of the trade cycle, with borrowing used only to finance investment. During recession, incomes are falling and tax revenue will fall too. Unemployment is rising and benefit payments increase. The result will be an increasing *budget deficit.* As the economy recovers this process goes into reverse and it will be possible to generate a surplus which offsets the earlier deficit. Any borrowing which is additional to this should be spent on investment projects which have the potential to increase incomes in the future.

goods are tangible products, in contrast to services. Goods are physical objects.

go-slow: a type of industrial action. Employees continue to work, but only do what is absolutely necessary under the terms of their contract. This is also sometimes called a *work to rule.*

government: a political body which has authority over a group of people. It may be local or national in scope.

government borrowing is used whenever the revenue from taxation is less than total government expenditure. It can include sales of *bonds* (long-term borrowing), sales of *Treasury bills* (short-term borrowing) and the use of National Savings. (See also *budget deficit.*)

government debt: the total amount outstanding in terms of *bonds, Treasury bills* and National Savings bonds. (See also *National Debt.*)

government economic objectives are the main economic policy goals of the government of the day. All governments have at least some objectives in the four main categories of government economic activity.

- Provision of services – *public goods* (such as a police service and a legal system) must be provided by governments and *merit goods* (such as education and health care) may also be made available.
- Reallocation of resources is needed, to deter harmful activities (such as smoking) and encourage useful activities (such as setting up a small business).
- *Income redistribution* – taxing better off people and providing benefits and services for poorer people.
- Economic stabilisation – the use of *fiscal policy* to keep aggregate demand growing in a steady but sustainable way.

Conservative governments tend to want to reduce the scope of government economic policy by cutting both taxes and expenditure. They have in the past perceived inflation as a higher priority than unemployment. They tend to be less *interventionist.*

Income redistribution and the alleviation of poverty is always going to be a higher priority for Labour governments than for Conservative governments.

Economic objectives often conflict with one another. Tax cuts cannot easily be combined with increased spending on health care. (See also *conflicting objectives.*)

government expenditure: the sum total of all spending by both local and national government. In 2000 this was roughly 39% of GDP. (See Figure on page 139.)

government failure occurs when governments act to deal with *market failure,* but in the process create further *distortions* in the market. Very broadly, government failure may be said to occur when government intervention makes the situation worse rather than better. For example, *national insurance charges* raise revenue which can be used to pay benefits, but they also make it more expensive for employers to take on more labour. They thus tend to discourage job creation and raise unemployment.

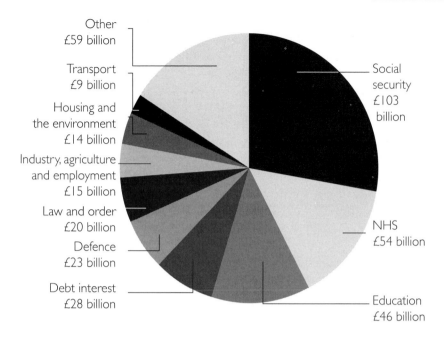

Other
£59 billion

Transport
£9 billion

Housing and
the environment
£14 billion

Industry, agriculture
and employment
£15 billion

Law and order
£20 billion

Defence
£23 billion

Debt interest
£28 billion

Social
security
£103
billion

NHS
£54 billion

Education
£46 billion

Source: *The Guardian*, 22.3.00

Government expenditure (see page 138)

government intervention is a loosely used term which usually refers to some way of influencing market forces and bringing about changes in production or consumption decisions. For example, the UK has an exceptionally high rate of home ownership and this has resulted from many years of government intervention in the market for mortgage finance. Until early 2000, mortgage interest payments were free of tax and therefore effectively subsidised. This gave most people with a steady income a strong incentive to buy a home. *Regulation*, tax incentives of all kinds and government support for industry are all varieties of intervention.

government procurement: all governments buy goods and services from private sector suppliers. Tanks, bandages and the construction of motorways are among the many possible examples. In this way, the government is an important customer for many firms. In the past it has been customary for governments to buy from suppliers in the same country. Now the *EU* and the *WTO* are working to require governments to open up all procurement contracts to competition from any potential supplier. This could mean that governments will buy imported goods at lower prices, thus increasing efficiency.

government securities provide governments with a way of borrowing to cover any shortfall between tax revenue and government expenditure. They consist mainly of *bonds* and *Treasury bills*.

government spending: see *public expenditure*.

gradualism means making policy changes by degrees. It contrasts with the notion of a 'short, sharp shock' which will bring about immediate changes. The choice between the two will depend on the government's perception of how difficult it will be for the economy to adjust to change.

The term gradualism may be used in a range of different contexts. In the early 1980s, governments favoured the use of monetary policy to give a clear message on inflation policy. This could mean raising interest rates very sharply. Nowadays, central banks favour small incremental changes in interest rates, based on a very careful reading of the economic indicators available. Borrowers adjust much more easily to such changes.

Gradualism has also been used in relation to the economic policies of *centrally planned economies* which were in transition to becoming market economies. Some have sold off their state-owned industries much faster than others. They have experienced higher unemployment than those that pursued a more gradual process of change.

grant: a payment from the government or a charity given to fund a specific project or service.

Great Depression: the slump of the 1930s. It began with the Wall Street Crash in 1929. Many people lost money then and this made them less willing to spend. This had important consequences.

- Confidence was destroyed and investment was badly affected.
- The *downward multiplier* effects continued for some years.
- Government policies were not helpful. Many governments cut spending which further reduced *aggregate demand.*
- Exports fell as aggregate demand fell everywhere. Many governments retaliated by imposing *import controls* and competing with each other to devalue their currencies. This reduced international trade.
- Unemployment in the UK peaked at 20%. In the US and Germany it peaked at 33%. Those who were in work experienced reduced incomes.

By 1934 the worst was over but the recovery was slow and faltering and it was not until rearmament began in 1937 that the depression finally came to an end. Meantime, in Germany the depression had contributed to the conditions which helped bring Hitler to power.

The work of *J M Keynes* at this time offered real insights into ways of alleviating depression. The lessons which were learnt were put into practice after World War II in the creation of the *Bretton Woods system* and in the moves towards freeing international trade which followed. In the late 1930s the US government under President Roosevelt got the message that governments could help with *deficit spending* on investment projects.

Green Paper: a consultation document issued by the government prior to formulating new policies. A White Paper sets out actual policy decisions.

green pound: an artificial exchange rate used for calculating payments to farmers out of the Common Agricultural Policy. If the green pound is devalued, food prices in British shops are likely to rise.

green revolution: the improvement in agricultural yields which occurred in many parts of the developing world after technical changes. Research led to improved seeds which could yield more grain. To achieve the increased yields, farmers needed:

- rural credit schemes so that they could buy the new seeds
- appropriate irrigation and fertilisers
- extension workers from agricultural colleges who could explain the new methods to farmers
- crop insurance (because the new methods were usually riskier than traditional ones).

The green revolution brought about dramatic increases in food grain production, notably in some parts of India. The process started with wheat but other products have been favourably affected too. Similar progress with seeds suited to arid climates is still awaited.

greenfield development: a term used for projects taking place on land not previously used for the same purpose. Usually it means that agricultural land is being used for industrial development or retail outlets.

greenhouse gases: the emissions of carbon dioxide and other substances which are leading to a build up of heat from the sun which cannot escape from the earth's atmosphere. The main causes are industrial pollution (part of it from power stations) and vehicle exhausts. Despite the work of many pressure groups, governments are so far unable to agree on the measures needed to reduce emission of greenhouse gases. Without an agreement which actually forces all governments to tax the activities which create the greenhouse gases, measures to reduce emissions are proceeding slowly and unevenly. (See also *fuel taxes.*)

Greenspan, Alan (b. 1926): Chairman of the US central bank, the Federal Reserve (the Fed), with overall responsibility for all *monetary policy decisions.* He trained as an economist and then worked for a number of big businesses and ran his own consultancy business in New York. From 1974 onwards he became an adviser to the US government. He was appointed to his present job by President Reagan in 1988 and began his fourth four-year term in 2000. He is widely credited with masterminding the long period of strong economic growth in the US which began in 1990. He has enjoyed the confidence of all the US presidents who have been and gone during his term of office at the Fed. Watch what happens when he eventually goes.

grey market: an unofficial market which is legal. It can be seen in operation when retailers wanting to sell branded goods find a market where they can obtain them more cheaply than they can by buying direct from the manufacturers. This exposes the fact that the manufacturers are price discriminating. When discovered, they generally object but they have no legal basis for this.

gross domestic fixed capital formation (GDFCF) is the sum total of all *investment* in infrastructure, buildings, plant, machinery, and vehicles in one year. It is an important indicator because it is strongly related to the future growth of *productive capacity.* It includes replacement investment but the higher it is, the more likely it is that it will lead to increases in *productivity.* It tends to be rather volatile because it is closely related to expectations and therefore to the phases of the *trade cycle.*

gross domestic product (GDP) is the value of everything produced in the economy for the year. It may be calculated from expenditure, in which case it is likely to be expressed in market prices. These include expenditure taxes. It can also be calculated from income or from the value of output. It is most commonly expressed at factor cost, i.e. the costs of all the inputs, which reflects the real resource costs of production.

gross investment: the total of all investment in buildings, plant, machinery and vehicles and infrastructure, including both replacement investment and new productive capacity. (See also *net investment.*)

gross national product (GNP) is calculated by adding total output (*gross domestic product* or *GDP*) to *net property income from abroad*. It corresponds to total spending power in the economy and is therefore a useful measure of the standard of living. Net property income from abroad is total interest payments, profits and dividends from money invested overseas, minus interest, profits and dividends earned by foreigners on investments in the UK.

gross profit is an accounting term which means sales revenue minus the costs associated with the actual production process (cost of sales). These do not include the overheads or *fixed costs* such as capital equipment, premises, management, marketing and so on. When these costs have been deducted, we have operating or net profit, which is closer to though not the same as the economist's definition of profit.

Group of Seven (G7) includes the governments of the seven richest nations: Japan, the US, Germany, France, Canada, Italy and the UK. Regular meetings allow matters of mutual interest to be discussed. Sometimes the governments work to co-ordinate their economic policies in order to try to stabilise the world economy. These meetings are widely reported in the press and can lead to significant progress in resolving world problems. If Canada and Italy are not invited, it is G5. When Russia is invited to participate it is known as G8. Were China also to be invited it would become G9.

growing populations: some economies have fast-growing populations. This means that their resources are increasing in quantity but also that they have more mouths to feed. In the US, population growth through continued high levels of immigration is a generally positive development. The increased labour supply helps to keep the economic growth process going. In Africa, high levels of population growth due to high birth rates have created some difficulty in improving per capita income and standards of living. The high rate of population growth may not continue in some countries if AIDS remains a serious problem.

growth: see *economic growth.*

growth rate: the percentage increase in GDP each year. This does tend to overstate the improvement in the standard of living because of the *costs of growth* which are not included.

hard currency includes a number of currencies which are easily convertible and widely accepted in payment everywhere. The US dollar, the pound and the yen are examples. Indian rupees and Chinese renminbi would usually be less acceptable.

hard landing: it is quite likely that after a period of rapidly growing aggregate demand, *monetary* and *fiscal policies* will be used to slow the economy down in order to avoid accelerating inflation. Because there are time lags in this process and because it is difficult for the authorities to decide the precise amount of change required at just the right moment, it can happen that the rapid growth is followed by an abrupt loss of business confidence and a rapid fall in investment accompanied by falling demand for a wide range of products. This will precipitate a *recession* with rising unemployment. This would be a hard landing. A soft landing would entail a slowdown in the rate of economic growth which did not actually reduce income growth to nothing or entail rising unemployment. Take a look at the US data for 2001. Did the economy have a hard or a soft landing?

hard loan: a loan given on normal commercial terms at the market rate of interest. In contrast, a *soft loan* would involve a lower rate of interest, perhaps with additional concessions. Soft loans are designed to assist developing countries. Projects with strong prospects of future profit can normally be financed with hard loans.

harmonisation in the European Union context means making all member countries' businesses subject to the same legal framework, i.e. harmonising laws and regulations. In this way the EU tries to create a 'level playing field' so that all firms compete on equal terms within the single *European market*. Harmonisation of the regulations governing actual products allows firms to standardise their production process and make one version of the product for the whole of the EU. This can lead to *economies of scale* and lower costs and prices.

Harrod-Domar model: a theory of *economic growth* which emphasises the importance of increasing capital inputs and therefore of generating savings which can be channelled towards investment in productive capacity. At the heart of the model is the constant capital-output ratio.

Although the theory was originally devised in the context of developed countries, it has been widely applied in developing countries. The idea was that if you knew the capital-output ratio, you could calculate the amount of capital needed to produce a given level of economic growth. It would then be possible to estimate the level of saving required to finance this level of investment.

In the late stages of the last century it became clear that this approach was rather simplistic. All countries do not have the same capital-output ratio. Furthermore, it is clear that in parts of Asia, growth has been greater than would have been expected on the basis of capital investment, even if investment in human capital is included. The diagram shows how some but not all of the gap between the growth rate of the Korean Republic and the growth rate in Ghana can be explained by differences in investment. Technical progress is obviously another important factor which can explain some of the remaining difference. Increased productivity and growth can come from other causes too, e.g. improved management techniques.

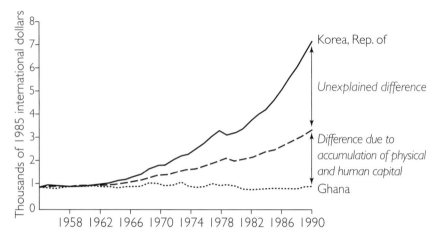

Source: *World Development Report,* 1998/9

In view of all this it is clear that the growth process is still not fully understood and there is no simple model which can be applied to all developing countries.

hazardous waste refers to the waste products of industrial processes which are harmful to people or the environment. In the past these have degraded soil and polluted water and air. *Regulation* of disposal is making this less likely. This means that firms are required to dispose of wastes safely and to bear the cost of doing so. This should mean that disposal costs become internalised (instead of being *external costs*) and are reflected in the price of the product. The desirable outcome is now occurring more often in developed countries. Developing and transitional economies still have weaker legislation on this.

headline inflation is inflation as measured by the *retail price index (RPI).* This includes some price changes which may be strictly temporary in their impact on the economy, such as mortgage interest payments. This is excluded from RPIX. Another measure of inflation, RPIY, excludes changes in indirect taxes, again in order to measure *underlying inflation.*

headline unemployment is the total number of registered unemployed, not seasonally adjusted. It will obviously exclude *disguised unemployment.*

Health and Safety at Work Act 1974 greatly strengthened the obligations of employers to ensure that employees' working conditions are safe. This raises the costs of production but reduces the risks associated with accidents and industrial health problems. The act is enforced by the Health and Safety Executive, a government-financed organisation which employs inspectors to investigate conditions in the workplace. Safety at work is now governed by the *Social Chapter* of the *Maastricht Treaty,* part of the 'level playing field' of the *single market* within the EU.

health insurance provides private health care outside the scope of the National Health Service to people who can and want to pay the premiums. It is quite often provided by employers as an additional element in the pay package, rather as they provide company cars.

heavy industry: this term does not have a precise definition but usually it refers to production of traditional, heavy products such as iron and steel, bulk chemicals, ships and vehicles on a large scale.

hedging is a way to minimise risks. Commodities or currencies can be bought now for delivery on a date in the future at an agreed price which removes some uncertainty. The importer who will need foreign currency at a date in the future will have it available at a known price. Similarly commodities which are known to be becoming available in the future can be sold in the future at a price which is agreed now. The alternative is to trade in the *spot* market at the current spot price and carry the risk that the price may change.

Contracts to buy/sell in the *forward markets* are known as *futures* contracts.

high-powered money means money which can form the basis for expansion of bank lending. This means that the money must be usable by banks as a liquid reserve.

hire purchase: a way of buying on credit. It is used for consumer durables and also by firms investing in an item of capital equipment. Specialist companies, often subsidiaries of banks, provide the finance. Loans of this kind are less used now than in the past. Consumers can often get bank loans, which are cheaper if they are well known to the bank. Firms are more likely to go for *leasing*, which is more or less the same as renting the equipment.

historic cost is the actual price paid and usually refers to items of capital equipment used by a business and recorded in its accounts. If there has been significant inflation, it matters whether the accountant uses historic costs or current costs, which would give the replacement cost of the item. When interpreting company accounts, it is necessary to know how the *assets* have been valued.

hit-and-run competition comes from firms which enter the market expecting to make immediate profits and then make a rapid exit from the market. This works only if the fixed costs of entry are relatively low. A fashion for the product may attract hit-and-run competition. Profits for the stable producer who has been in the market for a long time may be much reduced by this.

hoarding occurs when people or organisations keep money which is not earning interest or being used in a productive way. Savings kept under the mattress is a traditional example. Excessive current account balances would be another.

holding company: a firm that holds shares in other companies. Normally, it will have a controlling interest, i.e. more than 50% of the shares, and will have control without involvement in day-to-day decisions. Control may be exercised with a very light touch or may involve participation in all strategic decisions.

homeworking means working from home. This can mean being self-employed and working from home or taking in piecework such as sewing. Or it can mean using electronic communications to stay in touch with one or many other workplaces. Designers and computer programmers often work from home.

homogeneous products are identical. It is impossible to know whether the product came from one firm or another. A homogeneous product is an important feature of the model of *perfect competition*. The more homogeneous the products are, the stronger the competition is likely to be in the marketplace. Examples include many agricultural products, e.g. wheat, and many mineral products, e.g. iron ore.

In contrast, many businesses spend a great deal of time and money trying to persuade consumers that their products are different from others; theirs are *differentiated products*, the opposite of homogeneous.

horizontal integration involves a merger or take-over where both firms are engaged in the same type of production. They could both be involved in a single stage in the production process or they could have very similar end products. The features of integration have pros and cons.

- *Rationalisation* will enable the firms to exploit potential *economies of scale*. The fall in costs may make it possible to cut prices and benefit the consumer. But it may also increase *market power* by reducing competition.
- The two firms combined may be better able to stand up to competition from foreign producers. But they may also have a large share of the domestic market and this may mean that they will be referred to the *Competition Commission*.

Horizontal integration has occurred in many industries. Hotels, chemicals and travel companies provide examples.

horizontal merger means the integration of two firms which supply very similar products. (See also *horizontal integration*.)

host country: countries which attract foreign direct investment. Most governments are keen to be in this position because the investment creates jobs and income and may bring useful *technology transfer*. Foreign companies often provide training for employees. In the UK, Wales has been particularly successful as a host country and the employment generated has helped to fill the gap left by *declining industries*.

For developing countries, foreign investment has particular pros and cons.

- The investor may help to increase exports, bringing in much-needed foreign exchange. However, the profits will be repatriated to the parent company or its shareholders in developed countries, creating an invisible outflow in the balance of payments.
- Technology transfer may or may not happen. If it does, it will help to create a pool of new skills which will benefit the host country economy. But some multinationals set up in developing countries simply to take advantage of the cheap labour available, give little training and move on to other locations if wage rates rise.

hostile takeover bid: an attempt to take over a firm which is resisted by the existing board of directors. In order to fight off the bid, the board may recommend shareholders not to sell. There are stringent rules about how the battle may be fought. In 1998 the Bank of Scotland made a hostile bid for the then National Westminster Bank. The latter finally accepted a rival bid from the Royal Bank of Scotland after a six-month process of bid and counterbid.

hot money: speculative flows on foreign exchange markets. It is possible to hold large cash balances in order to gamble on changes in *exchange rates*. For example, during the Asian financial crisis in 1997-1998, large quantities of yen and other Asian currencies were sold. As exchange rates fell, more and more holders of the currencies lost confidence and they in turn sold. Later, when the exchange rates had stabilised at a lower level, they bought the currencies again. Money which moves from one capital market to another in search of the best rate of return is termed hot money.

household: the basic economic decision-taking unit. Economists tend to talk about households rather than individuals because their consumption patterns have more in common than, say, those of a teenager living at home and a single person living alone.

housing association: a not-for-profit organisation which exists to provide low-cost housing. Flats and houses may be rented or sold on concessional terms or some combination of the two. Finance comes partly from the public sector, partly from charitable donations and partly from banks and other commercial sources.

housing benefit: a payment made on the basis of need to cover rent. Where rents are very high, as in London, housing benefit in combination with other welfare payments can contribute to the *poverty trap*.

HRM: see *human resource management.*

human capital consists of knowledge and skills acquired by individuals. It may be acquired in a formal way through education or employers' training programmes. Or it may be the result of accumulated experience or on-the-job training, as with an apprenticeship. Investing in human capital makes people more productive and can increase their earnings, provided there is a demand for their particular skills and knowledge. It is an important element in the process of *economic growth.*

Some skills and knowledge are firm specific and of particular importance to the relevant employer.

human development index: a measure of the quality of life constructed by the United Nations Development Programme. It takes into account not just income but also a range of other criteria such as literacy, life expectancy, clean water and gender issues. Canada and the Scandinavian countries usually rank among the highest. It can be instructive to compare the rankings with those based on GDP. Individual countries have a great variety of reasons for discrepancies between the two.

human resource management (HRM): that part of the management process which involves the ways in which people are used and developed. Careful development and use of new skills can be very important in knowledge-based industries, so HRM has tended to become a higher priority for management generally in recent years.

hyperinflation: very rapidly rising prices. There is no precise dividing line between inflation and hyperinflation, but no doubt about when it is a real problem. Over 100% a year would probably be regarded as hyperinflation by most people.

Germany in 1923 experienced hyperinflation which peaked at 23 000%. At that level, people lose all confidence in money as a *store of value.* Many Latin American countries have experienced it. Russia and Yugoslavia in the early 1990s both had problems. Hyperinflation can have dire consequences because wealth is redistributed in favour of those with debts and against savers who are holding assets denominated in money terms, such as bank balances and building society accounts.

hypothecation is the term for earmarking of tax revenue from a particular source for a specific item of *government expenditure*. It is newsworthy in the UK because it would be possible to have a 1p or 2p addition to the standard rate of income tax and spend it on improving the National Health Service. Other suggestions have been made in relation to fuel taxes and road building or other transport spending.

hypothesis: a theoretical connection between two variables, which can be tested against the facts. For example, we might suspect that the purchase of yachts is related to income. By examining the increase in real incomes which occurs when the economy is growing and comparing this with the trend in yacht sales, we might find that the hypothesis was supported by the evidence.

hysteresis can be used to describe a sequence of events in which a change takes place but there are difficulties and time lags in the adjustment process and, because of this, the outcome is not necessarily what we would have predicted on the basis of economic theory. For example, economic theory suggests that unemployment will lead to falling or slow-growing wage rates. Eventually this will provide employers with some incentive to hire labour again. However, people who have been unemployed for a long time may be deskilled and have great difficulty in finding work because of this, even when the economy has picked up.

IBRD: see *International Bank for Reconstruction and Development*, commonly known as the World Bank.

IFC: see *International Finance Corporation*.

ILO: see *International Labour Organisation*.

IMF: see *International Monetary Fund*.

immobilities occur when people are unable to take up a job which is available because they are living in another area (*geographical immobility*) or because they do not have the right skills for the job (*occupational immobility*). Immobilities are a form of *market imperfection*. They impede the process of reallocating resources in response to changes in consumer demand.

imperfect competition occurs when there are a number of competing firms, but the market lacks some or all of the features of *perfect competition*. Broadly there are three types of imperfect competition: *duopoly*, *oligopoly* and *monopolistic competition*. In a duopoly there are just two firms competing. Oligopoly describes a situation where there are several firms in the market. In both cases, the market will be characterised by *interdependence*: the competing firms will base their decisions on what the others are doing, or might do in the future. There is likely to be much non-price competition. Under monopolistic competition there are many competitors, each selling a *differentiated product*.

imperfect information is a market imperfection as a result of which competition is impaired by lack of easily available information. The consumer who does not know where to find a product at the cheapest price will pay more, and this protects the producer from the competition which might exist if information were fuller. Similarly, the firm which does not know where to find the cheapest inputs will have costs higher than necessary, which reduces efficiency.

imperfect knowledge: see *imperfect information*.

imperfect market occurs when there are *imperfections*, i.e. distortions in the market such that competition is not as forceful as it might be. An imperfect market departs in one or more ways from the conditions of *perfect competition*. It will generally not achieve *technical and allocative efficiency*. For example, firms which have a degree of monopoly within their markets may not be forced to seek the most efficient methods of producing and as a result, prices may be higher than they need be.

imperfections occur in an imperfect market, and include *immobilities*, *imperfect information*, *government intervention*, *barriers to entry*, small numbers of buyers or sellers and any other source of distortions which may interfere with the operation of competitive market forces. (See also *imperfect market*.)

import controls: *tariffs*, *quotas* or other controls which can be used to reduce imports. Tariffs are *import duties*: there must be a payment to the government before they can be brought into the country. Quotas are physical limits for specific products, setting a maximum amount each year which can be imported. *Non-tariff barriers* include quotas and also many other regulations which have the effect of making it more difficult to import. For example, quality requirements may be used to exclude unwanted imports. Import controls are generally being reduced over the years by WTO negotiations.

import duty: a *tariff* levied on an imported item at the point of entry to the country. (See also *import controls*.)

import penetration: imports as a percentage share of the market for that product. For example in the car industry, import penetration is roughly 66% in the UK.

import propensity: the percentage of total income spent on imports. A very open economy may spend a large part of total income on imports. For example, Belgium spends roughly 70% of GDP on imports while the UK spends roughly 30% and the US, 13%.

import substitution: some developing countries have sought to industrialise by reducing imports and developing domestic industries which would replace them. Although this has been occasionally successful, in general the protected domestic industries have never become efficient enough to compete on world markets. So the countries which concentrated on producing the goods in which they had a *comparative advantage* and exporting them performed better. Brazil was an exponent of import substitution for many years but has largely abandoned it in recent times.

imported inflation means a general rise in prices which occurs because prices are rising in other countries. This means that import prices will rise, thus raising the cost of imported inputs for the production process. The effect of these, together with price rises for imported consumer goods, will feed into the *RPI*.

imports: goods and services bought from overseas producers.

incentives: financial and other rewards which can influence the decisions of firms and individuals. Favourable tax treatment of *investment* spending can induce firms to invest more. Increased taxes on tobacco give smokers an incentive to give up. On a wider level, the term may be used in connection with groups of people who, for example, lack the incentive to work because they are in the *poverty trap*.

Incentives can be vital in ensuring that the *allocation of resources* reflects the pattern of consumer demand. People may need an incentive to move from one kind of production to another; this could be a *pay differential* which encourages them to switch jobs.

incidence of taxation analyses the extent to which a specific expenditure tax falls upon the consumer or the producer. Depending on the *price elasticity of demand* for the product, the producer may or may not be able to pass the tax on to the consumer by raising the price.

A tax will shift the supply curve upwards by the exact amount of the tax. The more inelastic the demand is, the easier it will be for the seller to pass the tax on to the consumer in the form of a higher price (P1 in the diagram). If demand is elastic, then consumers will simply buy less of the product as the price rises and the producer will have to absorb at least a part of the tax (Ep minus f2 in the second diagram). Taxes on items with elastic demand will reduce the quantity bought and have little effect on the price, while taxes on items with inelastic demand will discourage consumption relatively little but lead to an increase in price close to the amount of the tax.

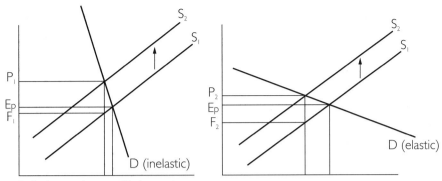

Ep is the market equilibrium price
P$_1$ and P$_2$ are the prices to the consumer after tax
F$_1$ and F$_2$ are the prices received by the producer after tax has been paid F

Incidence of taxation (See page 150)

income is a flow of money which acts as a reward for the services of a *factor of production*. Wages and salaries are a reward to labour and are described as earned income. Unearned income includes rent, interest and profit: rent is a reward for the owner of land or property. Profit gives a return on capital invested and also rewards the efforts of *entrepreneurs*. Interest is a return on a capital sum which is loaned to someone else.

For firms, income comes from sales revenue plus the return on any investments. For the economy as a whole, income is the total income derived from all activities and is measured most often using GDP.

income distribution: see *distribution of income*.

income effect: when there is a change in a price, that change will have an income effect and a substitution effect. The *substitution effect* shows how quantity consumed changes in response to the change in that price compared to all other prices. Thus if foreign holidays become more expensive, the substitution effect will lead to more holidays being taken closer to home. The income effect shows the effect on consumption of the change in real income which occurs when a price changes. The rise in the price of foreign holidays causes a fall in real income because it reduces purchasing power. This will mean a tendency for consumption of everything, not just foreign holidays, to fall. Items with very low prices will have a very small income effect. *Inferior goods* have a negative income effect.

income elasticity of demand measures the responsiveness of quantity demanded to a change in income.

FORMULA: $\dfrac{\text{percentage change in quantity demanded}}{\text{percentage change in incomes}}$ = income elasticity

There are several important factors to consider in examining the income elasticity of demand for particular products.

Is income elasticity positive or negative?

- Positive income elasticity implies that as income rises, so does demand for the product. We can easily think up examples: people will want more weekend breaks, restaurant meals and books as their incomes rise. So a rise in income will lead to a rise in quantity demanded. Both the top and bottom of the formula will be positive, giving a positive income elasticity.
- With some products, there will be very little sensitivity to income changes. Take toothpaste, for example. A change in income will make no difference at all. Income elasticity will be zero.
- On the other hand, demand for some products will go down as income rises. Bus services, for example, faced decreasing demand as more people became able to afford cars. The formula gives a negative percentage for change in quantity demanded over a positive figure for change in income. The result is a negative income elasticity.
- Products with positive income elasticity, like cars, are called *normal goods*. Products with negative income elasticity are called *inferior goods*. These are relatively few in number compared to normal goods.
- Positive income elasticity may be high or low. For many products, rising incomes will lead to a modest increase in quantity demanded. Many food items would fall into this category, with income elasticity positive but less than one. For some products, a rise in income will increase demand greatly and income elasticity will be greater than one.
- Income elasticities can change significantly over time. The motorbike, for instance, was a great success in the UK as incomes rose to the point where people could afford one as opposed to a bicycle. As incomes rose further, a small car became affordable and the demand for motorbikes fell, making it an *inferior good* at this point. Then, as incomes rose to the point where the motorbike became a recreational vehicle, income elasticity became positive once more.

Businesses selling goods and services with low income elasticity will be less vulnerable during a *recession* than those selling goods and services with high income elasticities. Producers of biscuits might hardly notice a recession while producers of yachts may go out of business due to lack of demand.

Worked example: It has been estimated that a 10% increase in incomes will lead to a 3% increase in demand for fruit. What is its income elasticity of demand?

$$\text{Income elasticity of demand} = \frac{\%\text{ change in quantity demanded}}{\%\text{ change in incomes}}$$

so in this example $\dfrac{+3}{+10} = +0.3$

---

income method: the calculation of national income by adding up all income earned by *factors of production*, i.e. wages and salaries, interest, profit and rents.

income redistribution means taxing high incomes much more than low incomes and providing benefits for those with little or no income of their own. The objective is to achieve a more equal distribution of income across society as a whole.

Progressive income taxes will achieve the first outcome. Providing more generous unemployment benefits, disability and child allowances and *income support* will achieve the second. *Means-tested benefits* may be used to ensure that the greatest help is given to the most needy.

Some income redistribution measures have been challenged on the grounds that they reduce the incentive to work. Where most benefits are means tested, there can be a poverty trap which is very difficult to escape. Recent policies on benefits have sought to address this by trying to ensure that everyone is actually better off working. The *Working Families Tax Credit* addresses this. (See also *income tax*).

income support: a benefit payment designed to ensure that everyone has a minimum acceptable income. Income support is *means-tested* and supplements other kinds of benefits such as the state pension and unemployment benefit. For example, a person who is unemployed but has not made enough national insurance contributions to qualify for unemployment benefit will be given income support.

income tax is a *direct tax* levied on the incomes of individuals. There is a personal allowance, which is tax free, and a 10% rate band which is designed to ensure that people on very low incomes pay very little income tax. Tax rates are announced annually in the Budget by the Chancellor of the Exchequer. The following example uses the bands and the tax rates set in the 2000 Budget.

Income between	Tax rate (%)
0–£4335	0
£4336–£5866	10
£5867– £32 836	22 (basic rate)
£32 837 upwards	40 (higher rate)

Worked example:

	James earns £15 000 per year		Jane earns £40 000 per year	
	Tax %	Tax due	Tax %	Tax due
0–£4335	0	0	0	0
£4336–£5,866	10	£150	10	£150
£5867–£32,836	22	£2009	22	£5933
£32 837 upwards	40	0	40	£2865
Total tax		£2159		£8948
As % of income		14.4%		22.4%

Income tax is a *progressive tax*, which means that it takes a higher proportion of a higher income and a lower proportion of a lower income. (*Regressive taxes* do the reverse, while proportional taxes are neutral in this respect.) Income tax thus has a major role to play in *income redistribution*.

If tax rates are kept constant, tax revenues will vary with incomes and will fluctuate over the course of the *trade cycle*. Income tax plays a part in the operation of *automatic stabilisers*, which help to reduce fluctuations in the level of aggregate demand.

High marginal income tax rates are usually resented by those who have to pay them. It is sometimes said that they create a disincentive to work hard. There is no statistical evidence for this.

Income tax is an important revenue raiser for the government, contributing roughly a quarter of total tax revenue at the present time.

incomes policy was used during the 1960s and 1970s as a way of controlling inflation. Usually, it meant that pay increases were limited to a certain percentage. Such policies were never very successful because they prevented wages from adjusting fully to market forces. Also, they were politically unpopular with both political wings, for different reasons. The right disliked the way they interfered with market forces; the left disliked the way they interfered with free *collective bargaining*.

increasing returns to scale occur if output can be increased using a proportionally smaller quantity of inputs. It will tend to be associated with *economies of scale*.

indebtedness is the extent to which a business or a government owes money to banks or international organisations.

independent variable: where there is a relationship between two variables, one may be determined by something else and thus be termed independent. In the relationship between income and consumption, consumption is seen as depending on income, while income, the independent variable, is determined by a whole range of other things such as the level of *investment*, the level of *government spending* and the level of exports. It is therefore treated as being independent.

indexation: see *index-linked*.

index linked means that the value in question will be changed in line with the retail price index. Pensions are now index linked so that their purchasing power is kept constant and keeps pace with inflation. Index-linked National Savings Certificates have their maturity values raised in line with the RPI. It is possible to index link wage rates but this is unusual because changes in supply and demand in the labour market make it desirable for wage rates to be more flexible.

index numbers can be created for any time series so that comparisons can be made more easily. A base year is required and the value for this year becomes 100. In each subsequent year, the percentage change from the base year is added to 100. There are many important indices.

- The *retail price index* gives a measure of average price rises. It is built up from a large number of price changes for products which are frequently bought. These are made into a *weighted average* to ensure that the products which figure largest in the average shopper's buys are given the most importance in the index.
- Stock Exchange indices such as the *Footsie 100* are also weighted averages, where the most frequently traded shares are given the largest weights.
- The *sterling exchange rate index* is a weighted average of exchange rate changes. The currencies of the UK's most important trading partners are given the largest weights.

These and other index numbers put a lot of complex information into a single series. They can be more easily interpreted than the raw data.

indicative planning is a process whereby the government produces a plan for the whole economy which may help individual businesses and organisations to make their own plans in order to fit in with it. Indicative planning was widely practised during the 1960s and is now rather out of fashion.

indicators help to show what is happening in the economy. *Leading indicators* foreshadow changes to come: an increase in machine tool production might indicate that an increase in output is likely. The level of vacancies would show a sharp rise if skill shortages were developing in the labour market.

indifference curve: a line graph showing a set of combinations of two products, each of which is equally acceptable to the consumer. As part of the revealed preference theory, indifference curves can be used to analyse the effect of price changes.

indirect controls: a way of controlling a variable by controlling its price. Pollution can be controlled directly by regulating the levels which are allowed and prosecuting firms which go over that level. Or it can be controlled *indirectly* by selling permits to pollute. This gives firms an incentive to avoid polluting. In the past, the Bank of England would place direct controls on the amounts that banks could lend. Now the Bank just raises interest rates which discourages borrowers from wanting loans – an indirect control.

indirect taxes are paid when goods and services are bought, i.e. they are expenditure taxes. Examples include *VAT* and *excise duty*. In contrast, direct taxes are levied on income and profits. In general, an indirect tax will be a *regressive tax*, having a bigger impact on poorer than on richer people. However, VAT is less regressive than it appears because many necessities are exempt or zero rated. In 1979, the UK shifted the burden of taxation away from direct taxation to indirect, on the grounds that direct taxes are a disincentive to working harder or longer.

individual bargaining, in contrast to *collective bargaining* with a *trade union* as intermediary, involves direct negotiations between employee and employer to determine pay and conditions. Some people, especially those with scarce skills, do not feel the need for a trade union to negotiate on their behalf. For some, there is no union readily available. Individual bargaining is on the increase.

individual savings accounts (ISAs): a type of tax-free savings scheme designed to encourage more people to save. ISAs can include cash savings, shares and life assurance policies. The interest received is not taxed.

indivisibility: a situation in which the different items of equipment needed for production come in different sizes, so that larger scale items are not used at full capacity. This can be a problem for small-scale producers, whose *average fixed costs* will be higher as a result. In this situation, expanding output would lead to *economies of scale*.

induced expenditure is spending, the level of which is determined by the level of income. Consumption, saving and tax revenue are all induced, within the framework of the basic Keynesian model of the macro-economy.

induction: a process by which relationships may be inferred from specific observations. The process may start with an examination of the data and from this a *hypothesis* may be worked out.

industrial action occurs when the workforce seeks to disrupt production as a way of bringing pressure to bear on employers. The objective is to secure better pay and/or conditions. Industrial action could take the form of a strike, a *work to rule* or a *go-slow*.

industrial democracy involves devising ways in which employees can participate in the decision-making process. Employees may elect a representative to sit on the board of directors. This person may or may not have voting rights. There may be a works council, which brings management and trade unions together at regular meetings. Provision for this is contained in the *Social Chapter* of the Maastricht Treaty. Some UK businesses have opposed this; others find the meetings useful.

The strongest form of industrial democracy is the *co-operative*. There, all employees have the right to participate in decision making, although in practice they may delegate this to a committee.

industrial dispute: a disagreement between management and trade union representatives. This will most often spring from negotiations about pay and conditions and may lead to industrial action if a ballot shows a majority of the workforce in favour. Alternatively, the parties may agree to go to *arbitration*.

industrial inertia refers to the way in which certain industries remain located in a particular region long after the original reason for their being there has ceased to exist. The classic example is the woollen industry in West Yorkshire, located there because of the easy availability of water power. Often the reason for industrial inertia lies in the *external economies of scale* which develop around an industry concentrated in one location. In many cases the main external economy will be a pool of skilled labour and local expertise.

industrial location: the place in which firms choose to locate when setting up their production facilities. The location may be based on important cost factors such as:

- access to motorways
- locally based input suppliers
- a pool of skilled labour
- sources of raw materials
- nearby markets.

However, nowadays, many industries are *footloose*, i.e. they can locate in many places without their cost structures being much affected.

In some cases, industrial location is determined by factors which were important in the past (see also *industrial inertia*). In some of these situations, *external economies of scale* have become important, particularly if there is local expertise which could be a significant input.

Industries using advanced technologies cluster together in science parks, often located close to universities where relevant research is under way. Then there is another kind of *cluster*, for which it is hard to find a logical reason. Antique shops are seldom found alone; they nearly always are one of a number up and down the high street, for example in country towns. It seems that if one is successful others will be attracted and together they attract people from further afield.

Governments can influence industrial location by offering grants and other inducements to firms which are considering setting up in areas where regeneration is a priority. The *assisted areas* have all had a legacy of *declining industries* and governments want to attract new firms which will create employment based on potentially prosperous ventures.

industrial policy can cover many different aspects of government economic policy.

- Regional policy can be used to regenerate areas which have suffered because *localised industries* have declined. Coal mining, iron and steel and shipbuilding have declined and left large areas with far fewer jobs than job seekers. Along with seaside resorts and a number of very remote regions, many of these places have been classified as *assisted areas*. They qualify for government or EU-provided inducements which may attract firms to locate in the area.
- Small firms policies can help to encourage firms to get started. Unemployed people with potential as entrepreneurs can get help from the *Enterprise Allowance Scheme*, as well as practical advice from government-funded bodies.
- Technology policies can be used to fund *research and development*. However, in the UK many commentators would hold that the government has not done enough.
- The *Private Finance Initiative* has been used to try to modernise UK infra-structure without relying too heavily on government funding. This was thought to offer a way of reducing the role of the government in the economy while still ensuring that services were provided.

industrial relations: the communication links which exist between employers and trade unions. Ideally, there will be some degree of trust between management and employees, which *employers' organisations* and *trade unions* can build upon. In practice, old animosities can be a problem in some workplaces. Also some firms still pay the absolute minimum they can get away with, though others have come to see concern for employees as important in leading to a loyal and committed workforce.

industrial union: a trade union whose members are all from a specific industry. For example, the Communication Workers Union draws its membership mainly from employees in telecommunications. In contrast, a general union such as the Transport and General Workers Union (TGWU) will have members from many industries.

industrialisation is the process by which a country may move from dependence on primary production to having a developed manufacturing sector. Many developing countries are in the process of this transition at the present time: for example, Mexico, India and Indonesia.

industry: an area of production defined usually by the product, e.g. the car industry or the chemical industry.

inefficiency: failing to maximise the value of output from a given quantity of inputs. If the quantity of output is less than it could be, *technical efficiency* is compromised. If the value of the output is less than it could be, the problem is with *allocative efficiency*. The problem then is that the output is not actually what consumers most want.

inelastic demand arises in situations where a change in price leads to a relatively small change in quantity demanded. Whatever the percentage change in price, the percentage change in quantity demanded will be less. *Price elasticity of demand* will be numerically less than one. This is shown in the diagram: inelastic demand can be represented by a fairly steeply sloping demand curve.

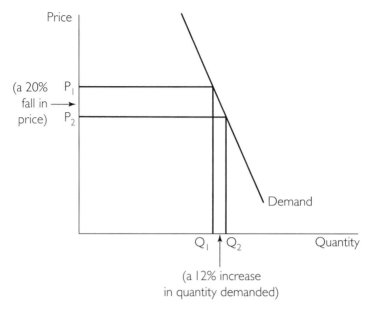

A 20% fall in price leads to a 12% increase in quantity demanded.

The change shown in the diagram indicates price elasticity of demand equal to 0.6, i.e. moderately inelastic demand.

There are two main reasons for inelastic demand.

- The product has few, if any, substitutes. When the price rises, people carry on buying the product because they cannot find a satisfactory substitute and they do not feel they can do without it. This would apply to bread, workclothes, and rail travel for commuters, as well as many other products.
- The product takes a small part of total income. This might apply to chocolates.

Where there is inelastic demand, a fall in price will lead to a fall in total revenue. Quantity demanded will not increase very much and therefore the increased quantity sold will be insufficient to offset the decrease in price. In the diagram, the shaded box showing lost revenue due to the price cut is larger than the shaded box showing revenue gained due to increased sales. Revenue gained through increased sales is less than revenue lost through the price cut. (See Figure on page 159).

(See also *price elasticity of demand*.)

inelastic supply: the quantity supplied has a relatively weak response to a change in price. If the price rises by a certain percentage, the quantity supplied will rise by less. Similarly, if the price falls, the resulting percentage fall in quantity supplied will be lower. Inelastic supply is often an important factor in the short run, because producers have not had time to adjust to the price change. (See also *supply elasticity*.)

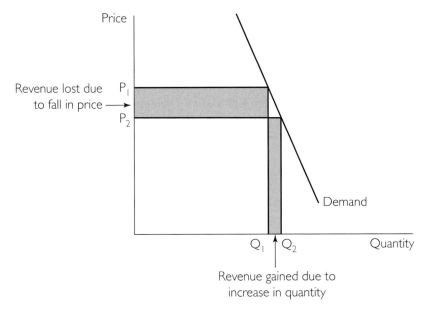

Inelastic demand means that a price cut involves falling sales revenue.

(See pages 157–158.)

inequality: a situation in which there are large differences in incomes and wealth within a society. Most developed countries in Europe have a lower level of inequality than the USA does. Inequality has tended to increase everywhere in recent years. Inequality can be reduced by *progressive taxes* and social security benefits. (See also *equity.*)

infant industries: very new firms, starting up in an industry which previously did not exist in that country, may take some time to become competitive. They will not at first be able to reap the *economies of scale* which are a feature of production in countries where the industry is well established. If they are to survive they will need to be protected from competition from imports, by means of *tariffs* or other *import controls*. This argument is most often used in relation to new industries in *developing countries*. However, there are drawbacks to using import controls to protect domestic industries. There may be considerable difficulty in deciding when the industry no longer needs protection; in the meantime consumers will be paying more for the product than they would for imports. The cost of protection to consumers may be very high.

inferior good: a product with negative *income elasticity of demand*. This means that a rise in incomes will lead to a fall in the quantity sold. Consumers will choose to buy less of the inferior good and more of normal goods, which they are now better able to afford. As incomes rose, people opted less and less to take holidays in UK seaside resorts (the inferior good) and went instead to Spain or other sunny countries. Producers of inferior goods may do well during *recessions*, when incomes are falling. Could holidays in Spain become an inferior good in the future?

inflation is an increase in prices generally. Money loses some of its value because its purchasing power falls. If the process accelerates to very high levels, there is said to be *hyperinflation*.

The causes of inflation are complex. Until the 20th century, inflation was very infrequent and the price level was as likely to fall as to rise. Until the late 1960s, inflation remained at a relatively low level in most developed countries, most of the time. Then it became much more volatile.

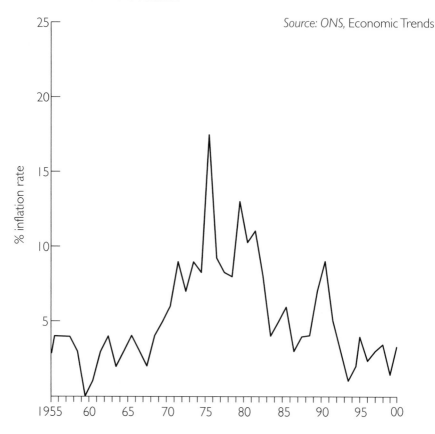

Source: ONS, Economic Trends

The precipitating cause of accelerating inflation is *excess demand* in the economy as a whole. This occurs when *aggregate demand* is growing faster than the capacity of the economy to supply. At first there will be evidence of skill shortages and it will become clear that sellers can raise prices and still sell the goods. Firms will raise wages to attract the scarce skills they need to increase output. Trade unions will find it easier to negotiate pay rises.

Once inflation is accelerating it will tend to continue because of people's *expectations*. All employees will try to protect their real earnings by negotiating an increase equal to what they expect inflation to be. (See also *inflationary expectations* and *inflationary spiral.*)

The *monetarist* view of inflation holds that it is caused by excessive increases in the money supply. As bank lending increases, borrowers are able to increase spending, leading to the excess demand already described.

Inflation has numerous consequences:

- Borrowers gain. So for firms and households which have borrowed substantially, inflation makes the debt smaller in real terms. Incomes and sales revenue rise in line with inflation, while debt repayments stay the same, becoming more affordable. At various times during the past 30 years, home owners typically made large capital gains as the value of their homes rose while the scale of their debt fell.
- Creditors and savers lose. When the money they have lent is paid back, it will have lost some of its value. The purchasing power of money held in the bank will be reduced. There may or may not be a large enough rise in interest rates to compensate for this.
- Inflation increases uncertainty. While a stable rate of inflation may appear predictable, in practice, the higher the rate of inflation, the more volatile it has proved to be. This makes planning difficult for firms and individuals.

Contractionary policies may be used to control inflation. Strict control of the growth of the money supply reduces aggregate demand and pressures in the labour market. In time, people's expectations of inflation will fall and they will accept lower pay increases. However, this process in the early 1980s and 1990s proved to be slow and to entail a considerable rise in unemployment. *Incomes policies* were favoured in the 1960s and 1970s.

Inflation is currently subdued and some have even suggested that it may be dead. It is too soon to be sure about this. There may still be inflationary pressures ready to build up in the economy if *skill shortages* become persistent. Exchange rate changes or commodity price rises could have an impact. The *Monetary Policy Committee* of the Bank of England comments on this regularly.

inflation targeting: during the 1980s, counter-inflation policy targeted first the *money supply* and later the exchange rate. Both of these have considerable impact on the inflation rate. However, during the 1990s, the UK and a number of other countries began to target inflation directly. In 1995 the target for the underlying rate of inflation was set at 2.5%. When the Monetary Policy Committee was set up in 1997 this target was retained and the committee was instructed to adjust interest rates so as to keep inflation close to the target. In fact, because there is a long time lag between a change in interest rates and a change in the rate of inflation, the MPC examines detailed forecasts for inflation.

If the inflation rate deviates by more than 1% from the target, the MPC must write an open letter explaining the deviation and setting out its strategy for bringing the rate back under control.

inflationary expectations are the views which people may hold as to whether and by how much prices will rise in the future. Usually, people expect the rate of inflation to be similar the next year to what it was in the past year. So they will seek to obtain a pay increase which will maintain or improve their real incomes, i.e. keep pace with inflation. If inflation is accelerating this can be a real problem. As it rises, employees and trade unions will be increasing their demands for higher pay. This will in turn raise costs and prices. In order to get the rate of inflation down again, some way must be found to convince people that it will be brought down and that they should adjust their expectations. This is very hard to do. In the past accelerating inflation has been brought under control by large interest rate increases which led to painful recessions. The resulting unemployment caused people to adjust their expectations over a period of years.

inflationary gap occurs when *aggregate demand* is greater than aggregate supply and the economy is already producing its *full-capacity output.*

inflationary spiral describes the way price increases lead to demands for increased pay, which in turn raise costs, leading to further price increases. A period of buoyant demand in the economy can cause excess demand and rising prices. These create inflationary expectations with wage demands aimed at protecting the value of real incomes. Pay increases feed through into further price increases. (See also *wage–price spiral.*)

informal economy: that part of economic activity which is not recorded in official statistics. This includes all kinds of voluntary and domestic work and work done for cash payments which are not declared for tax purposes. Some of this is legal but some consists of tax evasion or leads to fraudulent benefit claims. The amount of income which is not declared is difficult to determine and estimates vary within the range of 5–10% of GDP. The value of voluntary work is impossible to quantify.

information failure can lead to a type of *market failure.* The *allocation of resources* may be less than optimal because people lack full information. Consumers may simply choose a selection of goods and services which omits items which would make them better off and includes items which make them worse off, because there are some things that they do not know about these products. For example, they may choose to curtail their education, not realising by how much it might increase future income. Or they may go on smoking because they underestimate the health effects. The allocation of resources can be improved if education is provided free as a *merit good* and if tobacco is taxed as a *demerit good.*

information provision: where *information failure* is responsible for *market failure,* governments can require sellers to improve the information given to buyers. For example, consumer protection law contains all kinds of provisions to ensure that labelling is accurate and not misleading. In some cases, the information which the consumer needs is very complex and it may be necessary to get advice, e.g. about mortgages and insurance policies.

infrastructure includes all the transport and communications links and the basic services which are used by firms and households. Gas, electricity, telephones, water and drainage are included along with roads, rail and air links. Lack of an efficient infrastructure raises costs for firms, as well as creating inconvenience. So the provision of infrastructure is an essential element in *international competitiveness.*

Infrastructure requires a great deal of *capital* investment both for construction and maintenance and for improvements, so it is hard for poorer *developing countries* to make progress in providing it. This puts local producers at an automatic disadvantage.

Most of the infrastructure is provided by regulated utility companies. Some items, e.g. roads, are provided directly by government.

inheritance tax is currently levied on estates of more than £231 000 at a rate of 40%. It thus works to create a more equal distribution of wealth.

injections are spending flows which add to the circular flow of money. They include investment, government expenditure and exports. When injections increase, there will be an increase in aggregate demand, which will have a *multiplier* effect on the economy. They are balanced by withdrawals (also called leakages) from the circular flow, namely saving, taxes and imports.

Inland Revenue: the government department responsible for collecting income taxes and capital gains tax.

innovation means the development of a new idea so that it can be made into a new product or a new technique.

- Product innovation means a new product. It may be based on a new design or on new technologies or maybe just a new idea. Micro scooters provide an example. This is not exactly a new product – scooters have been made for children for generations. But new materials and technologies have transformed the scooter, making it lighter, faster and easy to fold up and carry. As such, consumer enthusiasm for it has been greatly increased.
- Process innovation means a new way of producing. Sometimes it involves the invention of new kinds of machinery which produce in a different way. Other kinds of process innovation might just involve a different way of doing things, different management strategies, new job descriptions or better ways of sharing responsibilities. Process innovation can lead to big cost savings and often to lower product prices. It is a major source of *competitive advantage* for individual firms.

Both product and process innovation play a major part in improving standards of living. The telephone is not a new product but today's instrument is very much cheaper and more efficient than its predecessors. Process innovation is of crucial importance in leading to the growth of *productivity* and ultimately to long-term *economic growth*.

inorganic growth can help a firm to grow larger by merging with or taking over other companies. The objective is to expand without having to undertake complex and costly investment projects.

inputs include anything used in the production process: land, labour and capital, raw materials, components, energy; the list could be extended.

insider dealing or trading: using inside information to make a profit. People often have information which they acquire at work which makes it possible for them to make profits for themselves. If you know that your employer is about to make a take over bid for a company and that the shares are currently priced somewhat below the bid value, you could rush out and buy the shares and sell them later at a handsome profit. This is illegal, because effectively, you would be defrauding the original shareholder, who would get a relatively poor price for the shares.

insolvency occurs when a firm is unable to pay its debts. In technical terms, its liabilities are greater than its assets. In practical terms, it cannot raise enough cash to pay the bills as they come in. This will usually follow a period when losses have been made. It is illegal to continue trading once it becomes clear that the firm is insolvent. Under the insolvency laws, an official *receiver* may then be appointed. This person may be able to reorganise the business. If there is no way to save it, it may go into *liquidation*.

institutional investors are the pension funds, insurance companies and unit trust groups which invest their capital in shares. Because of the huge scale of their investments, they have enormous influence, far exceeding that of all the small individual shareholders put together. It is sometimes thought that they encourage firms to pursue short-term profit at the expense of long-term investment.

insurance is the principle by which risks are shared between all those who wish to protect themselves from unforeseen eventualities. To insure against a risk, a premium is paid. The insurance company then pays compensation if the risky event happens. The premiums paid provide the necessary funds for compensation, together with an amount which covers the insurance companies' administrative costs.

insurance companies provide different types of insurance cover. Their accumulated premiums are invested in a range of assets. This makes them very important as *institutional investors* on the Stock Exchange.

intangible assets: those assets of a business which cannot be seen or touched. They include brands, patents, established markets (goodwill) and copyright items. These can be given a market value, e.g. when a takeover is contemplated and the price of the share offer clearly includes some allowance for these assets. However, their value is often uncertain.

integrated transport policy: a policy which would develop a variety of transport facilities to meet the overall needs of the public to get from one place to another. Instead of responding to rising demand for roads, rail travel and so on in a piecemeal fashion, the government would produce an integrated plan which meshed developments so that provision could be made for pedestrians, cyclists, drivers, passengers and rail and air travellers, with fewer negative *externalities* developing than at present. Progress to date is disappointing because an effective integrated policy is likely to require some measures which will annoy motorists.

integration is a term used in two ways. It may refer to the bringing together of two or more companies, either by takeover or merger. (See also *vertical integration, horizontal integration* and *conglomerate* mergers.)

Alternatively it may refer to the way in which the economies of different nation states become *interdependent*. For example, the EU is a powerful force for integration within Europe.

intellectual property: ideas which have originated from an individual or firm. They can be protected by a patent if they involve a product or by copyright if they involve books, articles or music. Trademarks and logos can also be protected by law. The patented idea cannot be used without the permission of the owner of the patent. Anything which is original and has copyright cannot be copied without permission. Some of the hottest intellectual property issues currently concern the illegal copying of copyright musical items. Often, intellectual property rights can only be protected by legal action which may be difficult and expensive.

Intellectual property may give its owner some degree of *market power*. However, the protection given by the law is essential to preserving the incentive to innovate and produce new ideas. Few authors would bother to write if their work could not be protected by copyright. No drug companies would research new drugs if they could not be patented.

Inter-American Development Bank: provides development finance to Latin American and Caribbean countries. It provides funds at both commercial and concessional rates of interest.

inter-bank market is the mechanism by which banks lend to each other on a very short-term basis to cover temporary deficits in their payments to each other.

interdependence refers to the way in which the economies of nation states have become increasingly reliant on one another in recent years, through the growth of trade and capital movements. This integration means that they are more vulnerable to adverse events in the economies of their trading partners but they are also more likely to gain from positive trends. For example, if the US economy grows more slowly, many countries fear that they may experience falling demand because the US is an important market for their exports.

interdependence between firms describes the way businesses in an *oligopoly* will each take decisions in the light of the behaviour, or the expected reactions, of the other firms in the industry. For example, if one firm cuts prices, others may follow suit because if they do not, they will lose market share.

interest is the return on *capital* which has been lent. The terms of a loan will usually specify a fixed percentage rate or they may provide for the rate to rise and fall with interest rates generally. Interest rations the amount of financial capital available amongst potential borrowers, in rather the same way as prices ration the goods and services available among competing buyers. Similarly, interest provides savers with the incentive to make their funds available to others. If they lend it (or deposit it in a bank which will lend it) they will be rewarded with interest payments.

interest rates define the amount which has to be paid in exchange for borrowing money. They will vary according to the riskiness of the loan. So, the highest interest rates are charged on unpaid balances on a credit card or on hire purchase loans. Bank loans are cheaper but the rate will depend on the bank's assessment of the risk involved. Mortgage rates are lower still, because the property can be repossessed in the event of default. Lowest of all are the rates charged by the Bank of England to the banks.

Lenders who are prepared to take some risks will get a higher rate of interest in return for the use of their funds than they would if they wanted to minimise the risk.

Interest rates are a key feature in many consumption and production decisions.

- If borrowing is for consumption, it is important to look at the total cost: the price plus the interest payable.
- A person who has funds but does not want to lend them will find that there is an *opportunity cost* – the interest which could have been earned.
- A firm which invests its *retained profits* in the business must be careful. The return on the investment should be at least equal to the interest rate which it could have got on this money if it had been placed in a bank account. This is the opportunity cost of the capital invested.
- A firm which borrows to invest must be sure that the returns on the investment will be greater than the interest payable on the loan.

Interest rates are the main feature of *monetary policy*. The Bank of England, in common with many other central banks, does not have any easy way of controlling the supply of money, i.e. the amount banks are prepared to lend. But through its control of interest rates, it can influence the demand for money, that is, the amount businesses and individuals want to borrow. This has a significant effect on the level of *aggregate demand*.

intermediate goods are inputs to the production process which have already undergone some processing or are manufactured. They include all kinds of components such as car exhaust pipes and partly processed materials such as the bulk chemicals used to make plastic products.

intermediate technology can be used in situations where high-technology methods of production are not appropriate. For example, in developing countries where wages are low it is often not cost effective to use capital-intensive approaches. In addition, such an approach may worsen poverty by creating job losses. Intermediate technology uses imaginative ways of making people more productive but does not require expensive imported equipment. A wheelbarrow may be an improvement, for moving soil, on the traditional Indian method of a basket carried on the head. It does not reduce employment in the way that a JCB might.

internal costs are the costs that appear in the firm's accounts. In contrast, *external costs* are the ones which are paid for by third parties. So internal costs cover labour and capital costs and the cost of inputs. The external costs arise from any pollution or congestion caused by the production process and any other costs to the community.

internal economies of scale: the many factors which cause costs to fall as output rises. They originate within the individual firm.

- Technical economies arise when it is possible to use larger, more efficient machinery. Because new machines will be expensive, it must be possible to spread these high fixed costs across a large quantity of output. Also, large producers will encounter fewer *indivisibilities* as they combine equipment of varying scales into a single sequence of processes. Where storage is required, large containers work out cheaper than small ones: these are called economies of increased dimensions. (This arises because volume increases by more than the cost of the container's surface area.) Further technical economies may be possible if large organisations rationalise production facilities, concentrating different items in the product range at specific sites. The car industry does this, each plant specialising in one or two models which will then be shipped all over the EU. Lastly, technical economies can accrue to large firms which can afford *research and development* departments. The cost of these can be spread thinly across the large quantity of output.
- Managerial economies arise when growing firms can hire specialists, working to find and train exactly the right person for a narrow specialist role. Smaller firms need people who are versatile rather than specialists. A deeper *division of labour* is possible in larger firms.
- Financial economies mean that the larger firm can access funds for *investment* more easily and often at a lower rate of interest. Public companies can raise share capital from the public at large.

- Commercial economies are possible if the firm can benefit from bulk buying of inputs and bulk transport of the output. In this category there are also marketing economies. Big firms can afford national advertising campaigns, using the most effective medium for the product in question. The high fixed costs will again be spread thinly.

(See also *economies of scale.*)

internal finance: using funds for investment which have come from the firm's own activities. The main source of funds will be *retained profit.* This is sometimes called corporate saving. The funds may be accumulated over several years while expansion is being planned, then perhaps combined with *external finance* when the plan is carried out.

internal growth occurs when a firm expands its own output. The alternative approach, *external growth,* would involve taking over or merging with other firms. This is sometimes called *organic growth* and depends on the firm's ability to capture a larger share of the market.

internal trade: trade within the economy, as opposed to international trade. These two are similar in that there are buyers and sellers, transport costs and a process of *specialisation.* However, with internal trade all producers are competing under similar conditions. The legal system is well known to all, all use the same currency and all face the same situation as to *interest rates,* tax rates and the state of the macro-economy. With international trade there are exchange rate risks and transaction costs, the trade cycle in the other country may be different and so on. This is an interesting distinction because the EU is gradually becoming more like a single market and within the euro zone, it could be argued that all trade is internal.

internalising externalities means finding a way to turn an *external cost* into an internal cost. For example, if a firm has been emitting harmful products through chimneys into the air, it can be required by law to clean up its emissions. It will have to install new equipment capable of doing this job and this will add to its costs of production – its internal costs. Meanwhile the people who suffered from the air pollution will no longer be experiencing the external cost. This is an example of the operation of the *'polluter pays' principle.*

International Bank for Reconstruction and Development (IBRD) is the proper name of what is usually known as the World Bank. It was set up in 1947 along with the *International Monetary Fund.* Initially it was designed to provide finance for the post-war reconstruction of Europe and Japan. Quite quickly its primary focus shifted to the *developing countries.* It borrows funds on Western capital markets and lends them to developing countries for projects of many kinds including infrastructure, agriculture, industry, education and health. It charges commercial interest rates, but lends for purposes and in countries which banks might usually find too risky. Loans are often conditional on the adoption of particular policies, which may be unpopular. However, this does mean that governments can shift the blame for necessary but unpalatable policies onto the World Bank.

Some of the World Bank's projects have been controversial. Although now anxious to promote environmentally sound policies, it has not always been so. Through its 'soft loan' arm, the *International Development Agency,* it lends to the poorest countries at concessional rates of interest. It also undertakes extensive research and advises developing country governments on economic policy.

international capital flows are large sums of money which are moved from one economy to another. There are two possible motives:

- Firms and individuals may be moving large bank deposits from one financial centre to another in order to take advantage of higher interest rates or to buy shares which have attractive profit prospects. (This is sometimes called *hot money*.)

- Firms may be investing directly in new productive capacities in other countries. Many firms prefer to locate production overseas, close to the market. Alternatively, they may want to locate production in a country with lower labour costs, from which they will then import.

All international capital flows are liable to lead to exchange rate changes. A capital outflow increases the supply of the currency in question and encourages exchange rate depreciation. A capital inflow will have the opposite effect. (See *exchange rate determination.*)

international competitiveness depends on a wide range of factors and determines how successful a firm is in selling exports and competing with imports. Price may be an important consideration for some products. Prices relative to those of the overseas competition will be affected by differing cost structures and by exchange rate changes. If the exchange rate depreciates, export prices can be cut.

Other important factors include design, quality, reliability and after-sales service – all the component aspects of *competitive advantage*. For some producers an important question concerns how effectively they have tailored the product to the needs of the market in question.

For some countries competitiveness is based on low labour costs. But countries with very high labour costs continue to compete well by relying on design and quality advantages as well as technical expertise.

Some multinational firms locate the labour-intensive parts of the production process in countries where labour is cheap (e.g. component assembly can be carried out in the Far East) while the capital-intensive stages of production stay in the country where they are based.

International Development Agency (IDA) is part of the *International Bank for Reconstruction and Development* (World Bank), undertaking lending on concessional terms. Interest rates may be lower on these loans and they may be waived altogether for a period of time. These loans are available only to the poorest developing countries and some of the projects supported are not strictly commercial, although they may have an important role in the development process.

International Finance Corporation (IFC): an international investment bank which is part of the World Bank Group. It was set up to lend to private sector organisations in developing countries. The World Bank itself lends only to projects organised by governments or with government backing. (See also *International Bank for Reconstruction and Development.*)

International Labour Organisation (ILO): a member organisation of the United Nations, the ILO exists to help improve working conditions throughout the world. It maintains relationships with trade unions as well as governments and seeks to promote social justice in the workplace.

International Monetary Fund (IMF) was set up at the Bretton Woods conference in 1944 and was designed to co-ordinate the international monetary system. Until 1972, it oversaw the system of fixed exchange rates which was in operation. Its objectives were to ensure the stability of the system and provide adequate finance to support the growth of world trade. Stability can itself promote trade, because it reduces uncertainty and makes forward planning easier and less risky.

Member countries contribute funds in proportion to the size of their economies. If they have problems with a persistent balance of trade deficit, they may negotiate a loan from the IMF. This will help to finance the deficit in the short term and allow time for economic policies to produce a long-term solution. Usually the IMF sends a team of inspectors to the borrower country; they advise on the conditions upon which the loan is provided. These conditions are likely to include cuts in public expenditure and control of monetary growth. The availability of loans helps to ensure that exchange rate changes are not excessively destabilising.

Since 1972, most exchange rates have floated. The IMF has continued to act as co-ordinator of the international monetary system, ensuring that the growth of liquidity was sufficient to finance world trade. Its role as a source of loans has increasingly been confined to developing countries. It continues to provide surveillance of all member economies, acting as a source of information and advice. It has had an important role in organising the developed countries' response to the *Debt Problem*.

During the *Asian financial crisis*, the IMF had a strong role in helping with funds and policy advice. However, its advice was widely criticised. In particular, the advice given to Indonesia to cut government spending and accept much higher import prices led to widespread political unrest which was anything but stabilising in its impact.

international trade means importing and exporting. Through *specialisation*, countries are able to increase both consumer choice and the total quantity of output overall. The theory of *comparative advantage* shows how trade is associated with increased output.

In the long run, there is a very clear link between international trade and *economic growth* (see bar chart on page 170). Being able to buy a cheap imported substitute for a dearer domestic product can increase many people's purchasing power, giving them higher real incomes. However, in the short run, some people may lose out as growing international competition forces the less competitive firms out of business and makes their employees redundant. This can lead to *protectionism*, a movement to reduce trade through import controls. (See Figure on page 170.)

interrelationships between markets: many markets have connections, in that changes in one market will have some impact on other markets. Changes in some product markets will have an effect on the labour market – falling demand for seaside holidays in the UK, for example, has left many resorts with high unemployment. Falling demand for butter has been balanced by rising demand for margarine. Similarly rising wage rates affect cost structures and competitiveness in some sectors.

intervention (in foreign currency markets) occurs when a central bank steps in to buy or sell a currency in order to stabilise its exchange rate. (See also *fixed exchange rate*.)

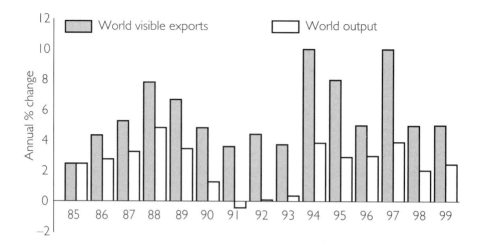

International trade (see page 169). Source: WTO, Annual Report

interventionist: a person who supports action by the government to influence and control market forces. A lively appreciation of the forces lying behind the various types of *market failure* can lead people to support interventions, for example in the form of *employment protection* laws, subsidies to groups which pursue social and community objectives and active involvement in the production process. Interventionists tend to be associated with left-wing political groups. (At the time of writing the Socialist Workers Party is collecting signatures for a petition to renationalise the railways.) Conservative voters would be more likely to support a *laissez faire* viewpoint.

interventionist policies are designed to manipulate or override market forces in such a way that a variety of political objectives can be achieved. Left to themselves, market systems tend to deliver marked inequalities in incomes, fluctuations in incomes over the course of the trade cycle and a variety of *market failures* which lead to long-term problems for society and the environment. The ultimate intervention was the nationalisation of many industries after World War II, so that the government was actually responsible for a considerable amount of production.

Although governments have become significantly less interventionist in recent years, some sectors are still subject to very significant intervention. *Regulation* of utilities, *competition policy*, the *Common Agricultural Policy*, *regional* and *environmental policies* are just a few areas where intervention is very visible. Nowadays, the intervention is often indirect, where it would in the past have been direct, influencing rather than controlling market forces.

When Margaret Thatcher's Conservative government came to power, the new Prime Minister believed that government should stand back from the detailed working of the economy because markets are the most efficient way to allocate resources. Government's role, she argued, is simply to provide an efficient background against which markets can work. The theory on which this is based is called *supply-side economics.*

invention means devising a new product or process. If it really is new, it can be *patented*, giving its owner some rights over its development. Invention is not the same as *innovation*, which means developing the product to the point where it is saleable.

inventory means stock.

inverse relationship: when two variables are related, so that they move in opposite directions, they are said to be inversely related. For example, quantity demanded is usually inversely related to price. As the price rises, consumers will be discouraged from buying the product.

investment means spending now on something that can be expected to generate an income in the future. It is a term which is used rather loosely and in many different contexts.

- Most importantly, investment means spending on capital equipment which can be used to create products which will sell. Investment will increase *productivity* and may cut costs or contribute to improving quality.
- Investment may also be directed towards increasing *human capital*. Improved skills and knowledge bring high rates of return on investment in human capital.
- Just to confuse you, people talk about investing on the *stock market*. If they are simply buying shares from the previous owner, no real investment has taken place although there has been a change of ownership. If they are buying shares which are part of a new share issue, the proceeds of which will be spent on an investment in new productive capacity, then they are financing an investment by the firm from which they bought the shares.
- Investment in *stocks* and work in progress refers to the stocks of inputs and outputs which manufacturers must hold. These are an investment in that they can be sold in the future or at least they can be made into products which will sell.

On the macro-economic level, investment is important because it increases productive capacity and productivity and promotes *economic growth*. Investment spending is an *injection* into the *circular flow of money* and will have an upward *multiplier* effect on income. Most governments want to encourage investment.

investment appraisal: the process of deciding whether a proposed investment will actually be worthwhile. For big projects, there are various ways of estimating the future income stream which can be expected. This must be compared with the *interest* payments which will be needed where loan finance is involved. Even where *internal finance* is being used care is needed to see that the returns are at least equal to the *opportunity cost* of the capital invested.

investment income: income derived from profits and dividends or, if the *investment* is in property, rents. It can also include interest on loans and *bonds*.

investment trust: a company which invests its shareholders' funds in a range of different stocks and shares. This means that the shareholders get the benefits in terms of *dividends* and capital gains from the trust's choice of shares. But because they are holding a wide range of shares indirectly, they spread the risks.

invisible balance means the balance between invisible imports and invisible exports. In the UK the invisible balance is usually in surplus and helps to balance a visible deficit.

invisible export: the sale of a service to a customer based overseas. Financial services, insurance, air travel and tourism all generate revenue from invisible exports.

invisible hand: the term used by *Adam Smith* to describe how the market system allocates resources. A decrease in demand for a product will mean that stocks build up as orders fall, so the producers begin to make losses. In time they will cut production and fewer resources will be devoted to the product which has become less popular. The reverse happens when demand increases. There will be a rise in the price so that *profits* will increase. More firms will want to produce for the buoyant market. Resources will be attracted to the industry. In this way the *profit-signalling mechanism* in the marketplace will invisibly secure an allocation of resources which balances supply and demand.

invisible import: services bought from abroad.

invisible trade means imports and exports of services. Invisible trade is recorded in the balance of payments alongside visible trade. The invisible account includes financial services, insurance, tourism, shipping and air travel, interest, profit, dividends and personal transfers. For the UK, the net surplus on invisibles helps to offset frequent visible deficits.

involuntary unemployment includes all those unemployed people who have made determined efforts to find work and will accept what work they are offered. In contrast, voluntary unemployment refers to those who will refuse the work that is available because they do not consider it suitable or sufficiently well paid.

inward investment is *foreign direct investment* which is coming in to the host country from abroad. Many *multinationals* have brought inward investment to the UK, including Nissan, Toyota, Hitachi, Ford, Peugeot and so on.

There has been a big increase in inward investment, which is one element in the process of *globalisation*.

inward-looking trade strategies emphasise self-sufficiency and the development of industries which can compete with imports. There may be a policy of *import substitution*, so that scarce foreign exchange is saved by the development of domestic industries which can provide these goods. It will probably be necessary to protect these *infant industries*, which means that imports will be subject to tariffs and other import controls. In contrast, free trade policies emphasise the benefits of competition.

The resource cost of developing new industries in which the country does not have a *comparative advantage* can be very high. Some Latin American countries tried this approach in the past without great success.

irrigation: the use of extra water sources to supplement rainfall and grow crops which need more water than can be provided by the natural climate. Irrigation increases agricultural *productivity*, especially when used together with appropriate seed strains and fertilisers.

ISA: see *individual savings accounts*.

J

Japanisation: the tendency of western firms to adopt Japanese management strategies. These include emphasis on long-term planning, training and quality issues and *lean production*.

jargon: the language used by specialists to convey ideas. Certain words are given precise meanings which are somewhat different from those commonly understood. Some terms are invented to facilitate the identification of new ideas.

J-curve: the short-term response of the current account of the balance of payments to a sharp fall in the exchange rate. *Depreciation* makes imports dearer and exports cheaper. Other things being equal, exports will rise and imports will fall. However, this takes time and during the process of adjustment, as buyers react gradually to price changes, imports will cost more and exports bring in little more than they did before. So the current account may actually worsen before it gets better.

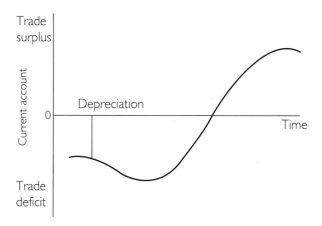

J-curve

JIT: see *just in time*.

job security: the extent to which employees can rely on their jobs continuing. It is generally thought that jobs are less secure than they used to be. The evidence for this is not very strong.

jobseekers' allowance: the benefit paid to someone who is unemployed for the first six months.

joint costs: costs which are shared between two different products which are in *joint supply*. This makes it difficult to decide what the average cost of each product is. For example, diesel and petrol are produced from crude oil; apportioning costs is difficult.

joint demand occurs when two items are consumed together, i.e. are complements. Examples might be shoes and shoe laces or CDs and CD players. An increase in sales of one may lead to an increase in sales of the other.

joint supply occurs when the production of one good also entails the production of another. This often happens in the chemical industry where one chemical may be produced as a by-product of another. Meat and leather provide another example. A fall in the market price of one may affect the quantity supplied of the other.

joint venture: a collaborative project in which two separate firms set up production facilities which will be operated jointly. Each can contribute specialist knowledge or skills. It is often used to help firms set up in business abroad. Joint ventures have proved to be a useful way for developed country businesses to invest in developing countries with which they are not familiar (e.g. China and India).

Jubilee 2000: the movement to persuade developed country governments to find ways of reducing the debt owed by the poorest and least developed countries. The objective was to clear all the debts of the world's 22 poorest countries before the end of 2000. In the event, the debt was reduced from $2.9bn to $2.1bn. Jubilee Plus is continuing the campaign. (See also *Debt Problem.*)

junk bond: a fixed interest loan with a high interest rate but also a substantial degree of risk for the lender. Junk bonds were for a time used to finance takeovers in the US. Some of these were not successful.

just in time (JIT): an approach to organising stocks of inputs and output. With very careful planning, it is possible to arrange deliveries in such a way that production can continue with much lower levels of stocks. This saves the cost of financing and storing stocks. Computerised stock control and good relations with supplier companies make this approach easier. Pioneered in Japan, JIT has helped many firms to cut costs. Good industrial relations are essential, to ensure that production is steady and continuous.

K

Kennedy round: the round of trade negotiations held under the *GATT*, 1964-1967. The outcome was a cut in most tariffs on manufactured goods of about one third. This began in earnest the long period of trade liberalisation which encouraged the growth of trade in the last decades of the century.

Keynes, J M (1883–1946): an economist whose influence during his lifetime and after his death was really second to none. In 1919, he wrote the *Economic Consequences of the Peace*, which criticised the terms imposed on Germany after World War I. His warnings turned out to be prophetic. In 1936, Keynes published his General Theory of Employment, Interest and Money. This work grew out of his deep concern about the unemployment and the poverty brought about by the Great Depression.

Keynes' best known work was built on his finding that a low level of *aggregate demand* did not necessarily correct itself and could persist for some time. This was in contrast to the classical view, which was that wages would fall during a depression until employers again began to take on labour. In this way unemployment would diminish on its own. To deal with the problem of *demand deficiency*, Keynes advocated deficit spending by the government. Expansionary *fiscal* and *monetary policies* could be used to increase aggregate demand. These ideas were influential all over the world, in particular during the period 1945-1970. (See also *Keynesian*.)

Keynes combined teaching and writing as an academic economist with advising the Treasury on the practicalities of economic management, over a very long period. But perhaps his most important contribution was in the thinking and negotiation which underpinned the creation of the international organisations that were set up after World War II (the World Bank and the IMF). He was instrumental in the setting up of the *International Monetary Fund* just before his death. His approach to economic policy has had a lasting impact and is still visible from time to time in the policy pronouncements of politicians. His work on unemployment in the 1930s reflected a profound concern for the welfare of the unemployed. At the same time he was a strong advocate of prudent management of the monetary system.

Keynesian: people and ideas associated with the work of *J M Keynes*. After his death, many economists developed Keynes' ideas, seeking to apply them to new situations. In the process, they probably drifted some way from Keynes' original intentions. Certainly, the new situations they were analysing were very different from the world Keynes had analysed in the 1930s. The main thrust of Keynesian ideas included:

- a strong commitment to maintaining a level of *aggregate demand* at which unemployment rates would be relatively low
- active use of *fiscal* and *monetary policies* to control the level of aggregate demand. At one stage the process was known as *fine tuning* because it was believed that this approach could be used to promote economic growth and keep unemployment down without encouraging inflation or a balance of payments deficit.

Whereas the classical economists believed that unemployment would lead to falling wage rates, which would in turn increase the quantity of labour demanded by employers, and gradually eliminate unemployment, Keynes showed that a fall in wages might reduce consumption and so cause the economy to settle at an equilibrium level of output well below that of full employment. Hence the need for increased injections to raise aggregate demand. Increased government expenditure could be financed by borrowing until such time as the economy recovered.

For a time, Keynesians were at odds with the group of economists known as *monetarists*, who saw government expenditure as a source of inflationary pressures and emphasised the importance of controlling the growth of the money stock in order to prevent inflation from accelerating. During the early 1990s, the debate came to hinge upon the impact of rising aggregate demand on the labour market. Keeping large numbers of people unemployed can help to reduce inflationary pressures, but it also has serious implications for the welfare of the unemployed themselves. Improved understanding of the inflationary process and of the impact of *supply constraints* has made the debate between Keynesians and monetarists increasingly irrelevant.

kinked demand curve: a theory which is used to analyse firms' behaviour in an *oligopoly* with no *collusion* between firms. It is observed that where there are just a few firms in competition with one another, raising product prices would mean a significant loss of sales because buyers would switch to competing products for which the price had stayed the same. This means that the upper part of the demand (or average revenue) curve would be highly elastic. However, a price cut would have little effect on sales because competing firms would follow suit with price cuts of their own. This would mean that the demand curve in this range would be very inelastic. The outcome of this analysis is a kinked demand curve and a tendency for prices to be quite stable as none of the firms in the industry has much incentive to change prices.

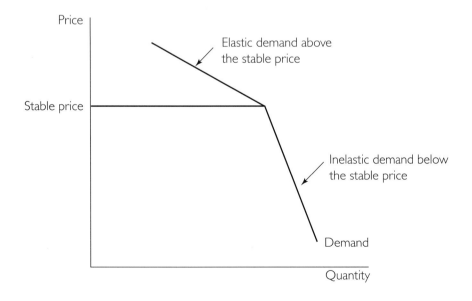

Kondratieff cycle: the idea that there is a very long-term 50–60-year trade cycle, operating alongside the kind of 5–10 year cycle which can be observed over the past few decades. The theory is named after its Russian originator. It is impossible to test the theory properly because comparable records do not go back far enough. The experience of growing prosperity over the past decade has diminished the attention paid to the Kondratieff cycle.

L

labour, demand for: the demand for labour reflects the demand for the product and is thus a *derived demand*. There will be a demand schedule for labour just as there is a demand schedule for the product and the numbers employed will depend partly on the going wage rate. At any given wage, more labour will be demanded if the price of the product rises or if more can be sold.

If labour *productivity* rises, there are a number of possible outcomes. Costs will fall, so prices may be cut, sales may rise and more labour will be demanded. Alternatively, the increased productivity may make it possible to pay higher wages but in that case costs will not fall.

The demand for labour is thus closely related to the product market and changes in the pattern of demand work their way through the labour market into the overall allocation of resources. There is also a close relationship between the demand for labour and the price of capital. If wages rise relative to the price of labour-saving capital equipment, employers will tend to substitute capital for labour and the quantity of labour demanded will fall.

labour flexibility: the extent to which it is possible for employers to use their workforces in a flexible way. This requires that:

- employees are trained for and capable of doing a range of different jobs
- they are willing to do different jobs as required and are not constrained by trade union agreements
- industrial relations in the work place are sufficiently trusting and amicable for flexible working not to be regarded as threatening.

Some employers have high expectations of employees in this respect. However, if it makes it possible to increase *productivity*, it may also be possible to raise wage rates.

labour force: the number of people available for work. This can be influenced by:

- birth rates in the past
- the number of people in education
- the retirement age
- the social security system and the extent to which poverty traps create disincentives
- the availability of child care.

When jobs are being created, as in the UK and the euro zone during 1999 and 2000, discouraged workers and women who were not previously seeking work may rejoin the labour force.

Labour Force Survey: the quarterly government survey of employment and *unemployment*. It uses sample surveys to measure the number of people unemployed and actively seeking work and also the number of people who are not actively seeking a job but would like to work. It is thought to provide a more accurate measure of unemployment than the *claimant count*, which gives us the headline total for unemployment on a monthly basis, derived from the numbers claiming benefits.

labour intensive refers to production processes which use relatively more labour than capital. Typical examples of labour-intensive production include many services, arts and crafts production and some manufacturing processes in situations where labour is cheap relative to capital.

labour market consists of the demand for labour coming from employers and the supply of labour coming from individuals who want to work. The interaction of these groups creates market forces which determine the price of labour or the wage rate. Although we often speak of the labour market as a whole, in practical terms the labour market consists of a large number of separate but linked markets for different kinds of labour. The local authority looking for a competent computer specialist who can look after its networks is in a rather different market from the cleaning agency which makes office-cleaning arrangements for its clients. However, in many instances these smaller markets are interlinked. (See also *wage determination*.)

labour market failure refers to any imperfection in the labour market which impedes the movement of people away from the products with declining demand towards products with growing demand. The most important of these are *occupational* and *geographical immobilities*. Because they have inappropriate skills or live in a place where there is no demand for their services, people made redundant from a declining industry may be unable to find alternative work.

labour market flexibility refers to the ease with which people are able to change jobs or adapt to changed circumstances in other ways. There are a number of examples:

- the trend towards greater labour market flexibility in recent years means that some people now have part-time contracts which allow the employer to vary the number and the timing of the hours worked
- improved education and training generally make individuals more flexible, so that they are relatively easily able to move to an alternative occupation
- any measure which improves *labour mobility* will be likely to increase flexibility. The US labour market is usually thought to be more flexible than the UK labour market. Within the EU, the UK and the Netherlands are thought to have the most flexible labour markets, but all are becoming more flexible.

Lack of flexibility can be due to *employment protection* law which may make it difficult for employers to make people redundant when demand for the product is falling.

labour mobility refers to the ease with which people can change jobs. Occupational mobility reflects the extent to which people can move to a different job. It depends on the ease with which they can be retrained and on their general level of education. Geographical mobility reflects the ease with which people can move from an area with limited employment opportunities to one with more jobs available. This depends on the availability of housing for rent, differentials in the cost of housing between the prosperous area and the area of high unemployment and people's willingness to move.

labour supply curve: the relationship between the quantity of labour supplied and the going wage. Higher wage rates can induce people to work longer hours. The supply of labour can be affected by the *participation rate*, by the structure of social security payments and by the rate of immigration. A growing labour supply has for many countries provided a stimulus to growth. Immigration into the US has always been seen as one of the strengths of the US economy. (See also *backward sloping supply curve of labour.*)

Laffer curve: the relationship between the rate of tax and the revenue derived from it, which makes a curve showing rising revenue as the rate is increased. The tax makes the activity in question less worthwhile so if rates are raised further the revenue falls again. This idea has been used in the past as an argument for cutting tax rates, because high marginal tax rates are sometimes thought to discourage hard work. However, there is no statistical evidence for this supposition, though there is evidence that lower tax rates discourage *tax evasion* and *tax avoidance.*

lagging indicator is an economic variable which changes after the event which caused it to occur. Unemployment is lagged in this way to the *trade cycle,* perhaps by about 12–18 months. Firms are often unwilling to take on more labour at the first signs of recovery; they want to be sure that the improvement will be sustained. Similarly, they wait as long as they can before making people redundant; by the time they do the economy may be well into recession.

lags may occur whenever a change in one variable has an impact on another, but after a lapse of time. It is usual for decision takers to take time to adjust to new circumstances. A change in prices will usually lead to a change in the quantity demanded but only after existing contracts have been completed.

laissez-faire: an approach to government intervention which favours minimal government involvement in the economy. All decisions are taken in direct response to market forces. If *perfect competition* were the rule in all markets, a laissez-faire approach would get the best allocation of resources for all. However, the existence of large numbers of *market imperfections,* distortions and market failures means that nowadays most people think that governments should have competition policies, environmental regulations and some degree of income redistribution.

During the 1960s and 1970s, a good deal of *government intervention* took place. However, since the early 1980s there has been a swing back towards less interventionist policies, associated with Thatcherism in the UK and with the transition to market economies in Eastern Europe and Russia.

land: natural resources. Land can be used for agriculture or buildings. It can be improved, making it more productive, e.g. by drainage. It can be degraded, e.g. by overgrazing or pollution.

landfill waste tax: a tax on the amount of waste dumped in landfill sites. It was introduced in 1996, as a way of internalising an *external cost* to society: the polluter has to pay. It is being gradually increased, to provide bigger incentives to minimise waste.

law of diminishing returns: see *diminishing returns.*

LDC: see *less developed countries.*

lead time: the time that elapses between one event and the next. For example, the lead time between the decision to design a new model of a car and its arrival on the market can be quite long. Japanese producers have developed an advantage because they have been able to shorten lead times, giving a swifter response to changes in market demand.

leading indicator means a variable which foreshadows subsequent events in the economy. The CBI Industrial Trends Survey collects data on business optimism, which can be a useful indicator of pessimism leading to falling demand for investment goods. Share prices similarly can foreshadow falling demand generally.

leakages are savings, taxation and imports, which leak out of the *circular flow of money* and reduce aggregate demand. (See also *withdrawals.*)

lean production: the collection of strategies that have been broadly characterised by the term *Japanisation.* These include *just-in-time* stock control, emphasis on quality control, fast response to market changes and shorter lead times in product development. Usually these measures require a well-trained workforce and good *industrial relations.* For some firms, these approaches have brought substantial cost cuts.

Learning and Skills Councils: the bodies responsible for ensuring that local training opportunities meet local needs. They are composed of representatives of local businesses and work in collaboration with Colleges of Further Education to set up appropriate courses.

lease: a contract giving a buyer the right to use something for a specified length of time. Usually this applies to property, most often to flats or industrial premises. The property reverts to the freeholder when the lease runs out.

leasing: a way of investing in new equipment without having to buy it. It involves a long-term contract to rent the equipment. It requires much less finance because the equipment will not be bought outright. Companies such as easyJet and Virgin have leased aircraft, particularly in the early days of their operation. Earth-moving equipment and vans are often leased.

least developed countries: the 41 countries identified by the UN in 1990 as having the lowest per capita incomes. Many countries in Africa south of the Sahara are included. Together they account for 8% of the world's population but only 0.7% of world GDP. (See also *less developed countries.*)

leisure industries: an important sector in modern economies, which includes cultural activities, sport and entertainment. Generally speaking, the sector has enjoyed strong growth in recent years and is characterised by high *income elasticity of demand.*

lemon: a product which does not work as expected.

lender of last resort: an important function of the Bank of England, which guarantees to lend to banks which find themselves temporarily unable to meet their customers' requests for withdrawals. This does not mean that the Bank will bail out any bank at any time; a bank which has been mismanaged or involved in fraud may still fail or be sold, as in the case of Barings in early 1995. But it does mean that the Bank will try to ensure the stability of the banking system as a whole.

less developed countries (LDC): a general term which covers all those countries which have relatively low levels of GNP, poorly developed *infrastructure* and a large part of their resources engaged in agricultural production. The World Bank defines as low-income countries those which in 1998 had per capita GNP of less than US$785 a year. These are sometimes described as the least developed countries. Middle-income countries are defined as those with between $786 and $9655 per capita income in 1998. Malaysia and Mexico belong to the latter group, a number of which might be described as being well on the way to being developed countries. (See also *developing countries* and *low-income countries*.)

level playing field: a situation in which all firms are competing on the same terms. Conditions which might make the playing field less level would include:

- government subsidies to some firms. This has been a particular problem in the iron and steel industry, where there has been world overcapacity and some governments have helped their domestic producers. The US has taken great exception to some European governments' subsidies
- health and safety requirements which raise firms' costs of production. Hence the harmonisation of employment law across the EU, as part of the *single market* provisions. The single market is in fact an attempt to create a level playing field for all EU firms
- differences in fuel taxes. UK hauliers think that high fuel taxes in the UK put them at a disadvantage when competing with other EU hauliers who face lower fuel taxes.

There are a great many other ways in which playing fields are not level.

Lewis model: a theory of economic development set out in the 1950s by Sir Arthur Lewis. He saw *developing countries* as being characterised by a *dual economy* with a capitalist and a subsistence sector. The capitalist sector may be either privately or publicly owned. The subsistence sector would have abundant labour, such that the capitalist sector could draw on an unlimited supply of people willing to work at the going wage rate. The *marginal product* of labour in the subsistence sector would be zero because of *underemployment*. The capitalist sector, consisting of industry, mines and plantations, could therefore expand without any rise in wages.

In the capitalist sector, profit-maximising decisions mean that a surplus develops and can be reinvested. This will increase the *productivity* of the labour employed and in turn the surplus. The capitalist sector will again reinvest and draw in labour from the subsistence sector, at the same wage as before. The surplus will continue to grow and be reinvested until eventually all the surplus labour in the subsistence sector has been absorbed. At that point wages will start to rise.

This theory was important in the 1960s and 1970s but was widely criticised because in time, the process of development was found to be rather different. Small farmers did in fact invest energetically. Wage rates in the capitalist sector rose long before all the surplus labour in the subsistence sector was absorbed. Nevertheless, you may still be able to observe some of the features of the Lewis model, for example in India and China.

liability: a legal obligation to pay a debt. Liabilities appear in the accounts of banks and companies. They imply the existence of some form of loan or responsibility to cover debts in the future. (See also *limited liability*.)

liberalisation: movement towards a *free market* system. This means that market forces will become more important in determining the way decisions are taken. This can be important within the economy and also in international trade.

- In the domestic economy it is accomplished by allowing prices and quantities to be determined by *market forces*. The role of the government in production is reduced, e.g. by privatisation. Controls of any kind are avoided. Competition is encouraged. Perhaps the least liberalised market in the UK is that for agricultural products covered by the CAP. Guaranteed minimum prices mean that the impact of market forces is greatly reduced by EU action.

- Internationally, liberalisation means eliminating or reducing the impact of tariffs and non-tariff barriers. This brings us closer to free trade, in which decisions to buy and sell are based entirely on market prices. The World Trade Organisation encourages liberalisation by organising worldwide negotiations to reduce import controls.

licensing: firms which have a patent or copyright may license other firms to use their intellectual property in exchange for a royalty payment. This is a good way to increase the returns on their investment without having to set up extensive production facilities in other countries.

life expectancy: the number of years that a person can expect to live. This is usually calculated for each country. It may be calculated as life expectancy at birth or at any later age. There have been big increases in life expectancy in a number of developing countries.

limited company: a firm that has limited liability. This means that the owners of the firm cannot be made to use their personal wealth to pay the debts of the business. This is important because without limited liability, many people who want to set up in business would be deterred by the risk to their families of losing all that they have. It is in society's interests to encourage entrepreneurship which creates incomes and jobs.

limited liability means that the owners of the company, i.e. the shareholders, can lose only the amount of money they put into the business if it becomes insolvent. They cannot be asked to pay the company's debts out of their personal resources. This limits the risks which people are taking when they invest in setting up a business or buy shares. (See also *private limited company* and *public limited company*.)

liquid assets are either money or something that can very quickly be sold for money at a price which involves little or no loss. In the case of a bank, liquid assets would include cash and any kind of very short-term loan.

liquid reserves: holdings of cash or liquid assets which can be kept in reserve and used to pay bills as they become due.

liquidation means that the firm has closed down, usually because it is *insolvent* and cannot pay its debts. Its assets will be sold for what they are worth. This may follow a court case brought about by a creditor asking for compulsory liquidation in an attempt to get debts paid. The court will then appoint a *receiver* who will sell either the firm or its assets in order to raise the necessary cash. Voluntary liquidation is possible if the owner of the business simply wants to cease trading.

liquidity: the extent to which a firm or an individual has an adequate supply of cash or of assets which can easily be sold and turned into cash. Assets which can only be sold at a loss or after time spent searching for a buyer are not regarded as being liquid. Firms need enough liquidity to pay their bills when they become due, as indeed do individuals. Insufficient liquidity may be the result of the bank being unwilling to lend any more.

liquidity preference: within the *Keynesian* theoretical framework, liquidity preference describes the demand for money. There are three elements:

- transactions demand for money arises from the need to pay for regular
  purchases
- precautionary demand leads people to hold money balances in order to be
  prepared for unexpected expenses
- speculative demand for money reflects people's desire to hold money as an
  alternative to other assets. (Money balances of this sort are called idle balances.) When interest rates are low, people will hold more money as there
  is little incentive for them to buy interest-bearing assets such as *bonds*.

These three elements in the demand for money give a downward-sloping demand
curve. Other things being equal, demand for money will increase if interest rates fall
because the opportunity cost of holding it is lower. A rise in incomes will increase
demand for money as people make more purchases. This means that the demand
curve for money will shift to the right.

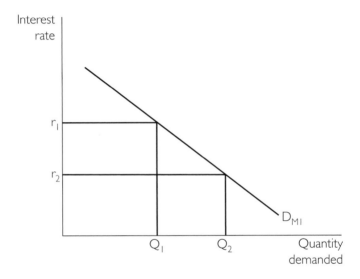

Falling interest rates increased the quantity of money demanded

listed company: a firm which is a *public limited company (PLC)* so that its shares can
be bought on the Stock Exchange. This gives it access to finance from a large body
of potential shareholders, but may make the business less easy to control than if it
were a *private limited company.*

literacy rate: the percentage of the adult population able to read and write.
Increasing literacy rates can be an important element in the process of economic
development. The lifetime returns (in terms of increased pay) to learning to read
and write are high.

living standards: see *standard of living.*

Lloyds: the market for *insurance* in London. Its members provide insurance of all kinds all over the world. The risks are carried by the 'names', wealthy individuals who are prepared to cover potential losses. In normal circumstances, they make excellent rates of return but if losses are made, they may be very large indeed. Insurance contributes significantly to the UK's invisible exports.

loan capital: funds for investment which come from borrowing. In contrast, share capital (also called equity finance) comes from selling shares in the company.

loanable funds theory explains the level of the *interest rate* by analysing its connections with the supply of funds from savings and the demand for funds for investment. Savings arise as people consume less than their total income. They generally deposit their savings in the banks. Investors are looking for finance to cover the cost of new plant and machinery. The interaction of the demand for funds to pay for investment projects and the supply of funds from savings will determine the interest rate – the price of funds in the money and capital markets. Banks act as intermediaries in bringing supply and demand together.

This theory has its roots in *classical economic* theory. Its explanatory power needs to be seen in the context of the modern economy in which interest rates are also much influenced by *monetary policy*.

local content: the percentage of total inputs which has been bought from local suppliers. This can be important when determining the *tariff* which must be paid. If the product were wholly imported then the full tariff would be payable. Sometimes there is a minimum proportion of local content for goods manufactured within the EU which is acceptable for tariff-free entry to other member countries.

local government is responsible in the UK for most school education, social services, local roads, planning and a range of other services. Changes in local government, and the trend towards unitary authorities (single authorities responsible for all locally provided services), may affect the way these services are organised.

local multiplier: when spending in one particular area increases, then a local multiplier effect will be observed. Extra spending will generate employment: if a new bridge is being built, people will be employed to do the building. These people will then spend some of their earnings locally, thus creating further demand and increased employment in the immediate area.

localised industry: where one area has a particular advantage for an industry, that industry will tend to develop there rather than in other locations. In the past the existence of coal often created an industrial area involving steel making and engineering. *Industrial inertia* may mean that these industries have continued to be located in the same place. Other possible local advantages include a supply of appropriately skilled labour with a tradition in the industry concerned.

location of industry: see *industrial location*.

Lomé Conventions of the EU allow many of the ex-colonies of EU states to have preferential access to EU markets. Four separate conventions, the most recent in 1990, have provided a forum for the negotiation of these arrangements with *ACP states*. They compensate to some extent for the loss of the trading arrangements which these countries lost through the development of the EU. They are not especially generous, given that the countries concerned are mostly very poor. India is not included in these trading arrangements.

London International Financial Futures and Options Exchange, known as LIFFE (pronounced 'life') for short, is the financial market where companies can buy currencies or *financial assets* forward. The latter include bonds and other financial assets. *Forward markets* such as this allow people to enter into contracts to buy at a specified price at a date sometime in the future. In this way they can reduce the risks associated with changing exchange rates and interest rates.

long-run: the period of time in which all factors of production can be varied. For example, it is possible to invest in new capital equipment and build new factories. Similarly, some businesses may enter or exit from the marketplace, so changing the size of the industry.

long-run equilibrium under perfect competition: the equilibrium price and quantity produced, which will be at the point where average total costs are at a minimum. Only normal profit can be made. Price will be exactly equal to average total cost. (See also *perfect competition.*)

long-run Phillips curve: the long-run relationship between inflation and unemployment. This idea is usually associated with the *expectations-augmented Phillips curve.* If there is a non-accelerating inflation rate of unemployment, i.e. a level of unemployment at which prices are not pushed up by excess demand (NAIRU), then this will be a vertical line. The level of unemployment given by this line will be that which is associated with *structural unemployment,* which cannot be reduced in the long run by extra spending. The argument is that this is the long-term rate of unemployment whatever the rate of inflation.

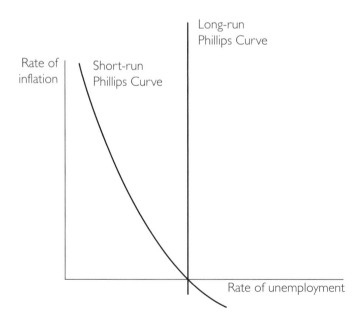

long-run supply curve shows the quantities which will be supplied at a range of different prices in the long-run. Firms can adjust fully to price changes in the long-run. Whereas in the short-run supply may be quite inelastic because there is not time to expand production in the most economical way, in the long-run the supply of some products may be almost perfectly elastic, because firms can simply duplicate efficient facilities for production and expand to meet the demand.

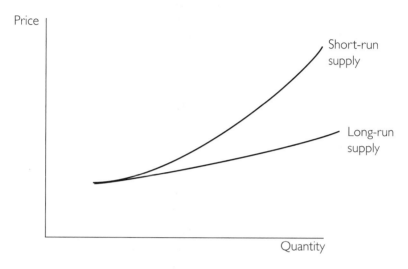

long-run trend rate of growth: the rate of growth of output which can realistically be achieved over a long period. In the UK this is about 2.2% per year. It is a moving average of growth rates over a period of time, typically the 30 years shown in the diagram. It represents the average rate of growth of productive capacity for the whole economy. It is influenced by:

- the level of investment
- improvements in education and training
- increased technical knowledge
- innovation generally.

Improved management techniques can also have some impact. Shocks to the economy such as oil price changes or serious loss of business confidence, which lead to falling aggregate demand and recession on a serious scale, will tend to reduce the long-term trend growth rate. Similarly, accelerating inflation which leads to very tight monetary policies which take a long time to work through the economic system can have the same effect. It follows that *macro-economic stability* can help to raise long-term growth rates. (See Figure on page 188.)

long-term unemployed are people who have been unemployed for more than a year. The number or proportion of long-term unemployed has policy implications:

- they may become discouraged and cease to make active efforts to find work
- they may become deskilled or lose their work habits
- as a result, they may for practical purposes have dropped out of the labour market.

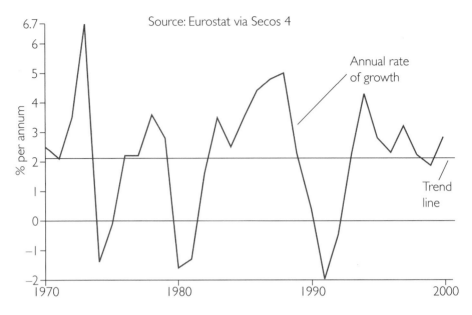

Source: Eurostat via Secos 4

Long-run trend rate of growth (see page 187)

To the extent that these consequences have followed upon long-term unemployment, governments have to consider retraining or policies to reduce *geographical immobility*.

Lorenz curve: a graphical representation showing inequality. In the diagram, the Lorenz curve will run along the 45° line if, for example, the range of percentages of the population are the same as the share of total income which they receive. The more unequal the distribution of income, the more the Lorenz curve will be bowed out below the 45° line. For example, at point A, 20% of the population have 10% of the total income. So the closer the curve is to the 45° line, the greater is the degree of equality and vice versa. Lorenz curves can be used to compare other frequency distributions which are not equal, such as the number of firms and cumulative market shares. The *Gini coefficient* is the area between the Lorenz curve and the 45° line and gives a measure of inequality. (See Figure on page 189.)

loss: the difference between total costs and sales revenue. Loss indicates that demand for the product is declining. The *profit-signalling mechanism* is working in reverse, indicating that resources should be reallocated away from the product in question. It may have gone out of fashion or there may be a competing producer who can create and sell the product at a lower price. The firm in question may cut production or it may exit from the marketplace. It may then switch to a more profitable product or go out of business altogether.

loss leader is something sold at a price below the cost of production. The objective would be to sell other products at a profitable price. Loss leaders are often to be seen in supermarkets, where they may attract customers who then go on to fill up their baskets with goods sold at a profit-maximising price.

low-income countries are classified by the World Bank as those with per capita incomes of US$785 or less per year. 2.4 billion people live in low-income countries, a high proportion of the world's total population of 6 billion. The largest low-income countries are India and Indonesia. Many of the very poorest countries are in Africa south of the Sahara. China has moved into the bottom end of the middle-income group in recent years, but still has huge numbers of poor people living in the countryside rather than the more prosperous cities. For comparison, Portugal is just rich enough to be classified in the high-income group. The Republic of Korea is just below the borderline in the middle-income group. The World Bank ranks per capita incomes across the world.

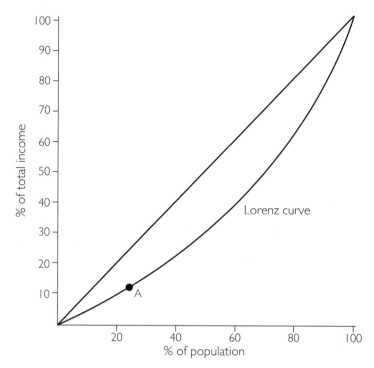

Lorenz curve (see page 188)

Country	Per capita income, US$	Rank, 1999
USA	30 600	8
UK	22 640	22
Portugal	10 660	47
Republic of Korea	8490	51
China	780	140
Ukraine	750	143
Turkmenistan	660	148
Indonesia	580	150
India	450	162
Sierra Leone	150	203

Source: World Bank, World Development Report, 2000

While many African countries suffer from extreme poverty, many countries which are making the transition from central planning to a market economy are also in the low-income category. For many of the poorest countries, war is partly responsible for their plight.

Ltd: see *limited liability*.

M0 is known as *narrow money* and is one measure of the money supply. It consists of:

- notes and coins in circulation with the public and in banks' cash machines (which is actually most of M0)
- banks' balances with the Bank of England, kept mainly for the purpose of settling debts.

Although cash is not a very important component of the money supply in a modern economy (it is currently about 4% of the total), M0 can be a useful indicator at times.

M4: *broad money*, the main measure of the money supply in the UK. It includes all the money which is being kept for spending purposes or as a *store of value*. It includes:

- M0
- all sterling bank deposits in the UK
- all building society deposits.

The rate of growth of M4 is an important indicator for the *Monetary Policy Committee* of the Bank of England when it is deciding interest rate policy.

Maastricht Treaty is named after the city in the Netherlands where it was negotiated in late 1991. Its official name is The Treaty on European Union. It had five significant elements:

- Its main provision was the detailed plan for Economic and Monetary Union (EMU).
- The funds which are used to assist poorer areas of the EU were expanded.
- It initiated the Social Chapter, a separate section of the agreement which created a system of regulations covering employee health and safety, workplace conditions, equal pay and employee participation.
- Provision was made to develop a common foreign and security policy.
- Arrangements were made to co-operate in matters of crime prevention, immigration and policing.

The Treaty came into force in late 1993 but was subsequently much modified by the *Treaty of Amsterdam*, which came into force in 1997.

macro-economic performance: the progress made by the economy as a whole. An initial measure of performance would be the rate of *economic growth*. However, there is really more to performance than this:

- the *long-run trend rate of growth* would show how productive capacity is growing over time
- *inflation* and *unemployment* rates would give a guide as to how stable the economy is
- non-income measures of welfare would provide qualitative evidence, e.g. ownership of consumer durables and access to health care and education
- measures of *income distribution* would show whether all members of society are participating in improved standards of living

- data on the environment would clarify the extent to which *economic growth* is sustainable.

macro-economic policy aims to bring about desirable outcomes by influencing the economy as a whole. The objective might be to raise the rate of economic growth or to make the economy more stable, by making adjustments in the level of *aggregate demand*. This could be done by making changes in:

- *fiscal policy*, using tax changes or government expenditure changes. Reducing taxes and increasing expenditure will increase aggregate demand and tend to stimulate the economy. Provided there are some unemployed resources, output will increase
- *monetary policy*, using interest rate changes to influence levels of spending on investment and consumer goods, will also affect aggregate demand and activity in the economy as a whole
- *exchange rate* policy may also be used because a falling exchange rate may stimulate demand for exports and discourage imports. Alternatively, a rising exchange rate may make imports cheaper and tend to reduce inflationary pressures.

In all macro-economic policy decisions, it is important to consider how close the economy is to *full-capacity output*. *Expansionary policies* used when the economy is close to full-capacity output and there are *supply constraints* will encourage inflation to accelerate. Equally, if *unemployment* is largely structural in nature, expansionary policies will not help. They may defeat the objectives which the government is aiming for. In these circumstances *supply-side policies* may provide a more appropriate strategy. (See also *demand management*.)

macro-economic stabilisation: market economies experience *trade cycles*, in which output fluctuates and unemployment and falling incomes can become a problem. Governments use macro-economic policies to stabilise the economy, attempting to avoid sharp fluctuations. Two types of policy can be identified:

- *automatic stabilisers* may be in operation. As incomes rise, tax revenues rise, reducing the growth of aggregate demand in the upswing of the trade cycle. Similarly, unemployment will be falling and government expenditure on benefits will fall too.
- *discretionary policies* allow governments to make an explicit decision to raise or lower tax rates or government expenditure. During a recession, they may choose to cut taxes and raise spending levels, as the Conservative government did in 1991.

The main difficulty with stabilisation policies is that it is not always easy for governments or central banks to gauge the precise amount of change which will have the desired effect. Statistical errors and time lags in the operation of policies make for uncertainty. Although at the time of writing it is thought that *Alan Greenspan* has once again been skilful in deciding US macro-economic policy, hindsight may tell you a different story. (See also *soft landing*.)

macro-economics relates to the economy as a whole. It is concerned with *aggregate demand* and aggregate supply and with total consumption, investment and expenditure. Aggregate demand is the total of demand from all sources, including consumption, investment, government spending and exports. Aggregate supply means total output for all producers in the economy. Important elements in macro-economics include:

- the *trade cycle* – the fluctuations in output over time which are a feature of most market economies
- *international trade* – the study of imports and exports and exchange rates
- the financial system including banking and the role of money.

The study of the macro-economy leads on to consideration of *macro-economic policy*. As there are areas of macro-economics which are still poorly understood, policy pre-scriptions can be controversial.

Malthus, Thomas (1766-1834): an economist who argued that population would grow faster than the capacity of the economy to provide food. There would be a long-run tendency for standards of living to fall. He was partly responsible for the view of economics as 'the gloomy science'. In fact, new technologies and falling birth rates have in many places improved standards of living hugely for most peo-ple. Parts of Africa south of the Sahara have not yet been able to join in this process, though many might in the fairly near future if peaceful conditions could be established.

managed exchange rate: a floating exchange rate may still be managed to ensure that day-to-day fluctuations are kept to a minimum. The central bank buys when the exchange rate is falling and sells when it is rising, so as to keep the exchange rate from deviating too far from its current market level. (See also *fixed exchange rate*.)

management buyout (MBO) occurs when the managers buy all of the shares in the company. For example, the managers of the Wensleydale Cheese factory in Yorkshire bought it when its then owners, Dairy Crest, were planning to close it down. Not only did they save the factory, they expanded production and set up a tourist attraction with strong links to Wallace and Gromit of Wrong Trousers fame. This was a highly successful MBO in which the new owners had a big incentive to try out new strategies. Other MBOs have been less successful, some based on excessive reliance on borrowed money. Sometimes the MBO is able to operate more efficiently because the original situation involved some *diseconomies of scale*.

managerial economies: see *internal economies of scale*.

manual worker: one who carries out practical tasks, such as might be found on a building site or a factory assembly line. The category is a very large one, including skilled, semiskilled and unskilled employees.

margin: the amount of profit, usually defined precisely as profit as a percentage of sales revenue.

marginal analysis: economic theory analyses decisions taken at the margin. That is to say, people usually decide not whether to do something at all but whether to do a little more or a little less. They may produce, or consume, more or less. Producing a little more will bring in *marginal revenue* and have a *marginal cost*. The profit-max-imising producer will carry on producing up to the point where these two are equal. This is economically efficient because the price a consumer is prepared to pay for that last unit is exactly equal to the real resource cost of producing it.

marginal concept: the idea that a small change in any variable will lead to small changes in other variables. This provides a way of analysing the size and direction of change, and of predicting the impact of change. (See also *marginal analysis.*)

marginal cost: the cost of one more unit of output. In the short run, only *variable costs* will alter, so for example the marginal cost of producing one more bicycle will reflect the extra labour and component costs of increasing output. In the long run, if factories are running at full-capacity, the marginal cost may reflect the *fixed cost* of building a new factory or assembly line. The marginal cost of one more hairdo will be almost entirely labour but if the shop is always fully booked, it may involve opening another shop. Normally, the term marginal cost is used to mean additional variable cost.

The formula for marginal cost can be used to focus attention on the additional cost of one more unit or of a batch of units.

$$\text{FORMULA:} \quad \text{marginal cost} = \frac{\text{change in total cost}}{\text{change in output}}$$

Marginal cost may rise if firms are constantly increasing output with a given amount of capital. They may no longer be using labour and capital in optimum proportions. To get more of the relevant variable factors of production may mean paying more. To increase output, the firm may have to pay its employees at overtime rates, perhaps time-and-a-half pay.

The marginal cost curve always cuts the average cost curve at its lowest point. When MC is less than ATC, the latter will be falling. The additional cost of increasing output is so low that it increases efficiency. Similarly when MC is greater than ATC, it will be dragging it up – average cost will be above the minimum, i.e. the point at which *technical efficiency* is maximised.

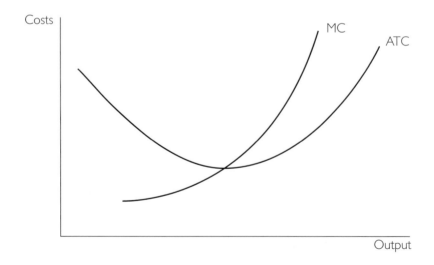

marginal cost pricing: an item may be priced at its marginal cost, thus ensuring that the price is equal to the *opportunity cost* of the resources foregone in producing it. This principle has been used in the pricing of goods produced in the public sector. The drawback is that the price may fail to reflect some of the fixed costs of production and so lead to losses being made.

marginal efficiency of capital or investment: the extra revenue generated by one more unit of capital invested. This will need to be at least equal the interest rate on borrowed funds if the investment is to be seen as worthwhile. From this can be derived the theory of the demand for investment funds, which is a part of the basic *Keynesian model* of the macro-economy. New technologies can increase the marginal efficiency of capital at any interest rate.

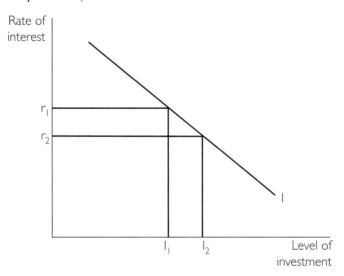

A fall in the rate of interest will lead to a rise in the level of investment

marginal factor cost: the extra cost of the *factors of production* needed to produce one more unit of output. In most cases the marginal factor cost will refer to the labour cost of increasing output.

marginal firm: if prices increase, marginal firms will be drawn in to the industry. For example, an increase in the price which people are prepared to pay for vitamin supplements will give potential producers an incentive to start making vitamin supplements. However, unless they are actually able to do this efficiently in the long run and compete with other firms, they may drop out again quite quickly, especially if the price falls again.

marginal land: some land which is used for particular crops or livestock will be of rather poor quality for the purpose. If the price of the product falls, that land will be withdrawn from production. Similarly, if prices rise, some marginal land will be brought back into production.

marginal physical product (MPP): the number of units of output resulting from a small increase in the input of a factor of production. (See also *marginal product.*)

marginal product: the extra output generated by the input of one more unit of a factor of production. For example, if a firm producing micro-scooters takes on one more employee, the extra output they can produce is the marginal product of the additional labour.

marginal productivity theory gives one explanation of how wages are determined. The theory is that wages will be equal to the value of the marginal product of labour. Profit-maximising employers will hire people up to the point where the cost of doing so (the wage) is just equal to the value of the output added. Although this can be quite helpful in giving an understanding of the forces underlying the demand for labour, it has little practical usefulness in that it is usually rather hard to tell exactly how much output one particular person has added to the total. (See also *marginal revenue product* and *wage determination.*)

marginal propensity to consume (MPC): the proportion of an increase in income which will be spent on consumption. It is important within the Keynesian model of the macro-economy because, along with the *marginal rate of tax* and the *marginal propensity to import* (i.e. the *marginal rate of leakage*), it helps to determine the size of the *multiplier.* The higher the marginal propensity to consume, the larger the multiplier will be.

marginal propensity to import: that proportion of an increase in income which is spent on imports.

marginal propensity to save: that proportion of an increase in income which is saved.

marginal rate of leakage: that proportion of an increase in income which leaks out of the circular flow of money in the form of savings, taxes and imports. The marginal propensity to consume and the marginal rate of leakage together are equal to one by definition. So a high marginal rate of leakage will be associated with a small multiplier.

marginal rate of tax: the proportion of an increase in income which is taken in tax. This may be used as a macro- or a micro-economic concept.

marginal revenue: the extra revenue which comes from selling one more unit of output. In a highly competitive situation this will usually be the price of the product. Where the firm has some monopoly power, it may be less than the price, because selling one more unit of output may entail reducing the price. (See also *profit-maximising output.*)

marginal revenue product (MRP): the extra sales revenue generated by the input of one more unit of a factor of production. This will be equal to the *marginal physical product* multiplied by the price of the product, provided the firm is operating in competitive markets.

FORMULA: MRP = MPP × price

The MRP of labour can be important in determining how many people will be hired.

In the diagram, the MRP slopes downwards to the right because each extra person using the existing quantity of fixed factors will lead to diminishing increases in output. It pays employers to take on more labour up to the point where MRP is exactly equal to the going wage rate. Below this level of output, MRP will be greater than the wage rate and profits could be increased by taking on more people. It follows that the MRP curve is also the employer's demand curve for labour.

The demand for labour is a derived demand, which depends on the demand for the final product. A rise in the price of the final product will increase MRP and cause the MRP curve to shift to the right. At any given wage rate, more labour will be demanded. (See also *wage determination.*)

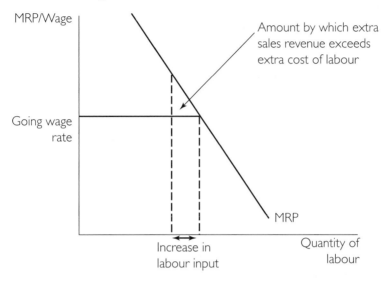

Marginal revenue product

marginal social benefit: includes all the extra benefits which result from an increase in the output of a particular product, whether they are felt by the person who bought the product or by some third party. It thus takes in any *positive externalities.* If people spend money on extra clothes, they benefit from feeling good in them. There is an additional benefit to anyone else who appreciates their appearance. The marginal social benefit of devoting additional land to sheep farming in mountain areas includes the benefit of the meat and wool produced and also the benefit to people who like to see the countryside farmed in the traditional way. See Figure on page 198.

marginal social cost includes all the costs of producing one more unit of output, whether they be the costs of production incurred by the business or the *external costs,* which may be borne by third parties. So the marginal social cost of producing more electricity in coal-fired power stations includes the cost of the coal and other inputs and also the cost to people in the neighbourhood of the increased atmospheric pollution. This may show up in health problems or any other problem caused by pollution.

Marginal social costs and benefits can be compared diagrammatically. If output is below the level Q, the marginal social benefits of extra consumption would outweigh the marginal social costs. From the point of view of society, it would make sense for output to be increased. (See Figure on page 198.)

marginal utility: the extra satisfaction derived from the consumption of one more unit of an item. The concept of utility helps us to understand the nature of demand, but is limited in its practical usefulness because we cannot measure it objectively.

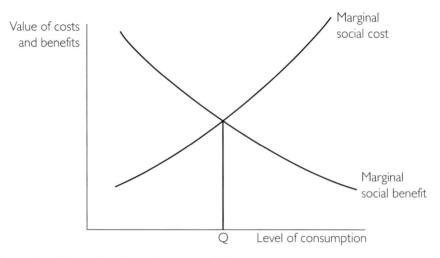

Marginal social benefit and cost (see page 197)

market: all the buyers and all the sellers of a product and the way in which they are able to interact. A market may be located in a particular place or it may merely have a way for buyers and sellers to communicate. The market will allocate resources among competing buyers. The interaction of buyers and sellers will lead to an *equilibrium price* at which *market clearing* will take place. Markets will be created wherever there are people who have a product which potential buyers want. In recent years markets have developed in Internet banking, new kinds of recreational drugs and perhaps also babies for adoption. Some markets are generally left free to operate according to market forces, others are often regulated or controlled by governments. (Try making a list of markets in each category.)

market access: in general, most sellers have access to markets for their products. However, some markets may be closed because of distance, *trade barriers* or inability to compete effectively. Lifting trade barriers can create much larger markets for some producers, e.g. within the EU.

market capitalisation: the value of a firm as measured by the number of shares it has multiplied by their current market price.

market clearing: the process by which price changes until the amount which sellers wish to sell is exactly equal to the amount which buyers demand. If this process does not occur, then there is said to be market failure. The market clears at the equilibrium price, by definition. Situations in which the market does not clear are known as *excess demand* or *excess supply*, depending on the circumstances. (See Figure on page 199.)

market concentration: see *concentration ratio.*

market demand: see *demand* and *demand curve.*

market dominance: the situation in which a single firm dominates the market. This means that it will be a *price leader* and all other producers in the field will tend to adapt their decisions to the behaviour of the dominant firm. This is likely under *oligopoly* conditions, where the dominant firm has a large market share. Competition will be rather limited.

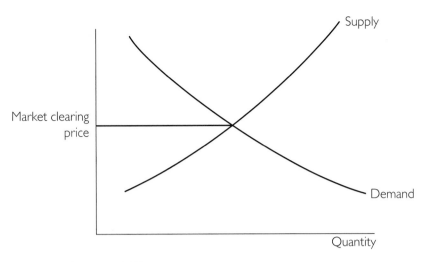

Market clearing (see page 198)
The market clears at the equilibrium price

market economy: an economy in which the majority of decisions about the allocation of resources are taken in response to market forces. The *price mechanism* shows when and where people are prepared to pay more for a product and this creates an incentive for firms to produce and sell more. A market economy will have a number of attractive features.

- The price mechanism will operate in product markets and also in the markets for factors of production. Prices will signal the value of each resource to both buyers and sellers. These prices will be the basis for individual and firm-level decisions.
- The price mechanism will guide resources towards their highest value uses, i.e. those where buyers are prepared to pay the highest price for them. So, for example, the most profitable retailers will offer the highest prices for high street retail outlets.
- Competition ensures that costs are kept down to a minimum and *technical efficiency* is encouraged, with products available at lowest possible prices to consumers.
- High prices will signal the existence of profitable markets. Firms will respond to the incentive and enter the market. The increase in quantity supplied will satisfy consumer demand and eventually prices will drop back to around the minimum average cost (provided the market is competitive). How much do you think the price of micro-scooters has dropped between their initial introduction and the present time?
- Changes in the pattern of consumer demand will lead to changes in the allocation of resources. *Consumer sovereignty* will ultimately determine the allocation of resources and there will be *allocative efficiency*.

The problem with markets is that they do not always work as hoped. They provide no guarantee that everyone will enjoy a reasonable standard of living. Many markets are not competitive. There are all kinds of reasons for *market failure*.

Some leaders have opted for *centrally planned economies*. However, these proved to be disappointing in terms of the extent to which they were able to improve standards of living, as well as in greatly limiting personal freedoms. The current conventional wisdom is that market economies produce the best rate of economic growth and governments can regulate markets to reduce the worst excesses associated with *market failure*.

market equilibrium: the point at which the quantity sellers wish to sell is equal to the quantity buyers wish to buy. The equilibrium price equates supply and demand and brings about market clearing. There is no *excess supply* or *excess demand*.

market failure occurs when market imperfections lead to an allocation of resources which is less efficient than it might be. For example:

- *imperfect competition* can lead to firms not striving to minimise costs and prices
- some goods may not be produced at all unless the government steps in – these are *public goods* such as the legal system
- *merit goods* such as education and health care may be consumed in smaller quantities than would be most effective from society's point of view, if available only through the market
- *externalities* may lead to high *social costs* which affect third parties, who are not producers or consumers of the product
- the market may fail to clear, as is the case where large numbers of people are unemployed.

Government intervention can correct market failures but does not always do so in the most efficient way due to *government failure*.

market forces are the forces of supply and demand in the marketplace. When demand is growing, other things being equal, the price will rise. If supply is rising but demand is constant, prices will tend to be pushed downwards. Market forces lead to price changes which reflect underlying changes in demand and supply. They influence the *allocation of resources* so that production is in line with consumer demand and reflects the real resource cost of production.

market imperfections come in many forms, each of which is a departure from the conditions of *perfect competition*. The main ones are:

- few firms in the market
- differentiated products
- imperfect information
- immobile factors of production.

market leadership refers to the way in which a *dominant firm* may be able to lead the market in setting prices and sometimes by determining the design and quality of the product. This is most likely to happen where there is an *oligopoly*, with one firm which has a particularly *large market share*.

market makers find buyers and sellers for stocks and shares. As it may not be possible to match a buyer with a seller immediately, market makers often have to take the customer's order on to their own books. Hence they are 'making a market' in the shares. Formerly they were known as stockjobbers and were forbidden to deal directly with the public, that function being performed by stockbrokers.

market mechanism is the process by which *market forces* determine prices, which in turn determine the decisions that are made by firms and households. Prices reflect both the strength of consumer demand and the total costs of production. Levels of production reflect the quantity demanded at a price which is sufficient to cover the full costs of production.

The outcome is an *allocation of resources* which is both technically efficient and allocatively efficient. However, this holds true only if the market mechanism is working under conditions of *perfect competition*. Market imperfections will tend to reduce the efficiency of the allocation of resources in practice.

market model: the theory which explains the working of supply and demand in competitive markets. It analyses market forces and their interaction, taking in the resulting consumer decisions and the response of firms.

market niche: a small, specialised market with particular requirements.

market orientation: a tendency on the part of the firm to tailor the product and the way it is sold to the precise needs of the buyer.

market period: the period of time in which the quantity supplied cannot be altered. For example, the quantity of a crop product such as potatoes cannot be altered until the next season. This means that supply is perfectly inelastic, i.e. the quantity is fixed. The length of the market period will vary from product to product. For some manufactured products it will barely exist.

market power: the degree to which a firm has power over its market. This means that to some degree the seller is able to determine the price charged. Market power develops when:

- a seller is able to distinguish what is offered for sale from that which is on offer elsewhere (product differentiation)
- there is little competition from other sellers
- there is a *monopsony* buyer which has more influence in the market than the seller does.

A person with scarce skills which are in strong demand will have some power in the labour market because buyers of those skills are competing to hire the few people who have them.

Marketing strategies can be used to increase market power and reduce the threat from competing products. Market power opens up the possibility of being able to determine the price at which the product sells and is a feature of *oligopoly*, where a small number of firms each have a significant *market share*. The *Competition Commission* exists to reduce market power wherever it threatens to work against the interests of the consumer.

Several sources of market power can be seen in the position of the large supermarket chains. Typically, they have market power in relation to suppliers because they can negotiate very favourable prices. Most of their suppliers will be operating in much more competitive markets, being relatively small-scale producers. They also have some market power in relation to consumers because many of the latter have only limited choices about where they can shop. Market power can develop wherever competing substitutes are hard to find. It will always mean that price elasticity of demand is relatively low.

market price is the price prevailing in the market. The implication is that the price has been determined by market forces, i.e. supply and demand, and is not influenced by government intervention of any kind.

market saturation occurs when almost everyone owns the product in question. It applies to washing machines and other products where normally each consumer wants just one. Once this point has been reached, future demand will be for replacement only. The market will be smaller than it was when new customers were buying.

market share: a firm's percentage share of the total market. Where there are many competitors this will be insignificant. In an *oligopoly* situation, several firms may have a significant percentage. In the UK, a monopoly is defined as a firm with 25% or more of the market. Many firms strive to increase market share because this can increase their *market power*.

market share maximisation: a possible goal for firms, which in some cases may be more important than *profit maximisation*. Economists usually assume that all firms strive to maximise profits and in some cases this is undoubtedly broadly true. However, increased market share can bring many benefits:

- firms may improve their position relative to that of a particular competitor
- they may establish a reputation which is conducive to long-run profitability and survival
- they may increase their *market power*
- managers may relish the personal power and influence that comes with a substantial market share.

market-sharing agreement: an arrangement by which a group of firms agree to avoid competing directly in some markets. Normally this would only happen if there is an oligopoly and there are *barriers to entry* preventing new entrants from coming into the market.

The agreement might take the form of a geographical share-out. Each firm would be able to sell in a particular area without facing strong competition. Or the firms might each sell a limited range of products so that there would not be too many close substitutes.

Market-sharing agreements are defined by the Office of Fair Trading as *restrictive practices* and are illegal under competition law. Only in exceptional circumstances are they tolerated. Cement manufacturers have in the past tried to maintain agreements but have been prosecuted successfully.

market size: the total market, i.e. the maximum possible level of sales if all potential buyers are included. Markets grow when:

- new technologies are making it possible to reduce prices
- tastes are changing in favour of the product
- incomes are rising (if the product has income-elastic demand)
- competing substitutes are becoming more expensive.

market structure refers to the number of competing firms in the market. There may be:

- *perfect competition* or something resembling it in many respects, as with many farm products
- *monopolistic competition*, for example hairdressers
- *oligopoly*, as with supermarkets
- *duopoly*, for example most soap products come from one of two suppliers
- *monopoly*, as with water supply.

These are theoretical structures and in practice, a much fuzzier picture emerges. For example, it is possible to argue about whether the computer hardware industry is an oligopoly or whether it really has important elements of monopolistic competition.

market system: the form of market organisation in which the decisions of firms and households are made on the basis of the market forces of supply and demand. A *market economy* will allocate resources largely on this basis, although some government intervention and regulation will also be important and will influence market conditions.

market value is the price which an item might fetch in the open market. In other words, it is what someone is prepared to pay for the item in question. It tells the owner the price at which it might sell. It is important to remember that a resource may have some perceived intrinsic value, especially to its owner, yet have a market value of absolutely nothing. An old easy chair, for example, may still be comfortable to sit in but will not sell at any price because no one else wants it.

marketing: the process by which firms seek to ensure that they actually sell as much output as possible. In a few cases, firms seek out a particular market rather than try to maximise sales. For example, they may concentrate on a market in which they can charge high prices.

Business success often depends upon a close understanding of the market and this can lead to serious efforts actually to provide the types of products most wanted by consumers. However, much marketing effort is actually aimed at exploiting *market imperfections*:

- products may be increasingly differentiated from one another, in order to capture some consumer loyalty
- advertising may become an important part of *product differentiation*
- pricing policies may be designed to drive competitors from the marketplace.

Marshall, A (1842–1924): an economist who worked mainly at Cambridge, laying the foundations of micro-economic theory. He invented the term price elasticity and developed the price theory which students of economics still learn.

Marshall-Lerner condition states that for an exchange rate devaluation to be successful in improving the balance of payments, the sum of the demand elasticities for exports and imports must be greater than one (ignoring the minus sign). Elasticities are important in determining the outcome of a devaluation (or a depreciation). If the demand for exports is price inelastic, the percentage increase in quantity demanded of exports will be lower than the percentage decrease in price. This means that export revenue will fall. If the demand for imports is price inelastic, people will tend to carry on buying them even though the price has risen. The import bill will rise. If the combined elasticities of demand for imports and exports are between 0 and –1, the balance of payments deficit will actually get larger after devaluation/depreciation. If demand is more elastic, the deficit will fall.

Marx, K (1818–1883): the thinker and writer who did most of all to promote the ideal of social equality. He perceived capitalism as one stage in economic development, because it would eventually bring about its own destruction. It would create the conditions in which revolution supported by workers would overthrow capitalism and replace it with the collective ownership of the means of production. Workers would be paid according to their needs rather than their market power and in this way capitalists (owners of capital) would no longer be able to exploit their employees by paying them less than the value of what they produced.

The development of communism in Russia (from 1917) and later in Eastern Europe and China (from 1948) was based on Marx's thinking. In all cases communist revolutions created much more egalitarian societies than those which preceded them. But the system was eventually found wanting because most of the countries involved experienced rather low economic growth rates. This meant that they were unable to reduce poverty as effectively as many capitalist economies had done. When free elections were held in Russia and Eastern Europe in 1989, the communist party attracted relatively few votes and the economies concerned began the transition to the market system. China, Cuba, North Korea and Vietnam still have communist governments but with the exception of North Korea are becoming steadily more market oriented. Watch this space.

Marx was banished from his native Germany in 1849, for his political activities, and settled in London where he did most of his writing in the Reading Room of the British Museum. He died long before his ideas came to fruition.

mass production: manufacture of a standardised product which can be carried out on a large scale, reaping significant *economies of scale*. Typically it might involve an assembly line making a product which can be widely advertised. Henry Ford was the famous initiator of mass production with the Model T car assembly line in Detroit, later set up at Dagenham also.

Computer-controlled manufacturing has made it much easier and cheaper to vary the features of the product and sometimes, to produce only to order. Mass production of standardised products is therefore much less prevalent than it was. *Flexible specialisation* has to some extent taken its place.

massaging statistics: the process of creating intelligible data series. Data is often inconsistent, with changes in the way it is collected and items that are missing altogether. Statisticians use their skills to construct reasonably comparable data series with as few inaccuracies and gaps as possible. Unfortunately, some governments sometimes use this process as an opportunity to make the data give a message of which they approve. This may diverge somewhat from the most truthful approach. For example, during the 1980s the UK government changed the way unemployment data was recorded in order to make unemployment rates look lower than they were. At this time it was necessary to use OECD data to get a more accurate picture. Governments with no democratic foundations and no free press are particularly suspect.

material progress: growth in the standard of living which can be measured by conventional means such as the rate of growth of per capita GDP. Progress which might not be captured by such data might include life expectancy and easy access to education and health care.

mature economies are those which have been fully industrialised for some time and are now experiencing a shift of resources into the service sector. The USA and the UK are examples of economies where the manufacturing sector has tended to shrink while a number of services have shown above-average growth rates. Financial services, tourism, health care and a variety of personal and professional services have all been growing. (See also *deindustrialisation.*)

maturity date: the date on which a *bond* becomes due for repayment.

mean: see *arithmetic mean.*

means-tested benefits are social security payments which are available only to those whose incomes are below a certain level; for example income support.

median: the middle observation in any data series. It is an important measure of the average in data series which have many extreme values. For example, the median income is sometimes more useful than the arithmetic mean income because it is not distorted by very high incomes which drag the mean upwards.

mediation: see *conciliation.*

medium of exchange: a function of money, which allows people to exchange their labour or other factors of production for the goods and services they want to consume. Without money as a medium of exchange, we should be reduced to bartering and straight swaps of one item for another, which would be very inconvenient.

merchant bank: a bank which specialises in supplying financial services to firms, most often large ones. Their original role was in financing international trade, lending to firms which were exporting and therefore had to face a long gap between paying production costs and receiving sales revenue. They still do this. Other services offered include:

- advising on and organising share issues
- stockbroking
- providing venture capital, i.e. loans to relatively risky new ventures
- advising on and helping to organise mergers and takeovers.

There have been many mergers in the financial sector and merchant banks are often financial conglomerates. These are made up of many specialist departments offering different types of services.

merger: the combining of two firms under one management. Whilst a *takeover* may involve a hostile bid by one company for another, which may be bitterly opposed by the one which is going to lose its independence, a merger is normally brought about by mutual agreement. A merger may have a number of advantages, depending on the nature of the companies concerned.

- A *horizontal merger* involves two firms operating in the same market. It will increase *market share*, possibly giving the merged company some *market power*. It may therefore be referred to the *Competition Commission*.

Rationalisation of production facilities may make it possible to reap *economies of scale*. The merger of SmithKline Beecham and Glaxo Wellcome in 2000 to form the giant pharmaceutical company Glaxo SmithKline provides an example. By merging their research efforts they could cut costs and further savings became possible from rationalisation. But the resulting company was so large that the US competition authorities created stiff conditions for the merger to be approved.

- A vertical merger may give the new company control over more of the production and distribution process. A manufacturer may merge with a supplier company or a distribution network.
- A *conglomerate* merger involves firms with very different products. The assumption is that the new firm will have an advantage in terms of management skills or access to finance. In the past this has not always turned out to be of real benefit and some conglomerate mergers have ended in *divestment*.

merit goods are provided by the government for those who are deemed to need them. Examples include health care, education and social services. The logic for government provision is that there is likely to be *market failure* in the sense that these services will be underproduced and consumed if decisions are based on market forces. Many of the people who would benefit from health care and education would have insufficient income to buy the services for themselves. Yet it is in the interests of society as a whole that the population have good health and education. Government provision ensures that everyone likely to benefit does so.

methodology: the range and structure of thinking processes which are used to make the subject clearer. In economics, methodology relates to the formation and testing of hypotheses and the development of theories about relationships between variables.

MFA: see *Multi-Fibre Arrangement*.

micro-credit refers to the provision of small-scale loans to poor people living in very deprived circumstances in developing countries. It enables them to set up small businesses. Originally pioneered in Bangladesh, the provision of micro-credit has been found to be a cost-effective way of providing development finance. Often, the credit has been targeted specifically at women, who have generally proved reliable about paying it back. The schemes set up to administer the loans are often co-operative in nature. Successful schemes are now operational in rural China and a number of other countries.

micro-economic models are theoretical systems of thinking which help to explain the working of markets. Each model consists of a set of relationships which can be used to analyse changes in the marketplace. If the relationships have been defined accurately in terms which match reasonably closely to the real world, it is possible to predict the outcomes of a variety of different possible changes.

micro-economics studies how the component parts of the economy work. It includes price theory, the theory of the firm and the study of labour markets. It provides a theoretical framework for analysis of decisions made by firms and individuals concerning consumption, production and the way factors of production are to be put to use. Analysis may be of one particular market (*partial equilibrium analysis*) or it may involve the interrelationships between different markets (*general equilibrium* *analysis*). The former would, for example, look at the way an increase in demand for bicycles might affect the price and quantity of bicycles sold, while the latter would go on to look at the impact on numbers employed in the industry and their wage rates and the secondary effects on any other products.

Micro-economics can be used to address a wide range of questions:

- What should be produced?
- What factors of production should be used in the production process?
- How do consumers choose what to consume?
- What determines the level of income received by individuals?

middle-income countries are those with per capita incomes lying between the low and the high-income categories. The World Bank defines middle-income countries as those with per capita incomes between US$786 and US$9655. Many middle-income countries such as Thailand and the Republic of Korea are growing fast despite occasional bad years.

migrants' remittances: migrant workers who go abroad often send quite large sums of money back to relatives in their country of origin. For some countries, these remittances are a valuable source of foreign exchange. For example, Bangladesh and India both receive substantial inflows.

migration occurs when people move from one area to another or from one country to another with the intention of working. People tend to move from areas where incomes are low to areas where some employers are having difficulty recruiting at the going wage rate. Some international migration is illegal; where this is the case labour laws will not apply to those that find work and pay and working conditions may be very poor.

minimum efficient scale (MES): the lowest level of output at which costs can be kept at their minimum. In the diagram this is the lowest output at which average total cost is minimised. For most goods, efficient production is possible across a range of

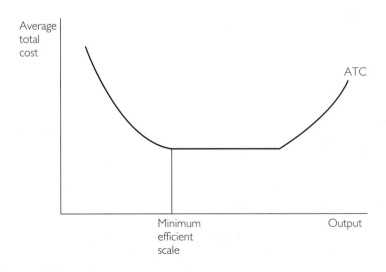

Minimum efficient scale

output levels, so the average total cost has a flat-bottomed U-shape and the minimum efficient scale is on the extreme left of the bottom of the curve.

minimum guaranteed prices may be used where there is government intervention in a market, with the objective of increasing the market price. For example, the *Common Agricultural Policy* of the EU requires intervention in the markets for farm products in such a way that the price cannot drop below a certain level.

minimum unit cost: at a certain level of output, costs of production will be the lowest possible.

minimum wage: the minimum rate of pay per hour which must by law be paid by employers. This was introduced in 1999 at £3.60 and raised to £4.10 in 2001. A lower rate applies for those aged 18-21. There is no minimum for under-18s.

The impact of the minimum wage varies greatly from one region to another. Few employers will be able to hire even unskilled people in London at the minimum wage anyway but it may have more impact in less prosperous regions. The objective is to prevent employers from paying very low wages.

Economists have tended to argue that a minimum wage will reduce the level of employment if it is above the equilibrium wage rate. It may lead to an excess supply of labour. At lower wage rates, employers might take on more labour. (See diagram.) However, there is no strong evidence yet that the introduction of the minimum wage in the UK has significantly reduced employment. After it was introduced, unemployment fell anyway. Employers interviewed since then mostly say their employment levels have not been affected. A minority of economists argue that the minimum wage will give employers more incentive to train employees so as to increase their *productivity*. If true, this would improve *competitiveness*.

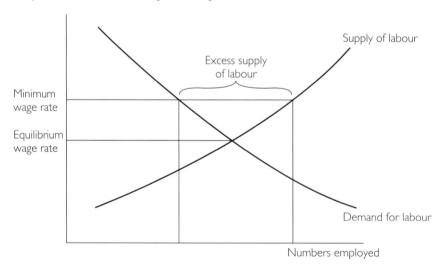

Minimum wage rate may reduce employment

Minimum wages cannot raise the incomes of those who are not in work, who are likely to be among the very poorest.

misery index: the sum of the inflation rate and the unemployment rate.

mixed economy: one in which there is both a *public sector* and a *private sector*. In practice almost all economies are mixed economies. It is difficult to imagine a country where all allocation decisions are taken on the basis of market forces and there are very few fully *centrally planned economies* now.

The relative proportions of activity falling into the private or the public sector vary very much from one country to another. China still has a very large number of state-owned enterprises but even there, there are plans to sell off many of them. Most European countries have drastically reduced their public sectors since 1980, mainly through *privatisation*. In the US, the public sector has always been much smaller than it was in the EU.

As public ownership has diminished, regulation has increased. This means that the private sector makes production decisions on the basis of market forces but within the constraints created by employment and competition law and other forms of regulation.

mobility refers to the extent to which people can move from one job to another and also from one location to another. The more mobile people are, the more flexible the labour market will be. A *flexible labour market* makes it easier for resources to move out of one less profitable line of production and into another more profitable activity. It increases *allocative efficiency*. *Occupational immobility* and *geographical immobility* both can lead to *structural unemployment* and an economy which has difficulty in adjusting to changes in the marketplace.

model: a simplified structure which mimics real-world trends in a way that makes them easier to analyse. The structure is based upon assumptions which allow us to isolate each individual change and analyse it without the complication of several different trends operating at once. The model is defined by a set of relationships which can be set out as equations or represented on a graph. For example, models which describe what happens in a market will use the relationship between price and quantity demanded as a starting point.

Macro-economic models involve a great many variables and equations and are very complex, requiring large computers to generate their predictions. (See also *Treasury model*.)

Models do not necessarily have to be realistic in order to be useful. Neither the model of *perfect competition* nor the model of *comparative advantage* is in the least realistic, but both perform a useful function in providing insights into the way the world works. Perfect competition provides a yardstick against which the competitiveness of individual markets can be assessed. Comparative advantage makes a link between international trade and economic growth and has some explanatory power.

monetarism is an approach to the analysis of macro-economic trends which emphasises the link between the money supply and the rate of inflation. It suggests a very direct relationship between the two. The strongest proponent of monetarism was the American economist *Milton Friedman*.

Monetarists tend to be rather pessimistic about the government's chances of bringing about any improvement in economic management. They see the control of inflation as a far more important objective of government policy than reducing unemployment. Their views have been contrasted with those of the Keynesians, for whom unemployment has generally been the top priority. The differences of view hinge on the question of the extent to which monetary growth should be controlled.

In practical terms, strict adherence to monetarism involves very careful control of the money supply. This requires willingness to raise *interest rates* very sharply if inflation threatens to accelerate. High interest rates will discourage spending and reduce aggregate demand and may lead to *recession*. During the 1980s there was much debate as to whether wage demands would automatically moderate in response to high interest rates. Monetarists held that they would. In contrast, the Keynesian view was that they would not, until unemployment rose substantially. When interest rates were raised in 1980, unemployment did increase greatly in the UK, over a period of years.

The useful thing that monetarism accomplished during the 1980s was to draw attention to the role of expectations in determining rates of inflation. This made for clearer thinking about the problems.

monetarist model: the macro-economic approach which defines the money supply as being a crucial determinant of the rate of inflation. (See also *monetarism.*)

monetary base: the amount of cash held by the public and by the banking system, which can serve as the basis for the expansion of bank lending. It corresponds to M0, the narrow measure of the money supply.

monetary policy uses changes in *interest rates* to control the demand for money and hence the rate of increase of bank lending. This in turn will influence the level of demand in the economy as a whole. High interest rates discourage borrowing for consumption, investment and house purchase.

The importance of monetary policy was enhanced when Conservative UK governments made tax cuts an important objective. This meant that fiscal changes were unlikely to be made for reasons of macro-economic control. So the main mechanism for altering the level of *aggregate demand* was monetary policy.

The Bank of England, in common with other central banks, has for some years found it difficult to control the supply of money (the amount of credit created) directly, so the thrust of monetary policy has been through control of the demand for money. The Bank will announce a change in its official interest rate. Borrowers will economise and reduce their demand for loans as fast as they are able. The growth of bank credit will be reduced. This means that borrowers, be they investors or home buyers, bear the brunt of a tight monetary policy.

The experience of 1988–1990 provides a useful example. In 1988, inflation was accelerating and the economy was clearly overheating. Interest rates were raised quite sharply. The increased cost of borrowing made businesses cut back their investment plans, reducing injections into the economy and producing a *downward multiplier* effect which ended in *recession*, 1990–1991. At the same time, the cost of mortgages became much higher and many people had difficulty in making their monthly payments. There was an immediate drop in consumer spending, because more of home-buyers' incomes were being spent on the interest payments. People who were not in debt were virtually unaffected by government policy, until it began to slow down the whole economy.

It is important to remember that monetary policy will always operate with a time lag. Most spending decisions take time and the full effects of a change in interest rates may take up to two years to work their way through the economy.

In May 1997 the Chancellor of the Exchequer made the Bank of England much more independent of the government. Monetary policy is now decided by the *Monetary Policy Committee* of the Bank of England. (See also *inflation targeting.*)

Monetary Policy Committee: the group of nine Bank of England officials and independent experts which decides *monetary policy.* The committee meets monthly to agree any change to interest rates. If it wishes rates to change it will announce a change in the official interest rate. The Governor of the Bank of England takes the chair and minutes are published two weeks later. The votes of individual members of the committee will be recorded in the minutes. This ensures that monetary policy can be decided without political interference.

The MPC's target for the underlying rate of the inflation is currently 2.5%. If the rate diverges by more than 1% from this, they will have to write to the Chancellor of the Exchequer explaining why and what should be done. The MPC itself has decided that earnings growth must be kept below 4.5% if inflation is to be kept low.

monetary squeeze describes a monetary policy which attempts to restrict spending in the economy by raising interest rates and thus limiting the amount of credit.

monetary system: the structure which provides the money needed to make the economy function effectively. The component parts of the system are:

- the banking system
- the central bank
- the body which supervises the banking system, which in the UK is the Financial Services Authority (FSA).

monetary union: see *Economic and Monetary Union.*

money: anything which is generally acceptable as a means of payment. Money is usually defined according to its functions. These are: a medium of exchange, a unit of account, a store of value and a standard of deferred payments. Keep in mind that these functions may be affected when money loses its value during a period of *rapid inflation.*

In the UK money is defined in two ways:

- narrow money, measured by *M0*
- broad money, measured by *M4.*

money at call: money lent in the *money markets* for a very short time, overnight or on the basis that the lender can ask for it to be repaid at any time.

money illusion refers to the mistake people make when they confuse an increase in money values with an increase in real values. It is most obvious when people complain about increasing prices while overlooking the fact that they have had an increase in income. It is possible that they may think they have had an increase in real income when in fact prices have risen by the same percentage as their income.

money income means income measured in money terms without allowance being made for inflation. In contrast, *real income* means income measured in terms of its purchasing power (i.e. in constant prices). The amount of the adjustment required depends on the rate of inflation.

money laundering occurs when people who acquired money in an illegal way want to disguise its origins. Drug dealing, tax evasion and other crimes lead people to move money around until it appears to have been generated by a legitimate activity.

money market: the market for short-term loans of various kinds. There is no particular place for this: most communications will be by telephone or electronic.

money multiplier: the amount by which bank lending can be increased if there is an increase in the *monetary base*, i.e. the amount of cash in the banking system.

money supply means the amount of money available to the general public and the banking system. This is an important macro-economic variable because it can affect the capacity of firms and individuals to spend.

In the UK there are two measures of money supply:

- *M0* is the narrow measure of money. M0 is defined as notes and coin in circulation plus banks' balances held with the Bank of England. In itself this total is of no great significance, since only a small proportion of transactions are completed using notes and coin. However, it has been found to be a useful indicator at times.
- *M4* is notes and coin plus all UK residents' deposits with banks and building societies. This provides a broad measure of spending power and is the indicator which gives important evidence when *monetary policy* is being decided.

The money supply must be allowed to grow in line with output. The figures have to be interpreted with caution because they can be affected by a wide range of events and there is often considerable uncertainty about their true meaning. This makes monetary policy difficult at times. In recent years the money supply figures have received less attention in the press than they used to.

Monopolies and Mergers Commission: the old name for the *Competition Commission*.

monopolistic competition occurs when there are many firms in the industry, each selling a slightly *differentiated product*. The market is characterised by easy entry and exit, so that small businesses can easily be set up and there is thus strong competition. Yet each has a small degree of monopoly power because the differentiated product allows consumers to choose to buy from a particular producer. Restaurants, hairdressers, estate agents, potteries and many others illustrate situations of monopolistic competition. It merges into oligopoly if there are relatively few producers or a few large ones and many smaller ones. Building societies provide an example of the latter situation.

Easy entry and strong competition ensure that in the long run there can be no supernormal profit under monopolistic competition. Firms will produce at the profit maximising output, but average revenue (price) will be equal to average total cost. This indicates that there will be excess capacity. Firms could expand and reduce ATC. However the higher output would mean lower prices and losses would be made. The diagram illustrates the output at which profits are maximised but no super normal profit can be made.

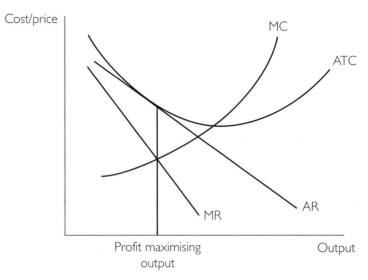

Under monopolistic competition average revenue just covers average cost

monopoly means a market in which there is a single supplier. In practice, this is unusual because in most markets there are alternatives or substitutes. However, if you consider Microsoft for a moment, you can see that some producers do have a great deal of monopoly power.

Monopoly is at the extreme end of the *spectrum of competition*. At the other end is *perfect competition*. Both ideas are fully expressed in theoretical models which define the precise conditions of each and predict how prices will be determined. However, the term is also used in connection with the legal definition of monopoly. In the UK, a firm with 25% of the market is said to have a monopoly and this will mean that it will be investigated by the *Competition Commission*.

The monopoly model has the following features, which can be shown diagrammatically.

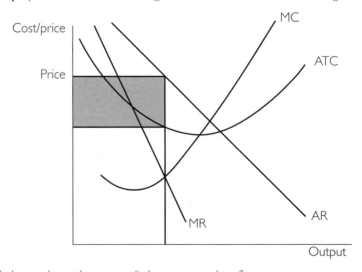

The shaded area shows the monopolist's supernormal profit

- In a monopoly, the demand for the firm's product is the market demand. So the demand curve (which is also the average revenue or AR curve) slopes downward to the right. The monopolist can choose the selling price and sell more or less, accordingly.
- The marginal revenue (MR) curve also slopes down and is always less than the average revenue. This reflects the fact that a price cut will always mean that average revenue falls.
- The profit-maximising output is at the point where marginal cost (MC) is equal to marginal revenue. If marginal cost is greater than marginal revenue, it will pay the monopolist to reduce output and raise the price.
- It follows that monopolists will have an incentive to keep output lower and prices higher than they would be under competitive conditions.
- The supernormal profit made by the monopolist is shown by the difference between total revenue and total cost or, as on the diagram, by the space between the price charged and the average total cost (ATC).
- Monopolists have no incentive to strive for efficiency, since they can sell the product even if production costs are higher than they really need to be.
- They have little incentive to strive for quality, again because they have a captive market.

Monopolies may end in taking advantage of consumers. The underlying logic of the monopoly model can be used to show why *competition policy* provides important protection for consumers. Equally, where *natural monopolies* are concerned, *regulation* will restrict their power.

monopoly legislation covers the full range of laws which restrict the ability of firms to develop monopoly power. It is operated through the *Office of Fair Trading* and the *Competition Commission* and also through the EU. As well as providing for the investigation of mergers and anti-competitive practices, the OFT deals with restrictive practices and restrictive trade agreements.

monopoly power: the *market power* which the single or dominant supplier has, in terms of being able to set prices. By restricting output, the monopolist may be able to set a higher price and increase both revenue and profit. (See also *monopoly*.)

monopoly profit: the supernormal profit which a monopolist can earn by virtue of the capacity to raise prices by restricting output. This is profit in excess of the full opportunity cost of all the resources used. (See also *monopoly*.)

monopsony: a single buyer. As with monopoly, it is unusual to find the extreme case of a single buyer but much less so to find a buyer with a dominant position in the marketplace. Large manufacturers are often in a dominant position with respect to their component suppliers and can force them to reduce their prices or accept rising costs when quality improvements are made. Supermarkets may do the same with small-scale food producers.

monopsonistic employers exist in areas where there is not much choice of jobs. They may exert monopsony power over their employees. This may enable them to hire people at lower wage rates than would be possible if they were competing for labour with other employers. The NHS is in some areas a monopsonistic employer of nursing staff.

moratorium: a temporary halt to the requirement to make interest payments or repay loans. This may happen if the lender prefers to allow the moratorium because this is the only way in which the borrower is going to be able to cope with the payments anyway. Rather than forcing the borrower into bankruptcy, it may seem better to wait for the debts to be paid. Borrowers then stand some chance of obtaining extra finance to tide them over. This usually applies to developing country governments but it can apply to individuals who are unable to make mortgage payments.

mortgage: a loan made for the purpose of buying property. The property will act as security in the event of the borrower being unable to make interest payments or repay the loan.

most favoured nation (MFN) is the provision often used in trade negotiations when a promise is made not to place *tariffs* on imports from the country concerned which are not levied on other trading partners' products.

movement along the demand curve: a change in price which leads to a change in quantity demanded but does not alter the position of the *demand curve*. A likely cause of this would be when the producer is able to cut costs, for example by investing in new technologies. This will shift the supply curve to the right (from S1 to S2 in the diagram) but the general conditions of demand and the demand curve itself will remain unchanged.

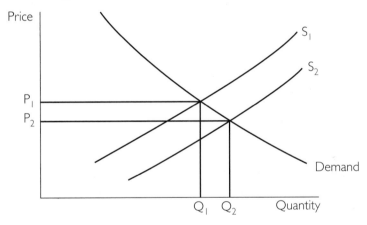

The fall in price leads to a rise in quantity demanded

moving average: an average which shows a long-term trend by calculating an average value for a number of years together and doing this for each successive year. A three-year moving average would average out the values for the year in question, the year before and the year after. This will smooth out the short-term fluctuations so that the long-term trend is more easily visible.

Multi-Fibre Arrangement is a trade agreement between the developed importing countries and some 80 developing country exporters of textile products. It involves a complex network of export and import *quotas*, designed to protect developed country textile manufacturers from competition. Typically, textiles are one of the easiest industries for developing countries to set up. They tend to have a *comparative advantage* because they can use their cheap and abundant labour. For this reason, they have posed a particular threat to developed country producers.

The MFA was tolerated to a certain extent by the *GATT*. Its avowed purpose was to allow developed country manufacturers time to adjust, rather than to provide permanent protection. Under the *Uruguay round* trade negotiations, it was to be phased out by 2005.

It remains to be seen whether the MFA will be gone by 2005, as some countries are moving slowly. The US has made a special bilateral agreement with the Chinese government to extend the quotas in relation to imports from China. This is part and parcel of China's negotiations to join the *WTO*.

When developing countries complain about the niggardliness of developed countries, the MFA is one of the things they have in mind. However, textile workers in developed countries are not well paid and they as well as the shareholders in textile companies still have some political clout. Recent research has shown that ending the MFA would substantially increase developing country exports.

The MFA has raised the price of clothing to consumers in the UK. This may worry you if you often buy clothes.

multilateral negotiations or agreements involve a number of governments. Trading blocs such as the EU or the *North American Free Trade Agreement* require multilateral negotiation as do the rules of the *World Trade Organisation*.

multilateral trade involves trade, which need not be reciprocal, between a number of countries. For example, if China buys office equipment from the UK, while the USA buys toys from China and the UK buys computers from the USA, multilateral trade has taken place.

multinational: a firm which operates in a number of different countries. It could have retail outlets (like Body Shop) or manufacturing plants (like Nissan). Multinationals are usually involved in *foreign direct investment*, which may be very welcome to the *host country*. They bring both advantages and disadvantages.

- The investment increases productive capacity and provides jobs but the multinational may depart again if wage rates rise or other conditions become less favourable. Nissan for a time threatened to stop producing in the UK if there is a decision to remain outside EMU.
- Multinationals in developing countries may facilitate technology transfer or they may just use unskilled labour and pay low wages and maintain poor working conditions.nationals choose the cheapest location at which to manufacture them.
- Profits may be repatriated to the country where the multinational has its head office and various ways may be found to avoid paying taxes in the host country.
- Many consumers get the products they want at lower prices because multinationals choose the cheapest location at which to manufacture them.

multiplier: the amount by which an increase in *injections* into the *circular flow of money* will increase total income in the economy. If investment (I) or consumption (C) increases, this adds to aggregate demand and many firms will be able to sell more investment goods or consumer products. For example, a number of firms may start off large new investment programmes involving much new plant and machinery. As the producers of these investment goods expand, they will take on more labour. The newly employed people will have rising incomes and will consume more. This will again add to aggregate demand and many firms will now expand. The increased demand will proceed around the circular flow of money for some time.

However, each time demand increases, some of the increase in income will be used to increase savings (S) or tax revenue (T) or imports (M). These are all *withdrawals* from the circular flow of money and will reduce successive increases in aggregate demand.

The size of the multiplier will depend on the extent to which increasing incomes leak away into savings, taxation or imports.

The formula for the multiplier reflects this:

$$\text{Multiplier} = \frac{1}{\text{Marginal rate of leakage}}$$

A decrease in withdrawals may have the same effect. Similarly, increased withdrawals or reduced injections will lead to a downward multiplier effect, with a cumulative fall in income.

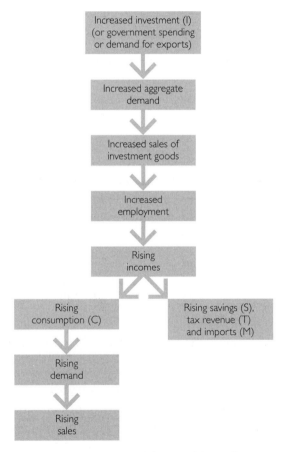

multi-skilling means that employees will be capable of doing a range of different tasks. This contrasts with the traditional situation in which people tended to have one craft skill and carry out only jobs associated with that skill. This sometimes requires more training but it means that the workforce will be more flexible and better able to adapt to changing circumstances, including changing patterns of demand.

NAFTA: see *North American Free Trade Agreement.*

NAIRU: see *non-accelerating inflation rate of unemployment.*

narrow money generally means the measure of money which is mainly cash. In the UK this means M0, which consists mainly of notes and coin held by the public and in cash machines.

NASDAQ: see *National Association of Securities Dealers Automated Quotation System.*

National Association of Securities Dealers Automated Quotation System (NASDAQ): originally a security market which traded in shares not listed on the Stock Exchange, it is now a big computer-based market dealing in all kinds of shares and competing strongly with the New York Stock Exchange.

National Debt: the sum total of all past debt accumulated by the government. It has tended over the long run to rise sharply during war time. In relation to national income, it has fallen during periods of rapid inflation. It is currently about 34% of GDP in the UK (low by international standards). In 2000 substantial repayments were made as tax revenue exceeded government expenditure.

national income means total income for the economy as a whole. It can be arrived at by three methods. The income approach sums all forms of income, wages, salaries, profits, rents, and net income from abroad. The expenditure approach sums consumption, investment, government expenditure and exports less imports. The output approach takes the total value of all output. All three methods in theory come to the same total, as they each reflect a different aspect of the circular flow of money. In practice, there are discrepancies which reflect the statistical problems of gathering the data.

national income statistics cover all the accounts on the macro-economy, drawn up by the Office for National Statistics, which show all the components of national income.

National Insurance is the scheme by which the government provides pensions and sickness and unemployment benefits. Its revenue comes from National Insurance charges (NICs) paid by employees, employers and the self-employed. Very low incomes are exempt. The rest pay a percentage of income, up to a certain maximum. Effectively, NICs are a tax. However, they are not sufficient to pay all the costs of social security payments, which have risen over the years. Pensions threaten to take a larger share of government spending as the population ages. Unemployment payments rise and fall with the rate of unemployment. When it was set up in the late 1940s, the scheme was intended to be self-financing but that is impossible now.

National Insurance charges (NICs): the payments made by employees and employers as their contributions to the funds needed to cover benefit payments. Employers' contributions raise the cost of employing labour. They may create some disincentive to employ people and thus contribute to unemployment so some attempts have been made to make them less onerous to employers. The employee's contribution effectively raises the marginal rate of tax: a pay increase will lead to higher tax payments and a higher NIC.

national minimum wage: see *minimum wage.*

national pay bargaining: negotiations between a trade union and an employers' association concerning a rate of pay which will apply across the country. It used to be the case that large numbers of employees had their pay determined in this way but many employers now negotiate directly with the union in the workplace or with individuals.

national product: the value of all income earned by factors of production owned by residents. It includes income from investments overseas and excludes interest and profits earned by foreign investments within the country concerned.

National Savings offer opportunities for people to save by lending to the government. In return they get a modest interest rate but total security and easy access to their money through post offices. From the government's point of view, National Savings provide a reasonably cheap source of finance.

nationalisation: the process by which governments take firms and industries into the *public sector.* The Labour government of 1945–1951 nationalised a number of industries. The objective was to run the industries concerned in the public interest. The nationalised industries included the railways, steelmaking, coalmining, British Airways and BP. Later shipbuilding, Rolls-Royce and British Leyland (which became Rover) joined the list. In time it became apparent that the public sector was not necessarily best placed to make the necessary business decisions. Many of the nationalised industries were prone to large losses and not just because many were declining industries.

After 1979 the then Conservative government began a programme of *privatisation* which returned most of the nationalised industries to the private sector. The ones which remain nationalised include the Civil Aviation Authority and the Post Office. They are, however, much more independent of the government than they used to be and moves to return them to the private sector are under way.

natural environment: the physical resources that surround us, as opposed to the business environment. The latter includes all the institutional structures which affect firms' decisions, the legal system and the state of the economy as a whole.

natural monopolies occur where a single supplier has an enormous cost advantage such that to have competing producers would actually raise costs. The most obvious example is water: two complete sets of mains water pipes would involve duplication of resources and raise costs. People used to use gas and electricity as examples of natural monopolies but firms are now competing, albeit in a regulated market. The existence of a natural monopoly has been used to justify *nationalisation* in the past. Now, it is the reason why privatised utilities all have *regulators,* which are supposed to protect consumers from the monopoly power of the utility companies.

natural rate of unemployment: see *non-accelerating inflation rate of unemployment.*

natural resources: include land and supplies of basic raw materials such as oil reserves. They may also include sites with development potential, which may for example be turned into deep water ports or hydro-electric schemes.

natural wastage: the inevitable fall in the number of people employed by a firm, as people retire or leave of their own accord. It can be used as a painless way of reducing the labour force without compulsory redundancies.

near money: assets which can very quickly be sold to generate cash, with no real risk of losing their value. Usually this means *Treasury bills* or *bank bills*.

needs and wants: the preferences for particular consumer goods and services that people use as their basis for making the decisions that create a demand for various products. They figure in the process of *choice* which is necessary because people have unlimited needs and wants but a limited income with which to buy them. This is the fundamental feature of scarcity, with which economics as a subject is deeply concerned.

negative equity can be found when people have borrowed to finance a house purchase, only to find that house prices subsequently fall. The size of their loan may then be greater than the value of the property.

negative externalities occur when an economic activity affects third parties, i.e. people other than the producers or the consumers, in some way which reduces their quality of life. For example, a polluting factory creates a negative externality for people living in the area affected by the pollution. They may encounter health problems which are a cost to the community. This cost is not borne by the producers or the consumers. The price of the product to the consumer is lower than it would be if it covered all of its *social costs* and the producer's profits may be higher than they would be if the social cost were included in the costs of production.

negative income tax: a unified tax and benefits system, such that people could be taxed or receive benefits according to a single set of rules. Its attraction is that it could be used to eliminate the *poverty trap* which sometimes means that people lose money by taking a job. Although the UK does not at present have a unified system, it is moving in that direction with the *Working Families Tax Credit* which reduces the impact of the poverty trap.

negative relation: an inverse relationship, such that as one variable rises the related one falls. For example, generally speaking, as the price of a product rises, the quantity demanded will fall.

negotiation is a method of reaching agreement, used where both parties have some bargaining power. The obvious example concerns a trade union and an employer, who will negotiate in order to agree an acceptable wage rate.

neoclassical economics: a set of economic ideas developed by a number of economists in the 1870s and further refined by *Alfred Marshall*. The general thrust of neoclassical economics lies in the study of market forces, supply and demand and the theory of competition. This approach analyses the way individuals achieve their objectives and how firms maximise profits. The price mechanism is seen as the fundamental determinant of the way in which the optimum *allocation of resources* is achieved. Heavy use is made of *marginal analysis*, in order to study the way in which markets create an optimum allocation of resources. (See also *technical efficiency* and *allocative efficiency*.)

neo-Keynesians: those economists who have generally followed the teaching of J M Keynes and sought to develop his ideas in the context of recent economic conditions.

There is some debate about how closely Keynesians have in fact adhered to the original ideas of Keynes.

net exports means the amount by which exports (both visible and invisible) exceed imports. If imports are greater than exports net exports will be negative.

net foreign assets means all assets held overseas by UK residents less all assets held in the UK by people living abroad. These assets include bank balances, shares, factories, retail outlets and any other production facilities. In many cases the owners will be companies rather than individuals. For example, the Japanese company Nissan has a big factory in Sunderland while the UK company BP has extensive oil production facilities in Alaska.

net investment is gross (i.e. total) investment less *replacement investment* (also known as *capital consumption*). Net investment thus represents the value of the addition to total productive capacity which has taken place over the year. It gives a good indication of the extent to which the economy is able to increase *aggregate supply* in the future.

net national product: the value of all output for the economy as a whole, less the amount of capital which has worn out during the year. This is *gross national product less capital consumption.*

net present value (NPV) is the value now of a flow of income which can be expected in the future. It can be calculated when it is desirable to know whether a particular investment project is worthwhile. It is one of a number of approaches to *investment appraisal*, known as *discounted cash flow*. Income in the future is worth less than money now, so the income flows must be discounted. A discount rate, which is rather similar to an *interest rate* in that it reflects the opportunity cost of the funds to be used for the investment, is used for this.

net profit is defined as *gross profit* less overhead costs (which are usually similar to fixed costs). An alternative approach defines it as total sales revenue less total costs. It is often called operating profit in company accounts.

net property income from abroad is a term found in the *national income statistics* which refers to interest and profits on foreign investments. It means total interest and profit received by UK residents on their foreign investments, less total interest and profit paid to foreign residents on their investments in the UK. (See also *gross national product.*)

net wealth: an individual's total *assets*, less any debts.

New Deal: a policy to deal with youth *unemployment* and long-term unemployment, introduced in 1998. People aged 18-24 who have been unemployed for more than six months are eligible. Unemployed people over the age of 25 are included if they have been unemployed for more than two years. During the first four months, people receive help and advice in seeking a job. Then they will be offered one of four options:

- subsidised employment
- voluntary work
- work with an environmental task force
- a one-year course of training.

The first three options all last for six months. So far, the evidence suggests that the New Deal has been on the whole a success. However, a judgement as to whether it is a cost-effective way of reducing unemployment will have to await further detailed research. Part of the problem is that it is difficult to keep track of everyone who has passed through the scheme for long enough to assess the impact it has had on their lives. It seems likely that during the period of falling unemployment from 1998-2000 it has done something to relieve some kinds of skill shortage and bring people onto the labour market in a more effective way.

new entrants: firms which set up in business in a particular industry for the first time. Usually they will be attracted by potential profits. These may arise because there has been an increase in demand for the product. This is part of the *price mechanism*, which creates incentives for firms to produce goods and services for which there is a demand. New entrants may be new businesses or well-established businesses venturing into a market which is new for them.

New International Economic Order (NIEO): the attempt, begun in 1974, to improve levels of aid and access to developed country markets for developing countries. The moving spirit behind this was the *United Nations Conference on Trade and Development.* The initial target was for 1% of developed countries' GDP to be devoted to flows of funds towards developing countries, which would include some government-provided aid and some private investment. This has never anywhere near been met and the percentage has tended to fall in recent years. Efforts to reduce trade barriers were not very successful either. There are some possibilities for the future if a new round of *trade negotiations* is set up.

new technology: new ways to:

- raise the level of output by investing in new machinery and other ways to produce
- bring new products to the marketplace
- improve the quality of existing products
- improve management techniques so that costs, and also prices, can be cut.

Innovation is one of the most powerful ways of increasing *productivity* and fostering *economic growth.* The implementation of new technologies has a critical effect in improving standards of living. Sometimes new technology is equated with advanced technology. In fact, some new technologies may be *intermediate technologies* put to new uses in situations where they were not previously in use. In some developing countries good results have been obtained with cookers built according to new designs and requiring less fuel. This economises on firewood, reducing the effort required to collect it and the environmental damage caused by too much cutting.

newly industrialised country (NIC): the term used in the past for a *newly industrialised economy (NIE).*

newly industrialised economy (NIE): an economy which has recently experienced a high level of growth of manufactured output.

- Typically, a large part of manufacturing output will be exported.
- Low wage rates attract *foreign direct investment.*

- Investment may be encouraged by a high rate of domestic saving (as in Taiwan).
- Labour moves quite rapidly out of agriculture and into the *secondary sector* (as in the eastern provinces of China at the present time).
- New skills are acquired and a larger range of goods is produced.

The classic example of NIEs used to be the Asian tigers: Taiwan, Hong Kong, Singapore and the Korean Republic. Singapore now has a very high per capita income and the rest are not far behind. The NIEs today are numerous, still heavily concentrated in Asia, but including also some from Latin America such as Brazil and Mexico.

NIEs are characterised by their high level of manufactured output. As they continue to grow they will tend to develop larger service sectors.

NGOs: see *non-governmental organisations.*

NIEO: see *New International Economic Order.*

Nikkei Index is Japan's Stock Exchange Index, equivalent to London's Financial Times Stock Exchange (FT-SE100) index (Footsie).

NIMBY: see *not in my back yard.*

nominal GDP means *gross domestic product* at current prices. This means that no allowance has been made for *inflation.*

nominal value means value in money terms. No allowance is made for *inflation.* Nominal wages will increase over time. Some of this increase will be nominal, reflecting the current rate of inflation. The rest of the increase will be a *real* increase, reflecting an increase in the purchasing power of the wage.

Sometimes nominal value means face value: this can apply to shares which have a face value derived from their initial price and a current market price which may be higher or lower.

non-accelerating inflation rate of unemployment (NAIRU): the level of unemployment at which inflation is stable. Once unemployment falls below a certain level, some skills will be in short supply and there will be a tendency for wages to be bid up and for inflation to accelerate. This is known as *overfull employment.* It will be below the NAIRU level but may not last long before inflation becomes a problem. This type of argument is particularly associated with *monetarism* and with the work of *Milton Friedman.* But it has with some qualifications been widely accepted by economists who would not describe themselves as monetarists.

Higher rates of unemployment (above NAIRU) induce people to settle for moderate, or no, pay increases or even a pay cut. So there is a trade-off between inflation and unemployment (the *Phillips curve*). Competition for scarce jobs will gradually bring down pay increases and the rate of inflation. In extreme cases (as in Japan in 2001) prices will fall.

Structural unemployment, which is long term by its nature, tends to continue even when aggregate demand is sufficient to buy all of the current output. This is the main component of NAIRU. The existence of structural unemployment has little effect in forcing down pay rises. It is determined by the nature of the economy. If there are *immobilities* in the labour market, it may persist for a long time.

There is some debate about the actual level of NAIRU in the UK. It certainly rose during the 1970s and 1980s, probably because of the pace of *structural change*. It is thought to have fallen during the late 1990s. It may have been affected by:

- improved support and training embedded in the *New Deal*
- increased incentives to work provided by the *Working Families Tax Credit*
- availability for work tests used in the administration of unemployment benefits.

Structural unemployment can be reduced by training in areas of skill shortage and other measures which make it easier for people to suit themselves to the jobs available.

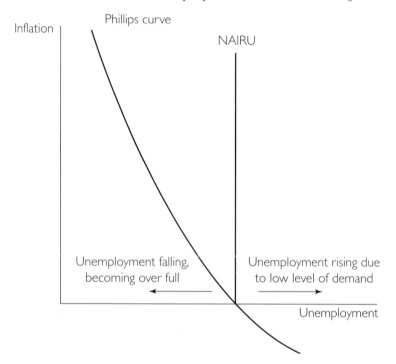

non-collusive oligopoly: a situation in which there is a small number of producers competing strongly with one another and making no attempt at collaboration or at *tacit agreement*. The market will exhibit interdependent behaviour in that each producer will be observing and reacting to the strategies of the other producers. There are three possible outcomes:

- the firm will assume that competitors will not react to its actions. It will do its best to maximise profit with a strategy which does not depend on competitors' reactions
- the firm will assume that competitors will react to its actions. This could lead to a situation in which there is a *kinked demand curve*. The firm will try to predict the reaction, using its own past experience, and allow for this in its forward planning

- the firm will try to predict what competitors will do and will devise a profit-maximising strategy which allows for new possibilities in the marketplace. This outcome will correspond to a *game theory* type of approach.

In practice, oligopolies often lead to price stability. However, there can be short periods of intense change, as when there is a *price war*, in which these types of market behaviour can be observed. For example, most newspaper prices are fairly stable most of the time, but *The Times* has been known to cut its price dramatically, precipitating a lot of reaction.

non-excludability: a feature of *public goods*, the consumption of which by one person does not exclude consumption by others. The security provided by the police force is one example. Provided there is a police force, all will benefit regardless of whether they have contributed to its financing.

non-executive directors are appointed to the board of directors of a public company on a part-time basis. Their purpose is to provide an independent voice and to observe and advise on the actions of the full-time managers. They have the potential to prevent fraudulent or dubious decisions. In practice, they are sometimes the cronies of the management.

non-governmental organisations are bodies which are associated neither with governments nor with firms in the private sector. For the most part they are charities or *pressure groups* which are non-profit making. Oxfam is a well-known example. They can be big spenders worldwide, although their local projects tend to be small scale. They are a significant presence at some meetings of international organisations such as the UN and the *WTO*, where they will normally have observer status. Some non-governmental organisations have been very critical of the process of globalisation on the grounds that it allows multinational corporations to pay low wages in poor countries. There is a long-run debate between those who focus on the way globalisation has created jobs and those who hope to see working conditions and pay improved through regulation and international agreement.

non-inflationary growth: rising output which does not lead to accelerating *inflation*. Economic growth can lead to a rise in demand for particular types of labour with scarce skills. This can bid up wages as employers compete for the available people. Costs of production then increase and these may be passed on to consumers in the form of higher prices.

Economic growth may not lead to inflation if:

- the supply of labour is growing
- training procedures are being improved
- labour is being used more efficiently and productivity is growing.

This can be shown diagrammatically with long-run aggregate supply increasing at the same time as aggregate demand. (See Figure on page 226.)

non-marketed activity: economic activities the products of which do not appear on any market. This includes housework and caring activities within the home, DIY activity, voluntary work and some health, education and personal social services provided free of charge by governments.

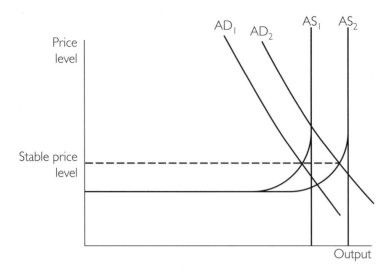

Non-inflationary growth (see page 225)
Aggregate supply rises to keep pace with aggregate demand

non-material progress: improvements in the standard of living which are not captured in GDP data. In developing countries these might, for example, relate to:

- longer life expectancy
- higher literacy rates
- improved water supplies
- fewer environmental hazards.

non-pecuniary advantages are the elements in the package of rewards for working which are not quantified in money terms as pay. They might include a company car, private health insurance and other similar rewards. They can create incentives to change jobs or undertake particular types of work.

non-performing debt: a debt upon which no *interest* is being paid and repayments are in arrears. Lenders will sometimes carry a non-performing debt on the books for some time before they give up hope of debt service payments being resumed.

non-price competition involves any kind of competitive activity other than reducing the price. It is a particular feature of market structures which fit the pattern of an *oligopoly*. It can mean competing on quality or design, through advertising or packaging or special offers of any kind. Oligopolists often use non-price competition because it reduces the risk of lower profits associated with price competition. Branding is a particularly visible form of non-price competition, in its attempts to enhance customer loyalty.

non-profit making organisations are run without profit as an objective, although they may try hard to cover all their costs. They include charities, some schools and a range of other organisations designed to operate in the public interest.

non-renewable resources: see *finite resources.*

non-rivalry refers to *public goods* which can be consumed by an unlimited number of people because the presence of one consumer does not exclude the enjoyment of the product by another. Public parks provide an example: people are generally not in competition with one another in order to consume their benefits. A number of people can enjoy them at the same time.

non-tariff barriers (NTBs) include *quotas* and other restrictions on trade which do not involve taxing imports. Many of them are contrary to either the spirit or the letter of international regulations under the *WTO*. Quotas involve an upper limit on the level of imports. Also included in the category of non-tariff barriers:

- a particular type of quota called a *voluntary export restraint (VER)*. This is negotiated with the exporting country's government
- technical regulations which force exporters to make specific changes to the product so that it is acceptable in that particular market. This raises costs for the exporter.

Because barriers to trade tend to reduce the level of trade, they also reduce the real incomes of the countries which employ them, by depriving consumers of cheap substitutes for domestically produced goods. They may be popular with voters, though, because they are thought to protect the jobs of domestic producers.

non-tradables are products which will not normally figure in international trade. They include some sorts of services which are unlikely to be consumed much by tourists and some very heavy construction materials. Usually, the markets for non-tradables are rather less competitive than those for tradable goods and services. Prices may be rather higher because there are fewer substitutes.

normal goods are those for which demand will increase when incomes increase. In other words, the *income elasticity of demand* for them is positive. They include a huge range of products, such as foreign holidays, restaurant meals, theatre visits, golf clubs and so on. In contrast, inferior goods experience falling demand when income rises. Examples include maincrop potatoes, basic models of consumer durables and so on.

normal profit: that level of profit which is just sufficient to keep the resources employed in making a particular product from being used for some other purpose. Any profit in excess of that amount, termed *supernormal profit*, will tend to attract additional resources into the industry; in other words there will be entry into the industry by new firms. If less than normal profit is earned, some resources will leave the industry to exploit more profitable opportunities producing other things. Normal profit is an important feature of *perfect competition*. The theory predicts that under perfectly competitive conditions, only normal profit will be earned in the long run, because the entry of new competitors will force prices back down to the level which just covers the costs of all resources used in production. (See also *profit-signalling mechanism*.)

normative: involving a value judgement. A normative statement is one which cannot be tested against the facts. It is likely to be a matter of opinion. It contrasts with a positive statement which can be tested against the evidence. 'The Chancellor ought to raise taxes and increase pensions' is a normative statement, because different people will have different opinions on it, depending perhaps on their age and values.

North American Free Trade Area (NAFTA) consists of the US, Canada and Mexico. As a *free trade area*, it is different from the EU because it does not have a *common external tariff* against the rest of the world. Also it does not on the whole attempt to harmonise its regulations. However, it has been successful since its inception in 1993 in increasing trade between member countries. As a major trading bloc, it has potential to influence future *trade negotiations* quite strongly.

no-strike agreement: a negotiated agreement between employees and management not to go on strike. This will usually be in return for some concessions as to pay and working conditions, as well as a commitment to go to *arbitration* in the event of a dispute which is not easily resolved.

not in my back yard (NIMBY) refers to the tendency of homeowners to oppose developments close to their homes. Examples might include new houses nearby, a new motorway or an airport extension or homes or hostels for ex-prisoners, hospital patients or homeless people.

The consequence of this type of action may be to raise property prices in the area. Restricting the availability of planning permissions reduces the number of homes which might be built in the area and drives up their price. Such action can therefore be very profitable for the people already there. Resisting other improvements which might benefit society as a whole may make it difficult to improve the *infrastructure* generally, with long-run implications for the social structure and the competitiveness of society as a whole.

obsolescence: when a product or a process is going out of date. While not yet completely obsolete, it is becoming so. For example, a piece of machinery may still be usable in the production process, but may be more expensive to operate than the latest technology.

occupational immobility occurs when people have been trained in a skill which is no longer in demand and have difficulty in retraining in a skill which is in demand. This may result in their being unemployed. This type of unemployment is known as *structural unemployment*. Policies to deal with it include projects such as the *New Deal*, which gives help in finding work as well as additional training.

OECD: see *Organisation for Economic Co-operation and Development*.

offer curve of labour: see *backward sloping supply curve of labour*.

Office of Fair Trading (OFT) was set up in 1973 to oversee all of the UK's competition policy. It operates in a range of areas. It:

- monitors changes in *market structures*, collecting data and investigating merger activity generally
- decides whether to refer takeovers to the *Competition Commission* for further investigation before approval can be given
- responds to complaints about anti-competitive activities (which usually come from competing firms)
- takes care of many aspects of *consumer protection*, including trades description.

The OFT was greatly strengthened by the 1998 Competition Act, which gave it new powers of investigation, including the power to stage a *dawn raid* if it is likely that a firm will try to obscure important evidence. Also, it can give a firm immunity from fines if it informs on other members of a *cartel*. And it can fine firms which collude up to 10% of their UK turnover for up to three years. A dawn raid on two bus company offices in late 2000 suggests that the OFT's shiny new teeth may be effective in discouraging collusion.

John Vickers, the Director General, said early in 2001 that the OFT would be using its new powers as soon as a really strong 'platform of evidence' was accumulated. More dawn raids were planned and several companies had asked for immunity from fines after providing information about cartels.

official development assistance is the *foreign aid* given by governments to developing countries in the form of grants and loans. This may come in the form of bilateral aid, from one government to another, or multilateral aid, from an international organisation funded by many countries. It does not include charitable donations or private investment.

official finance transactions are payments made by the Bank of England to offset inflows and outflows on the *balance of payments*.

official reserves are the reserves of foreign exchange held by the *central bank*. They may be used to defend the exchange rate if market forces are pushing it down. (See also *fixed exchange rate*.)

OFGEM, the Office of Gas and Electricity Markets, is the regulator for the gas and electricity industries. Both have had regulators since *privatisation* in the late 1980s. The two were combined in 2000, partly because some companies are supplying both products. OFGEM regulates the extent to which gas and electricity prices can be raised and also the value for money which customers get. It can require suppliers to restrain their activities in order to ensure that the market remains competitive. Because both industries are to some extent *natural monopolies*, regulation is needed to protect the interests of consumers.

Since 1999, neither British Gas nor the electricity suppliers have had a monopoly position; consumers can choose where to buy. Choice has brought potential savings of £60 per year on gas bills and £20-35 on electricity bills, depending on the area.

Regulation has at times brought OFGEM and its predecessors (Ofgas and Offer) into dispute with shareholders. To the extent that suppliers' profits may be reduced, shareholders sometimes object when prices cannot be raised.

OFLOT: the regulator for the National Lottery.

OFT: see *Office of Fair Trading*.

OFTEL is the regulator for the privatised telephone industry, set up at the time of privatisation in 1984. It has been instrumental in opening the telecommunications market to many competing suppliers. This has created strong price competition and brought down the cost of telephone calls. In spite of this, OFTEL is currently thought to have been rather soft on BT in the past. BT has moved slowly on opening up its telephone exchange facilities to other firms which want to develop broadband networks. UK companies are developing this technology quite fast but future progress depends on access to BT's system. OFTEL could perhaps have insisted more strongly that this must happen. This situation may now be changing. (See also *regulatory capture*.)

OFWAT is the regulator for the water industry, set up at the time of privatisation in 1989. In spite of its efforts to hold down price increases, many people think that the water companies continue to act like monopolies. Water remains a true *natural monopoly* in that it is not usually possible to choose between competing suppliers and the need for a pipe network makes duplication of facilities wasteful and inefficient. In fact, prices have risen in part because of the need for extensive investment in improved water supplies. It is hard to tell how effective regulation has been in this case.

oil crisis: a situation in which supplies of oil are threatened and prices rise as it becomes more scarce. The precipitating cause could be war in the Middle East, as in 1973. *OPEC* has in the past been able to restrict production with a view to raising prices.

Because demand for oil is very inelastic, a relatively small fall in production can bring about a much larger increase in prices. Shortages are likely to disrupt economic activity because of the crucial role of oil in industry and distribution. A very short oil crisis occurred in late 2000 when protesters blockaded refineries to prevent supplies of petrol reaching the public. The oil companies were quick to raise prices but came in for much public criticism and prices soon fell again.

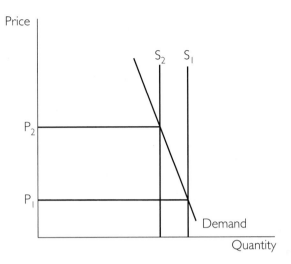

A small fall in quantity supplied leads to a large increase in price if demand is inelastic

oil price: the price of oil in the wholesale market, which is a significant indicator of future pressures on production costs and sometimes of impending *inflation*. The price is usually quoted in US dollars.

oligopoly: a market in which there are a few large firms competing with one another. It is characterised by:

- *differentiated products*, sometimes with well-known and easily distinguished brand names
- *barriers to entry*, such that it may be difficult or impossible for new entrants to come into the market
- the fact that firms may make *supernormal profits* in the long run, because of the barriers to entry
- the relatively small number of competing firms, which is likely to include *price makers* and *price takers*. The former will tend to set prices and the latter will tend to follow.

Oligopolies can have very stable prices, because firms will often favour *non-price competition*. They may seek to expand their market share on the strength of design or advertising. There may be *tacit agreement*, with no price cuts but intense efforts to promote products in other ways.

Occasionally, though, a price war may break out, in which one firm begins aggressive price-cutting strategies and others follow, each trying to undercut the other in a bid for increased market share. This is good for consumers in the short run but may lead to the least profitable firm going out of business. Then competition is reduced and a return to tacit agreement is likely. Petrol provides occasional examples of price wars.

Interdependent behaviour is an important feature of oligopoly, because the small number of competing firms watch each other closely, devising strategies which take into account the likely reaction of the others.

Some oligopolies have a number of large competitors, as with Coca Cola and other major soft drink suppliers, together with a large number of comparatively small suppliers which are price takers. (See also *concentration ratios, kinked demand curve, anti-competitive activities.*)

ombudsman: a person or body which investigates complaints from consumers in either the public or the private sector. Banking and insurance both have ombudsmen whose findings are not legally binding, but who can give the consumer view some strength.

OPEC: see *Organisation of Petroleum Exporting Countries.*

open economy: an economy in which foreign trade is important. Exports contribute significantly to aggregate demand and imports are a significant proportion of total purchases. For example, the UK economy is a more open economy than the US. Luxembourg is even more so.

open market operations involve *central banks* in buying and selling *bills* and *bonds.* The objective is to influence the money supply. They are used to buttress interest rate changes as part of *monetary policy.* When central banks buy bills and bonds for cash, they increase the amount of cash available to the banking system.

operating profit: the main accounting measure of a firm's profit. Total costs will be subtracted from total sales revenue so this is the accounting measure which comes closest to the economist's view of profit. However, the costs which are included may not cover all of the resources used so there is still a difference in the two concepts.

opportunity cost represents cost in terms of what could have been had as an alternative to the item actually chosen. For example, the opportunity cost of a new economics text book might be the cinema ticket which you could have had instead. So opportunity cost is the best or highest valued alternative that must be foregone.

The idea of opportunity cost may be applied in any situation where choices are being made. For example, consumers' decisions involve choices between items; one will be chosen and the one foregone is the opportunity cost. Similarly labour market decisions may involve choices between work and education or between two possible jobs. And the government may find that the opportunity cost of, say, more money for the NHS is less money for roads or social services.

Opportunity cost is also important in considering alternative investments. Even if the firm is using its own *retained profits* to fund the investment, it must allow for the interest which could have been earned if this money had been left in the bank. This is the opportunity cost of investing in, say, a new machine or office furniture. An investment which cannot equal the rate of return on a bank deposit is not a good use of funds.

optimise: to strive for the most favourable outcome. This could mean *profit maximisation* or maximising market share or any other objective.

optimum means simply the best possible outcome, i.e. buying your first choice of product, getting the best paid job possible for you, making the most profit you can.

optimum currency area: the best size for a single currency area. There is no simple answer to what this might be.

- A small currency area such as the UK will have to carry the risk of an unfavourable exchange rate change. Firms will face uncertainty: the exchange rate may float up, making export prices rise and leading to difficulties in maintaining competitiveness. There will be transactions costs associated with every trade deal. But the government will retain the option of allowing a *depreciation* which will enhance competitiveness. It will have a wider range of macro-economic policy choices. It will be able to set *interest rates* to suit the needs of the economy at any given time.

- In a large currency area such as the *euro zone*, all producers will know the price at which they can sell across a very large market. There will be much less uncertainty and no transactions costs. But if one member country loses competitiveness compared to other member countries, e.g. because of inflation, it will not be able to depreciate as a means of adjusting and regaining competitiveness. Interest rates will be determined by the *European Central Bank* with reference to the area as a whole and not to the needs of individual member countries.

In practice, large and small currency areas exist side by side. Think of the US and Switzerland, both with high standards of living and both able to compete very successfully with the rest of the world in their own specialist areas. West Virginia does not seek its own currency despite having rather low incomes relative to the rest of the US and Switzerland seems quite unlikely to seek to join the euro.

option: the right to buy or sell a *commodity, bonds* or currency at a specific time in the future, at a price agreed now.

order book: means literally the book in which a firm's orders are recorded. The term 'a long order book' means that the firm has enough work already arranged to last for a substantial period. It is an indication that the firm is working close to *full-capacity*.

ordinary share: a way of buying a small part of a *public limited company*, i.e. one which offers its shares to the general public. The firm gets finance for investment, while the shareholder gets a *dividend*. However, the shareholder runs the risk that the share price will fall or the company will become insolvent, in which case the money will probably be lost. Then again, the company may turn out to be profitable, the share price may rise and the dividends may offer a good rate of return.

organic growth: an expansion of the firm which is based on building up new production capacity within the existing business, rather than through merging with another firm.

Organisation for Economic Co-operation and Development (OECD) is a group of 29 member countries, mainly those with relatively high incomes. In recent years some *transitional economies* have joined, including Mexico, the Republic of Korea, Hungary, Poland and others. It is located in Paris and does much useful work in producing consistent data which can be used for international comparisons. Its main functions are:

- acting as a forum for discussion and co-operation in international economic policy, supported by research into economic problems. Meetings are attended by finance and trade ministers
- co-ordinating the provision of bilateral aid by the donor countries to the developing countries.

Organisation of Petroleum Exporting Countries (OPEC) is the group of oil-exporting countries drawn from the Middle East, South America and Africa. Its objective is to control supply in order to maintain prices but in this it has had very varied results. The US, Russia and European producers do not belong to it. In 1973 and in 1979 it operated as a very effective *cartel*, reducing supplies and forcing up oil prices so that producer countries' revenues were greatly increased. However, this price increase made new oilfields such as those in the North Sea and Alaska economic to develop, thus reducing the market power of the OPEC cartel. To a degree, Saudi Arabia is still able to influence the quantity of oil supplied. In late 2000 it increased supplies when prices rose to the point where governments felt that world-wide economic stability was threatened.

organised labour means the trade unions and their membership. In contrast, employees who choose not to join a union and negotiate independently or accept the going wage are not part of organised labour.

other things being equal: see *ceteris paribus*.

output: the endproduct of a firm, resulting from an economic process. Output can be valued according to its price in the market or stated in volume terms. *Productivity* means output per person employed and is a measure of efficiency.

output gap: see *deflationary gap*.

output method: a way of calculating *gross domestic product* by evaluating total output. All output is valued at either market prices or factor cost. Care is taken to avoid double counting, by using the value added method. Value added by each firm is counted, to arrive at a total. The alternative methods of calculating GDP are the *income method* and the *expenditure method*.

outsourcing is the process by which firms buy services, component inputs or even finished products from independent suppliers, rather than produce them themselves. This practice increased as many businesses have found it cheaper to rely on other producers than try to do everything themselves. Sometimes new cheap sources of inputs can be found overseas; this has been an important element in *globalisation*.

outward-looking trade strategies: trade policies which encourage exports and allow imports. These have become important in *developing countries* because some of the countries which adopted such policies have been very successful. Singapore is an example, now having per capita income near to the highest in the world and a very high percentage of output exported. In contrast, countries which adopted *import substitution* policies have tended to grow more slowly.

overcapacity occurs when demand for the product is less than the capacity of the firms in the industry to supply. Usually this happens because demand has fallen. There is currently world overcapacity in the steel industry and in the car industry. Demand for steel has fallen as alternative materials have become available and supply has increased as newly competitive producers in developing countries invested. The outcome for British Steel was a merger with its Dutch competitor, to become Corus. *Rationalisation* followed with the closure of the large Llanwern steel production plant in South Wales. In the car industry also mergers and rationalisation of production facilities have been a feature of recent experience.

overconsumption occurs when the price of the product does not reflect the full costs of the product. Prices may not include *external costs*. For example, it can be argued that cigarettes are overconsumed because buyers do not take full account of the health effects of smoking and the price does not fully reflect the health care costs of tobacco-related illnesses. Taxes go some way towards this, of course. We may be overconsuming petrol because we are not allowing for the long-term environmental effects of our behaviour. Overconsumption can be associated with *information failure*.

overdraft: a loan facility which allows individuals or firms to borrow from the bank only just the amount they need at any time. If borrowing needs vary from day to day this arrangement saves interest payments when loan needs are low. Usually the bank will set a maximum limit on the size of the overdraft.

overfull employment: a level of employment which is going to lead to inflationary pressures. This will be above the *natural rate of unemployment* (NAIRU) by definition. At this level of employment, employers are competing for people with scarce skills and they will tend to bid up wages in an attempt to get the people they want in order to expand production. Costs will increase and this will be passed on to consumers in the form of higher prices. There is *excess demand*. Any further growth in aggregate demand will lead to accelerating inflation rather than rising output because aggregate supply cannot increase fast enough to keep pace.

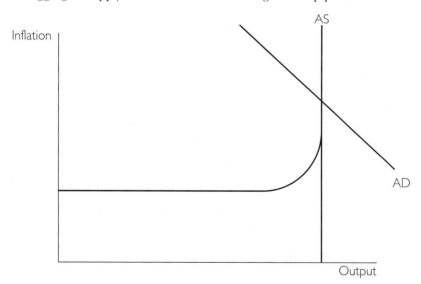

Aggregate demand exceeds aggregate supply, wages are bid up and inflation accelerates

overheads are similar to *fixed costs* in that they are not related to the level of output. They include salaries of people not actually involved in production, capital equipment, rent, heating and lighting.

overheating occurs when *aggregate demand* exceeds *aggregate supply*. The *excess demand* which results reflects the fact that *supply constraints* are preventing producers from increasing output. There will be a tendency for *inflation* to accelerate and for imports to rise as the pressure of demand increases. (See also *overfull employment.*)

overmanning: using more labour in the production process than is strictly necessary. It can occur when firms are run inefficiently yet survive because they have a degree of monopoly power. Or it can occur when agreements are made between unions and management not to make people redundant. This means that employees are kept on the payroll even though it would be possible to supply the existing quantity of the product without their help.

overproduction occurs when there are *external costs* which are not included in the cost and price structure of the product. For example, a producer which manages to keep costs down by emitting polluting waste into the air or rivers will have accounting costs which are lower than the full *social cost* of production. This will make the product look artificially cheap and firms will be able to sell more of it than they would if the price reflected the externality. Internalising these costs by making the firm clean up its emissions will raise the internal costs and prices and lead to an equilibrium output which reflects demand at the resulting price level.

overshooting: when the economy is changing fast, some variables have a tendency to overshoot, i.e. adjust more than is necessary. For example, if there is a glut, prices may actually fall too far and a temporary shortage will follow. An overvalued exchange rate may also fall too far, down below the level needed to balance imports and exports. Share prices may do the same. In each case, markets fail to clear, there is then a price adjustment but initially it overshoots, leading to a later correction which adjusts prices more closely to the long-run equilibrium.

overtime: time spent at work in addition to the hours which are part of the normal working week. Typically, the working week will be 38-40 hours and any time spent over that will attract overtime payments for manual workers and some clerical occupations. Managerial groups and professionals seldom get overtime payments.

overtime ban: industrial action that allows a normal working week but bans any overtime. This leaves wages close to normal but may disrupt the production process if employers would have required overtime.

overvalued currency: an *exchange rate* level which is above that at which exports and imports would automatically balance. Export prices will be high and firms will have difficulty in competing. Similarly import prices will be low and people will increase their imports. There will be a current account deficit.

In time, the resulting low level of demand for the currency, and high level of supply, will tend to push the exchange rate down again if it is floating fairly freely. Market forces will create downward pressure. This may or may not be counteracted by central bank action to maintain the exchange rate by buying it and so supporting its value. (See Figure on page 237.)

owner occupation: ownership of the property by the person who is living in it. In the UK this is the commonest form of housing arrangement.

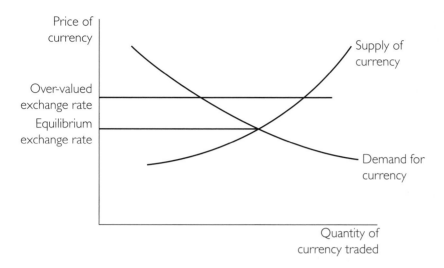

Overvalued currency (see page 236)
The overvalued exchange rate is above its long-run equilibrium level.

ownership rights usually allow owners to decide how their property will be used. This works well with a tin of soup – you can decide when to consume it. It is more complex with land – you will have to get planning permission to develop it. If you own a property, you will be taxed on the rent from it. Ownership rights are an important aspect of the *free market economy*.

ozone layer: a layer of the atmosphere which protects living things from radiation. It has been affected by emissions of CFCs. The use of these is now controlled by international agreement, but there is some question as to how effective these currently are. CFCs used to be a clear *negative externality* in the production of refrigeration equipment.

packaging: one of the elements in *non-price competition*. Along with advertising, product design, quality and customer service, it can be a part of the competitive process in an *imperfect market*.

paradox of thrift: when people start to save a larger part of their incomes, the resulting withdrawal from the *circular flow of money* has a *downward multiplier* effect on aggregate demand, which eventually leads to a fall in the level of saving. This is a prediction of the basic Keynesian model of the macro-economy, in which saving is directly related to income because a rise in the rate of saving implies a fall in consumption.

parallel imports are branded goods which are imported by a distributor who is not connected with the manufacturer. These importers look for price differences between countries, buying where the product can be obtained most cheaply. They will then be able to sell at a higher price in countries where the 'official' distribution network charges more. Parallel imports encourage price competition, e.g. in the car market where prices have tended to be higher in the UK than on the continent. They are not to be confused with *pirate products*, which are illegal copies of branded goods, e.g. expensive perfumes. However, they are very unpopular with manufacturers because they reveal their efforts at *price discrimination*.

Pareto efficiency, or Pareto optimality, refers to a situation in which it is impossible to make anyone better off without making someone else worse off. This means that there must be an optimal *allocation of resources*, such that inputs are used in the most efficient way (*technical efficiency*) and output yields the maximum possible utility to consumers (*allocative efficiency*).

Pareto, Vilfredo, (1848-1923): an Italian professor of Economics who set out the Pareto criterion for efficiency. His work centred on the workings of the market economy and on the ideas of *technical* and *allocative efficiency*. The Pareto criterion states that there is a clear improvement in welfare if at least one person can be made better off without making anyone else worse off. This idea has provided an important foundation for later work in *welfare economics* and *cost–benefit* analysis.

Pareto's reasoning does not take into account the distribution of income. Also, it assumes a situation of *perfect competition*; nevertheless, it provides important insights into the way markets work.

parity is a term used in the context of exchange rates. We may speak of a fixed parity, meaning a value for the exchange rate which will be kept fixed.

partial equilibrium analysis examines individual markets on the assumption that events in that market can be viewed in isolation from all other markets. This is easier to do than the alternative, *general equilibrium* analysis, which requires the inclusion of all the knock-on effects which occur in other related markets and takes in the labour and capital markets as well as the product market.

participation rate: the proportion of the population which is either in work or registered unemployed. It is thus a measure of the size of the total workforce available and the extent to which the population is economically active. This in turn depends on the age at which people cease full-time education, the retirement age and the extent to which parents take time out from employment to look after children.

partnership is a type of business organisation owned by two or more people. They will be able to raise more capital together than they could as *sole traders*. But they will not have *limited liability*, so they may have to meet all of their debts out of their own resources if the business is not successful. This means that trust between the partners is essential. Partnerships are common in accountancy and the law.

par value: see *nominal value*.

patent: a legal right to the *monopoly* of a new product or process. The newness of the invention must be demonstrated in the application to the Patent Office. Once the patent is obtained, the holder can use the process or manufacture the product, or license other firms to make it, for up to 20 years.

Patents can be very valuable, as with certain drugs for which pharmaceutical companies hold the patent. Glaxo made enormous profits from the development of Zantac before its patent ran out. They are economically important because they provide a significant incentive to innovate. Without patent protection, few innovations would be developed and *productivity* would probably grow much more slowly than it has. However, the patent holder must be prepared to defend the right in court, which can be very expensive. Patents are one element in the general term *intellectual property rights*.

pattern of trade: the way in which an economy trades with different parts of the world and in different products. The UK pattern of trade has the following features:

- increasing trade with the EU
- the US and Germany are the two single most important trading partners.
- a high proportion of exports consist of services, particularly financial services.

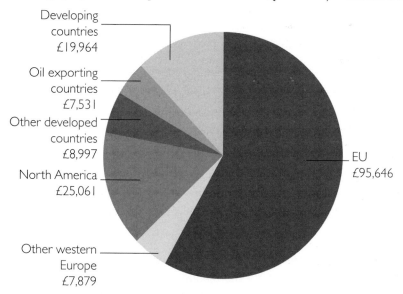

Source: ONS, Annual Abstract of Statistics, 2000

Exports from the UK by destination, 1998, £ million

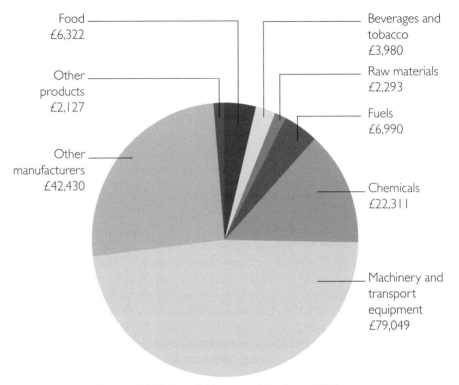

Food £6,322

Other products £2,127

Other manufacturers £42,430

Beverages and tobacco £3,980

Raw materials £2,293

Fuels £6,990

Chemicals £22,311

Machinery and transport equipment £79,049

Source: ONS, Annual Abstract of Statistics, 2000

UK visible exports, by commodity, 1998, £ million (see page 239)

pay differentials: the differences in wages and salaries between specific occupations and industries. Differentials reflect education and training which lead to differences in *productivity*. They are also important indicators of market forces in the labour market. They create important incentives. High pay sends a signal to the market that more people are required in that particular occupation.

- Pay can act as an incentive to move into an occupation for which demand is growing. Some computer programmers are very highly paid because they possess very scarce skills. The high pay should in time act as an incentive which will attract more people to get the appropriate training.
- Pay differentials between regions create an incentive to move. Higher pay in South East England attracts more people into the area.
- Low pay indicates declining demand and sometimes encourages people to retrain or move to another region.

Pay differentials do not always perform their function of reallocating resources very efficiently. Sometimes the differentials are insufficient to compensate for the bother of retraining or moving, so that excess supply and demand in the labour market may persist.

Differentials can reflect innate abilities. *Labour market flexibility* requires that differentials do actually induce people to move to where they are needed.

PAYE stands for 'pay as you earn'. It is the system by which employers deduct income tax from pay at source.

payments in kind: that part of the pay package which comes in the form of goods and services. Examples include a company car, private health insurance, season tickets and so on.

payroll tax: a tax paid by the employer which rises with the number of employees. The common example is the social security taxes which exist in most countries of the European Union. In the UK these are called employers' *National Insurance contributions*. They have the effect of raising the costs of employing labour. They therefore have the potential to reduce employment if the employer is likely to look for labour-saving ways of producing.

pay round: the process of negotiating the annual pay increase. Some national pay agreements act as standards which other negotiators will try to achieve later in the year.

peace dividend: the money saved when the end of the Cold War reduced the need for defence spending by governments.

peak pricing may be used where there are substantial variations in demand over the course of time. For example, rail fares are set in such a way that it costs more to travel during the rush hour. This is a way of raising revenue and charging higher prices to those customers who put the most pressure on the capacity of the organisation to provide for them. (See also *price discrimination*.)

pension funds are *financial intermediaries* which channel money from the premiums of people who want pensions into a variety of investments in firms. Payments are paid monthly into pension schemes by large numbers of people who have occupational pensions. The pension funds invest in shares, property and government bonds, spreading the risks associated with any one investment. Along with insurance companies and investment trusts, the pension funds are known as *institutional investors*. They are a very important source of funds for investment and have considerable influence with the firms of which they are shareholders.

per capita means 'per head', as in *per capita income*, meaning income per person. It is usually used as an average of the whole population.

per capita income means income per person and is an important measure of the standard of living. In *constant price terms*, it is widely used for international comparisons. It is based on either GNP or GDP so it must be interpreted with the caution required for all standard national income measures. In particular, care is needed where exchange rate changes have occurred. Allowance may have to be made for environmental degradation or deterioration in the quality of life as measured in other ways.

percentile: a one-hundredth part of a set of observations. A person who is among the highest 1% in terms of income earned may be said to be in the top percentile. The 50th percentile corresponds to the median observation, and so on.

perfect competition is an economic model of a market situation characterised by a large number of firms all making the same product. Many markets for farm products such as cauliflowers or wheat are broadly similar to perfect competition. Some commodity markets also have many similarities to it. The model itself has the following features:

- many buyers and sellers, all of whom are *price takers*. They are able to sell as much as they can produce at the going market price
- no one seller's product is distinguishable from another's. All produce a *homogeneous product*
- there is *free entry* to and exit from the market. New firms can start up production easily
- there is *perfect knowledge*, meaning that all buyers and sellers have full information about products and prices. All producers have access to the same technologies
- factors of production are perfectly mobile – they are able to move from one line of production to another without difficulty
- in the long run, only *normal profit* can be earned. Any *supernormal profit* will be competed away by new entrants to the market, forcing prices down to the minimum average total cost.

Technical efficiency can be achieved under perfect competition because there will always be many sellers competing and they will need to keep costs to a minimum in order to survive. *Allocative efficiency* can be achieved because free entry to the market means that there will always be a producer seeking to meet consumer demand at a price which reflects costs of production.

As with all firms, profit is maximised where *marginal cost* is equal to *marginal revenue.* Marginal revenue is always equal to price.

Many of the important features of perfect competition can be shown diagrammatically. The diagram shows the long run equilibrium.

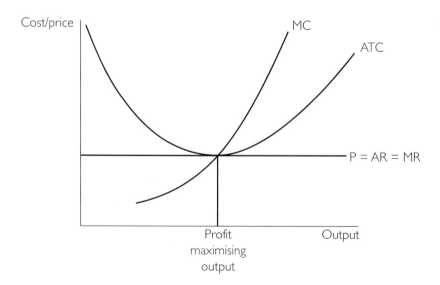

In looking at the diagram, keep in mind that:

- firms can sell all they produce at the going market price. This means that the firm faces a horizontal perfectly elastic demand curve, which also corresponds with the marginal and average revenue

- competition forces firms to minimise costs, so all firms will produce at the point on the average total cost curve where costs are at a minimum. This will be the lowest possible price at which they can stay in business
- in the long run, prices will always be forced down to this level by competition. At this point, marginal cost will equal marginal revenue and this will be the output at which profits are maximised. So the long-run equilibrium price under perfect competition will be the minimum average total cost of the product.

New entrants will always force the price to the level of minimum average total cost, so that only normal profit can be earned. (See also *short-run equilibrium under perfect competition*.)

perfect knowledge is a condition of *perfect competition* implying that both consumers and producers are fully informed about the conditions in the market and about the best ways of producing. Consumers know all about the prices and availability of the products they may purchase and producers are all able to use the best technology available at the time.

Perfect competition (see pages 241–242)

perfect market: a market in which the conditions are those of perfect competition, with many suppliers, a *homogeneous product* and *perfect knowledge.*

perfect mobility is a condition of *perfect competition* and means that both labour and capital can move from one use to another. People will be able to move from one occupation to another without difficulty and also move to a different geographical area. Funds for investment will be able to move out of a less profitable use and into a more profitable activity.

perfectly elastic demand: sellers can sell all they produce at the going price. For each one, the market is very large compared to the size of the firm. This is one of the conditions of *perfect competition.*

perfectly elastic supply: the quantity supplied is theoretically limitless. In the long run, the supply of many products can be increased indefinitely. There is no problem about finding the resources to expand production at the same price. Some manufactured products are like this, e.g. plastic toys. However, this would only be the case in the long run. The long-run supply curve would be a horizontal line.

perfectly inelastic demand: consumers demand a fixed quantity. Price has no effect on this quantity. At any reasonable price, this applies to kitchen salt. The demand curve will be a vertical line, at the single quantity demanded.

perfectly inelastic supply means that there is a fixed supply. This holds for many products in the *market period*. Prices will be entirely demand determined. The supply of housing is fixed in the short run, because it takes time to build or convert more. In the long run, high prices would induce builders to expand supply. (See diagram on page 244.)

performance-related pay (PRP) means linking pay to some measure of performance, e.g. sales or output. This can act as an incentive to achieve particular business objectives.

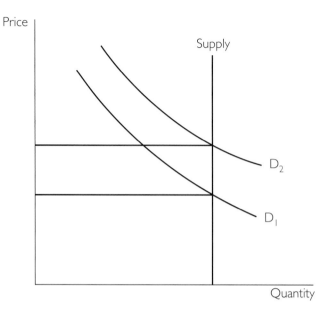

Perfectly inelastic supply of homes in the short run; increasing demand from D_1 to D_2 will drive up prices (see page 243)

periphery: remote regions of the economy which are disadvantaged by difficult communications and relatively low incomes. West Cornwall is an example, being a long way by road and rail from the economic core of the UK which centres on South East England, the West Midlands and West Yorkshire. Firms tend not to set up production facilities in peripheral areas. If traditional forms of production decline, employment opportunities are reduced and a *downward multiplier* effect may follow. Many peripheral areas qualify for EU Objective 1 funding which can help to regenerate them. (See also *assisted areas.*)

permanent income hypothesis: a theory of the determination of the level of consumption, which holds that consumption is directly related to expectation of income over the long run. This theory was set out by *Friedman* and contrasts with the view of *Keynes*, who saw consumption as depending on current income.

personal allowance: the amount of an individual's income which is free of income tax. This amount is usually raised in line with inflation in the *Budget*, unless the Chancellor wants to increase the real level of tax revenue.

personal disposable income is the income which remains to individuals to spend as they wish, after all direct taxes have been deducted.

personal preferences: individual consumer choices which determine the level of *demand* for each product.

personal sector: that part of the economy which consists of transactions made by individuals. The corporate sector involves all decisions by businesses and these two and the financial sector together constitute the private sector.

petroleum revenue tax is levied on the profits from the production of oil within the jurisdiction of the UK government. The oil companies can offset the cost of exploration against the tax.

Phillips curve: the name given to the trade-off between *inflation* and *unemployment.* The nature of this trade-off is complex and sometimes also controversial. It rests broadly on the experience of the *trade cycle*, in which periods of accelerating inflation tend to be associated with falling unemployment during a boom. During recession inflation will usually slow down and unemployment will rise.

The relationship between inflation and unemployment was first studied in detail by A W Phillips (1914–1975). In 1958 he published his investigation of annual data for the previous 100 years, showing a strong inverse relationship between the two. During the period of high unemployment in the 1930s, prices had actually fallen so the relationship looked broadly like the diagram below. The point where the curve cuts the zero-inflation line is a debatable question.

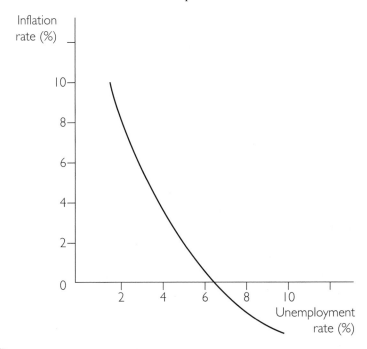

The Phillips curve

During the 1970s, the idea of a straight trade-off between inflation and unemployment fell into disrepute because the two increased together for a time. This happened when oil prices were rising and there were expectations of accelerating inflation. For more detail see the entry on *expectations-augmented Phillips curve.* (This is tricky to follow and you may not need to know it in detail.)

The problem of the 1970s – *stagflation* – was eventually defeated by the very tight monetary policies of the 1980s, which were closely associated with high and rising unemployment. From about 1980, you can begin to see a trade-off emerging again in the annual data.

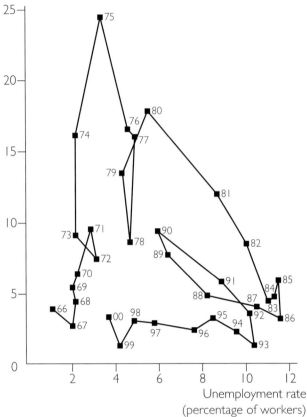

Source: ONS, Economic Trends

Inflation and unemployment

The relationship between inflation and unemployment is important in policy making but it keeps changing. Just to keep us all puzzled, in the late 1990s unemployment fell without inflation accelerating. It is likely that there is still a short-run trade-off between inflation and unemployment, but it may be at a lower level of unemployment than previously. In fact, some say that inflation is dead. Think about the points on the graph for 2001 onwards. Where are they and what do they suggest?

physical capital means tangible investments in production facilities of all kinds which will bring in an income stream in the future. They include buildings, shops, tankers, machinery and office equipment, along with many other examples. In contrast, *human capital* is embodied in the skills and education of people.

picketing means standing outside a place of work and discouraging people who want to carry on working during an *industrial dispute*. It is strictly controlled by law, which tends to limit the powers of trade unions.

picking winners: from time to time governments imagine that they can identify firms with good long-run profit potential and encourage them with the provision of subsidies or cost advantages such as low business rates. As these firms are often already in difficulty, subsequent success has been elusive. The most famous target for government support was British Leyland, which eventually became Rover after which it was first bought and then sold by BMW. Although bits of the company have been very profitable at times, the firm has had a lot of problems over the years and the government support was very expensive. Some people think the *market system* should decide which firms are the winners.

piece rate: wages based on the amount produced. It tends to be associated with poorly paid work.

pirate products: imitations of famous brands. These are illegal because brands are generally protected by trade marks which can only be used for the genuine article. The *intellectual property rights* of the owner of the trade mark are being infringed and legal action may follow. However, many firms find it very difficult to identify the sources of pirate products. They may come from countries with low wages and weak systems of commercial law.

planned economy: an economy in which all the resource allocation decisions are taken by government departments. So decisions about what is to be produced, and how, and how it will be distributed, all become a matter for the bureaucracy. The only fully centrally planned economies remaining are North Korea and Cuba, but China and Vietnam are still centrally planned to a large degree and many countries' governments still plan centrally some parts of economic activity.

planning permission involves getting permission from the local authority before starting to build new homes, factories or retail outlets. The objective is to protect the countryside and ensure that designs are appropriate to the location. In practice, the process has made building land much more expensive than agricultural land. In some places the scarcity of land for development raises prices a great deal. High property prices in areas where labour is scarce can deter people from moving away from areas of high unemployment to places where they would be more likely to find work.

plant is capital equipment which is fixed in place in a factory or other production facility. It is a term usually used to describe facilities and machinery which have a very specific use, as with a chemical plant or car assembly line.

ploughed-back profit means profit retained within the firm. In contrast, the rest of the profit will be distributed to shareholders in the form of *dividends*. It is an important source of finance for investment in the future.

policy: a course of action planned by the government or by other decision takers.

policy conflict: it is frequently the case that policies conflict with one another in that the effect of one policy is to make another policy harder to achieve. For example, policies which are likely to reduce inflation are also likely to increase unemployment. Policies to persuade more firms and individuals to use the railways are likely to entail raising the cost of road use. This conflicts with the objective of keeping road use costs at a level acceptable to public opinion. There are many other examples. As Abraham Lincoln said, you can't please all the people all the time. (See also *macro-economic policy*.)

policy instrument: the means used to carry out a particular policy.

- Interest rates are the instrument used to implement *monetary policy*.

- Taxes and government expenditure can be used to create incentives and provide goods and services. *Incentives* are sometimes called *indirect controls*, because they work through their effect on people's decisions.
- Regulations are called *direct controls*, because they actually force people into a particular way of doing things, e.g. health and safety regulations.

policy package: some economic problems cannot be solved with a single policy. Supposing the government wanted to reduce air pollution by 50%. The causes of air pollution are quite varied so a range of policies would be required to deal with ozone, carbon monoxide, particulates and so on. The broader the policy objective, the more likely it is to require a policy package. Poverty, for example, has to be tackled in a whole range of ways.

poll tax: a fixed amount of tax which must be paid by each person as an individual. It was tried as a means of raising revenue for local authorities in England and Wales over the period 1990–93, but was highly unpopular. This was partly because poll taxes are *regressive*, i.e. they take a higher proportion of a poorer person's income and a lower proportion of a richer person's income.

'polluter pays' principle is the idea that polluting emissions should be taxed so that the businesses which create the pollution carry the full cost, i.e. both the private and the *social cost*, of the pollution they create.

pollution: impurities which are allowed to escape into the environment. Air pollution comes from vehicles, power stations and industries. Water pollution comes from farms, sewage and industries. Efforts are being made to ensure that polluters clean up more effectively. *Business responsibility* is often now described as entailing a commitment not to pollute or to control the level of pollution. In practice there is still much to be done.

pollution charges can be used to discourage pollution. Usually, such charges will be taxes on polluters, levied in proportion to the scale of their emissions. The climate levy in the UK forces firms to pay escalating amounts as pollution rises above set levels. This gives them an incentive to install equipment which will reduce the amount of pollution.

pollution permit: a licence given by the government which allows a firm to emit polluting substances up to a certain level. By allowing less than the amount of pollution currently occurring, the government can reduce pollution overall. Over time, levels allowed by the licences can be reduced. (See also *tradable permits*.)

population: all the people within a defined area or group. Most commonly it refers to countries or regions, but it can be used to refer to a more closely defined group, e.g. car owners or NHS users.

population change: a change in the number of people in a given population. Changes may occur because of:

- immigration or emigration. Immigration can be stimulating to an economy. Immigrants are often looking for work and can increase the supply of labour. They may relieve known labour shortages. Some may bring entrepreneurial vigour to a market system. It is clear that this happened to the US in the 19th century

- changes in birth rates and/or death rates. Falling death rates have typically had a big impact on the populations of developing countries. During the 1990s, for example, life expectancy in India rose from 59 to 62. Over the long run, this kind of change can make a big difference to populations.

During the development process, birth rates are at first high but infant mortality rates fall as incomes rise and health care improves. So families often become larger. In time, rising incomes lead people to want fewer children. They can be fairly sure their children will live. They may become eligible for welfare payments in old age. The critical need for children, as an insurance policy against poverty, diminishes. Birth rates fall. This process is advancing rapidly in many Asian developing countries, followed closely by some Latin American countries. In large parts of sub-Saharan Africa it has yet to appear.

population control: in countries with high birth rates, limiting population growth is very important because it can raise per capita incomes. Different strategies have been tried in different places. China has the one-child policy, which has been a success in urban areas but not in rural areas where two thirds of the population still live. The Indian government has tried to promote vasectomy. However, these types of measures have really had limited success until people's incomes rise fast enough to improve their standards of living significantly. Then they seem to manage to control family size regardless of government policy. Italy, Japan, Germany and a number of other developed countries are likely to face falling population trends in the future unless they decide to encourage immigration. At the present time there are many countries with *ageing populations*. (See also *population change*.)

population growth: the rate at which the population increases. This may come from immigration or from a rising birth rate or a falling death rate. (See also *population change*.)

Porter, Michael (born 1947) is an academic business specialist based at Harvard University. He has done a great deal of work on how both businesses and nations can develop a *competitive advantage*. In his book *The Competitive Advantage of Nations*, he and his associates set out in detail an analysis of the competitive positions of 10 countries, including the UK, the US and Japan. He showed the importance of *clusters*. These occur where there are a number of firms, relatively close together within one economy, which are competing strongly with one another on both domestic and world markets. The stimulus of competition forces each firm to find cost, technical and product advantages which increase efficiency. These advantages give all the competing firms a competitive edge relative to producers in other countries. It follows that competition policy is vital in promoting stronger competition between firms. The UK has an element of competitive advantage in speciality chemicals, pharmaceuticals and financial services.

portfolio: the full range of assets held by an individual or a firm. A wealthy individual or firm might have property, *shares*, bank balances, perhaps held in more than one currency, and fixed interest securities such as *bonds*. Many individuals might have a selection of these types of assets and a pension plan of some value too. A major objective would be to spread risks, sometimes described as not having all one's eggs in the same basket or *diversification*. For this reason, most people would hold shares in several companies rather than just one.

portfolio investment means buying *financial assets* rather than direct investment. The latter would involve actually setting up productive capacity such as factories or retail outlets. The former involves buying shares, property, bonds or other financial assets.

positional goods are things which by their nature are fixed in supply and therefore, ultimately, accessible only to those who can afford to pay rising prices if demand increases. Examples include quiet beaches and unrestricted rural views. As population pressures and economic growth continue, demand for such things increases while supply diminishes, pushing the price up and limiting access to the relatively few people who can buy themselves a privileged position. Another example might be a seat on the centre court at Wimbledon or any other item the desirability of which is increased by its scarcity.

positive externalities are the external benefits that may result from a course of action. Sometimes they are called spillover effects because they bring some benefit to a third party, someone who is neither a producer nor a consumer of the product. The firm which builds an office block of some architectural merit improves the appearance of the neighbourhood. In this way it benefits anyone who appreciates the improvement. (See also *externalities*.)

positive statements can be checked against the facts in order to decide whether they are true. They contrast with *normative* statements, which involve value judgements and will reflect personal opinions.

post-tax profit: profit after *corporation tax* has been deducted. This can be kept as *retained profit* to finance future expansion or distributed as *dividends* to shareholders.

poverty is a situation in which people's *standard of living* is low. It may be measured in either absolute or relative terms. *Absolute poverty* means that a person's basic human needs for food, clothing and shelter are not being met and a poor standard of health may also result. This applies to people suffering from malnutrition or without homes. *Relative poverty* depends on the standards being applied and implies that within a particular society a given standard of living is unacceptably low. So people may be described as living in relative poverty if they are unable to participate in activities which are considered normal in that society, even though they have enough to eat and somewhere to live. Thus poverty may mean having basic needs satisfied but being unable to go to a football match or spend a short time at the pub or pay for children's books or outings.

There is some evidence that poverty is on the increase because *income distribution* has widened in the past 15 years, worldwide, under the impact of market forces.

poverty line: an arbitrary dividing line which defines the income below which people are said to be living in poverty. This will vary from one country to another because exchange rates and prices do not necessarily coincide and because standards as to what is acceptable vary.

There is no single widely acceptable definition of world poverty but an income of less than US$1 per day is seen as unambiguously poor. Substantially reducing the number of people with incomes below this level has become a target for many organisations concerned with poverty, including the UN. There are currently around 1.2 billion people with less than a dollar a day, mainly living in rural areas.

In the UK, the income level at which benefits such as *income support* become available has been described as the poverty line. However, many people would argue that this level of income is insufficient to allow people to lead a normal life.

poverty trap: a situation in which a person may be worse off working than living on *means-tested benefits* because the marginal rate of taxation and the rate at which benefits are lost in combination remove the incentive effects of the earnings. This results from low *tax thresholds* combined with a sharp tapering off of means-tested benefits as income rises. Incentives have increased with the introduction of the *Working Families' Tax Credit*. (See also *replacement rate*.)

predatory pricing occurs when one firm sets its prices lower than those of its competitors, in the hope that one or more will be driven out of business because it cannot follow suit without making a loss which forces it to leave the market. The original firm can then raise prices to their old level again. Normally the price cutter will be a *market leader* with a chance of eliminating smaller competitors from the field and gaining *market power*. *The Times* tried this in 1997 and very nearly succeeded in driving *The Independent* out of business, but not quite. Being owned by News International, *The Times* could afford to make losses for a while. The *OFT* can investigate predatory pricing, but it is hard to prove.

preference shares are less risky than ordinary *shares* because, if the business fails, the preference shareholder will if possible be repaid first. Similarly, dividends will be paid first, in a year when profits are low, but the dividend will always be lower.

premium can mean either an insurance premium or an extra amount paid for a particularly attractive product or asset. An insurance premium is the amount paid for the insurance policy, i.e. the right to reimbursement if the event insured against actually happens.

present value is the name given to the current value of a future income stream. This may be calculated using a *discount rate* when an investment project is being considered. (See also *investment appraisal*.)

pressure group: an organisation which represents the interests of a particular group of people. Oxfam is a pressure group which works to reduce poverty in developing countries. Its members are all people with a particular concern about the issues involved. Pressure groups include *employers' organisations, trade unions,* community organisations and charities. They bring pressure to bear by lobbying wherever help towards their cause may be obtained. Oxfam lobbies government organisations and international organisations such as the *WTO*.

price: the money value of anything which is bought and sold in the marketplace, including goods, services, assets and factors of production. In competitive markets price is determined by market forces, i.e. supply and demand. Businesses with some monopoly power may be able to decide prices within limits. In some cases prices are decided by governments, e.g. prescription prices in the UK or all prices in a *centrally planned economy*. Mostly, prices are displayed and known in advance. In some cases, they may be negotiated, depending on the quantity bought or the means of payment, or there may be a haggling process in which the price emerges as a compromise.

price agreements are generally illegal under *competition law* but may be arrived at by a group of firms (a *cartel*) trying to reduce the impact of competition on each other. They may agree to keep prices above a certain minimum level. So long as they all stick to the agreement, they will be acting collectively like a *monopoly* and will be able to keep quantities sold lower and prices higher than they would be if there were strong competition. Under the 1998 Competition Act, a participant in a price agreement can go to the OFT with information so that it faces lower fines than the rest of the group if the OFT decides to prosecute.

price ceiling: a maximum price set by law. Most often this occurs where there is *regulation*, as with a *public utility*. In the past, rent controls have prevented rents from rising. The risk with a price ceiling is that if it is below the market clearing equilibrium, quantity supplied will in time be reduced.

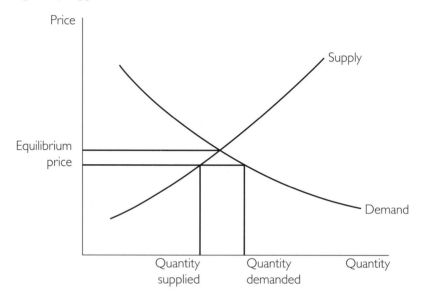

price competition means the rivalry between firms which use price as a way of attracting consumers. It contrasts with non-price competition, which involves other ways of attracting consumers, e.g. through advertising.

price discrimination: charging different prices in different markets where there are different price elasticities of demand. For example, rail operators charge commuters much more than they charge travellers who start out after the morning rush. For commuters, demand for rail services is very inelastic because there is usually no substitute: alternative ways of getting to work would take too long or it may be impossible to park a car. Keeping the price high means high sales revenue.

Other travellers have choices. They may be able to travel by bus or by car or avoid travelling altogether. There are substitutes and demand is price elastic. Low fares may induce them to travel by train, so maximising revenue. The marginal cost of taking an extra passenger in the middle of the day is usually zero, so offering low fares means extra revenue at no extra cost. (See also *price elasticity of demand* for diagrammatic explanation.)

Price discrimination will not work unless it is possible to separate the two different markets effectively.

price elastic: a change in price leads to a proportionately larger change in quantity demanded. (See also *price elasticity of demand.*)

price elasticity of demand measures the extent to which a change in price leads to a change in quantity demanded.

FORMULA: $$\frac{\text{percentage change in quantity demanded}}{\text{percentage change in price}}$$

For example, if the price of a good rises by 10%, and the quantity demanded then falls by 20% price elasticity is: $-20\% \div +10\% = -2$

If the number is greater than one the product is said to be price elastic. A number between zero and one is said to be price inelastic. If price elasticity is zero, it is termed unit elasticity of demand.

Price elasticity of demand is a negative number because an increase in prices causes a fall in quantity demanded and vice versa. There is an *inverse* relationship. As this is always true the minus sign is sometimes ignored in discussing the value of price elasticity. It should never be ignored when doing calculations.

Price elasticity of demand has a number of features:

- The most important factor in deciding elasticity of demand is whether *substitutes* are available. If there are, people will shop around and if the price rises, they will switch to an alternative. If there are no good substitutes, the demand will be inelastic. Often the elasticity depends on how tightly defined the product happens to be. The demand for toothpaste is inelastic because there are no acceptable substitutes so far as most people are concerned. But the demand for Colgate toothpaste may be quite elastic because a price rise may lead people to choose another brand.
- A second factor of relevance in determining price elasticity is the amount spent on the product in question. Where the price is low relative to the income available, demand is likely to be inelastic. Demand for a packet of crisps or a box of matches is usually inelastic.
- Time can be another factor. Sometimes information about price changes takes time to reach people. Then it may take a while for people to adjust to a price change. In the short run, a big increase in the price of petrol will make only a little difference to the demand for it. People who have cars will continue to use them for journeys they consider essential, getting to work, shopping and visiting family. In the long run, demand may be less inelastic. Some people will find alternative ways to travel and the car makers will have a bigger incentive to design fuel-efficient cars.
- There is a link between price elasticity of demand and sales revenue. If demand is elastic and prices rise, the greater-than-proportionate fall in quantity sold will mean that sales revenue will fall and vice versa. In the diagram, the box showing lost revenue is larger than the box showing gained revenue. With inelastic demand, a price increase will result in a rise in sales revenue. In the diagram on page 254, the box representing revenue gained is larger than the box representing revenue lost.

- Price elasticity of demand is of considerable significance because it may affect decisions about price. Raising the price of an item which has elastic demand may not help to cover rising costs. Also price elasticity affects the impact of certain indirect taxes, e.g. those on petrol, alcohol and tobacco (see also *tax incidence*) and of *tariffs* and *quotas* on imports.

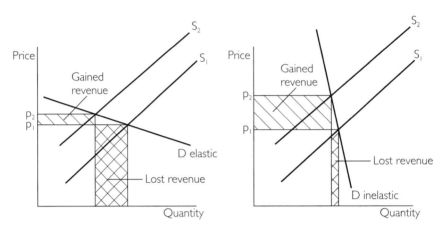

Price elasticity of demand

price elasticity of supply: see *supply elasticity*.

price fixing occurs when two or more firms agree to charge a minimum price. This is defined as an anti-competitive activity. (See also *price agreement*.)

price floor: a minimum price set by law. The commonest example comes from the guaranteed prices of the *Common Agricultural Policy* of the EU. Farmers receive a set price for most of their crop and animal products. The CAP authorities guarantee to buy all that is produced. If this is above the equilibrium market price, the outcome will be an excess supply which has to be bought and stored (in the diagram, Q_S-Q_D). In the past this has made the CAP very expensive and has raised food prices above the world level. Now the level of guaranteed prices has been reduced somewhat. (See Figure on page 255.)

price index: a way of measuring changes in the general level of prices using index numbers. The *retail price index* measures inflation generally. The wholesale price index measures changes in wholesale prices and provides a useful leading indicator of inflation.

price inelastic: see *inelastic demand*.

price leader: a firm with sufficient market power to decide on a price change which its competitors will tend to follow. This will be the *dominant firm* in the industry and perhaps also the largest. Often, all the competitors will be facing similar changes in costs and all follow the lead given by the price leader. This would be likely to occur in an *oligopoly* situation.

price level: the average level of prices of all consumer goods and services. This is measured by the *retail price index*.

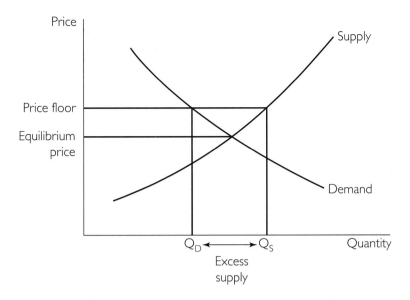

Price

Supply

Price floor

Equilibrium
price

Demand

Q_D ← → Q_S Quantity

Excess
supply

A price floor leading to excess supply (see page 254)

price maker: another term for *price leader*. It contrasts with *price taker*, the firm which follows the price leader.

price mechanism is the means by which resources are allocated in a *market economy*. Price rations the available resources among competing buyers. Rising demand tends to push up prices. This gives producers higher profits, which act as an incentive to increase the quantity supplied. Similarly, falling demand leads to lower prices and lower profits. If a loss is made, some producers will close down and the quantity supplied will fall.

The price mechanism works in the market for factors of production as well. If, for example, labour becomes scarce, wages in the occupation concerned will rise and costs of production will rise too. Producers will seek to pass the cost on to consumers in higher prices. Some people will switch to substitutes or reduce consumption. This may lead to lower levels of production.

As wages rose generally, the price of hiring servants rose. Quantity demanded fell. People did their own cleaning, in time switching to vacuum cleaners and other machines. A whole occupation more or less disappeared, changing the allocation of resources dramatically, though over a long period.

price reform: the process of moving from administered prices in a *centrally planned economy* towards market-determined prices. Administered prices do not always reflect the true *opportunity cost* of production. This means that some resources are under-valued and some overvalued, relative to what they are really worth in market terms. There may be *excess supply* or *excess demand* for some products. Price reform is quite difficult to achieve quickly because it has a big impact on people. For example, in most East European countries after 1989, many manufactured products could not compete with imports because they had been overpriced. The result was that much manufacturing capacity was closed down, leading to lower incomes and higher unemployment for a number of years.

price rigidity: the tendency of prices to stay the same and to change very little over time. This is most likely to happen in an *oligopoly*, where firms may try to avoid competing on price. Instead they will engage in non-price competition.

price sensitive means that the product has *elastic demand* with respect to price. A given change in price will lead to a proportionately higher change in quantity demanded. Some products are much more price sensitive than others. Compare the likely change in quantity demanded resulting from a 10% increase in price of petrol and skiing holidays.

price stability means that the price level rises slowly and the rate of inflation does not fluctuate greatly. The current target for the UK inflation rate is 2.5% per year. The Bank of England is charged with ensuring that it stays within 1% of this target. A low rate of inflation (rather than a zero rate) is generally thought to provide the best conditions for a flexible economy. Wage rates and prices often rise in response to increases in demand, creating incentives for resources to move into products for which consumer demand is increasing. Because both wages and prices tend to be sticky downwards at times, an increase of less than 2.5% (i.e. a relative fall) may be easier to achieve than an actual cut. It will still give the same useful signal of changes in demand which require resources to move from a declining industry into a line of production for which demand is growing.

price stickiness: the tendency for prices to rise but not often to fall. This does not really apply to individual products, where price cuts may be found. It refers to the tendency of the average price level to rise. (See also *price stability.*)

price subsidy: a payment to producers from the government which will enable them to charge a lower price for the product. Subsidies are often used to help sell EU exports of agricultural products. (See also *subsidy.*)

price supports are used where governments want to keep prices above their free market level. This can be done if the government is willing to buy the surplus which develops. The *Common Agricultural Policy* of the European Union provides an example of the extensive use of price supports. (See also *price floor.*)

price system: the mechanism which causes prices to rise when demand exceeds supply, and vice versa, so ensuring that prices send signals to producers about the nature of changes in consumer demand. This in turn enables the *allocation of resources* to change in response to consumers, thus preserving *consumer sovereignty*. (See also *price mechanism.*)

price taker: a firm which sells at the price prevailing in the market. It will face strong competition and will not be able to sell its product at a higher price. This may be because there is a *price maker*, a large and powerful producer, in an *oligopoly* market. Or it may be because there are many quite small producers, all competing strongly.

price theory: the area of economics which is concerned with the determination of price, through the study of demand and supply and their interaction. The focus of price theory is on *equilibrium* and disequilibrium prices and it seeks to predict the outcome of a variety of possible changes in the marketplace.

price transparency: a situation in which it is easy to compare the prices of differ-ent competing producers. EMU will make for greater price transparency within the euro zone, because prices will be given in the same currency in all countries. It will be easy to see if it would be cheaper to buy in another member country. This may be important in the car market, for example.

price war: a series of competing price cuts which are likely to lead to losses for some or all of the competitors. Price wars are usually associated with an *oligopoly*. They may be started by a dominant firm with a *predatory pricing* strategy and an objec-tive of driving one of the smaller players out of the market. They occur from time to time among newspapers, package holidays and petrol companies, among others. They usually do not last very long because profits are likely to be reduced for all. They will be followed by a much longer period of *price rigidity*.

prices and incomes policies were used in the past as a way to reduce the rate of inflation. Actual upper limits on rises were set by the government. The policies were not very successful.

primary products are produced directly from natural resources in agriculture, fishing, forestry, mining and quarrying and oil extraction.

primary product dependency arises when *developing countries* have to rely upon primary product exports for most of their foreign exchange needs. Many of them have large primary sectors, relative to their *secondary* and *tertiary sectors*. They have few if any manufactured products in which they have a *comparative advantage*. But many primary products have fluctuating prices and some of these exports therefore are not a very reliable source of revenue.

primary research is gathered directly from its source, rather than looked up in books and databases created by others. Firms often carry out their own market research using interviews: this is primary research. Investigating sources of data already collected is called desk research.

primary sector: all producers engaged in agriculture, fishing, forestry, mining, quarrying and oil extraction.

prisoner's dilemma: a *game theory* idea, based on the situation of two prisoners who must decide whether to confess, without knowing whether the other will or not, when confession carries the possibility of a lighter punishment. This is akin to com-petitors in a duopoly. They are not allowed to collude by law, but they will be greatly affected by each other's pricing strategies.

A *profit pay-off matrix* shows what will happen in all four different outcomes.

private benefits are the benefits which accrue to the individual buyer and seller of a product. In contrast, the *external benefits* are those which accrue to third parties. For example, if a large new factory is built, shopkeepers close to the area where employees of the new factory live will probably find that their profits are rising because of the increase in incomes in the area.

private costs are the costs of production which are borne by the business which produces the product. For example, private costs will include wages and salaries, interest and the costs of raw materials and components, as well as any research and development costs. They do not include *external costs*, i.e. those which are borne by third parties. These might be the costs to health and welfare of pollution which results from the production process.

private enterprise includes all economic activities which are undertaken for *profit* within the *private sector*. The owners of the business will be individuals operating as sole traders or as shareholders or other private sector organisations. In contrast, *public enterprise* involves the government. Private enterprise is normally subject to market forces, with decisions being made according to conditions of demand and supply.

Private Finance Initiative (PFI): a strategy begun in 1992 to invest in UK *infrastructure* using a mixture of private and public sector funding. The objective was to modernise the infrastructure without being committed to a big increase in government spending. It has been used to encourage private sector approaches to increasing the efficiency of building programmes in health, education and transport. Projects are run by private sector contractors, using private sector funds. The public sector body concerned undertakes to pay an annual fee for a given length of time (sometimes 20 years) which covers the costs. The most controversial such plan is to modernise the London Underground through a PFI. Is the outcome now known? It is too soon to say whether the costs of PFIs are worth the benefits. (See also *public–private initiatives.*)

private goods: items bought and consumed by individuals for their own benefit. Most goods and services come into this category. The distinguishing feature of private goods is that there is *rivalry* in consumption. Once consumed by one person they cannot be consumed by another. Other people are said to be excluded from consumption. There is rivalry in that consumers are competing with one another to obtain the goods they want. In contrast, *public goods* are those which must be provided by the public sector if we are to have them at all. No one will be excluded from benefiting from them and there will be no rivalry in consumption.

private limited company: a business set up under company law with shareholders and *limited liability*. It is private in that the shares cannot be bought or sold without the consent of all the existing shareholders.

private marginal cost: the extra cost of producing one more unit which is borne by the producer. (See also *marginal social cost.*)

private property: *assets* and goods owned by individuals who have a right to use them as they please which is recognised by the law. In contrast, public property is owned by local or national government. The right to use private property as the owner pleases is usually constrained to some degree, for example through planning permission.

private sector: all the firms which are owned by shareholders or individuals. Within the private sector, decisions are made on the basis of *market forces*, with businesses responding to the conditions of supply and demand so that changes in consumer demand will be reflected in decisions about what to produce. Approximately 61% of economic activity was conducted in the private sector in 2000–1, with the other 39% being public sector activity. Some activities, e.g. street cleaning, are financed by local or national government but actually carried out by the private sector.

privatisation: transferring economic activity out of the public sector and into the private sector. Privatisation was an important element in the policies of the Conservative government elected in 1979 although it took several years after that to get under way. Privatisation took several forms:

- The nationalised industries were sold to the public, mainly from 1984 onwards. During the late 1940s, many industries had been nationalised, including coal mining, the railways, British Airways, BT, gas, electricity and water. Iron and steel had been nationalised in 1966. Some of these which did not necessarily face strong competition were given regulatory bodies to protect the interests of consumers, e.g. OFGEM.
- Tenants of council houses were given the right to buy their homes at favourable prices. Between 1979 and 1997, 1.4 million dwellings were sold.
- Some public services were contracted out to the private sector, e.g. buses, school meals and refuse collection.

Many of the nationalised industries were actually declining and privatisation made it somewhat easier to close down parts of them. Others were very profitable, e.g. BT, and their sale sparked off a big increase in the number of people who actually owned shares. At the time privatisation was somewhat controversial but few people now favour renationalising the industries concerned. On the whole they have become more efficient when subjected to market forces. Some closures, particularly in coal mining, created a great deal of unemployment for a number of years. The cost to the government of maintaining these jobs would have been very high if they had stayed in public ownership and kept going.

There are still many controversial issues pertaining to privatisation. Some people are doubtful about:

- privatised companies' commitment to public safety
- the pay rises received by some of the chief executives
- the pay cuts experienced by some local authority employees who are now working for private sector employers
- some price increases, e.g. for water
- the impact of regulation
- and doubtless by the time you read this some other issues too.

process innovation: improvements in the way a product is produced, arising from new technologies. This is a powerful way to cut costs and become more efficient for many businesses. It can lead to big increases in *productivity*.

procurement means the purchase of goods and services by governments. Very large contracts are involved, e.g. for aircraft for the defence forces. In the past it has been quite normal for governments to favour domestic producers, but procurement contracts are being gradually opened up to competition within the EU. The issues may be discussed further within the *WTO*.

producer goods are goods bought as inputs into the production process for consumer goods and services.

producer objectives: see *business objectives*.

producer price index: an average measure of the prices of goods and services sold on a business-to-business basis. There are two distinct types:

- the average price of inputs to firms' production processes
- the average price of output sold wholesale.

These indices give an early warning of rising costs which could feed through into accelerating inflation.

producer surplus: the segment of consumer surplus which will be lost to the consumer if the industry becomes a monopoly. *Consumer surplus* is the area under the demand curve but above the price line, defined for competitive conditions. If the industry now becomes a monopoly, the price will rise as the firm cuts back production to take advantage of its position. Consumer surplus will be reduced. Part of this reduction (the price increase × quantity sold) becomes the producer surplus. This is a gain for the firm at the expense of the consumer.

product differentiation: see *differentiated product.*

production means the use of real resources to contribute to the creation of a final product. It applies to both goods and services. In practice, however, it is most often used when considering *primary products* and manufactures.

production function: a mathematical relationship which links the quantities of inputs to the production process to the quantity of output.

production possibility curve: see *production possibility frontier.*

production possibility frontier: the set of combinations of products which can be produced within an economy if all resources are being fully utilised. It is usually shown in diagrammatic form as being a curve, showing possible combinations of two goods. This curve will be concave to the origin, because resources vary as to the efficiency with which they can be used to produce particular items. Giving up some of one product may be possible but may not lead to much more of the other product being produced, if all the resources suited to its production have already been used.

Combinations of products outside the frontier (e.g. at point A) are impossible because they require more resources than are currently available. Combinations of products inside the frontier (e.g. at point B) entail unemployment of labour or capital or both. If the quantity of resources available increases, e.g. as a result of investment, then the frontier may shift outwards, allowing more of both goods to be produced. (See Figure on page 261.)

productive capacity refers to the ability of the economy to produce. An increase in productive capacity, which might result from an increase in investment, implies that it will be possible to increase output.

productive efficiency: see *technical efficiency.*

productivity measures the efficiency with which resources are used. The most commonly used productivity measure is output per person employed. When people speak of productivity, this is usually what they mean. However, it is possible also to measure output per unit of capital employed – the productivity of capital.

Productivity can be measured within the individual firm or for the economy as a whole.

On the international level, differing levels of productivity growth (efficiency) are important in explaining variations in industrial performance and rates of economic growth. These in turn have a major impact on standards of living.

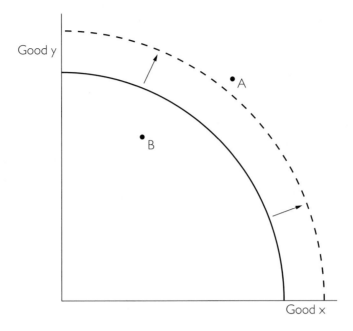

Production possibility frontier (see page 260)

In recent years, productivity growth in the UK has improved. Productivity grows for a number of reasons including:

- increased capital investment, so that labour inputs are working with better quality or larger amounts of capital equipment
- technological change, so that production processes are more efficient
- improved management techniques, so that people work more effectively together. Examples of the possibilities would be *multi-skilling* and *teamwork*.

Rising productivity can cause unemployment, which may persist for a number of years, if demand does not rise as fast as the productivity gains. (This happened in the UK in the early 1980s.) Despite this, it is difficult for an economy to grow healthily in the long run without productivity improvements. In the period 1960–1980, UK productivity grew very slowly compared to other developed countries. Recent experience has been much improved, though still not without cause for concern in some areas.

Productivity increase, 1994–2000

US	Japan*	France*	Germany	Italy*	UK
15.5	4.0	6.4	7.2	7.7	10.0

*1994–1999

Source: National Institute Economic Review, 4/2000

productivity bonus: a cash incentive to keep production at or above a target level. Some employers try to link pay increases to productivity in order to keep *unit costs* from rising and stay competitive.

productivity deal: part of a pay negotiation which links the pay increase to productivity improvements. These may involve changed ways of working which help to use the workforce more efficiently.

profit: a simple definition of profit is what is left from sales revenue after costs have been deducted. Profit is also a return on capital invested: it compensates the owner of the capital for the loss of the capital for any other potential use.

Economists distinguish *normal* and *supernormal profit*. The former is that amount of profit which is just sufficient to keep the resources employed in their current use. The latter is profit in excess of this amount and indicates that buyers are prepared to pay a price above the costs of all the resources used in production. In time this will attract more resources into production and increase output in line with consumer demand. (See also *profit-signalling mechanism.*)

> FORMULA: revenue – costs = profit

profit and loss account: part of a firm's annual report and accounts which gives a record of costs and revenues for the year. *Gross profit, operating (or net) profit,* profit before and after tax and *retained profit* will all be shown.

profit margin: profit as a percentage of sales revenue.

profit maximisation: in economic theory it is usually assumed that firms always maximise profits. Although many firms do have other objectives, profit is necessary for survival and is also likely to be a consequence of pursuing these other objectives. So the assumption can still give useful predictions. In practice:

- many firms look for long-term profit and may not maximise profits in the short run. Sales maximisation may be their main objective in the short run and this may bring with it increased *market power*
- other firms may take quite the opposite view, neglecting long-term planning in order to maximise profit in the short run. This is sometimes called *short-termism*
- another possible strategy is *satisficing* – earning enough profit to stay comfortably in business. Small businesses sometimes ignore opportunities to expand because they are comfortable with their existing scale of production.

The theoretical profit-maximising output for any firm will be at the point where *marginal cost* is equal to *marginal revenue*. Under *perfect competition*, marginal revenue will be equal to price (diagram A). Under *imperfect competition*, marginal revenue will tend to fall as output and sales increase, because prices will fall (diagram B). In both cases, at point A on the diagram, profits are less than they could be if output was increased, because the extra output would cost less than the revenue brought in. At point B profits are less than they could be (and losses may be made) because output above the profit-maximising level costs more to produce than it gains in revenue. (See Figure on page 263.)

Diagram A

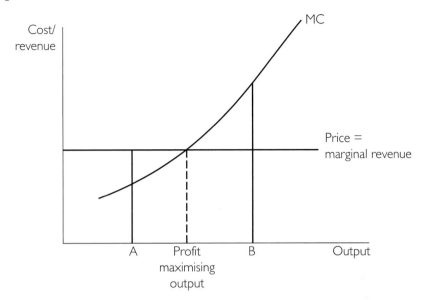

Diagram B

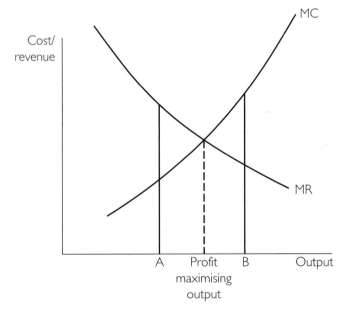

profit motive: the objective of the *entrepreneur*, who will seek sales revenue over and above the level of costs of production, as a reward for taking risks and organising the business. Economic analysis usually rests on an assumption that all entrepreneurs are motivated by profit. In fact, although it is important to make a profit to ensure long-term survival, many businesses have other motives as well. (See also *profit maximisation*.)

profit pay-off matrix: this is a game theory tool which can be used in a *duopoly* or *oligopoly* situation to show how each firm's best strategy depends on the reactions of competing firms. Firms are said to be interdependent.

Using the diagram below, within the matrix, firm X has the lower triangle in each quadrant and firm Y the higher triangle. HP is the high price strategy and LP the low price strategy. If both firms X and Y maintain high prices, profits will be 10 each, as in the top left quadrant of the diagram. If X thinks Y may keep to the high price, it will be better off cutting its price. It will make profits of 14, while Y will make 2. Alternatively, if Y takes this position and X maintains a high price, the position will be reversed. If in fact both cut prices together, both will have reduced profits of 6 each. (This is the *price war* type of outcome.) The least risky course of action is to stick to a high price strategy – hence *price rigidity* is very likely in this situation.

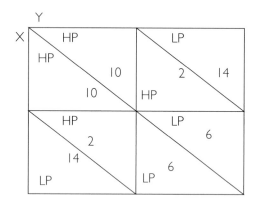

profit-related pay: earnings which are directly related to the *profit* levels of the employer. While this can give the employee an incentive and a stake in the company, it may be hard for them to see their role in increasing profits. It is not a widely used strategy.

profit-signalling mechanism: when demand for a product is increasing, prices will tend to rise and the product therefore becomes more profitable. This encourages entrepreneurs to expand output in profitable lines of production by moving resources into them. When losses are being made the reverse happens: resources will be moved out of the unprofitable lines. In this way profits signal the existence of unsatisfied consumer demand and ensure that the allocation of resources falls into line with the pattern of consumer demand. This link between the pattern of demand and the allocation of resources is an important element in the working of the *market system*.

progressive tax: one which takes in tax a higher proportion of high incomes than it does of low incomes. The most important example is *income tax*. Having a tax-free allowance, then a band of income which is taxed at 10%, means that people on lower incomes are taxed less, while people on higher incomes will pay tax at the standard rate of 22% or the higher rate of 40%.

property income is the return to land or capital (unearned income) as opposed to the return to labour (earned income). It could come in the form of *dividends* from ownership of shares or rents from property, interest on loans or bank deposits or profits made in business.

property rights: owners of *assets* have a right to charge people who want to make use of those assets. For example, owners of fishing rights may charge for the use of them by other people. The term is often used in connection with *intellectual property rights* such as copyright and patents.

proportional tax: a tax which takes an equal proportion of income whatever the person's income level.

protectionism involves any policy which protects domestic producers from international competition. Measures used might include any barrier to trade: *quotas, tariffs* and *non-tariff barriers*. These will raise the price of the imports to which they apply, so reducing the threat to domestic producers.

Protectionism can reduce the benefits of free trade in terms of consumer access to cheap products and enhanced economic growth. It is therefore discouraged by WTO rules and has been reduced through international trade negotiations. There are still many protectionist measures operating in some countries and it has a significant effect on the trading prospects of some of the *developing countries*.

The most notorious period of protectionism was between the wars, during the *Great Depression*, when country after country put up barriers in the hope that unemployment would not increase. The barriers made unemployment worse: they reduced exports for all concerned.

There has been an increase in protectionism in some product areas in recent years. *Voluntary export restraints* in the EU and USA have been placed on imports from the Far East of cars, steel and electronic goods. Despite the benefits of trade generally, people with vested interests in certain industries are sometimes able to bring pressure to bear on their MPs or Congressional representatives so that they will support protectionist measures.

proven reserves: known amounts of crude oil which are underground (or under the sea) which would be economic to extract at current oil prices. There is much more oil which could be retrieved economically if the price were to rise.

PSBR: public sector borrowing requirement, the old name for PSNCR, the *public sector net cash requirement*.

PSDR: see *public sector debt repayment*.

PSNCR: see *public sector net cash requirement*.

public borrowing means borrowing by the government to finance current and capital expenditure.

public choice: the choice of goods and services to be provided by the government. Overall, this is a matter of great complexity. Governments respond to public opinion and to media views to a degree, but many of the more complex decisions have to be made in the context of the relationship between the government and the civil service.

public corporation: the legal basis for the formation of a *nationalised industry*. The BBC is an example.

public enterprise refers to state-owned organisations, i.e. *nationalised industries*, which produce for the market, for example the Post Office (for now).

public expenditure is spending by the government, for example on social security, defence, education and health. Public expenditure in 2000 was approximately 39% of GDP. (See also *fiscal policy* and *government expenditure*.)

public finance refers to government expenditure and the ways in which it is financed through taxation and the *public sector net cash requirement*.

public goods are items which must be provided by society as a whole for two reasons. No one can be excluded from benefiting from them and their consumption by one person does not prevent their consumption by someone else, i.e. they are non-rivalrors. Examples include street lighting, defence and the police force.

public interest: the interests of society as a whole. The term is usually used in relation to the actions of the public sector, in particular of the remaining nationalised industries and the regulatory bodies set up to monitor the privatised industries (e.g. OFGEM). These are charged with acting in the public interest. This needs constant reinterpretation in the light of changing circumstances but can be loosely defined as protecting the consumer and the community from hidden or unnecessary costs.

public limited company (PLC): a company with *limited liability* and shares which can be bought by the general public. PLCs are the only type of company which can be quoted on the *Stock Exchange*. The drawbacks of being a quoted company are illustrated by Richard Branson of Virgin. He decided that having become a public company he wished to return to the status of *private limited company* again to avoid the loss of control and the share price fluctuations which accompany quotations on the Stock Exchange. (See also *divorce of ownership and control*.)

public ownership refers to *nationalised industries*, which produce for the market but are owned by the government and are therefore part of the *public sector*.

public–private initiatives are projects which aim to use a mixture of public and private finance to invest in the development of public services. Many are related to public transport developments. A particularly controversial scheme involves the London Underground which is badly in need of expensive modernisation. The nature of this initiative is as yet undecided. (See also *Private Finance Initiative*.)

public sector: that part of the economy which is organised directly or indirectly by national or local government. It includes the civil service, the NHS, all the services run by local government (e.g. education and refuse collection) and the few remaining *nationalised industries*. Decisions will tend to be made in the public interest, rather than on the basis of profitability, although some activities are required to cover their costs (as with the Post Office).

public sector borrowing: total borrowing by the *public sector*. The *public sector net cash requirement* shows the amount of borrowing needed in the current year. The *National Debt* is the total loan outstanding. If there is a surplus of tax revenue over government expenditure, there will be a PSDR, *public sector debt repayment*. This will reduce the National Debt.

public sector borrowing requirement (PSBR): the old name for the *public sector net cash requirement (PSNCR)*.

public sector debt repayment (PSDR): if government expenditure is less than tax revenue, then the government will be able to pay off some of its debts. This occurred from 1987–1990, partly because the government was receiving large payments for shares in the privatised industries. It occurred again in 1999–2000 as the economy grew and tax revenues rose.

public sector net cash requirement (PSNCR) is the amount by which *government expenditure* exceeds revenue from taxation and other income. It varies from year to year, depending on government policies at the time and on the state of the *trade cycle*.

The PSNCR is funded by borrowing. The mechanism for borrowing may be the sale of *Treasury bonds* or *bills* or the encouragement of *National Savings*. High levels of borrowing may necessitate high interest rates, in order to encourage people and organisations to buy Treasury bonds. This can be a problem if the result is to make borrowing more expensive for businesses which want to invest. It also means that there is a link between the way government expenditures are financed and *monetary policy*. High levels of borrowing can make it difficult to pursue prudent monetary policies in order to reduce inflation. Borrowing increases in times of *recession* as tax revenues tend to fall and expenditure on benefits increases. The reverse may happen in a boom.

Public sector net cash requirement (PSNCR) as % of GDP

1996	1997	1998	1999	2000	2001 (est)
+3.6	+1.0	−0.4	−3.6	−3.5	−0.8

Source: Treasury

A negative figure implies that there is a *public sector debt repayment*. Some governments at times have difficulty in keeping borrowing under control. One of the requirements for entry to EMU is that borrowing be less than 3% of GDP per year.

public spending: see *government expenditure*.

public utility: the suppliers of basic services to homes and businesses, including water, gas and electricity. These are *privatised industries* with *regulators* to protect consumers from the *market power* of the companies.

public works: expenditure by the government on *infrastructure* or socially useful projects, which may be of particular value in times of high unemployment.

pump priming: a term used much in the past to describe government spending which may be able to increase economic activity in a depressed area. For example, building new roads creates jobs for unemployed people; it may also improve communications and have a *multiplier* effect.

purchasing power: the real value of a given sum of money in terms of what it will buy. Inflation causes the purchasing power of the currency to fall.

purchasing power parity: an approach to international comparisons of standards of living which takes into account price levels in different countries. It uses exchange rates which have been adjusted to give accurate comparisons of purchasing power.

quality assurance: all measures taken to ensure that quality standards are actually reached.

quality control: checking the quality of a product. Usually this term is applied in manufacturing processes, meaning checking that both inputs and outputs are made to the correct specifications.

quality of life: recent research into the cost-effectiveness of particular medical treatments now measures quality of life achieved. This is an improvement on merely measuring mortality rates because it takes into account what people can do as a result of their treatments and not just whether they are alive.

quango: see *quasi-autonomous non-governmental organisation.*

quantity demanded: the specific amount of a product which consumers want to buy at a particular price. This is different from *demand,* which refers to the amounts demanded at a range of different prices (the *demand curve*).

quantity of money: the amount of money available in the economy. (See also *M0* and *M4.*)

quantity theory of money: the theory which links the quantity of money in circulation with the rate of *inflation.* The simplest version of this is given by the *equation of exchange.* This states that MV = PT, where M is the quantity of money, V is the *velocity of circulation,* P is the price level and T is the number of transactions. (In itself, this is in fact an identity: it is true by definition.) The theory holds that if M rises while V and T are constant, P will also rise.

This theory was important in economics in the early part of the 20th century but was superseded when Keynes and other economists observed that V and T might not be stable. It was replaced by a more sophisticated theory relating money and prices, developed by the proponents of *monetarism,* of whom the most notable was *Milton Friedman.* These ideas were influential during the early 1980s and became associated with Margaret Thatcher's time as prime minister. The policy prescription which resulted from monetarism was one of strict monetary control which would bring down the rate of inflation.

quartile: the observation which lies one quarter of the way through the population being studied. It is similar to the median or middle observation. The upper quartile will be three quarters of the way through the population, in ascending order. The lower quartile will be one quarter of the way through. This means that, say, people with incomes below the lower quartile level will be the quarter of the population with the lowest incomes.

quasi-autonomous non-governmental organisations (quangos) are bodies appointed by the government which are nevertheless independent of it. Their objectives are clearly laid down by the government but they are not subject to regular interference by it in their actual operation. They have been used to try to reduce the size of central government. The Equal Opportunities Commission is an example.

quasi-public goods: goods which have some features of *public goods*.

quaternary sector means all those firms working in the field of information technology.

quintile: the observation one fifth of the way through the population. So the lowest quintile would be the observation 20% of the way up a population arranged in ascending order. The term is also often used to refer to fifths of the total population.

quota (IMF): the money paid into the *International Monetary Fund* by each member country. This will determine its voting power and the amount which can be borrowed in the event of a balance of payments emergency.

quotas (import): an *import control* which places a fixed limit on the quantity of the good which can be imported. The objective is usually to protect domestic producers. The supply of the imports will be reduced and the price will usually rise.

The more inelastic the demand for the imported product, the more the price is likely to rise. Above the level of the quota, the supply is fixed and the price is demand determined.

A common form of quota is the *voluntary export restraint* (VER); these have been placed on imports of cars, electronic goods and steel to the EU and the USA from the Far East. Quotas are strongly discouraged by the *WTO* but are nevertheless widespread in some product areas. This is because there has been support in recent years for protectionist policies on the grounds that they may save jobs. In reality it is likely that the loss of output caused by the restraint on trade is more serious for standards of living than the loss of jobs. (See diagram below.)

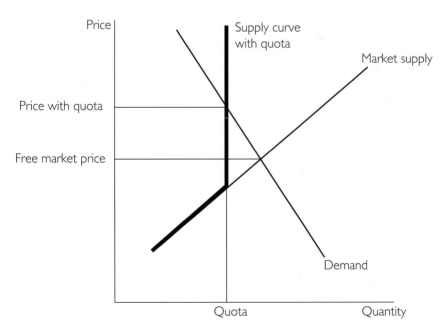

The effect of a quota

Quotas are an important element in the *Multi-Fibre Arrangement*, which is designed to reduce imports of textiles into all developed countries. It is due to be phased out by 2005. When this happens, basic clothing prices in the UK should fall.

quoted company: a firm that has its shares listed on the *Stock Exchange*.

R

R and D: see *research and development.*

race relations legislation makes it illegal to discriminate against people at work on grounds of colour, race, ethnic or national origin. The Commission for Racial Equality can investigate and pursue employers or *trade unions* which are thought to discriminate.

racial discrimination means refusing a job or a promotion to someone on grounds of race. Although it is illegal, recent studies show that it is still occurring. It is sometimes difficult to prove in individual cases. Unemployment rates amongst different ethnic groups are too large to be explained entirely by differences in qualifications.

random sample: a sample selected at random from a population being researched, so that it is likely to be representative of the population as a whole.

rate of interest: the amount which will have to be paid annually for the loan of funds. This will be higher for risky borrowers than it is for known, reputable borrowers. The lowest interest rates are those used by banks when they lend to each other. (See also *interest rates.*)

rate of return: a measure of the profit earned in relation to capital invested. Various definitions of profit may be used and comparisons of different investments may be made in order to determine which is most profitable.

rate support grant: the block grant from central government to local authorities. It means that not all of local spending needs to be financed by local taxes (i.e. by *council tax* and the *Uniform Business Rate*). It also allows the government to provide extra money to those areas with the greatest needs. In recent years it has been reduced somewhat.

rates are taxes paid by businesses to the local authority in their area and are usually known as the *Uniform Business Rate*. Rates used to be payable on all properties but now individuals pay *council tax*.

rational expectations: an economic theory which holds that because people learn from past experience, their reactions can be predicted, for example in relation to inflation. The theory was an important element in the body of thinking known as *monetarism*, which was particularly influential in the early 1980s. After that it became clear that people sometimes take some time to learn from past experience and therefore there may be long time lags in their reactions.

rationalisation: closing down parts of a firm which duplicate functions. This often happens after a merger but may happen wherever the firm is trying actively to cut costs. When the Royal Bank of Scotland bought the National Westminster Bank, rationalisation (i.e. closing branches) was planned in areas where both banks had branches located close together.

Sometimes rationalisation is used as an excuse for redundancies which the employers wanted anyway.

rationing: a limit on the amount that can be consumed. This term appears in a number of contexts, for example:

- when essential consumer goods were rationed by the UK government, during World War II
- when referring to the way the *price mechanism* rations consumer goods according to ability to pay
- in relation to the NHS, which is forced to ration certain health-care procedures because there is not enough money for everyone to have all the treatments from which they might possibly benefit.

Rationing can lead to the development of alternative markets. During World War II, the rationing system was respected by most people but *black markets* did develop, selling foodstuffs which had been produced on the quiet. NHS rationing does send some people off to the market for private health care, through which they can get faster treatment. Economic theory predicts that if there is someone who wants to sell the product and someone who wants to buy it, a market will develop.

raw materials: *commodities* in an unprocessed state which will be inputs to the production process.

real means that the item in question is being expressed in a way which removes the effects of inflation. (See also *real incomes.*) For example, real earnings show the actual change in the *purchasing power* of what people are earning. In contrast, *nominal values* are expressed in money terms, without allowance for inflation.

real GDP means a figure for total output in the economy which has been adjusted to allow for *inflation.*

real incomes are money incomes adjusted to allow for inflation. The figures must be deflated to constant prices using *index numbers.*

$$\text{FORMULA:} \quad \text{real income} = \frac{\text{money income} \times \text{base year index}}{\text{current year index}}$$

Worked example: If money income has increased by 20%, from £20 000 to £24 000, while the price level has risen by a total of 15%, how much has income increased in real terms and in constant prices?

To convert the new money income to the base year prices, it must be deflated using a price index. This means the index for the base year is 100. For the current year it is therefore 115.

$$\text{Real income} = \frac{£24,000 \times 100}{115} = £20\ 870$$

---

real interest rates reflect the actual rate of interest paid on a capital sum after allowance for the effects of inflation. Usually, the rate of *inflation* is deducted from the actual (nominal) interest rate, to arrive at the real rate of interest. Some of the nominal interest rate is in fact compensation for the fact that the capital sum is losing some of its value each year because of inflation. What is left is in fact the real rate of interest.

$$\text{FORMULA:} \quad \text{real interest rate} = \text{nominal interest rate} - \text{rate of inflation}$$

So a nominal rate of interest of, say, 7% with a rate of inflation of 2% implies a real rate of interest of 5%.

real national income: total income for the economy as a whole adjusted to *constant prices* to allow for the effects of rising prices.

real resources are all the things which can be used to create products for which there is a demand. So they include the *factors of production, land, labour and capital, human capital* and *natural resources.*

real terms: the use of *constant prices* to give values in terms of their purchasing power, making due allowance for the rate of *inflation.* Output in money terms can be deflated to constant prices in the same way as *real income.*

real values show changing values over time with the effects of *inflation* removed. This means they will be expressed in constant prices, using a base year. (See also *real incomes.*)

realignment (of currencies) occurs when governments from a number of countries with *fixed exchange rates* agree to change them because they have become out of line with the forces of supply and demand brought about by changes in trade and *capital movements.* This applied to the members of the *European Monetary System* (forerunner of the *EMU*) as they worked towards *convergence.*

reallocation of resources: when the pattern of consumer demand changes, resources are reallocated in line with the new pattern of demand, through the price mechanism. This process was first described by Adam Smith, who characterised it as the *invisible hand.* Reallocating resources is not always easy; it may entail some *structural unemployment* as some industries decline while others grow and people take time to adjust to the new composition of output.

receiver is appointed when a firm becomes *insolvent,* i.e. it does not have enough *assets* to cover all of its debts. The receiver will try to sell the company or as much of it as possible in order to raise money to pay off the debts. Receivers are sometimes called insolvency practitioners.

recession is the downswing of the *trade cycle* during which aggregate demand is growing slowly, if at all, and may be beginning to decline. There will be little sign of business confidence, so investment will be falling. *Inflation* will slow as people compete to get the few jobs available and pay increases become smaller. *Unemployment* will start to rise after a time lag. In the UK, the boom of the late 1980s was followed by a severe recession, with output actually falling during 1991. By then, aggregate demand was well below the level needed to absorb all of *full-capacity output* and unemployment was growing quite fast.

From 1993 until late 2000, the UK and the US enjoyed steady and fast economic growth respectively. What happened next?

reciprocity is the principle by which countries agree to grant the same trade concessions to their trading partners as they are receiving from them. When governments are negotiating trade arrangements through the *WTO* this principle is often important in securing agreement.

recovery is the upswing phase of the *trade cycle.* At first *aggregate demand* and output will grow slowly. *Investment* will begin to recover from its previous very low level.

There will be little inflation at this stage. For a while, *unemployment* may continue to rise because employers will be reluctant to take on more people until they are certain that the rise in demand will be sustained. (There is a time lag of 12–18 months between changes in output and changes in employment.) Later in the recovery, optimism returns and investment grows faster. There will be a *multiplier* effect.

During the 1990s, after the 1990-1991 recession, there was a long period of recovery. For many firms, confidence was slow in returning even though the economy as a whole was recovering. Not until 1994 did all firms regard themselves as having emerged from recession.

recycling means reusing existing resources, rather than using raw materials. It usually applies to paper, plastic or metallic products. The decision whether or not to recycle usually entails careful consideration of the costs and benefits of doing so. Waste products have to be collected, sorted and processed and the cost of these processes can be more than the cost of raw materials.

redeployment means moving to a different job offered by the same employer. When *structural change* is under way and people are being made redundant, redeployment can reduce the number of actual *redundancies* required. It may happen as a result of *rationalisation* or of declining demand for one product when the firm has other products for which demand is stable or growing.

redistribution of income: see *income redistribution.*

redundancy: job losses that result from fewer employees being needed. It may be the result of declining demand for the product or of *rationalisation*. Sometimes the firm will be investing in new equipment which is more efficient than the old. There will be a shift to more *capital-intensive* production. This will increase productivity and wages may rise but fewer people are needed. If redundancy payments are attractive enough it may be possible for some or all of the redundancies to be voluntary.

reflation means stimulating aggregate demand by using *expansionary policies* in order to increase the rate of economic growth and reduce unemployment. These could be *fiscal policies* such as tax cuts or increases in government spending or *monetary policies* such as reducing interest rates.

Regional Development Agencies (RDAs): the bodies responsible for implementing *regional policy*. Scotland, Wales and Northern Ireland have had them for some time; the nine English RDAs were set up in 1999. The English RDAs administer a part of the *Single Regeneration Budget*. The objectives are to enhance competitiveness within each region and to create job opportunities in areas where they are scarce.

regional policies are designed to address inequalities between regions. Incomes and unemployment vary considerably. In particular, the policies aim to address the problems created by localised industries' decline. The areas most in need of support are defined as the *assisted areas*; the boundary lines for these were redrawn in 2000 to reflect current needs more accurately.

The policies are administered partly through the government's regional offices and partly through the *Regional Development Agencies*. In order to reduce the duplication of effort through different ministries, there is now a *Single Regeneration Budget*.

The amount of money spent on regional assistance by the UK government has declined over the past 20 years, but the EU contribution is now larger than it was. The decline in the UK budget reflects concerns about the effectiveness of regional policies.

- Although altogether 800 000 jobs have been created in the assisted areas since the 1960s, the cost of each job has been estimated at £40 000.
- Some assistance has been given to firms which would have located in the assisted areas anyway.

regional unemployment is one element of *structural unemployment*: it is associated with the decline of localised industries which have in the past been big employers and have experienced a fall in demand for their products. Shipbuilding, iron and steel and coal are the industries most affected; in all three cases production was concentrated in locations which had been very favourable in the past. Falling demand arising partly from international competition brought many redundancies concentrated in a relatively short space of time. The adjustment process was a difficult one because of the lack of alternative job opportunities. Another example comes from Merseyside, where 100 000 jobs were lost on the docks between 1970 and 1990. Shipping traffic gradually shifted away from Liverpool towards air transport and towards the ports facing Europe rather than the US. The unemployment has persisted: it can take a long time for the local economy to adjust.

Registrar of Companies keeps records of all *private* and *public limited companies* in the UK. The information is available at Companies' House.

regressive tax: one which takes a larger proportion of low incomes than it does of high incomes. Expenditure taxes are all broadly regressive. To the extent that people on lower incomes are likely to save less, poorer people will find that expenditure taxes take more of their total income. Everyone who smokes 100 cigarettes a week will pay the same tax; it will be a large proportion of a poor person's income, a smaller proportion the higher the income.

The regressiveness of *VAT* is greatly reduced by the fact that it does not apply to food eaten at home, housing and public transport.

regulation covers a wide range of legal and other rules which apply to firms. Some come from national governments, some from the EU and some from trade associations which guarantee certain standards for their member firms. Regulation includes:

- health and safety regulations which might apply to electrical goods or to toys
- *consumer protection* which requires sellers to maintain standards
- employee protection which provides some guaranteed rights in the workplace
- competition law which requires firms to compete freely with one another
- rules for the privatised industries set up by their *regulators*, which watch prices and value for money.

Firms often complain of excessive regulation but modern societies have numerous reasons for maintaining extensive sets of rules. *Compliance costs* can be high but the rules protect large numbers of people.

regulator: an independent body set up by the government to ensure that privatised industries with an element of monopoly in their markets do not exploit consumers by overcharging and do make strenuous efforts to keep their costs down. An important element in their actions has been price caps. For example, BT has been required to keep its price increases below the rate of inflation; this is a relatively easy objective, since the industry is enjoying increased efficiency due to technical change and some prices have fallen. (See also *OFGEM, OFTEL, OFWAT.*)

regulatory capture: it is possible for regulators to be influenced by the firms they are supposed to regulate. This may make them prone to favour the interests of the industry rather than those of the consumer. OFTEL has been accused of tolerating too many *anti-competitive* practices at BT. In particular, some people think it has been too sympathetic to BT over its slow progress in offering access to the use of its telephone exchanges to other companies. Regulatory capture is particularly likely where the individual regulators stay in post for a long time and become closely associated with particular managers.

relative export prices: export prices compared to those of competitors or to world prices. Low relative export prices indicate a high degree of *competitiveness.*

relative inflation rates involve a comparison of *inflation* rates between countries. A high inflation rate relative to those of competing countries will mean that the exchange rate will become overvalued. As prices rise, exports will become dearer and are likely to fall while imports will become cheaper and may rise. *Depreciation* may follow.

relative interest rates involve a comparison of interest rates with those offered by other *financial intermediaries* or with those in other countries.

- Interest rates may be high or low in general but vary between one bank or building society and another and between different sorts of loans. Interest rates on very risky loans will always tend to be relatively high.
- Where one country has a higher interest rate than other countries, it will tend to attract deposits from abroad (provided its currency is one which the depositors are willing to hold). There are large amounts of capital which can be moved at short notice if an interest rate differential opens up, making the change worthwhile. (See also *capital inflow* and *capital outflow.*)

relative poverty means lacking the income needed to lead a normal life in the society concerned. It reflects the variations in expectations between countries. In developing countries there may be large numbers of people who are living in *absolute poverty* and so do not have the basic necessities of life: nourishing food, clothing and shelter. In *developed countries* almost everyone has these basic necessities, but many people do not have opportunities for leisure pursuits or reading books; their housing may be damp or in an area where safety is questionable. In the UK it is estimated that one fifth of all children are living in relative poverty which will have an adverse effect on their opportunities as adults.

relative price: a price may stay the same in money terms but rise or fall in relation to that of another if the price of the other good changes. Prices change in relation to one another because of market forces. These will vary from one market to another depending on changes in the pattern of consumer demand and in supply conditions. For example, the Millennium Dome attracted enough visitors for other visitor attractions, such as theme parks, to notice a fall-off in their business. Some of them reacted to this with various special offers, which amounted to a price cut. This would make the Dome look relatively expensive to potential visitors. Changing relative prices makes competing products look more or less attractive and are a part of the *price mechanism* which determines the *allocation of resources*.

relative wage rates mean wages in comparison with those in other occupations, with other employers or with the price of other inputs such as capital. They reflect differentials between different jobs, which are important in determining how labour is allocated between different possible products. Changing patterns of demand and changes in supply conditions will work through prices to affect the relative cost of wage rates and the allocation of resources.

For example, wage rates may stay the same while the price of capital equipment may fall due to technological developments. Decisions about how much capital to acquire and how much labour to employ depend on their relative prices. The fall in capital prices and the relative rise in the wage rate may lead to capital being substituted for labour in the production process and fewer people being employed. Production will be more *capital intensive.*

relativities are comparisons between levels of pay in different grades, occupations or industries. They are used in pay negotiations to establish what might be an appropriate pay rise. For example, a pay rise at Ford may be used to establish relativities in other car companies or in manufacturing generally.

relocation of labour refers to measures which might encourage geographical *mobility* of labour. These could include:

- relaxing restrictions on planning permission in areas where work is plentiful, so that more houses could be built
- offering more council housing in areas with job vacancies
- improving transport systems so that longer journeys to work become practical.

renewable resources are natural resources which can be regenerated. For example, forests which are regularly replanted after felling has taken place are renewable and hydro-electric power is renewable because it is continuously available. In contrast, electricity from a gas- or coal-fired power station is not a renewable resource because fossil fuels which have been used are not replaceable – they have been taken from the earth's crust. Wind power is controversial. It is available whenever the wind is blowing so is theoretically renewable but wind farms do spoil the view, which is not so easy to renew.

rent is the payment made for temporary use of a property. Income from rent is the return on the capital invested in the property. *Economic rent* has a specialised meaning: it is a payment made for a factor of production which is fixed in supply and therefore receives more than its *transfer earnings*. The economic rent reflects its scarcity in relation to the demand for it.

rent seeking: looking for ways to persuade the government to change the rules and regulations so that more profit can be made. This might involve trying to get the OFT to agree to some kind of *restrictive practice* being allowed or to negotiate a subsidy.

replacement investment: the level of investment needed to maintain the existing stock of capital equipment. This is sometimes known as *capital consumption. Gross investment* less *replacement investment* gives the level of net investment. This is the addition to the capital stock, which takes place each year.

replacement rate: the percentage of a person's income, when employed, which would be replaced by benefits if he or she is unemployed. Despite benefits which top up pay for people with families on low pay, there were still 595 000 people in 1998 who had replacement rates of 70% or more. The Working Families Tax Credit should reduce this percentage.

repo rate: the technical term for the Bank of England's official interest rate. It is the interest rate charged to banks which borrow from it whenever they are short of funds. Repo is short for 'sale and repurchase', the mechanism by which the Bank lends. The banks sell bills and bonds to the Bank at a discount equal to the repo rate, with an agreement that they will be bought back by the banks within about two weeks. It is thus a very short-term loan. Because the banks need to borrow in this way on a regular basis, the repo rate underpins the structure of interest rates generally and gives the Bank of England its controlling influence over the rates charged to borrowers.

repossession: when a borrower is unable to make interest and debt repayments on a loan which has been given specifically for the purchase of a home or a consumer durable the property is security for the loan and may be taken back by the lender to cover the outstanding debt.

resale price maintenance describes the way in which manufacturers sometimes try to set a minimum price for the product. It was made illegal to try to enforce these prices in 1964. This brought about much stronger competition between retailers, which generally favoured the large supermarket chains and caused small shops to suffer.

research and development (R and D): scientific research followed up with the development of products or processes which are either new, better or cheaper. R and D is an important aspect of innovation and of the process of *economic growth*, leading to rising standards of living as quality products become more accessible. The UK still spends relatively little on R and D, which may explain why *productivity* growth sometimes lags behind that of competitor countries. Current government policies call for tax incentives which may induce firms to spend more on R and D, but these are not yet fully developed.

Some economists argue that the firms most likely to spend on R and D are the ones in an *oligopoly* situation, where new product development can confer significant advantages. Some innovations can be protected by *patents* and this creates another type of incentive.

reserve assets: the assets held by banks which are very liquid and available for use when people want to withdraw their deposits. They include cash balances and very short-term loans.

reserve requirements: the reserve asset ratios which specify how much money banks must keep easily accessible in the form of liquid *reserve assets*. Central banks can vary these requirements. They are used in the *supervision* process which is an essential aspect of banking *regulation*.

reserves is a term usually used to refer to the foreign currency reserves held by the *central bank*. These may be used to manage the level of the exchange rate, so that its value is kept stable.

resource allocation: see *allocation of resources*.

resources: sources of inputs available to the economy for use in producing goods and services. Ultimately, the quantity of real resources available depends on the quantity of land, labour and capital and the extent to which changing technologies can improve the ways in which they are used.

restrictive practice is a term used in two different contexts. It can be:

- any method of interfering with the free play of market forces. Firms may try to reduce the market supply, which will tend to drive up prices. Or they may try to make a *market-sharing agreement*. This will reduce the amount of competition and again, help to keep the price high. However, it will only be legal if it can be justified to and registered with the OFT.
- regulations which prevent employers from using their employees in flexible ways. For example, there may job demarcations which mean that certain jobs are reserved for employees with specific craft skills, e.g. electricians. This is much less common than it used to be because firms have negotiated flexible working arrangements with trade unions and have given employees extra training to bring about *multi-skilling*.

restructuring means changing the departmental organisation of the firm or *rationalising* production. The objective is usually to cut costs but it may also involve reducing the output of some products which are not very profitable and increasing the output of others which are more so. It may involve closing down some factories or branches.

retail banks: the banks which cater for the needs of individuals and small businesses. They include the traditional banks, Barclays, Lloyds TSB and HSBC and a number of banks which used to be building societies, such as Abbey National. The remaining building societies also offer many retail banking services. In contrast, *merchant banks* deal mainly with the long-term needs of large businesses.

retail co-operatives were set up to give consumers better value for money at a time in the 19th century when prices in the shops were much less competitive than they are now. Profits went to the customers themselves, who were members of the co-op.

retail price index (RPI): the main measure of inflation in the UK. It is a *weighted average* of price changes based on average levels of spending on a wide range of consumer goods and services.

The Family Expenditure Survey carries out regular surveys of prices and spending patterns, using a representative range of different types of households. From this weights are calculated. For example, with weights totalling 1000, food is given 128 and housing 193, while fuel and light takes 34.

The base year is given the value 100. Price relatives are constructed for each product included, showing the price change from the base year. These are combined with the weights to arrive at the weighted average for the overall change in prices.

The formula for the construction of an index number is:

$$\text{Index} = \frac{\Sigma(\text{price relative} \times \text{weights})}{\Sigma \text{weights}},$$

where the price relative is the index of the change in the individual price. (Σ means 'the sum of'.) If Year 1 is to be the base year and if there are just two products, a price index for them can be constructed in the following way. This gives the average increase in prices and reflects the relative importance of each item in the total budget.

Product	Year 1 price	Year 2 price	Price relative	Weight	P.R. × weight
Potatoes	16p	20p	125	6	750
T-shirts	£4	£4.40	110	4	440

$$\text{Index} = \frac{750 + 440}{10} = 119$$

A number of different price indices are constructed for particular purposes. The RPI is the main measure. In addition there are:

- the Pensioner Price Index, which uses a different selection of goods and services which reflect pensioner habits and excludes housing, reflecting the prices which actually have most impact on pensioners
- RPIX, which measures inflation but without mortgage interest payments. This makes it possible to measure price changes without the impact of changes in interest rates which can distort the overall change
- RPIY, which measures inflation without mortgage interest payments and also excludes changes in council tax, VAT, import duties and the taxes on cars, airport use and insurance.

retained profit is profit kept by the firm rather than being distributed to shareholders as *dividends*. It will usually be used to finance new investments or the replacement of worn-out equipment. This is known as *internal finance*.

retraining: giving people who are part of the way through their working lives different or improved skills which are likely to be in demand in the future. Where people are *occupationally immobile*, this can enable them to take the jobs which are available.

return on capital employed (ROCE) is profit as a percentage of capital employed. It provides a measure of the rate of return on capital invested.

returns to scale: the relationship between the level of output and the quantity of inputs needed to produce it. If there are possible *economies of scale*, there will be *increasing returns to scale*. A given increase in output will require a proportionately smaller quantity of inputs in order to produce it.

revaluation refers to a rise in the value of the currency in relation to all other currencies. This might occur if there is a fixed exchange rate. It is likely to happen if the country has a long-standing surplus on the current account of the balance of payments.

revenue is the total value of sales made within a given period.

      FORMULA: revenue = price × quantity sold

revenue maximisation is one possible goal for a firm operating under imperfect *competition*. It may wish to expand its market share and therefore prefer revenue maximisation to profit maximisation. It will expand output up to the point where the marginal revenue is zero. This will be higher than the profit-maximising output. To sell all it has produced, the firm will need to reduce prices below what could be charged at the profit-maximising level of output. However, depending on its market power, it may still be able to make *supernormal profit*.

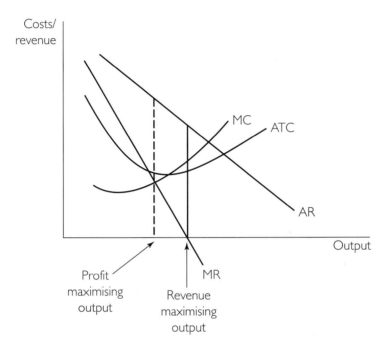

Ricardo, David (1772–1823): an economist whose most enduring contribution was the Theory of Comparative Advantage. This shows how each country will have a *comparative advantage* in producing different goods and services and if each specialises in the products in which it has the comparative advantage, it will be possible to increase total output, thus making everyone at least somewhat better off.

rights issue: an opportunity given to existing shareholders to buy more shares. From the firm's point of view this may be a relatively cheap way to raise extra finance. From the shareholder's point of view the outcome depends upon what happens after this to the share price.

risk: the possibility that events will not turn out exactly as expected. Risks are quantifiable, and probabilities can be assigned to them. Sometimes it is possible to insure against them, the insurers using the probability of their happening as a basis for setting the insurance premium. In contrast, uncertainty is not quantifiable.

rivalrous marketing: where a small number of firms are competing fiercely, their marketing strategies may be quite clearly targeted at each other's products. Advertising may be designed to invite unfavourable comparisons. Products may be designed so that they compete directly. This type of behaviour is very typical of an *oligopoly*, where a small number of large firms compete on price and on a number of non-price features.

rivalry: a term used in two contexts:

- Competition between firms may lead to intense rivalry as each seeks to outdo the other in the marketplace. This is a likely outcome where there is an *oligopoly* or a *duopoly*, where each firm is using both price and *non-price competition* and is intensely preoccupied with increasing market share.
- Rivalry in consumption refers to the fact that *private goods* can only be used by the household that bought them. Other people are excluded from consuming them. In contrast, *public goods* such as defence or street lighting are not rivalrous in this way. Once they are provided, everyone can benefit from them.

road pricing: a system for ensuring that the costs of road use are paid for entirely by the road users. The technology for tracking road use now exists and the only thing preventing its implementation is its political unpopularity.

It has a number of advantages:

- Prices could be set at a level which discouraged users from driving their cars in congested places unless the benefits to them outweighed the costs, so reducing the total amount of traffic.
- Congestion would be reduced and traffic would move faster, saving the economic costs of delay caused by congestion.
- Funds raised could be used to improve public transport.

There are some uncertainties as to what price levels would actually reduce congestion and as to how the technology would actually work in practice.

robots are electronically controlled machines which can perform precision manufacturing tasks with a high degree of reliability. They can be used to increase *productivity* in some manufacturing processes.

ROCE: see *return on capital employed*.

Rostow's model set out a sequence of phases in the development process which he saw as affecting all *developing countries* over a period of time. These were:

- the traditional society in which most people are living in rural areas and dependent on agriculture for their living
- the transition stage in which some manufacturing has begun to develop
- the take-off, during which investment increases rapidly and the country begins to develop its resources and its infrastructure much more actively, leading to self-sustained economic growth

- the drive to maturity, when both manufacturing and service sector production expand
- the stage of high mass consumption, corresponding to the position of the developed countries.

Although the idea of the take-off period proved to be helpful in providing real insights, the overall sequence has been widely criticised. There is much variation in the development experience and many countries have followed a rather different pattern. Not all developing countries have started out on the development process from the position of a traditional society. *Mature economies* continue to alter, undergoing a continuous process of structural change, and their economies differ greatly from each other.

Royal Commission on Environmental Pollution reported in 1994, setting targets for the reduction of transport-related pollutants. It stated that carbon dioxide emissions in 2000 should be no more than they were in 1990 and that by 2020, they would be just 80% of 1990 levels. The main weapon for achieving cuts in emissions of all greenhouse gases was to be an increase in fuel taxes, using the *fuel tax escalator*. This provided for increases above those required by the rate of inflation at each annual Budget. It proved to be rather unpopular and the 2000 budget switched to a lower rate of increase. At the time of writing the drivers appear to have settled for more global warming.

royalty: an agreed percentage of sales revenue paid to the owner of a patent or copyright for the use of the idea, process, name or work.

RPI: see *retail price index*.

RPIX and RPIY: RPIX is the retail price index excluding mortgage interest payments, thus giving a measure of inflation which is not distorted by interest rate changes. RPIY excludes *indirect taxes* as well as mortgage interest.

rustbelt: a large stretch of the North Eastern US which has suffered from declining industries.

sacking: dismissal by an employer. This may be for a breach of contract or *redundancy*.

salary: monthly payment by an employer. From the point of view of economic theory, salaries are exactly the same as wages, i.e. a payment for the services of labour.

sales maximisation: the highest output possible without making a loss. This can be an objective for the firm in certain circumstances.

- It may happen in an *oligopoly*, when a firm engaged in a price war has to decide by how much it can afford to cut its price, with a view to maintaining market share.
- *Satisficing* could also produce this result. Imagine a firm with a local market, very much a part of its surrounding community, which could present its product as an expensive, upmarket item but instead chooses to produce all it can with the facilities it has and sell it at a price which makes a *normal profit*.

In the diagram, output will be at the level where average revenue is exactly equal to average total cost.

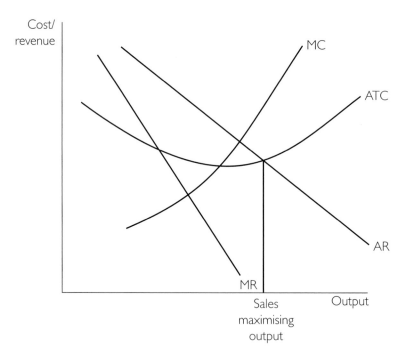

sales promotion: bringing the product to consumers' attention. It is particularly visible in an *oligopoly*, where there is much non-price competition. It includes:

- advertising and packaging, both of which can be used to create an image for the product which eventually may become an element in the product itself
- branding, which can be used to promote the product on quality expectations, style or reliability
- personal selling, which may persuade consumers
- free offers, competitions etc. which may be used briefly to attract customers who, it is hoped, will then develop some brand loyalty.

sales revenue: the total value of output sold.

FORMULA: quantity sold × price = sales revenue

Sometimes sales revenue is called total revenue or just revenue. When prices change, revenue will be affected and the size of the effect will depend on the price elasticity of demand. (See also *average revenue*.)

sales revenue maximisation: see *revenue maximisation*.

sales tax: a tax on goods sold which is included in the price to the customer. Examples include VAT and excise taxes.

sales turnover: an everyday business term for *sales revenue*.

sanctions are rules made by international organisations or pressure groups which prohibit trade with countries which are behaving in ways which are considered unacceptable. The United Nations may place sanctions on a country which is considered to be behaving aggressively, as with Serbia in recent years. South Africa was eventually forced by sanctions to abandon overtly racist policies. It is possible to prohibit trade in particular items, e.g. arms.

satisficing: taking business decisions which lead to an adequate *rate of return*, rather than *profit maximising*. There are a number of reasons why this *business objective* may seem to be the best option.

- Small businesses may not want to grow, because the owner of the business is happy making a living and does not want the risks and anxiety of a more dynamic approach.
- Very large firms in an *oligopoly* situation may prefer not to be seen to be making very high profits. These could attract new entrants to the market, which would intensify competition. (This is the situation in a *contestable market*, where barriers to entry are relatively low.) High profits might also attract the attention of the OFT, which may leave well alone if the firm is offering good value for money.

saving: the amount of *disposable income* which is not spent on consumption but kept for the future. Saving is a withdrawal from the *circular flow of money*. In the short run an increase in saving will reduce *aggregate demand*, other things being equal. Saving is normally measured by the *savings ratio*.

Saving can provide finance for investment. Over the long run this can be important in promoting economic growth. Japan, Taiwan and other Asian countries have high savings ratios which have contributed to high levels of investment.

In the basic *Keynesian model*, saving is directly related to the level of income. (See also *average propensity to save* and *marginal propensity to save*.) At very low levels of income, there will be dissaving – past savings will be run down in order to provide funds for essential consumption. At higher incomes, if consumers save more and spend less then aggregate demand may be insufficient to sustain business confidence and output may fall.

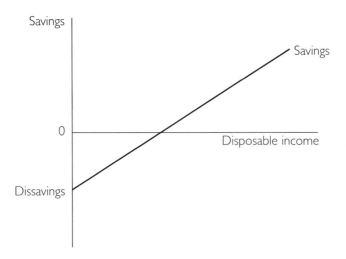

savings ratio measures the rate of saving, i.e. saving as a proportion of GDP. In the long term, the growth of an economy depends upon a high rate of saving, although in the short term a rise in the savings ratio can cut consumer spending and reduce *aggregate demand.*

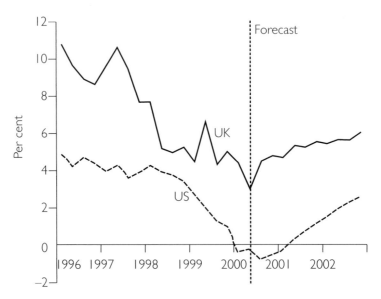

Source: National Institute Economic Review, 4/2000

The savings ratio in the US and the UK

In the past savings were thought to be at least partly determined by interest rates. That link now appears rather weak. Savings could be determined by expectations, so that the threat of rising unemployment might make saving increase. However, this has proved to be a weak link too. A stronger connection can be made between the savings ratio and the rate of *inflation*. A higher rate of inflation can erode the value of money-denominated assets and therefore lead people to save more for a while in order to rebuild the real value of their assets.

scale of production: some production, e.g. of cars, will be undertaken on a large scale, because mass production is cheaper – there are *economies of scale*. For other products, small-scale production works quite well. For some products, production may work well on either a small or a large scale. Pottery can be produced by one person skilled in the craft, making hand-made pots, or in a factory with a large output.

As output increases, it is possible for the producer to encounter *diseconomies of scale*, which will mean that average costs are rising.

scarce resources: *factors of production* and *raw materials* which are scarce in relation to the scale of human needs and wants. The scarcer they are, the more the price will tend to rise as people compete to obtain what they want.

scarcity: the term used to describe the fact that people's wants and needs always exceed the resources available to satisfy them. In practice, choices must be made and those choices determine the *allocation of resources*.

Schengen countries: the EU member countries which have opted to eliminate border immigration controls on their internal frontiers. Only the UK and Ireland have stayed outside this agreement. The fundamental principle of free movement of people wanting to live and work in other parts of the EU is not affected by this.

science park: industrial estates located close to universities. Easy access to expert knowledge can provide *external economies of scale* for the firms in the science park.

SDRs: see *Special Drawing Rights.*

SEAQ: see *Stock Exchange Automated Quotation System.*

seasonal adjustment removes regular seasonal changes from data so that the underlying trend can be seen clearly. *Unemployment* figures are usually seasonally adjusted so that monthly figures show the changes which are brought about by macro-economic factors.

seasonal unemployment: unemployment which rises and falls according to a seasonal pattern. Wintry weather can lead to *unemployment* of construction workers or of people employed in tourism.

secondary action means industrial action in workplaces different from those of the original dispute. In the past, employees in other industries might come out in support of the employees in dispute. This is now illegal.

secondary sector: all firms engaged in manufacturing. Several trends have been discernible in the UK:

- The secondary sector faces competition from imports. Some products lose their *comparative advantage* as developing countries become cheaper sources of standard consumer goods and semi-manufactures (processed raw materials).

- Other products have lost their comparative advantage to imports coming mainly from developed countries, such as cars.
- Some manufacturers compete very successfully and have expanded exports in a wide range of products, such as speciality chemicals.
- Most manufacturing has become more *capital-intensive.* Productivity has increased. Employment in the secondary sector has fallen dramatically.
- In developing countries, it is common for the secondary sector to be growing fastest.

(See also *sectoral change.*)

sector: the economy can be divided up into sectors, each of which consists of a group of decision takers with features in common. For example, one distinction is between the *private sector*, the *public sector* and the overseas sector. The economy can also be divided up into the personal sector, the corporate sector and the government sector. The personal sector consists of all individuals, the corporate sector of all businesses.

sectoral changes are the differences that develop over time in the relative size of the *primary, secondary* and *tertiary* sectors. In a mature economy such as the UK, the secondary sector is typically smaller than the *tertiary* (service) sector in terms of the number of people employed and also in terms of the value of output. An important reason for the falling numbers employed in the primary and secondary sectors is the substitution of capital for labour, leading to more *capital-intensive* production. In both there has been a big increase in *productivity.*

UK GDP by sector, %

	1960	1980	1996
Agriculture	6.0	3.1	1.9
Industry	41.0	36.5	29.4
(manufacturing)	30.4	24.7	21.3
Services	53.0	60.4	68.6

Source: OECD

Employment in the UK, % of total

	1964	1979	1990	1997
Primary	5.1	3.0	2.1	1.4
Secondary	46.9	38.5	26.6	22.4
Tertiary	47.8	58.5	71.3	76.3

Source: ONS, Annual Abstracts

securities is a general term covering financial contracts such as *bonds, shares* and *derivatives.* In each case, a sum of money changes hands in return for an income stream which may be in the form of interest or dividends. Often, owners of securities take some risk as to possible changes in capital value, should they wish to sell them.

segmented labour markets: the labour market consists of a number of different occupational groups, between which there is relatively little movement because of *occupational immobility.* This means that pay differs quite substantially between groups, depending upon the bargaining power of each group. Some professional organisations have a degree of control over the supply of their labour and are able to keep pay high.

Some trade unions have bargaining power because most people in a particular occupation are union members. (This is less often the case now than it was before trade unions were weakened by changes in the law.) The AEEU (the Amalgamated Engineering and Electrical Union) was able to raise substantially the pay for its electricians working on prestige projects in London, e.g. the Millennium Dome, during 1999. At the other extreme, many employees in catering are poorly paid. They are often not unionised and many work for relatively small employers so they have very limited bargaining power.

self-employment refers to people who work freelance or in their own business, either alone or with some employees. The numbers involved tend to increase during a *recession*, as jobs with employers become harder to find. In mid-2000, 12.2% (3.4 million) of the labour force was self-employed.

self-fulfilling prophecy: a situation in which the expectation of an event may actually help to bring it about. The best example concerns the increase in *investment* which follows upon resurgent confidence during the recovery phase of the *trade cycle*. During recession, firms' expectations are gloomy. Demand is stagnant or perhaps falling, new production capacity is not needed and investment is very low. In time, however, *aggregate demand* will begin to rise and firms' expectations will become more optimistic. Investment will seem worthwhile and will start to rise, so there will be an upward *multiplier* effect and incomes will rise by more than the initial injection into the circular flow of money. Investment will increase again, fulfilling the promise of the expectations.

self-regulation means that the industry itself imposes standards and codes of conduct which encourage firms to act in a responsible way. It is essentially a form of consumer protection which is operated by the firms themselves. Sometimes self-regulation is the industry's response to the threat of regulation by the government.

sellers' market: a market in which there are more buyers than sellers, so that the sellers can raise the price and still sell. The term applies most often in a housing boom, when prices are rising steadily.

separation of ownership from control: see *divorce of ownership and control.*

services: products which consist of something done, rather than a tangible object. They include retailing, hotels and catering, hairdressing, transport, technical services and financial services, among many others. The line between a good and a service can be blurred. As I write this book I am part of a long process in manufacturing it. It is a good and if someone throws it at you, it will hurt. But the ONS would probably think I am offering professional services to the publisher.

service sector: see *tertiary sector.*

set-aside: the scheme by which farmers are paid not to cultivate a portion of their land. The *Common Agricultural Policy* of the EU currently has a set-aside policy, as does the US government. This is to ensure that farmers in the country concerned do not produce so much that farm prices fall and farm incomes are reduced.

sex discrimination means preferring men to women applicants for a job or for promotion. Although it is illegal under the Sex Discrimination Act of 1975, it is still clear that it is happening, particularly in some sectors. Part of the problem is that proving it is difficult. Employers who discriminate are missing the opportunity to appoint the best person for the job and may have higher costs of production as a result. There is ample evidence that on average, full-time women employees are paid less than their male equivalents. The difference is not explained by differences in qualifications.

share: a contribution to the capital needed by a firm, by virtue of which the shareholder becomes a part owner of the firm in perpetuity. A share certificate is issued, entitling the shareholder to a *dividend*. This will normally be paid once or twice a year and will vary depending on the profits earned during that year. (In a very bad year it may be zero.)

Shares in a *public limited company* can be sold on the *Stock Exchange* but the price will be uncertain and will depend on expectations of future profitability or likely growth in the share price. Some high-technology shares seldom pay dividends but may offer some prospect of capital gains due to a rising share price.

Shares in a *private limited company* can be sold with the permission of the rest of the shareholders.

share options are opportunities for particular employees to buy shares in the firm at a price fixed on a certain date. If the share price rises, the employee can exercise the right, making an immediate capital gain. If the price falls, they lose nothing. This can provide a substantial incentive to key employees. It can also lead to enormous rewards to managers who may in fact have contributed no more to the success of the firm than has the workforce as a whole.

share price index: a measure of the average change in share prices over time. In London, there are the Financial Times Actuaries All-Share Index, covering all the shares traded, and the Financial Times-Stock Exchange 100 Share Index (the Footsie) which covers 100 equities with over £1 billion of market capitalisation. In Japan there is the Nikkei index. New York has the Dow Jones and the NASDAQ index, which is part of the National Association of Securities Dealers Automated Quotation system, which competes with the New York Stock Exchange.

shareholders are the legal owners of the firm. They receive a share of the profits in the form of dividends. They are also entitled to go to the *annual general meeting (AGM)* of the firm where they will approve the accounts, elect directors and get the opportunity to ask questions. Many shares are owned not by individuals but by financial intermediaries such as insurance companies and pension finds. Individual shareholders often do not exercise their rights to ask questions but some buy a few shares with the main intention of using their rights to question the directors on the firm's *ethical policy*.

shift in aggregate demand: an increase in the amount of aggregate demand at all price levels. This is likely to happen because consumption, investment, exports or government expenditure, or some combination of these, has changed. If there is an increase in aggregate demand, it will be possible for output to increase so long as the appropriate resources are available (AD2). If the economy is approaching *full-capacity output* (AD3), pressure on resources will cause inflation to accelerate as *supply constraints* develop.

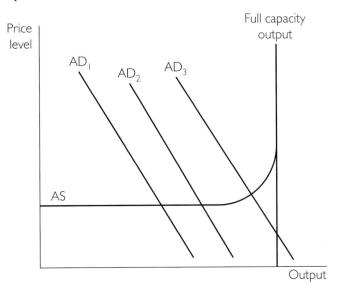

shift in aggregate supply: a change in the potential of the economy to supply goods and services. Usually this will increase over time as technology and *investment* create new productive capacity. (See also *economic growth*.)

shift in the demand curve: the demand curve, which shows the relationship between price and quantity demanded, will shift if there is a change in market conditions. This might result from a change in incomes, a change in the price of a substitute product or a complement or a change in tastes or fashion. For example, an increase in incomes will shift the demand curve for designer clothes to the right. More will be sold at any given price. (See also *demand curve*.)

shift in the supply curve: the supply curve shows the relationship between price and quantity supplied. The curve shifts if there is a change in costs of production. For example, an improvement in technology or investment in new capital equipment will shift the supply curve to the right. A larger quantity will be supplied at any given price. There may also be a shift in the supply curve if some other product becomes more profitable, diverting resources towards the most profitable items. (See also *supply curve*.)

shift work means that different teams of employees work one after the other, using the same space and equipment for two or three eight-hour shifts in each 24-hour period. All essential services work like this. In manufacturing, shift work makes sense if the equipment is very expensive relative to other costs, because it makes the fullest possible use of the large capital *investment*. It may also be used if orders are coming in faster than one day shift can handle. Work during anti-social hours will usually have to be compensated at higher rates of pay, so the decision to work shifts requires a careful evaluation of the costs. The car industry may or may not work shifts according to the level of demand.

shocks are events which have a major impact on the economy, such that many things change. Examples include the reunification of Germany, which created a major shock for Germany and a somewhat smaller one for its EU partners, and the oil price rises of 1974 and 1979. A change in commodity prices will be a major shock for a country which depends on export revenue from the sale of that commodity.

shortage: a situation in which demand exceeds supply. Usually, with a *market system*, the shortage will cause prices to rise, creating an incentive for producers to supply a larger quantity, and *equilibrium* will quite quickly be restored. A shortage will persist if for some reason the price cannot rise. (See also *excess demand*.)

short run: a time period in which only some variables may change. For example, the short run may be the time in which inputs only of *variable factors of production* can be altered. The input of fixed factors cannot be changed. So more employees might be put to work with the same stock of equipment. In contrast, in the long run, inputs of all factors of production may be changed. The definition of the short run may change according to the context in which it is being used.

short-run equilibrium under perfect competition is a situation in which demand has changed, so that the price is not at its usual level. This is a signal that consumers want to buy more or less of the product. There are many firms under *perfect competition* and *entry* and *exit* are easy, so a change in profits will bring a fairly swift change in output, restoring the system to the long-run equilibrium.

If your exam board requires diagrammatic detail on this, read on.

- If demand has increased, price and *marginal revenue rise*. There is a new, higher short-run equilibrium at the output where marginal cost is equal to marginal revenue. Firms already in the industry will make *supernormal profit* (sometimes referred to as *economic profit*) which is over and above the long-run opportunity cost of the resources used. In the diagram, it is the shaded area between price and average cost. This will attract new entrants to the industry, so that added competition will force the price back down to its long-run equilibrium level, P1.

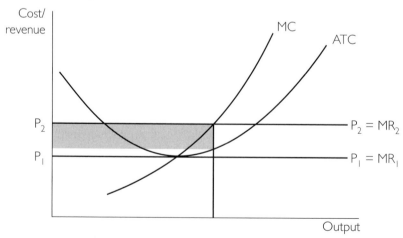

Short-run equilibrium after an increase in demand

- The converse may happen. Demand has decreased and the price has fallen. Firms will be making losses (equal to the difference between ATC and price). There will be a new short-run equilibrium where the price is equal to or more than the level of average variable cost. So long as their fixed factors of production keep on running, firms will continue to produce because their variable costs (AVC) are covered. As their fixed factors of production wear out, some of them will go out of business rather than replace their capital equipment. As firms exit the market, competition will be less forceful and the price will gradually rise to its long-run equilibrium level, P1, at which both fixed and variable costs are fully covered.

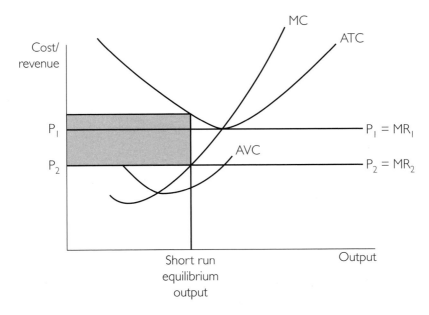

At the short-run equilibrium output, variable costs are covered

(See also *perfect competition.*)

short-run Phillips curve: the trade-off between inflation and unemployment which can be observed over a period of a few years. This term is used when it is assumed that the long-run Phillips curve is a vertical line which corresponds to the *non-accelerating inflation rate of unemployment.* (See also *Phillips curve.*)

short-termism describes a tendency on the part of firms to plan for short-run profit maximisation rather than long-run growth. The main problematic consequence will be to reduce investment in projects which pay off only in the long run, and in research and development. This may mean that quality and technical prowess are threatened. Sometimes the shareholders are blamed for wanting to see good results quickly.

short-time working: during a *recession* or a period of reduced demand for any reason, firms may reduce the length of the working week to perhaps three or four days.

sight deposits: another name for current accounts.

Silicon Valley: the area in California in which numerous new electronic and software products have been developed and produced.

simulation: the use of a model of a firm or of the economy, which imitates what happens in the real world. It can be used to explore the effects of a variety of changes. Simulations are usually based on a set of equations which describe the relationships between different variables.

single currency: the euro is the single currency of the 12 EU countries which have joined together in the *Economic and Monetary Union* (EMU). From 2002, national currencies will go out of use and the *European Central Bank* will issue notes and coins. The costs and risks associated with foreign exchange transactions will be eliminated within the member countries. It is possible that euro transactions will increase in the three EU countries which are outside EMU (UK, Sweden and Denmark) even if they do not join soon. At the time of writing the UK government is still undecided about joining. The economy must of course meet the *convergence criteria*. Also, Chancellor Gordon Brown has outlined his five economic tests:

- Will EMU create better conditions for *foreign direct investment* in the UK?
- How will the UK financial services sector be affected?
- Are the euro zone and the UK *trade cycles* moving reasonably closely together?
- Will EMU be flexible enough to cope with problems as they emerge?
- Will joining lead to higher growth, greater stability and low unemployment?

Will these give us the answer?

single European market: the agreement to create a unified market across the European Union. The overall objective was to make it genuinely possible for goods, people and capital to move around freely. Part of this entailed the removal of restrictions encountered when crossing member countries' borders. The overall effect of the measures was to make the EU much more like a single economy. They came into force at the start of 1993. Specific changes included the following:

- Foreign exchange controls were abolished, making financial integration much easier, so that capital could move around. This opened up the financial markets of all member countries to all the banks.
- Many *regulations* were harmonised, so that firms could produce to specifications common to all member countries. This meant that products could be standardised for the whole of the EU. It removed many *non-tariff barriers* to trade.
- Qualifications which are recognised in one member country are generally recognised throughout the EU.
- Common systems were established in the fields of transport and communication.
- Qualified majority voting was introduced in the *Council of Ministers* and the *European Parliament* was given added powers. This reflected the general view that closer economic integration would require more effective political systems.

In many respects, the single market is still incomplete because full harmonisation has not yet been achieved. However, movement towards the single market has been significant.

Single Regeneration Budget: since 1994, a range of government departments all concerned with regenerating *depressed areas* have been brought together under the auspices of the Department of Trade and Industry. Its largest single element is the Challenge Fund, which has been taken over by the *Regional Development Agencies*. The Challenge Fund allocates money to bidders planning employment, training, housing and crime prevention initiatives.

skill shortage: even when there is substantial unemployment, shortages may develop of people available for work and possessing the skills required. This is likely to happen if the economy has been growing and the employment of skilled people has been increasing. Employers may offer higher pay in order to attract the type of people they require.

Where skills are scarce, appropriately qualified people are in *inelastic supply*. An increase in pay may provide an incentive to acquire the skills but this will be a long-run process.

skills: any job-related competences possessed by an individual, who can use these to help produce a saleable product.

skills mismatch: a situation in which the people available for work have skills which are not those required by the employers who are seeking to hire people. This will be associated with *occupational immobility*. It occurs because people have been made redundant from *declining industries*. The skills required by growing industries are different. This is a feature of *structural change*.

slump: the low point of the *trade cycle*. *Recession* brings a slowdown characterised by gloomy expectations, low levels of investment, rising unemployment and eventually falling *aggregate demand* and output. If falling output persists for more than two quarters, there is said to be a depression or a slump. Output actually fell two years in a row in 1991 and 1992. The then Conservative government responded with a substantial increase in *government expenditure*, involving a much-increased public sector deficit which helped to revive demand.

During a slump, aggregate demand is well below the level of full-capacity output.

small and medium-sized enterprises (SMEs) are defined as all firms with less than 250 employees. Small firms are those with less than 50 employees; medium-sized have between 50 and 250. These firms are thought to be very important in creating new jobs.

SME: see *small and medium-sized enterprises*.

Smith, Adam (1723–1790) was a Scottish professor of moral philosophy who pioneered much of the thinking in classical economics and laid down the fundamentals of the working of market economies. In his book *The Wealth of Nations* (Penguin, 1982), published in 1776, he explained the process of specialisation and the *division of labour*. He showed how the market mechanism could promote technical and allocative efficiency. He wrote about the *invisible hand*, which allocates resources amongst alternative uses, and showed how self-interest pursued in a free market would lead

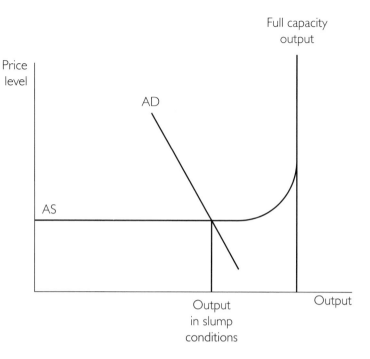

Slump (see page 295)

to consumer satisfaction. Although in using this reasoning, Smith was assuming that markets would be highly competitive, he was well aware of the tendency among producers to collude in order to secure a higher price.

snouts in the trough is an expression designed to highlight the way human beings can be impelled by greed. It has been freely used in describing the disquiet of people who object to senior managers receiving pay rises much larger than those awarded to the workforce. There have been suggestions in the press that these pay rises may not actually be necessary in order to secure the most talented managers.

social benefits are all of the benefits from consumption of a particular item, not just those received by the buyer. They therefore include the external benefits which may be obtained by third parties, i.e. people who neither bought nor sold the item. For example, the social benefits of a pretty front garden include the benefits obtained by the owner of it, together with the benefits of any passers-by who happen to enjoy looking at the garden.

FORMULA: internal benefits + external benefits = social benefits

(See also *marginal social costs.*)

social capital: *infrastructure* which is provided by governments and is very necessary for economic growth, but cannot always be provided on a profitable basis by the private sector. It includes education, health care and some transport and communications facilities.

Social Chapter: that part of the *Treaty of Amsterdam* which deals with social issues, including working conditions, *employment protection* and *employee involvement.* Until 1997, the UK chose to opt out of the Social Chapter, but is now committed to the implementation of its provisions. There is still some debate about whether employment protection is fully consistent with a dynamic process of job creation.

Social Charter: set up in the late 1980s within the European Union, this defined a set of objectives towards which all member countries would work. The idea was to harmonise social legislation as well as the economic framework. It covered 12 areas: freedom of movement, social protection, vocational training, health and safety, elderly people, protection of children, disabled people, sexual equality, living and working conditions, employment and remuneration, collective bargaining, information, consultation and participation. Many of its objectives were embodied later in the *Social Chapter* of the *Treaty of Amsterdam.*

social cost measures the cost to the whole of society of a production process or business decision. This means that not only are the firm's *internal costs* accounted for, but also the costs imposed on society as a consequence of the action (such as pollution or unemployment). These latter costs are external to the company.

FORMULA: internal costs + external costs = social costs

(See also *marginal social costs.*)

social development refers to the need for improvements in the social infrastructure of developing countries. It is related to important elements in the improvement of welfare such as the availability of clean water supplies, of health care and of education. Strictly speaking, these do have important economic dimensions but they are generally seen as part of the social development process.

social exclusion is about the way in which some members of society seem to be permanently excluded from benefiting from rising standards of living. This problem develops because people who are living in poor housing with few job prospects often have children who are at a real disadvantage too. There is a cycle which is hard to break.

social overhead capital: see *social capital.*

social responsibilities refer to a firm's duties towards its employees, customers, society and the environment, which it may or may not accept. Some firms see social responsibility as being very much in their own interests in the long run. Others will try to evade responsibility with a view to maximising short-run profits.

social security is the system by which governments provide for people in need. Unemployment benefits, pensions, income support and various other income supplements are payable to people in certain circumstances. Payments may be *means tested*, as with income support, or handed over as of right, as with pensions. Social security payments have increased enormously in all developed countries in recent years, partly because of ageing populations and partly because *unemployment* has been higher since 1980 than it was before.

Social security is part of what is called the *welfare state.* Increasing numbers of benefits are now being means tested because of rising expenditure on *universal benefits.*

social welfare concerns the well-being of people and how it may be improved. It involves *normative* aspects of economics which are directed towards deciding the way in which resources should be allocated so as to maximise welfare.

socialism is a social and economic system which involves collective ownership of the means of production and a major role for the state in the provision of services which can improve people's welfare. In its extreme form of communism it dominated the *centrally planned economies* of Eastern Europe until 1989. China, North Korea and Cuba are still to a large degree governed in this way. In its social democratic form, socialism has been an important underlying principle for a number of left-of-centre political parties in Western Europe.

soft currency: a currency which is not always completely freely convertible. This means that countries will not want to hold the currency as part of their foreign exchange reserves.

soft landing: after a prolonged period of economic growth, there may well be a progression through the *trade cycle* and into *recession*. An objective for policy makers at this point is to aim for a soft landing, i.e. a downturn which leads to a slower, sustainable rate of economic growth but not a recession. The US may or may not achieve this in the years following the slowdown which began in 2000. If it does not, other countries may be adversely affected because the US is such a large market for other countries' exports.

soft loan: a loan which is made on concessional terms, so that the interest rate is lower than the market rate or there is a 'holiday' during which no repayments are necessary. Soft loans are made to developing countries as part of their aid packages.

sole trader: an individual who runs a small business, who may or may not have employees, but does not have *limited liability*.

solvency: a situation in which a firm has enough assets to cover all of its outstanding debts. In contrast, insolvency implies that the firm cannot cover its debts and may be forced into *liquidation*.

sources of finance: businesses which are investing need finance, which may be internal or external. *Internal finance* can come from retained profit, working capital or the sale of assets. *External finance* may come from bank loans or from a new issue of shares.

sovereign debt: debts owed by governments rather than by private sector organisations. Many developing country governments have borrowed from banks. These debts are different from loans to the private sector because the borrowers cannot be pursued through the courts if they do not pay the interest or make repayments. (See also the *Debt Problem*.)

spare capacity: a situation in which a firm has equipment which is not fully utilised. It could expand output very quickly if there was a demand for it.

Special Deposits: a now defunct requirement by the Bank of England that banks deposit cash with them in quantities which would constrain their capacity to lend. It has not been used since 1980.

Special Drawing Rights (SDRs): IMF member governments can use SDRs to settle debts with each other. They are a form of international money which exists only on paper and only for use by the IMF and governments. They are used to help countries with balance of payments problems.

specialisation: the process by which individuals, firms and economies concentrate on producing those goods and services in which they have an advantage. Further specialisation is possible as production processes are broken up into a sequence of different tasks. This was described by *Adam Smith* in his account of the *division of labour* at the pin factory where each employee had a different job.

Specialisation has the potential to lead to increasing the output that can be obtained from a given quantity of resources. It is closely connected to the theory of *comparative advantage.*

Taken to extremes, specialisation can involve some jobs becoming very repetitive and boring, for example, assembly processes in manufacturing. One management response to this has been *teamwork* and *multi-skilling* – which can provide employees with more variety and the firm with a more flexible labour force.

specific tax: an indirect tax which is a fixed amount per unit of output. Petrol, alcohol and tobacco – the products with excise taxes - are taxed like this. In contrast, an ad valorem tax is one with a percentage rate, like VAT.

spectrum of competition: the range of market systems which can be anything between *perfect competition* and *monopoly*. At one extreme there is the situation of many competing producers with easy entry into the market; hairdressing would be one example. At the other extreme there is the single business which dominates the market and cannot be challenged because new entrants to the market have difficulty in getting started because of *barriers to entry*. Microsoft is currently the best-known example.

Perfect competion	Monopolistic competion	Oligopoly	Duopoly	Monopoly

speculation involves buying or selling something in the expectation of a price change and so making a profit. Foreign exchange dealers who expect the *exchange rate* to fall will sell quickly, then when the price has fallen they can buy back the currency at a much lower price than they sold at, so making a profit on the deal.

speculative capital flows consist of large money balances which their owners can move from one currency to another. If they suspect that one currency will depreciate, they will sell it and move into another which is likely to appreciate. Of course, if many people sell the currency which is expected to depreciate, this is just what will happen – there will be a *self-fulfilling prophecy*. Speculative capital flows can create major problems for central banks and governments but they cannot be stopped without disrupting normal capital movements as well. They draw attention to the importance of confidence in keeping economic systems reasonably stable.

spillover effects: the effects of certain production decisions which have an impact on third parties, who are neither producers nor consumers of the product in question. They are the same as *externalities.*

spot market: a term used to describe a commodity or foreign exchange market where the deals are made and completed there and then and delivery is immediate.

In contrast, in the *forward market* deals are made in which the price is agreed now, but the delivery of the goods concerned takes place perhaps three months later.

spot price: the price in the *spot market*. This means the price which must be paid for a consignment of a commodity for delivery immediately.

SRB: see *Single Regeneration Budget*.

stabilisation policy aims to keep the economy growing in a sustainable way and prevent a cycle of *boom* and *recession*. It uses *fiscal* and *monetary policies* to influence the level of aggregate demand and prevent both overheating and rising unemployment. Stabilisation policies are not always successful because the time lags in the economy and weaknesses of some of the data can make it very difficult to predict how much policy change is required. Stabilisation policies can be used for electoral reasons in ways which are ultimately destabilising, but this has been made much less likely since the Bank of England became responsible for monetary policy in 1997.

stagflation means a combination of *stagnation* and *inflation* happening together. This was a phenomenon associated with the 1970s. Whereas normally there is a trade-off between inflation and unemployment, stagflation led to the two rising together. Because trade unions expected further inflation, they wanted to negotiate pay rises big enough to preserve and increase real incomes. But at the same time, unemployment was rising because of recession. Competition in the labour market might have depressed pay rises. In this instance, efforts to maintain real incomes overrode competition from unemployed people for the available jobs. This experience led to detailed study of the role of *expectations* in the determination of inflation and a fuller appreciation of their impact.

stagnation: a situation in which the economy is growing very slowly or not at all.

stakeholders: people with a strong interest in a particular firm, including employees, shareholders, consumers, suppliers and the community. Firms which take *business responsibility* seriously recognise obligations to all of these groups.

standard of living refers to the well-being of the population but does not have a precise meaning. A serious attempt to assess progress in this area requires inspection of a wide range of data, including:

- measures of real income such as GDP at *constant prices*, to assess the economic component of the standard of living
- per capita income, if population growth is rapid
- measures of social welfare such as mortality rates, life expectancy, participation in education, access to health care and clean water and so on
- in some cases, data for the *distribution of income* would add detail to the picture. The presence or absence of a *social security* system may also be relevant.

International comparisons of the standard of living can be confused by exchange rate variations. The World Bank produces data based on *purchasing power parity* which gives a clearer picture. The UN's Human Development Report also provides useful data.

standardised products are those which are mass produced to uniform specifications. This type of production opens up possibilities of reaping economies of scale.

For example, the use of standardised parts in vehicles reduces stockholding costs and design costs. Paradoxically, computer-controlled manufacture has made it easier for firms to manufacture small batches of items, so cars now come in a bewildering array of models with many variations, many of which are produced more or less to order. These two trends are occurring side by side.

state-owned enterprises include all the organisations which sell a good or a service for a price and are in the public sector. This category was large until many such enterprises were privatised from 1981 onwards. The best remaining example in the UK is the Post Office.

state planning: the process by which, in a *centrally planned economy*, decisions are made about how resources will be allocated. This will be an administrative process which overrides market forces as to both prices and quantities.

state provision covers all the goods and services provided (i.e. paid for) by the public sector. The actual delivery of these goods and services may be undertaken by either the public or the private sector. Refuse collection is provided by the local authority and may be carried out by it too, or it may be put out to *tender* with the private sector. Many home helps now come from private operators working for the local authority.

statistics: the data which record events in the economy and can show trends in a range of important variables. They make it possible to predict likely levels of growth, inflation and unemployment but may be subject to errors and uncertainties and may only become available with a *time lag*.

sterling: another name for the pound, the UK's currency.

sterling exchange rate index: a measure of change in the foreign *exchange rate* which takes a weighted average of a basket of currencies. These are weighted according to their importance in the pattern of trade. It provides the simplest way of measuring competitiveness.

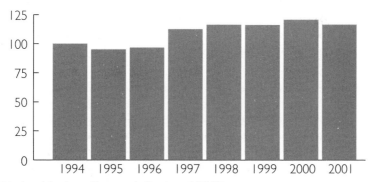

Source: National Institute Economic Review, 4/2000

sticky wages: a term which refers to the tendency of wages to go up but not down. *Trade union* negotiators will try to see that wage rates rise each year by the rate of *inflation* plus a real increase. In non-unionised occupations with no bargaining power, money wages may sometimes be held constant but this will mean that their purchasing power will go down by the rate of inflation. It is very rare for money wage rates to fall. Sticky wages can make the economy less flexible because they can obscure signals that labour should be being reallocated away from declining industries and towards products for which demand is growing.

stock: this term has two meanings:

- A stock, as opposed to a *flow*, means an amount held. Wealth is a stock, while income is a flow. Savings are the stock of past saving, whereas saving is a flow, i.e. the extra saving added this year to the stock of past savings.
- Stocks may be of inputs, work in progress or output. When aggregated for the whole economy, the level of stocks is important because it may reflect changes in the level of *aggregate demand* relative to output. Also, changes in stocks may impact upon the level of output. If demand has been falling, stocks will rise and de-stocking may become necessary. This means that the level of output will for a while fall below the level of demand and this may reduce the demand for labour, leading to rising unemployment.

Stock Exchange: a market on which *shares* and *bonds* (*securities*) can be bought and sold on a second-hand basis. This means there is always a way in which securities can be exchanged for money, although the price will not be known much in advance. Shareholders do not have to hold their shares indefinitely unless they want to.

The London Stock Exchange is very large, competing for international business with Frankfurt, Tokyo and New York. Stock exchanges help to ensure that funds are made available to firms to invest. A steady flow of investment finance is an important element in the process of *economic growth*.

Stock Exchange Automated Quotation System: a computer-based system which shows all buying and selling prices to all traders on the *stock exchange* simultaneously. It provides something like *perfect information* in the market.

stock market: see *Stock Exchange*.

stocks and shares: investments which can be bought and sold on the Stock Exchange. *Shares* or equities imply part ownership of the company by the shareholder; they pay *dividends*. The term 'stocks' in this context is thoroughly confusing; they may mean the same as shares (in the US) or they may mean a fixed interest loan like a *bond* (in the UK).

stop-go: a term used in the 1960s in relation to *macro-economic policies*. For a time it was thought that careful management of aggregate demand, using fiscal and monetary policies, could protect the economy from the fluctuations of the *trade cycle*. In fact, difficulties in operating fiscal and monetary policy, together with *time lags* in the provision of accurate data which could be the basis for decision taking, meant that governments got a reputation for doing 'too much, too late'. By 1979, when the Thatcher government came to power, demand management had acquired a bad reputation. In practice, however, governments have continued to use the same expansionary and contractionary policies as before.

Are governments getting better at it? Do better data and forecasting help? The mighty boom of the late 1980s and the subsequent slump in 1991–1992 suggest that there are still some problems with this approach. Can you give a verdict on Gordon Brown, providing evidence?

store of value: one of the uses of money. By keeping money safely, you can have the use of it later. However, it may lose its value to some extent if there is *inflation*. If there is hyperinflation, money will not be a store of value at all.

strike: a situation in which workers stop work in order to exert some power in an *industrial dispute*. Most often, this will be over pay but it can be about redundancies or unfair dismissal. Strikes may be official, i.e. sanctioned by the trade union, or unofficial. They are much more likely to occur in larger firms than in smaller ones. In recent years strikes have been fewer in number, partly because of the fear of unemployment and partly because the law now requires a secret ballot of union members as to whether they want to strike.

structural adjustment: a set of policies which has become associated with the *International Bank for Reconstruction and Development* (the World Bank) and the *International Monetary Fund* (IMF). The package of policies will depend upon the circumstances of the country concerned, but is likely to include:

- *devaluation/depreciation* of the currency
- cuts in government expenditure and reform of the tax system which will reduce the public sector deficit
- reduced trade restrictions and the encouragement of market forces in a number of contexts, sometimes through *privatisation*
- improved incentives to encourage increased agricultural production
- export incentives.

Often the World Bank and the IMF are in a position to dictate the policy prescription because of the country's need for development finance. Some of these measures have proved unpopular at times.

structural change is the process by which resources are reallocated away from the production of items for which demand is falling and towards items for which it is rising. This reallocation of resources leads to changes in the composition of output. It also entails major changes in employment patterns. Where a *localised industry* declines, it can cause whole communities to be affected by increased *unemployment*, often for many years. Coal and shipbuilding both provide examples of serious structural problems. However, without structural changes, the economy does not adapt to new patterns of demand and *technical efficiency* may be compromised as well.

structural unemployment occurs when people are made redundant from *declining industries* but lack the appropriate skills to enter a growing industry or are located a long way from the jobs available. Many declining industries such as coal and iron and steel are localised, so that the large excess supply of labour in a place with limited opportunities becomes a real problem.

Occupational immobilities and *geographical immobilities* make it difficult for people to find alternative jobs. Supply-side policies such as training and retraining may be needed to deal with these. *Regional policy* and regeneration measures can be helpful too. There has been a long-term and substantial increase in structural unemployment in many developed countries which governments have had little success in reducing. Unskilled people are particularly vulnerable and despite recent improvements, the problem remains grave in many parts of the EU.

structure of industry: the composition of output.

subcontracting: buying in inputs from another firm, rather than creating them in-house. Another term for this is *outsourcing*.

subsidiarity involves taking political decisions at the lowest appropriate level. In theory it should lead to a strengthening of the role of local authorities, which may be responsive to local needs. It may prove useful in the EU context in preserving the democratic process in distinctive regions. At present in the UK there is a tendency, despite devolution, to deal with some local issues at the central government level. Subsidiarity may be a good idea but it hasn't made a great deal of progress.

subsidiary: a firm that is owned by another firm (the holding or parent company). The subsidiary may be fairly independent of the parent company or it may be effectively controlled by it. There may be no independent accounts published so that the subsidiary's performance is hard to evaluate.

subsidy: a sum of money paid by governments to the producer, so that the price to the customer will be lower than it otherwise would have been. This may be done either for social reasons (e.g. to a railway as a provider of an essential service) or to raise incomes (e.g. hill sheep farmers) or to keep down prices of essential goods. In early 2001, the government gave £250 million to Rolls Royce, the aero-engine manufacturer, to develop a new type of engine. Although this will eventually be returned to the government in the form of a payment for each engine sold, this will take a long time and the subsidy will help RR to stay competitive. This type of subsidy is subject to EU approval.

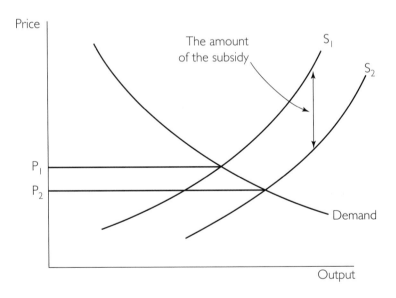

The subsidy shifts the supply curve to the right, making it possible to charge a lower price, P_2

subsistence agriculture: a system in which farmers supply all or most of their daily needs by their own efforts. They have little or no surplus which they can exchange for goods and services produced by others. They are likely therefore to have a very low standard of living.

subsistence level: an amount of real income which provides only just enough to keep the person alive in the long run.

substitutes: goods and services which are possible alternatives for the consumer, so that a change in the price of one will have some impact on demand for the other. Some substitutes will be much closer than others. For example, an own-brand tin of baked beans is quite a good substitute for a tin of Heinz beans. But a cauliflower, although it is another vegetable product, is probably not a very close substitute for any tin of beans. (See also *cross price elasticity of demand*.)

substitution effect: a change in price will lead to a substitution effect. If there is a fall in the price of housing (either because of interest rates or because of low levels of demand), some people will choose to buy a larger house rather than have an expensive holiday. This is the substitution effect of a fall in price. There will also be an *income effect*: because people actually have more real income as a result of the fall in the price of housing, they may buy more of a number of products, including housing.

sunk costs are costs which have already been paid for and which no longer figure in the decision-taking process. For example, once the product is brought to the market, research and development costs are sunk costs.

sunrise industry: one which is expected to grow quite fast. It may be one in which new technologies are important.

sunset industry: one which is declining because of lack of demand, perhaps caused by competition from new products.

supernormal profit: profit which is in excess of the amount needed to keep the resources in the industry, i.e. the full *opportunity cost* of all the resources used. When demand is rising, it will often be possible for the firm to make supernormal profit because it can raise the price and still sell the goods. This situation will continue until more firms have moved into the industry, thus competing and driving prices back down to the level where *normal profit* only is made. If there are *barriers to entry*, then the firm may make supernormal profit in the long as well as the short run, because the level of competition is reduced. In fact, any kind of market power will allow supernormal profits to be made; for example, brand names, such as Levi's, create loyalty which reduces the power of competition to force down profits. (See also *perfect competition* and *monopoly*.)

supplier relationships are important to firms which buy in many of their inputs from other businesses. In the context of a good relationship, it will be easier to negotiate quality improvements or *just-in-time* stock control procedures.

supply is one element in the market system: the market forces contributed by supply and demand together determine prices and quantities and the *allocation of resources*. Firms will supply goods and services in a range of quantities, depending on the price they can get for them. At any given price level, quantity supplied will be affected by input costs in general, by technological change and by government policies which affect taxes and subsidies. (See also *supply curve*.)

supply chain: the sequence of processes by which a final product is created. For many products, the supply chain takes in many different suppliers, often located in different countries. Many sophisticated manufactured products are built up in developed countries using intermediate products assembled in *developing countries* where wages are lower.

supply curve: the curve showing the quantities producers wish to supply at a range of different prices. It is normally shown sloping upwards to the right. This is because a higher price gives a business more of an incentive to produce and indicates possible higher profits (as at p2 and q2 on the diagram).

The supply curve will shift if there is a change in costs and it may then change its shape as well. For example, new technologies will tend to make the supply curve shift down and to the right, reflecting the fact that costs have fallen and possibly also *economies of scale* have been reaped. Then it may be possible to produce the larger quantity (q3 in the diagram) at the original price.

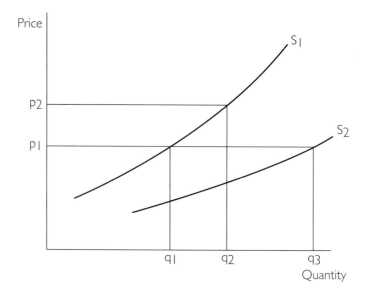

Supply curve

supply elasticity: the responsiveness of quantity supplied to a change in price. The formula is:

FORMULA: elasticity of supply $= \dfrac{\text{percentage change in quantity supplied}}{\text{percentage change in price}}$

Inelastic supply will be less than one, while elastic supply will be greater than one. Supply may be perfectly inelastic (i.e. equal to 0) in the market period simply because there has not been time to mobilise the resources needed to increase supply or to disband them if the price is falling. In the short run, supply can be increased by the addition of variable factors of production to the production process. In the long run, fixed factors of production can also be increased. So supply becomes more and more elastic the longer the time period. Housing is usually in inelastic supply: it takes time to build more; equally, if demand is falling the existing stock of housing will continue to stand for some time. This means that changes in demand may produce sharp fluctuations in price. Another example of inelastic supply occurs when scarce skills are in demand; it will take time to train more people and in the meantime the supply of the skills will be very inelastic.

If very scarce resources are needed to produce the item, then costs may rise as output increases, thus making supply rather inelastic. As depletable resources of mineral products are exploited, the price will rise and this means that supply is inelastic. In contrast, the supply of most manufactured products in the long run is highly elastic.

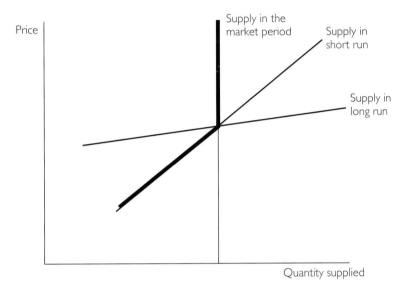

supply schedule: the set of prices and quantities which show how much producers are prepared to supply to the market at different prices.

supply of labour: the number of people available for work. The *participation rate* gives the percentage of the people who are working or available for work. The number of people who are actively looking for work depends on rates of pay, the likelihood of finding a job and the level of benefits paid to those out of work. Also important is the immigration policy at the time.

The supply of labour in any one occupation is greatly affected by pay. Higher pay will enlarge the number of people prepared to move to a new occupation or to retrain for it. It will also encourage those already working to work longer hours.

supply-side policies are based on the notion that economic growth can best be encouraged by helping markets to work more efficiently. They actually work to increase supply from a given quantity of real resources. This contrasts with the so-called *Keynesian* policies which are designed to influence the level of demand in the economy. Supply-side policies were originally favoured particularly by *monetarist* economists, who believed that policies to increase *aggregate demand* were potentially inflationary and could destabilise the economy. There are many possible supply-side measures.

- Policies which make the labour market more flexible: these involve restriction of trade union activities, which has led in the past to overmanning and demarcation problems. Supply-side enthusiasts also argue for some reduction in *employment protection.*
- Training and retraining: these address directly the *supply constraints* which usually exist to some degree, increasing the supply of skilled labour able to respond to job vacancies.
- Competition policy: by encouraging competition, it is possible to force firms to organise their production systems more efficiently, increasing the output from a given input.
- Reducing disincentives to work: some people have suggested reducing unemployment benefit and income support to this end. Marginal tax rates can be reduced, but the evidence that this actually makes people work harder is difficult to come by. In recent years the government has introduced new measures, such as the Working Families Tax Credit, to try to ensure that people with families are always better off working than not.
- Financial incentives to promote spending on research and development and encourage investment.
- Promoting competition in the financial sector, to encourage it to work more efficiently at channelling funds towards profitable opportunities.
- Privatisation: reducing the extent of the involvement of the public sector in economic activity can help to increase general efficiency in the industries concerned.

Many supply-side measures have in fact secured widespread support from all political parties. Support is not confined to the original Conservative monetarist enthusiasts. Measures such as improving training and retraining, helping people to find jobs and spending money on research and development can all help to increase *productivity* and employment, as well as fostering growth.

supply-side shocks: noticeable changes which have an impact on the quantity of goods and services supplied and the general price level at which they are available. The oil price rises of 1973 and 1979 were shocks in that many producers found their costs of production rising and prices were raised in turn. Oil-users' purchasing power was reduced. The impact of the changes was very considerable. A pleasanter kind of shock concerns the rapid impact of new technologies in the US during the late 1990s. This led to big increases in *productivity* in the industries concerned and increased prosperity for many people.

surplus: the amount by which revenue exceeds costs in *non-profit making organisations.*

surplus on current account: the amount by which *visible* and *invisible exports* together exceed visible and invisible imports.

sustainable growth is a term used in two different contexts:

- Growth which can be kept up at a steady rate over the long term is said to be sustainable. In contrast, unsustainable growth requires resources which will become increasingly scarce as growth proceeds. In particular, shortages of scarce skills will develop and when they do, wage rates will be bid up, costs will rise and *inflation* will accelerate. This will lead the government to damp down the growth process and the result may be a swing into *recession* which will last until such time as people's inflationary expectations have adjusted under the impact of the threat of unemployment. (This sequence of events was experienced in the UK between 1987 and 1992.) So sustainable growth must be at a rate such that the resources available at the time can meet the aggregate demand without input prices (including wages) being bid up through increasing scarcity.

- In the context of the environment, sustainable growth means growth which does not rely on exploiting resources which cannot be replaced. For example, the use of *depletable resources* such as oil can probably not be sustained indefinitely unless the rate of use can be slowed dramatically. The exploitation of hardwood forests cannot be sustained indefinitely unless the rate of use slows and more attention is given to replanting.

sweat shop: a workplace where the wages on offer are very low indeed and little attention is paid to the need for good working conditions. Unemployment may be high so that employees have little choice but to put up with the conditions. There will normally be no trade union and the employees may have difficult circumstances which reduce their capacity to resist *exploitation*. Sweat shops can probably be found more often in developing countries but there are still instances of such situations in some developed countries.

synergy means combining the positive qualities of two entities, so that their economic prowess emerges greater than the sum of their parts. It is often advanced as an argument for a merger, where the two firms have complementary strengths. Mergers sometimes disappoint in this respect and the outcome may be a *demerger* or divestment process.

tacit agreement means that an understanding has developed between two competing firms, but without any kind of personal contact or formal agreement. It is characteristic of an *oligopoly*. The sellers will simply not take action in any way which might increase the level of competition between them. Because there is no actual agreement, this is hard to prevent, even though it may have considerable impact on the buyer. It is possible for a long period of tacit agreement to follow a *price war* which the participants have found very damaging. They may just set their prices at similar levels and avoid further price competition.

Early in 2001, the *Competition Commission* announced that the big four banks – HSBC, Lloyds TSB, Barclays and the Royal Bank of Scotland – were operating a *complex monopoly* in services to small businesses. The Commission said that although they are not a *cartel*, their behaviour restricted competition. Since there was no suggestion of collusion, an element of tacit agreement was implied.

take-off: a stage in the process of economic development at which the economy becomes able to achieve sustained economic growth. An important element in this concerns the ability of the country to generate *savings* and to channel these towards well-planned *investment* and infrastructure projects. Also, the government must be able to provide reasonable education facilities and a reliable legal system. The thinking underlying the idea of a take-off stage is embodied in *Rostow's model.*

takeover: one firm buys a controlling share (i.e. at least 51%) of the shares of another firm. A takeover may be hostile or friendly, according to the attitude of the management of the firm taken over. These *acquisitions* are an important means by which firms can grow in size without having to go to the trouble of expanding their own operations. This is known as *inorganic growth.* It is often an easy way for the firm to increase its market power and its market share. Some takeovers may create so much market power that the OFT considers whether to refer the takeover to the *Competition Commission.*

takeover bid: the opening offer by a firm for the shares which it hopes to buy in order to achieve control of another company. To be successful, the bidder will have to make an offer better than the current market price for the shares. It may offer cash, some of its own shares or a combination of the two. If the response from the shareholders is insufficient to give it full control, the firm may make a higher bid. Sometimes there will be two competing bids for the target company.

tariff: a customs duty on an imported good. The effect of this tax is to make the price of the import higher, so competing domestic products will be relatively cheaper. The domestic producer will benefit from some *protection* against foreign competition.

The tariff can be an *ad valorem* or a *specific tax.* Import tariffs are discouraged, and some are banned, under *WTO* agreements. They raise prices to consumers and can reduce real incomes, especially if the exporting country decides to retaliate with tariffs of its own. This will reduce trade all round, reducing demand for exports generally.

The impact of tariffs depends on the elasticity of demand for the product. If demand is elastic, this implies that there are competing substitutes available from domestic producers and the tariff will cut imports considerably, as in diagram (a). It may be impossible for the importer even to pass on the full amount of the tariff to the consumer. An example of this might be a tariff on steel products. If, on the other hand, demand is inelastic, as in diagram (b), the price increase brought about by the tariff will be quite high but the fall in quantity demanded will be less than proportional because people carry on buying the import as they see few or no satisfactory substitutes. This might happen with a tariff on hi-fi equipment.

The general principle on which tariffs work is the same as that of *tax incidence.*

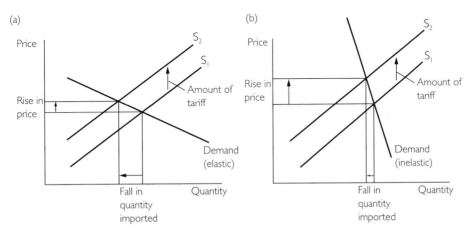

The impact of tariffs with elastic and inelastic demand

tax allowance: a specific amount which may be deducted from income before tax is calculated.

tax avoidance means reducing the tax bill by legal means. People with businesses can reduce their liability by deducting legitimate expenses. Firms and individuals may keep some of their assets in tax havens, where tax rates are much lower. *Transfer pricing* allows multinationals to avoid some profits tax by setting the prices of goods transferred from one country to another at levels which minimise the overall tax bill.

tax base includes all the sources of tax revenue. For example, profits are taxed to provide *corporation tax*, individuals are taxed to provide income tax and products are taxed to provide *VAT* revenues. Widening the tax base means devising ways of raising revenue which rely on different sources.

tax burden refers to the total amount of tax. When taken as a proportion of GDP, it is possible to compare the tax burden in different countries.

Current tax revenue as % of GDP, 1998

Australia	22.9
Belgium	43.3
France	39.2
Germany	26.6

Current tax revenue as % of GDP, 1998 *continued*

Italy	38.6
Netherlands	42.7
Sweden	35.8
UK	36.3
US	20.4

Source: World Bank, WDR 2000

tax evasion means paying less tax than is legally due. For example, a person might not declare all of their income and thus pay less income tax than they should. Or they may claim allowances to which they are not legally entitled.

tax expenditures occur when people are allowed to offset some of their *income* against tax allowances, which means that they pay less tax than they otherwise would. This reduces their tax liability and gives them more spending power.

tax haven: a country with low rates of *income* and *corporation tax*, such as the Cayman Islands.

tax incidence: see *incidence of taxation*.

tax rate: the marginal percentage rate at which an income or an expenditure tax will be levied. (See also *income tax*.)

tax relief: a reduction in tax which is designed to create an incentive. For example, deducting investment expenditure from total profit can reduce tax payable on profits and encourage firms to invest.

tax revenue is the money which is paid to the government in tax. The total is important because it influences both the amount which the government may spend and the amount which has to be borrowed (the *Public Sector Net Cash Requirement*).

The expected revenue from taxation is determined by the policies laid out in the *Budget* each March.

tax thresholds are determined by the size of the personal tax allowance, which is the amount of income people are allowed to earn before tax becomes payable. An increase in the personal allowance means that the tax threshold rises. There is another threshold at the point at which the person becomes liable for tax at the 40% rate.

tax yield: the revenue raised by a tax, less the cost of collecting it.

taxation: the process of raising finance for government expenditure through the use of direct and indirect taxes. *Direct taxes* are those levied on incomes, profits or wealth, while *indirect taxes* are levied on expenditure. In 2000, roughly 38% of GDP was paid in taxes of all kinds. The pie chart shows the relative importance of each tax. Excise taxes are those levied on specific products such as petrol, tobacco and alcohol. (See Figure on page 313.)

teamwork: the system by which production is carried out by teams of people who co-operate in order to achieve efficient ways of working. It may be associated with *multi-skilling*, whereby some members of the team can carry out a number of different tasks. Teamwork can help to alleviate the boredom of repetitive tasks, associated with too extreme a *division of labour*.

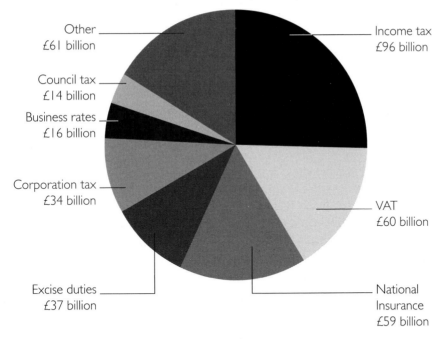

Other
£61 billion

Council tax
£14 billion

Business rates
£16 billion

Corporation tax
£34 billion

Excise duties
£37 billion

Income tax
£96 billion

VAT
£60 billion

National
Insurance
£59 billion

Source: *The Guardian*, 22.3.00

Taxation (see page 312)
Tax revenue, 2000–2001

technical or technological change refers to the process by which both products and the processes of production are developed and improved, as a result of increased scientific knowledge and the application of that knowledge to production.

- A technical breakthrough may make a new product development possible. Mobile phones are a relatively recent new product.
- Equally, technical change leads to new and cheaper methods of producing and this leads to costs falling and sometimes also falls in relative prices. Telephone calls have recently become cheaper because of improved equipment.

The process of implementing technical change is known as *innovation*. Technical change provides a substantial impetus to the process of *economic growth* because it makes it possible to increase *productivity*, i.e. to reduce the quantity of real resources needed to produce a particular item. The gains from technical change are most obvious in manufacturing, but there have also been major increases in productivity in the *primary sector* and in the *service sector*, for example as a result of using computer systems.

technical economies: see *internal economies of scale.*

technical efficiency: a production process is said to be technically efficient if the costs of production have been minimised by economising in the use of real resources. It is one element in *economic efficiency* and is achieved when average total cost is at its minimum point. *Economies of scale* are often important in achieving technical efficiency. To achieve it, factors of production must be combined in the most effective way.

technological unemployment occurs where people have been made redundant as the business invested in labour-saving capital equipment. However, they will only remain unemployed if they are also affected by *occupational* or *geographical immobility*.

teleworking means working at home, often by using electronic communications. This can benefit the employer by reducing the fixed costs per worker and may suit the employee personally. Teleworking has some potential to create a more flexible labour market because it provides a range of options to suit different situations.

tender: a system by which a number of competing firms will bid for a contract, saying exactly what they will provide and giving a price. The lowest price or best value bid will be accepted. Local authorities, central government and a variety of businesses all use the system from time to time, e.g. for building projects or provision of school meals or home helps.

terms of trade: the price of *exports* relative to the price of *imports*. It is measured by the terms of trade index.

$$\text{FORMULA:} \quad \text{terms of trade index} = \frac{\text{index of export prices}}{\text{index of import prices}} \times 100$$

The terms of trade improve if it becomes possible to buy more imports with the proceeds of a given quantity of exports, i.e. if import prices fall or if export prices rise. For example, if the price of copper rises, Zambian copper producers will receive a higher price for their exports and will be able to buy more imports. Similarly, if the price of copper stays the same but the price of imports rises, Zambia's terms of trade deteriorate.

There will be a change in the terms of trade if there is a change in the exchange rate. A *depreciation* leads to lower export prices and higher import prices. This implies a deterioration in the terms of trade. This leads to confusion, because the terminology suggests that deteriorating terms of trade are a bad thing. In fact, a depreciation may have the beneficial effect of making producers more competitive and lead in time to an improved *trade balance*.

term structure of interest rates means the whole range of *interest rates* which apply to all the different types of loans that exist. Broadly, interest rates depend on the length of the loan and the degree of risk associated with it. Money lent to the government when a *bond* is bought will have a very low rate of interest because it is certain that it will be paid back and that the interest will be paid in full and on time. Similarly money lent within the banking system overnight will also have a very low rate of interest. A credit card loan will have a very high rate of interest: non-repayment is quite likely. Loans to firms for investment purposes will lie somewhere in between.

tertiary sector: all the firms in the economy which produce services. It is much the largest sector in the UK, as also in the US. (See also *secondary sector*.)

Thatcherism: the set of policies, and their underlying philosophy, developed during Mrs Thatcher's period as Prime Minister (1979–90). Her objective was to set the economy free from government intervention and allow *market forces* much more of a role in determining the *allocation of resources*. The main policies were:

- *privatisation* of the nationalised industries
- the use of *monetary policy* to control inflation, a high priority at the time
- reduction of the power of the *trade unions*
- increases in incentives through tax cuts
- strengthening of *competition policy*
- *deregulation* of the private sector.

Of these, the implementation of the first three had substantial effects. The tax cuts certainly redistributed income towards the richer part of the population. On competition and deregulation, the effects of the change in policy are more debatable.

theory: a set of principles used to explain real-world events. Economic theory aims to provide insights into the nature of economic problems by simplifying sequences of events so that stage-by-stage analysis is possible. For example, the theory of *perfect competition* defines the nature of a very competitive market, allowing us to pinpoint the extent to which real markets diverge from the competitive model.

theory of the firm: a branch of economics which seeks to explain price and output decisions. It uses *marginal analysis* to explain the profit-maximising output of the firm. It examines the nature of the various market forms, covering *perfect competition, monopolistic competition, oligopoly* and *monopoly*. In recent years it has been extended to analyses of relationships between firms through *game theory*.

third parties: individuals or groups which are not the main parties in a transaction, but are affected by it. For example, if a paint factory is polluting the atmosphere and people living nearby are affected by the pollution, those people are third parties in the transaction which takes place between the producer and the consumer of the paint.

third world countries: another term for *developing countries*.

tied aid: aid given by developed countries to developing countries which carries a condition that it be spent on exports from the donor country. Sometimes this considerably reduces the value of the aid to the recipient. The donor's products may not be the ones most suited to the recipient country's situation.

tiger economies are those countries in the Far East which have been most successful in developing their economies and are at or close to per capita income levels associated with developed countries. They include Hong Kong, the Korean Republic, Singapore and Taiwan. Between 1960 and 1980, Singapore had an average annual rate of growth of 7.4%.

tight fiscal policy means using a tax increase and/or government expenditure cuts to reduce *aggregate demand* in the economy. This could be used if the economy has been growing unsustainably fast and *inflation* is accelerating. It could be combined with a *tight monetary policy*. The success of such a policy depends upon its being implemented at the right moment (rather than too late) and therefore upon having accurate forecasts about likely future changes. This is important because there will be *time lags* between the policy decision and its effect upon the economy, probably of between one and two years.

tight monetary policy involves high interest rates, so that borrowers will try to keep their loans down to a minimum. This is usually associated with *counter-inflation policy*. As borrowers try to reduce the amount they spend, aggregate demand will fall (or grow more slowly). Demand for the products of many firms will fall and they will cut production. In time they will reduce employment and incomes will fall. Consumption then falls, so that the process is repeated, with a downward *multiplier* effect. Competition for the few jobs available will reduce pressure on wages and the inflation rate will fall again but only after a time lag.

The success of such a policy depends upon its being implemented at the right moment (rather than too late) and therefore upon having accurate forecasts about likely future changes. This is important because there will be time lags between the policy decision and its effect upon the economy, probably of between one and two years. (See also *monetary policy*.)

time deposits: another term for deposit accounts, which pay interest but do not allow instant withdrawal of the funds.

time lag: a delay in the reaction of one *variable* to a change in another variable. For example, during the *trade cycle, unemployment* may start to fall only 12–18 months after output starts to rise at the end of a recession. An increase in *interest rates* will also have a delayed effect, spread over a period of perhaps a year, during which borrowers adjust their plans in response to the change.

time series data covers a period of time, so that a sequence of events can be described. Inflation data for a 20-year period would provide a time series. In contrast, cross-section data provides a series of observations drawn from a single time period. Rates of inflation in one year for 20 countries would be cross-section data and would enable international comparisons to be made.

Tokyo Round: the international trade negotiations which took place between 1973 and 1979. It reduced tariffs on manufactures traded mainly between developed countries by about a third, which led to substantial growth in trade and to enhanced economic growth. It did not reach agreement on reducing agricultural *protection* or on *non-tariff barriers*; these were addressed to some degree in the later *Uruguay Round* but remain a problem today.

total cost: all the costs of production to the firm, including *fixed costs* and *variable costs*.

total fixed cost: the full cost of all *fixed factors of production*, which include land and capital.

total revenue: sales revenue, for which the formula is:

Formula: total revenue = price × quantity sold

total variable cost: all the variable costs to the firm, which will include labour, raw materials, component inputs, energy and any other costs which vary with the level of production.

tradable permits: these allow certain businesses the right to pollute the atmosphere or water up to a certain point, but no more. If they are able to reduce their polluting activities below that level, they may be able to sell the permit to another business, enabling it to carry on with its polluting activities. Tradable permits are used to gradually reduce the overall level of pollution by granting fewer each year.

tradables: goods and services which figure in *international trade*. In fact, most goods and services can be traded to some degree, if only by being bought by tourists when visiting the country or, as in the case of education and health care, bought by people who travel to obtain them. The exceptions include some heavy building materials and some kinds of services, such as government-provided social services and administration.

trade agreements: international agreements about the rules under which trade takes place. These have all happened under the auspices first of GATT and, since 1995, of the *WTO*.

They cover *tariffs* and *non-tariff barriers* and dispute settlement mechanisms. The most important agreements grew out of the three major 'rounds' of negotiation, the *Kennedy Round*, the *Tokyo Round* and the *Uruguay Round*. These brought about successive reductions in the level of barriers to trade in many manufactured goods and made trade much freer. Only with the Uruguay Round was agricultural protection seriously addressed and much protection still continues untouched. An important principle in trade negotiation is that of *reciprocity*, meaning that countries must offer equal access to each other's markets.

trade barriers impede the trading process and include *tariffs, quotas* and other *non-tariff barriers*. Tariffs tax imports. Quotas place a physical limit on imports. *WTO* aims to reduce trade barriers over time. (See also *import controls*.)

trade creation occurs when a new *trading bloc* has been set up and businesses begin to take advantage of the opportunities arising from *free trade* between member countries. Because there are fewer *trade barriers*, new markets open up and businesses will try to extend into them. There will be increased *specialisation* and more *trade*.

trade credit: firms which are selling their products to other firms will often give them time to pay. This credit is interest free. It may be given to retailers who will find it hard to pay for the goods until they have been sold. The availability of the credit is one element in the value for money of the product being sold.

trade cycle: the fluctuations in output and employment which take the economy through a sequence of *boom, recession, slump* and *recovery*. The cycle varies in length and severity and must be looked at alongside the process of *economic growth*. This provides the background: a *long-run trend rate of growth*, around 2.2% in the UK, about which output growth fluctuates. The phases of the trade cycle do not form a neat, predictable pattern, but interact with other events to form a complex sequence.

- The boom phase occurs when there is unsustainably fast growth, which causes *supply constraints* and accelerating inflation. This last happened in the UK in 1988. It is sometimes called the Lawson boom, after the then Chancellor of the Exchequer. By cutting taxes when the economy was already growing strongly, in line with Conservative policy at the time, he inadvertently stoked up the boom.
- Booms may give way to recession anyway but in 1989 inflation was 7% and rising. Interest rates were raised and the economy was quickly slowed

down. Falling aggregate demand led to slower growth and, after a time lag, rising unemployment as firms tried to cope with slow sales.

- By 1991 and into 1992, income and output were actually falling, meaning that the recession had turned into a slump. Unemployment, lagged as usual, peaking at 10.3% in 1993. This type of unemployment is termed *cyclical* or *demand deficiency unemployment.*
- Recovery actually began with rising output in 1993, but rather slowly at first. Then unemployment, too, fell from 1994 onwards. The recovery was sustained and has not led to unsustainable growth, leading to suggestions that inflation may have ceased to be a problem.

The graph for economic growth (see page 89) shows the phases of the trade cycle described here quite clearly. In general, if the growth rate is falling and below the long-run trend, the economy will be experiencing recession. When output is actually falling, there is a slump. On average, the trade cycle is usually thought of as lasting roughly 10 years but its irregularity makes this only a very rough approximation.

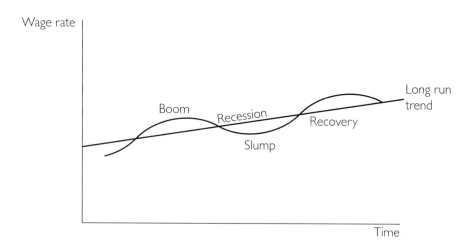

The phases of the trade cycle

trade deficit occurs when visible *imports* are greater than visible *exports.*

trade diversion: when a new *trading bloc* is created, trade diversion takes place because some member countries will shift to buying more from other member countries rather than from non-member countries. For example, when the UK joined the European Union, it began to buy more butter from France and less from New Zealand. The absence of *trade barriers* between member countries and the *common external tariff* give people an incentive to switch. NAFTA, the *North American Free Trade Area*, is demonstrating trade diversion at the present time, as people in the USA, Canada and Mexico will tend to buy more from each other and less from outside the area.

trade gap: a deficit on the *balance of trade.*

trade in goods: visible exports and imports which include primary products and semi-processed raw materials and manufactures.

trade in services: *invisible exports* and imports including tourism, financial services, transport services, education and so on.

trade liberalisation: the process of limiting and reducing *trade barriers* and drawing closer towards a situation of free trade. The impetus for this has come from the GATT/*WTO* and it has been carried out through the *Uruguay Round* of trade negotiations. It has resulted in reduced tariffs on a wide range of goods and services and restrictions on the use of quotas and other non-tariff barriers.

trade-offs: in making decisions people often have to consider that having more of one thing may mean having less of another.

- An important trade-off in *macro-economic policy* is between inflation and unemployment. It is often the case that lower unemployment can be achieved but at the price of accelerating inflation.
- Another trade-off involves *equity* and *efficiency*. Increased wage *differentials* lead to improved incentives but less equity in the *distribution of income*.

In making a decision which involves a trade-off, there will be an *opportunity cost*. For example, the opportunity cost of reducing the rate of inflation may be the increase in unemployment which results.

trade sanctions: restrictions on trade which are designed to discourage aggressive or discriminatory behaviour by governments. These may be agreed internationally through the UN or pursued by one or more individual governments. Iraq provides a long-standing example.

trade surplus occurs when the value of visible *exports* is greater than the value of visible *imports*.

trade union: an organisation that represents employees who can gain more from collective than from individual negotiation or action. Trade unions can ensure that their members have some redress when faced with an employer who is unconcerned about working conditions. There are three types of trade union:

- craft unions, which represent everyone with a particular skill, such as ASLEF, the Associated Society of Locomotive Engineers and Firemen
- industrial unions, which represent employees across a whole industry, such as the ISTC, the Iron and Steel Trades Confederation
- general unions, which represent any group which is not well represented by other unions, in particular the unskilled, such as the TGWU, the Transport and General Workers' Union.

Trade unions can operate at the level of the individual workplace or within a region or nationally. They represent their members in the negotiation of pay and conditions where collective bargaining is appropriate. They take a strong interest in health and safety issues. They can protect individuals against unfair dismissal, as well as protecting members from employers who are intent on keeping costs down rather than considering employee welfare.

In situations where trade unions find a common sense of purpose with management, they can be partners in the process of making the firm more competitive. Where management interests are seen as being different from those of employees and especially where the top management has secured very large pay rises, relations may be confrontational rather than collaborative. (See also *wage bargaining*.)

Trade union membership has fallen substantially. The reasons are:

- diminishing numbers of employees in *declining industries*, which had been for the most part strongly unionised
- increased *productivity* and falling employment in manufacturing generally
- increasing numbers of skilled and educated people who are able to negotiate for themselves just as effectively as a union might.

From a high of 13 million in 1980, trade union membership is now under 8 million.

Trade union power has diminished since legislation was passed in the early 1980s and later weakened the unions substantially. In particular, unions were required to hold a secret ballot before taking strike action and it became much more difficult to start unofficial strikes which had not been organised in accordance with the law. The trade unions were forced into a situation where confrontation with employers could no longer be sustained. The unions' capacity to help poorly paid people diminished, as did their bargaining power in negotiation. However, some employers began over the same period to see concern for the welfare of employees as an important element in responsible management.

trade war: a situation in which some governments put in place *import controls*, designed to protect domestic industries from foreign competition, and the exporting countries then retaliate with import controls of their own. This will tend to depress demand for exports generally and lead to falling levels of economic activity. The most serious instance of this occurred during the 1930s depression. The lessons learned then underlie continuing efforts at *trade liberalisation*, visible in trade negotiations in recent years.

Trades Union Congress (TUC): the umbrella organisation for UK trade unions. It formulates the overall policy stance of the trade union movement, representing it in discussions with government and the *Confederation of British Industry* and parallel organisations in other countries, especially within the EU. The anti-union legislation of the 1980s greatly reduced its influence but in the context of the *Social Chapter*, which sets out employment protection requirements across the EU, it has greater significance.

trading bloc: a group of countries that have agreed to *free trade* with each other.

training means developing knowledge and skills of direct relevance in the workplace. The Learning and Skills Councils (previously the Training and Enterprise Councils or TECs) organise local provision. The LSCs are run by local business representatives, working in collaboration with neighbouring further education colleges where off-the-job training will take place. The idea is that the LSCs are able to define local needs and ensure that they are met by a combination of on-the-job training and courses.

transaction costs: the actual cost of buying or selling something. One is most aware of these costs when buying a home or foreign currency. House purchase involves estate agents, solicitors and stamp duty. Buying foreign currency involves a fee to the seller. Effectively, transaction costs add to the price of the product.

transfer earnings: the wages which could be earned in the best alternative employment. For example, if a teacher was able to earn £20 000 working in a bank, that would be that person's transfer earnings.

transfer payments occur when government revenue from one part of society, e.g. taxpayers, is paid to another part. The best-known transfer payments are pensions and social security payments such as *income support*.

transfer pricing is used when products do not actually reach the marketplace but are transferred between one department and another of the firm. Pricing the product in this way at each stage of production may be useful in establishing internal costs of production. It is used by some *multinationals* when transferring the product from one country to another. By setting the price high in a low tax country and vice versa, they may be able to reduce the amount of profits tax they have to pay.

transitional economies are those which have previously had *centrally planned economies* and are now allowing *market forces* to operate at least in parts of the economy. Russia, Poland and many other East European countries are currently in transition.

transmission mechanism is the theoretical process which connects changes in the stock of money in the economy to the level of income and output. It shows how increased bank lending leads to increases in both consumption and investment, then in aggregate demand, and finally in the level of production. (See also *monetary policy.*)

transnational corporation: another name for a *multinational.*

transparency means an open and clear approach to all decisions. It can be important in ensuring that government policies are appropriate to the situation. If it is possible to see clearly what the proposed policy intends, how it works and who will implement it, then the consultation process which precedes implementation will probably ensure that the policy works well. Similarly, in business, transparency may be able to ensure support for wise decisions. In the euro zone, transparency refers to the fact that differentiated prices for a product will be immediately obvious, no longer obscured by exchange rates.

transport modes: the different methods of transport which are in use, including rail, road, sea and air, also inland waterways and pipelines.

Treasury: the government department at the heart of the government's policies on *taxation* and *government spending*. The Chancellor of the Exchequer has control of the Treasury and so also of *fiscal policy*. Because it has the power to withhold or spend money, it is the most influential of all departments. The annual spending round, where Ministers have to bid for money for their individual departments, can make or break a Minister's political career.

The Treasury has its own macro-economic forecasting model which can predict some changes fairly accurately, aiding decision making.

Treasury bills are short-term (three months) government securities. They are sold in order to cover any shortfall between government spending and tax revenue. Because they are so short-term, they provide a very flexible way for governments to borrow.

Treaty of Amsterdam: an EU agreement, completed in 1997, which came into force in 1998. Most of the issues addressed are more political than economic, although the *Social Chapter* was formally incorporated in it. Its main purpose was to create 'an area of freedom, security and justice' within the EU. The main points are as follows:

- It incorporated the Schengen agreement which abolishes border controls (the UK and Ireland opted out of this).
- It extended the principle of qualified majority voting, reducing the areas where national vetoes operate. This is intended to help decision taking when the EU is enlarged from 15 to perhaps 25 countries altogether.
- Systems to encourage joint EU action on organised crime were put in place.
- Common action on foreign and defence policy was planned.
- The powers of the European Parliament were extended.

Treaty of Rome: the initial agreement between the original six members of the then European Economic Community: Belgium, France, Germany, Italy, Luxembourg and the Netherlands. It came into force in 1958.

trend: the longer run direction of change which can be seen in *time series data*. A clear trend can be used to predict some future changes.

TUC: see *Trades Union Congress*.

turnover, or sales turnover, is the same as sales revenue.

unbalanced growth means avoiding the need to develop a range of industries all at once, as in the theory of *balanced growth*. Instead, it suggests that developing country governments should select industries with backward and forward linkages, for example processing locally produced raw materials or leading to the subsequent development of other industries. These can then be encouraged as a way of increasing growth rates. They may also identify bottlenecks in the economy and set up production facilities which address these directly.

This approach has gone out of fashion as the emphasis has shifted from public sector to private sector solutions to development problems.

The term unbalanced growth is sometimes used much more loosely, simply to mean economic growth which is much more evident in one sector of the economy than another. For example, many developing countries have a fairly well-developed industrial sector, while agriculture has developed relatively little.

uncertainty: the situation of not knowing what will happen in the future. In contrast, risk is easier to deal with because there are known probabilities of a range of possible events actually occurring. Uncertainty is by its nature impossible to quantify. Obviously uncertainty increases the further forward you try to look.

UNCTAD: see *United Nations Conference on Trade and Development.*

underconsumption applies to *merit goods,* for which demand will be lower than is socially most efficient, if people are left to provide them for themselves. It is in the best interests of society for people to be educated and have access to health care, because in this way the population as a whole will be kept healthy and productive. However, both education and health care are expensive and people on low incomes will not be able to pay for them in the optimum quantities. They will therefore be underconsumed unless provided by the government. This is an example of *market failure.*

underdeveloped country: see *developing country.*

underemployment occurs where people work but do not have opportunities sufficient to occupy them full-time. It is common in rural areas in developing economies where most people are dependent on agriculture but are not kept busy with it all year. The outcome is usually a low standard of living. (*Micro-credit* addresses this problem, providing opportunities for some additional occupations.) It also affects people in depressed areas where only part-time work is available.

underlying rate of inflation: the long-run trend rate of inflation. In the UK this is usually measured using the retail price index, minus the change in mortgage interest rates. This is also known as *RPIX.*

undervalued exchange rate: an *exchange rate* which is below its long-term equilibrium value. This means that exports are very competitive and therefore high and imports appear relatively dear and will be fairly low. The outcome is a current account surplus on the *balance of payments.* An undervalued exchange rate can be very helpful in encouraging the development of industries which export.

underwriting is the business of accepting risks which underpin the entire insurance industry. It can also apply to the way a merchant bank will guarantee that all the shares issued by a firm will be sold, by undertaking to buy them itself.

UNDP: see *United Nations Development Program*

unearned income: income derived from interest, dividends and rents, i.e. from assets which are owned, rather than from employment.

unemployment: the problem encountered when there are people able and willing to work but unable to find jobs. This leads to a loss of potential output. The two main categories of unemployment are *demand deficiency* (sometimes called cyclical) and *structural unemployment*. Since the early 1980s unemployment has been consistently higher than previously. This reflects the rapid structural changes which have taken place and the fact that counter-inflation policies have kept the level of aggregate demand below the level needed to employ more of the working population.

Policies to deal with unemployment can be varied:

- When the cause is lack of demand, *expansionary policies* may be appropriate.
- Structural unemployment requires measures which reduce *immobilities*. Training and retraining help.
- Regional policy can be used to help areas where major industries are declining.

In recent years attention has been focused on whether employment protection laws reduce the rate at which new jobs are being created, especially for unskilled jobs. Policies have emphasised the need for labour markets to be flexible. In the USA, unemployment fell steadily during the late 1990s, in contrast to the situation in most of the EU, where unemployment in a number of countries was above 10% for some time. This has been attributed to the very flexible labour market which exists in the USA.

Unemployment can be measured in different ways, giving different results. The *claimant count* is the number of people who register as unemployed, which excludes some people who are available for work but do not qualify for unemployment benefit. The figures based on the *Labour Force Survey*, or the ILO definition of unemployment, will include these.

unemployment benefit is the social security payment made to people who have become unemployed. It has recently been renamed the *jobseeker's allowance* and is now paid for a maximum of six months. The intention is to create an enhanced incentive to find work.

unfair competition: the use of methods of competing which in some way break rules which other competitors have to abide by. This can apply in a range of situations:

- some firms may resort to 'dirty tricks', e.g. bus companies have been known to timetable their buses just before the arrival times of other companies' buses, which can drive a smaller competitor out of business
- firms may be in receipt of government subsidies which their competitors cannot get
- firms may be able to cut costs by having lower health and safety standards than their competitors.

Some businesses compete with firms in countries with lower wage rates and mistakenly see this as unfair competition. In reality it simply reflects the relative *comparative advantages* of the competitors.

Uniform Business Rate: a tax paid to the local authority by businesses in its area. It is based on property values, at a rate set by central government. It can be a substantial fixed cost for firms.

union: see *trade union.*

union recognition involves employers in accepting collective bargaining with the union to which members of the workforce belong. By law employers need not do this unless they so choose, which means that in new firms, trade unions may have very little impact.

unit cost: the average cost of one unit of the product. Changes in unit costs are a useful measure of competitiveness.

unit elasticity means that *price elasticity of demand* is exactly equal to −1. The percentage change in quantity demanded is exactly the same as the percentage change in price. Price changes will make no difference to the amount of money spent on the product, because an increase in price will be offset by a decrease in quantity demanded. Someone who has a set amount of beer money to spend each week will have unit elasticity of demand.

unit labour cost: the cost of the labour needed to make one unit of output. This can be reduced in two ways, without cutting wages:

- by cutting the labour input, adopting a more capital-intensive way of producing
- by using labour more efficiently, e.g. by training in additional skills.

unit of account: one of the functions of money, by which it allows different values to be added and compared.

unit trust: a firm which sells its own shares to savers and invests the proceeds in the shares of a wide range of businesses which it hopes will be more profitable than the average. For people who want to buy shares without investing a great deal of cash, this approach reduces the risk of all their shares falling in price. In return, the unit trust will collect the difference between the dividends it receives and those it pays to its shareholders.

United Nations Conference on Trade and Development (UNCTAD): the organisation within the United Nations framework which tries to help the developing countries to secure improved trade agreements and aid payments. (So far its efforts have not been greatly rewarded.)

United Nations Development Program funds *soft loans* and technical assistance for developing countries. The latter usually consists of expatriate experts who can work with officials of the country concerned.

universal benefit: a *social security* payment which is given to all who qualify regardless of income. The most important example is the old age pension. In contrast, *means-tested benefits* are given only to those whose incomes are below a certain level, e.g. income support.

unlimited liability: the way in which businesses which do not have the legal status of a company will have to pay all of their debts from their owners' personal funds, if the business cannot cover its costs. Sole traders and partnerships are in this position.

unlimited wants: the endless needs and desires for goods and services which may be felt by consumers. Resources are scarce and all economic goods have a price, so that consumers have to choose which of their unlimited wants will be satisfied.

unofficial economy: see *black economy*.

unsecured loan: a loan which is not covered by any asset which could be used to repay it. A mortgage is secured in the sense that the home can be sold to pay off the debt. Unsecured loans are likely to have higher interest rates.

unsustainable growth: economic growth which is faster than the long-term trend rate of growth, which reflects the actual increase in the productive capacity of the economy. A period of unsustainable growth is likely to be followed by a period of slower than average growth. The UK is widely believed to have been growing at an unsustainable rate of growth in 1988 and also in 1993, in both cases at an annual rate of more than 4%. In both cases this was not sustained.

An alternative definition of unsustainable growth would emphasise the environmental considerations. It would be growth at a rate which involved the use of depletable resources which could not be continued in the long run because they would become progressively scarcer and therefore more expensive. Sustainable growth involves the management of resources so that they are replaced as they are used. For example, trees are replanted and reliance on fossil fuels is progressively reduced.

upturn: the point in the *trade cycle*, at the end of a slump, when some firms begin to be optimistic enough to consider new *investment* projects.

urban economy: that part of the economy which is based on developments in city areas. This will contrast with the predominantly agricultural rural economy. There will be a sharp contrast between the two in some developing countries, where the urban economy may be much more modern than the rural economy.

Uruguay Round: the trade negotiations which took place under the auspices of GATT (now *WTO*) and were put into effect at the beginning of 1995. (The negotiations originally began in Uruguay.) They had the effect of reducing trade barriers for a wide range of goods and services, including some which had previously been strongly protected by *tariffs* and *non-tariff barriers*.

utilities: industries which provide the *infrastructure* for the economy. They include water, energy and communication facilities. They used to be regarded as *natural monopolies*, so were given *regulators* on *privatisation*. Most are now facing some competition (but not water).

utility means satisfaction, to an economist. Some of the underlying theory behind our understanding of demand involves examining the utility which consumers derive from small extra amounts of the goods and services they consume and comparing this to the prices paid.

vacancies: job opportunities which are registered with job centres. This is not the number of job vacancies in existence, because many are not registered but are advertised independently in a wide range of publications and agencies. However, the changes in vacancies over time are a very useful indicator of the slackness or tightness of the labour market generally. A sharp rise in vacancies indicates that the economy may be running into *supply constraints* across a wide range of occupations. It could be the precursor to a rise in the rate of inflation.

In 1993, at the end of the early 1990s slump, monthly vacancy figures stood at around 117 000. By the time the economy had recovered in 1995, they were around 178 000. After five more years of reasonably steady growth, in 2000, the figure was 360 000.

value means economic worth. In realistic terms, the value of an asset or a product is what someone is prepared to pay for it, provided that price is at least equal to the price at which someone is willing to supply it. If it is not, the value is low and production will fall.

value added means the value of a firm's output, less the value of all the bought-in inputs. It is the value added by the firm's *factors of production*. It reflects the value of the services of labour, land and capital which have been used in creating the product.

Value Added Tax (VAT) is the main expenditure tax in the UK, levied at 17.5% on most goods and services. The tax is added by each producer, so that for a car, say, it is paid by the component manufacturer, the final product manufacturer and the car dealer. Each of these can get back the VAT paid on their inputs, so that the tax reflects the value added at each stage of production. Ultimately, of course, the full amount of the tax is paid by the consumer because it is included in the price of the product.

VAT is *regressive* in the sense that it will take a larger proportion of a poor person's income than of a rich person's income. In the UK it is less regressive than it appears because some goods and services are either exempt or zero rated. These include food eaten at home, housing, public transport and children's clothes which are likely together to account for a large proportion of the spending of the less well off.

value judgements: conclusions which are based on opinions rather than on verifiable facts. These will vary according to the value systems of the individual. Many value judgments can be traced to the personal position of the individual. For example, opposition to high marginal tax rates is much more common amongst the people who pay them than among non-taxpayers.

variable: a measurement that changes over time and in turn causes other changes to take place. In the macro-economy, changes in variables may be predicted by economic models. For example, the effect on spending of a tax change can be estimated. Changes in independent variables (such as tax rates) can be fed into the model, to give predictions about the effects on dependent variables (such as incomes and expenditure).

variable costs: the costs of production which vary directly with the amount of output. They include raw materials, components and the labour and energy which are used in the actual production process.

variable factors of production are those factors which can be varied in quantity in the short run. Raw material or component inputs are an example: the amount used will depend on the level of output and can be varied as necessary. Labour may be a variable factor, if the number of people employed or the hours worked can be varied according to the amount of work to be done. This might be the case if overtime was worked in order to increase output. Alternatively, labour may be a fixed factor, if the employees concerned will have to be kept on even if output falls.

VAT: see *value added tax.*

velocity of circulation: the ratio of the value of output to a particular measure of the stock of money in circulation in the economy. Over the years this may change, depending on the extent to which idle bank balances are held.

venture capital is finance for projects which could be very profitable but are also quite risky. It is usually organised by *merchant banks* as a source of finance for small and medium-sized firms which are not sufficiently well established to issue shares on the Stock Exchange.

VER: see *voluntary export restraint.*

vertical integration: amalgamation of two firms in the same industry which are specialised in different stages of the production process. The undertaker who set up a florists was becoming vertically integrated. Often, vertical integration involves a merger or takeover.

Backward vertical integration occurs when the firm buys a supplier. A manufacturer of plastic products might buy the firm which supplies the mouldings needed in the production process. Forward vertical integration occurs when a manufacturer takes over a distribution network, i.e. its customer.

vertical merger: see *vertical integration.*

vested interest refers to a situation in which someone is acting in a way which is influenced by their own material interest in the outcome. Farmers have a vested interest in the future of the Common Agricultural Policy. Teachers have a vested interest in the provision of more government funding for education. If they do not declare this interest their enthusiasm for particular outcomes may be misinterpreted.

visible balance: another name for the trade balance, i.e. visible exports minus visible imports.

visible trade is the export and import of goods only, services are not included. The difference between visible exports and visible imports is the *balance of trade.* (See also *balance of payments.*)

volume index: a measure of changes in output or exports which counts the changes in the actual quantity of goods and expresses these as an *index number.* It is a useful way to compare changes in exports when inflation or exchange rates make the data hard to interpret.

voluntary export restraints (VERs): a quota placed on imports from a particular country, with the agreement of that country's government. (See *quotas* for explanation of the likely impact.) They have been negotiated mainly with Japan, but also with countries such as Taiwan and South Korea. They apply mostly to manufactured goods such as cars and televisions. Their objective is to protect the domestic industry of the importing country. The exporting country may be persuaded to accept them if the alternative is a more damaging trade barrier. They are outside the rules of the *WTO* but nevertheless continue to exist in a number of countries.

voluntary unemployment includes anyone who has refused to take a job which is available and anyone who could work but is not actively seeking work. It is extremely difficult to measure voluntary unemployment and some economists even doubt that it exists. Some people will refuse work because they believe they should be able to get a better paid job or a different type of work. The concept of voluntary unemployment has been associated with some *monetarist* economists; a possible policy to deal with it is to reduce benefits.

wage bargaining may occur collectively or individually. The outcome depends heavily on the market power of individuals and the organisations concerned. Many people have no choice but simply to accept the going rate of pay, when neither they nor any trade union they might join has any bargaining power. Only a shortage of their particular skill, or of labour generally, will then raise their real earnings.

- A highly skilled employee may be able to negotiate pay if it is clear that these particular skills are scarce and badly needed by the employer.
- A *trade union* or a team of unions may negotiate directly with the employers over pay in that particular workplace or firm. National agreements covering all the company factories in the UK are found in the car industry.
- Trade unions may negotiate with employers' organisations to arrive at a national pay bargain which will apply to the whole industry.
- In the public sector, especially the NHS and in education, national pay agreements are the norm. Despite being strongly unionised, however, employees in the public sector tend not to have a great deal of bargaining power.

wage determination in practice reflects some combination of market forces in the occupation concerned and the relative bargaining power of any organisations involved. (See also *wage bargaining*.) For any particular occupation, analysis requires some understanding of both of these.

Assuming markets are competitive, pay will be determined by the interaction of supply and demand in the labour market. The important factors affecting demand are:

- the demand for the final product
- the price of capital equipment which could be substituted for labour
- the productivity of labour.

Factors affecting supply are:

- wage rates on offer in other occupations
- the non-monetary attractions of the work
- the amount of training required.

Some very unpleasant work is well paid because few people would accept it otherwise.

A growing industry which can charge relatively high prices will have a high level of demand for labour. Depending on the supply of labour, wage rates are likely to be higher than they would be in a declining industry. This can be seen clearly in the pay of computer software specialists, who are both scarce and very much in demand.

Increasing demand for particular skills takes the demand curve from D_1 to D_2. These skills are relatively scarce so the wage rate rises in order to attract the type of people needed. (See diagram on p.331.)

Changes in the supply of and demand for labour will be affected by elasticities. An increase in demand for construction workers during a boom will typically raise pay because the supply of suitably trained people is inelastic in the short run.

If you are studying the labour market options in the OCR or Edexcel specifications, make sure you understand the underlying relevance of *marginal revenue product* and *marginal productivity theory.*

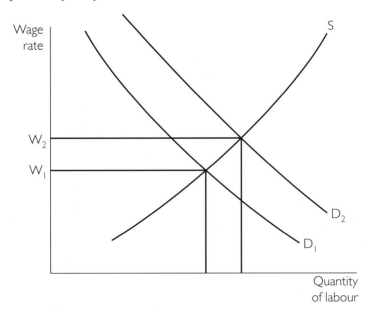

wage differentials: see *differentials.*

wage–price spiral: if wages are rising, costs of production will also be rising. Also, demand for consumer goods will also rise. Both trends are likely to cause *inflation*. This in turn will cause employees to negotiate higher wages and the cycle starts over again. Inflation becomes built into people's *expectations* and is therefore hard to stop. The only method of stopping people from expecting inflation which has been successful in recent years is to reduce aggregate demand to the point where unemployment rises, so that competition in the labour market for scarce jobs causes pay increases to slow down.

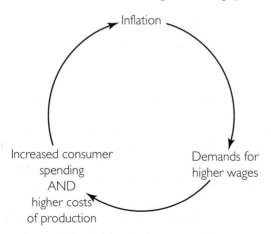

Wage–price spiral

wage rate: the price of labour. When wage rates change, the change may be real or it may be just a change in money wages which maintains their existing purchasing power.

wage rigidity: see *sticky wages*.

Wall Street Crash: during the 1920s the US stock market rose dramatically, taking prices beyond anything which reflected likely long-run value. The result was the 1929 crash. The loss of confidence which this caused was a major factor in the 1930s depression.

A similar but less dramatic cycle, of a long period of rapid share price increases followed by a correction which frightens people into selling all at once, has been seen since. Black Monday in the UK and the US in 1987 was like this, also for some Asian countries the crashes associated with the *Asian financial crisis* in 1997–1998.

war: Winston Churchill said 'If the human race wishes to have a prolonged and indefinite period of material prosperity, they have only got to behave in a peaceful and helpful way toward one another, and science will do for them all they wish and more than they can dream'.

wealth: the stock of *assets* held by an individual or organisation. These assets can be used to yield a stream of *income* in the future. They may consist of financial assets, such as bank balances or shares, or real assets, such as property.

wealth distribution: the way in which total *wealth* in the economy is shared out among the population as a whole. In most countries wealth is unevenly distributed. In the UK, roughly 36% of total wealth belongs to the wealthiest 10% of the population. 83% of all wealth belongs to 50% of the population. Widespread home ownership does do something to redistribute wealth.

wealth effect: the impact of increased *wealth* on consumer demand. When the US stock market was rising during the 1990s many ordinary people bought shares. As they saw their assets rise in value, they felt able to increase their consumption.

wealth tax: with a view to redistributing income and wealth, it is possible to tax wealth, although valuing some assets can be difficult. There is no direct wealth tax in the UK but *inheritance tax* does reduce large family holdings of wealth. *Capital gains tax* reduces the extent to which wealth can be accumulated through rising share and property prices.

weighted average: an average which takes into account the relative importance of its components. For example, the *retail price index* is a weighted average that gives larger weights to the prices of products on which a significant amount of income is spent.

Weights are regularly revised through the Family Expenditure Survey to ensure that they reflect current spending patterns.

welfare: a term usually used to refer to people's well-being. It is hard to measure. *National income statistics* are an imperfect guide. Sometimes, other measures are used, which might include life expectancy, child mortality or the ownership of certain *consumer durables*.

welfare economics: aspects of economics which are concerned with *welfare*. It is sometimes called *normative* economics because it addresses the question of how well the economy works to achieve certain desirable objectives. It takes in issues of *equity* and *efficiency*, including *Pareto efficiency*; issues associated with *market failure* and all kinds of *externalities*. In defining desirable objectives, welfare economics will include questions about what ought to happen, as well as questions about what does happen. It can therefore be used to explore areas of the subject which involve value judgements.

welfare state: the system of social security benefits and health care which was set up in the UK after 1945. It was designed to help all those in need, but is constantly threatened by efforts to cut costs and avoid raising taxes. The capacity to provide is affected by the ageing population, which increases demands on the welfare state.

white-collar union: a *trade union* representing clerical, professional or managerial staff.

White Paper: a government document which describes in detail proposed new policies and laws.

wholesale price index: a measure of changes in wholesale prices. It is useful because it may give an advance warning of impending changes in retail price levels.

wholesaling: buying large quantities of various products and selling them on in smaller quantities to retailers and other firms. Essentially, wholesalers are suppliers to other businesses. Although 'middlemen' are often thought to add to costs, businesses use wholesalers to save them the trouble of having to buy direct from a large number of producers. The fact that they exist shows that they have a role in increasing efficiency.

windfall: an unexpected gain. This could be an inheritance or an exceptional rise in the price of one's home or a much higher profit than usual. The point is that it is exceptional and not something that can be relied upon.

withdrawals occur when money is taken out of the *circular flow of national income*. They are also known as leakages and consist of taxes, imports and savings. In each case, the withdrawal leads to a lower level of aggregate demand for domestic output, i.e. they reduce spending power. A fall in withdrawals will lead to an increase in spending, as with a tax cut.

work in progress (WIP): goods and services which are part way through the production process. In manufacturing, stocks of work in progress may be kept. This may increase efficiency but it may also be costly because the stocks are lying idle rather than being finished and sold.

work to rule: a type of *industrial action* which involves working precisely according to the rules laid down in employment contracts. Usually this entails a loss of flexibility and reduced quality of communication between employees and with management. Employees can continue to draw their basic pay and production does not stop, but there may be a serious loss of goodwill in the workplace.

worker participation: see *employee involvement*.

working capital is the finance needed to pay for production costs until payment is received for the output. For some firms it is financed with an overdraft or it may be financed out of past *retained profit*.

Working Families Tax Credit: a benefit paid to people with families whose pay is low. It helps to ensure that people on low pay do have some incentive to work.

working population: all those who are working or actively seeking work. The UK's working population is currently increasing, from 28 million in 1997 to 29 million in 1999.

working time directive: a measure resulting from the EU's *Social Chapter*, which requires that employees work no more than 48 hours per week, averaged over a 17-week period. Individual employees are allowed to opt out of this if they wish.

works council: a body which brings together employees and management for discussion of matters of mutual interest. Employees can be briefed on management plans for the future. Issues affecting employee welfare (other than pay) can be raised. Likely topics include working conditions and health and safety issues. Works councils are consultative bodies with no capacity to take decisions but they may help to resolve issues before they become a problem. Under the EU's *Social Chapter*, they are compulsory for larger firms.

Not all UK managers welcome the advent of works councils. Those that have had them for some time say that they can be useful in providing a forum for discussion.

World Bank: see the *International Bank for Reconstruction and Development.*

World Development Report: an annual publication of the World Bank providing extensive data on growth and development issues.

World Trade Organisation: oversees and regulates the international trading environment. It replaced GATT, the *General Agreement on Tariffs and Trade,* early in 1995. As with GATT, its objectives are to promote freer trade. In practical terms it aims to reduce *trade barriers.* There have been successive rounds of tariff negotiations which have cut tariffs on a wide range of products and sought to eliminate quotas and reduce non-tariff barriers. (The last of these, the *Uruguay Round,* was the most far-reaching to date and was implemented from 1995.) Most of the world's nations belong to the WTO and participate in its work. In addition to reducing trade barriers, it has mechanisms for resolving international trade disputes. Although the WTO/GATT has been highly successful in reducing tariff barriers on trade in manufactures, there are still major restraints on trade in agricultural products which are being reduced only very slowly, if at all.

Some moves have been made to start a new round of trade negotiations. The future of these is very uncertain at the time of writing.

WTO: see *World Trade Organisation.*

X, Y, Z

x-inefficiency: the tendency for costs to rise because the organisation has few or no competitors. This is likely to occur if the producer has a degree of monopoly power, whether in the public or the private sector, which allows management to become careless about keeping costs to a minimum.

yield: the annual income derived from a *share* or a *bond*, as a proportion of its current market price.

zero sum game: a situation in which a gain made by one person or organisation can only be made at the expense of a loss to another. It can be important in *game theory*.

ECONOMICS AND BUSINESS REVISION LISTS

The following pages set out lists of terms to revise for examinations. There is a list for each module of the AQA, Edexcel and OCR specifications. When approaching exams, look up each word in the main text, making sure that you understand it and can memorise the definition.

AQA AS Module I Markets and market failure

Administrative costs
Allocation of resources
Capital
Choice
Commodity markets
Composite demand
Conflicting objectives
Consumption
Demand curve
De-merit goods
Derived demand
Distortions
Division of labour
Economic activity
Economic efficiency
Economic models
Economic resources
Economic welfare
Economies of scale
Elasticity of demand
Enterprise
Equilibrium market price
Exchange
Government intervention
Immobility
Imperfect knowledge
Incentive
Income distribution
Income elasticity of demand
Indirect taxation
Inefficiency
Inequality
Innovation
Inter-relationships between markets
Invention
Joint supply

Labour
Land
Margin
Marginal social cost
Market economy
Market failure
Market imperfections
Market mechanism
Market power
Merit goods
Micro-economic models
Misallocation of resources
Monopoly
Natural environment
Negative externalities
Non-excludability
Normative
Needs and wants
Opportunity cost
Over-production
Positive externalities
Positive statements
Price controls
Price elasticity of demand
Price elasticity of supply
Price mechanism
Private costs
Production
Production possibility curve
Profit signalling mechanism
Public goods
Rationing
Regulation
Scarcity
Shifts in the demand curve
Shifts in the supply curve

Social costs
Specialisation
State provision
Subsidy

Trade-offs
Unit costs
Value judgments
Wealth distribution

AQA AS Module 2 The national economy

Aggregate demand
Aggregate supply
Balance of payments
Budget (the)
Consumption
Current account
Economic activity
Economic growth
Economic incentives
Economic performance
Economic policy
Employment
Enterprise
Excess aggregate demand
Exchange rates
Exports
Factor mobility
Fiscal policy
Free market policies
GDP
Government expenditure
Government objectives
Imports
Index numbers

Inflation
Interest rates
Interventionist policies
Investment
Investment income
Long run
Long run trend rate of growth
Macro-economic policies
Monetary policy
Money supply
Policy conflicts
Production
Production possibility curve
Productive capacity
Real national income
Short run
Supply side policies
Surplus on current account
Taxation
Trade in goods
Trade in services
Transfer payments
Unemployment

AQA A2 Module 4 Working as an economist, EU

Assumptions
Common Agricultural Policy
Convergence criteria
Economic integration
Economies of scale
Economic analysis
Euro
Free movement of people
Harmonisation

Hypothesis
Inflation targeting
Monopoly power
Price transparency
Single European market
Specialisation
Trade creation
Trade diversion
Trading bloc

AQA A2 Module 5 Business economics and the distribution of income

Abnormal profit
Absolute poverty
Advertising
Allocative efficiency
Barriers to entry
Cartels
Collusive oligopoly
Competition policy
Concentration
Conduct
Consumer surplus
Contestable markets
Cost benefit analysis
Cost structure
Costs of production
Dead-weight losses
Demand
Demand for labour
Derived demand
Discrimination
Efficiency
Entry
Equity
Equality
Exit
External growth
Factor inputs
Free entry
Game theory
Government failure
Hit and run competition
Human capital
Income distribution
Interdependence between firms
Integration
Internal growth
Invention
Innovation
Kinked demand curve
Law of diminishing returns
Long run
Marginal cost

Marginal productivity theory
Marginal revenue
Market failure
Minimum efficient scale
Monopoly
Monopsonistic employers
Non-collusive oligopoly
Non-price competition
Normal profit
Oligopoly
Price agreements
Perfect competition
Pollution permits
Price discrimination
Price leadership
Price makers
Price takers
Price wars
Privatisation
Producer surplus
Product differentiation
Productive efficiency
Productivity
Profit maximisation
Property rights
Public ownership
Redistribution of income
Regulation
Regulatory capture
Relative poverty
Relative wage rates
Research and development
Revenue
Satisficing
Separation of ownership from control
Short run
Sunk costs
Super normal profit
Supply of labour
Technological change
Trade unions
Wealth distribution

AQA A2 Module 6 Government policy, the national and international economy

Balance of payments
Bank of England
Bank deposits
Budget balance
Capital account
Comparative advantage
Current account
Customs union
Cyclical instability
Equity
Economic and Monetary Union
Exchange rate
Exchange rate target
Fixed exchange rates
Floating exchange rates
Fiscal policy
Fisher equation
Globalisation
Index numbers
Inflation
Interest rates
International capital flows
International trade
Liquidity

Living standards
Long run
Long run trend rate of growth
Monetarist model
Monetary policy
Money supply
National income statistics
Natural rate of unemployment
Pattern of trade
Phillips curve
Policy conflicts
Policy instruments
Protectionism
Public expenditure
Quantity theory of money
Quotas
Short run
Supply side influences
Supply side shocks
Sustainable growth
Tariff
Taxation
Unemployment

AQA revision lists

Edexcel Unit 1 Markets – how they work

Absolute advantage
Allocation of resources
Average costs
Centrally planned economies
Commodities
Comparative advantage
Consumer preferences
Demand
Demand curve
Division of labour
Economies of scale
Efficiency
Elasticity of demand
Entry
Exit
Free market economy
Gains from trade

Incentive
Incidence of taxation
Income elasticity of demand
Indirect taxes
Inferior goods
Minimum guaranteed prices
Minimum wage
Mixed economy
Normal goods
Price elasticity of demand
Price mechanism
Shift of the demand curve
Subsidy
Supply
Supply curve
Supply elasticity
Transitional economies

Edexcel Unit 2 Markets – why they fail

Allocative efficiency
Average cost
Barriers to entry
Consumption
Demerit goods
Diseconomies of scale
Economies of scale
Environmental pollution
Entry
Exit
External benefits
External costs
External economies of scale
Externalities
Government intervention
Indirect taxes
Inequality
Marginal cost
Marginal social cost
Market dominance

Market failure
Market share
Merger
Merit goods
Monopoly
Ownership rights
Patents
Pollution permits
Private costs
Private marginal cost
Private sector
Production
Productive efficiency
Property rights
Public goods
Regulation
Social costs
Subsidy
Tradable permits
Welfare

Edexcel Unit 3 Managing the economy

Aggregate demand
Aggregate supply
Balance of payments
Claimant count
Consumption
Current account
Disequilibrium
Economic growth
Exchange rate
Exports
Flexibility
Full employment
Government expenditure
Gross domestic product
Imports
Income distribution
Index numbers
Inflation
Investment
Labour force survey

Long run
Multiplier
Nominal GDP
Phillips curve
Productivity
Real income
Retail price index
Shift in aggregate demand
Shift in aggregate supply
Short run
Skills
Standard of living
Supply side policies
Technical change
Time series
Trade in goods
Trade in services
Trade-offs
Unemployment

Edexcel Unit 4 Industrial economics

Allocative efficiency
Average cost
Average cost pricing
Backward integration
Barriers to entry
Cartels
Collusion
Competition
Competition policy
Concentration ratios
Conglomerate mergers
Constraints
Consumer surplus
Contestable markets
Corporate objectives
Cost-plus pricing
Economic efficiency
Economies of scale
Entry
Exit

External growth
Forward integration
Homogeneous products
Horizontal mergers
Imperfect competition
Internal growth
Law of diminishing returns
Marginal cost
Marginal revenue
Market share
Market structures
Mergers
Monopoly
Monopoly power
Multinationals
New entrants
Oftel
Ofwat
Oligopoly
Perfect competition

Predatory pricing
Price discrimination
Privatisation
Producer surplus
Productive efficiency
Profit maximisation
Regulation

Revenue maximisation
Sales maximisation
Sales promotion
Sunk costs
Takeover bid
Transnational corporation
Vertical integration

Edexcel Unit 5a Labour markets

Ageing population
Benefits
Collective bargaining
Deciles
Discrimination
Elasticity of demand for labour
Equal opportunities
Geographical immobility
Government expenditure
Government intervention
Incentives
Income effect
Income distribution
Inequality
Labour market
Labour market flexibility
Lorenz curve
Marginal product
Marginal rate of tax
Market imperfections

Migration
Monopsony
Occupational immobility
Owner occupation
Participation rates
Poverty
Productivity
Quintiles
Regional policies
Social Chapter
Substitution effect
Supply of labour
Taxation
Trade unions
Unemployment
Wage determination
Wage differentials
Wealth distribution
Working population

Edexcel Unit 5b Economic development

Absolute poverty
Aid
Bretton Woods
Corruption
Debt
Debt forgiveness
Deforestation
Development indicators
Economic development

Economic growth
Environmental degradation
Export promotion
External costs
External finance
Foreign direct investment
Government intervention
Human capital
IMF

Import substitution
International Monetary Fund
Life expectancy
Literacy rates
GDP per capita
Growing populations
Inward-looking trade strategies
Official development assistance
Outward-looking trade strategies
Physical capital
Population growth
Primary products

Primary product dependency
Private sector
Public sector
Quality of life
Relative poverty
Resource allocation
Social development
Structural adjustment
Technical change
Trade liberalisation
Welfare

Edexcel Unit 6 The global economy

Automatic fiscal policy
Balance of payments
CAP
Capital inflows
Capital mobility
Common Agricultural Policy
Competitiveness
Current account
Customs unions
Demand management
Deregulation
Direct taxes
Discretionary fiscal policy
Economic and Monetary Union
EMU
Exchange rate policy
External shocks
Fiscal policy
Fixed exchange rates
Floating exchange rates
Free trade areas
Globalisation
Import penetration
Indirect taxes
Inflation

Interdependence
Inward investment
Long run Phillips curve
Monetary policy
NAIRU
Non-tariff barriers
Protectionism
Public expenditure
Public sector borrowing
Quotas
Relative export prices
Relative inflation rates
Relative interest rates
Short run Phillips curve
Skills
Speculative capital flows
Supply side policies
Tariff
Taxation
Time lag
Trade barriers
Trading bloc
Unemployment
Unit costs
World Trade Organisation

Edexcel revision lists

OCR Module 2881 The market system

Average cost
Average revenue
Barriers to entry
Business objectives
Choice
Competitive markets
Consumer preferences
Consumer surplus
Cross price elasticity of demand
Demand curves
Economic problem
Economic resources
Effective demand
Economies of scale
Equilibrium price
Equilibrium quantity
Exchange
Factor markets
Labour market
Long run
Marginal concept
Marginal cost
Marginal revenue
Market demand
Market equilibrium
Market system
Market share maximisation
Market structures
Methodology
Money
Money market
Monopoly
Monopolistic competition
Movements along the demand curve
Oligopoly
Producer objectives
Producer surplus
Production
Product differentiation
Profit
Profit maximisation
Sales revenue maximisation
Satisficing
Shifts in the demand curve
Short run
Spectrum of competition
Supply elasticity
Total cost
Total revenue
Trade-offs

OCR Module 2882 Market failure and government intervention

Allocation of resources
Allocative efficiency
Competition policy
Cost-benefit analysis
De-merit goods
Distortions
Efficiency
Equity
Excludability
Externalities
Factor immobility
Government failure
Government intervention
Immobilities
Incentives
Information failures
Information provision
Intervention
Market dominance
Market failure
Market power
Merit goods
Minimum wage
Negative externalities
Non-excludability
Non-rivalry
Pareto efficiency
Pollution
Positive externalities
Price controls

Private goods
Production possibility frontier
Productive efficiency
Public goods
Regional unemployment
Regulation

Rivalry
Quasi-public goods
State provision
Structural unemployment
Subsidy

OCR Module 2883 The national and international economy

Aggregate demand
Aggregate supply
Aggregate supply curves
Balance of payments
Capital
Claimant count
Demand management
Developing countries
Economic growth
Economic performance
Economic policy
Equilibrium in the macro-economy
Exchange rate determination
Exchange rate policy
Exports
Fiscal policy
Gains from trade
GDP
Government expenditure
Government economic objectives
Import controls
Imports
Index numbers
Indicators
Inflation
Injections
Interest rates

Internal trade
Inter-relationships
Investment
Labour Force Survey
Labour
Land
Leakages
Long run
Monetary policy
Money supply
Multiplier
National income
Nominal values
Non-tariff barriers
Pattern of trade
Policy conflicts
Price stability
Protectionism
Quotas
Real values
Short run
Supply side policies
Sustainable growth
Tariff
Technological change
Unemployment

OCR Module 2884 Economics of work and leisure

Backward sloping supply curve of
labour
Bilateral monopoly
Competitive behaviour
Contestability
Demand for labour
Discrimination
Disequilibrium
Earnings
Economic rent
Elasticity of supply of labour
Employment
Geographical immobility
Human capital
Imperfect information
Income redistribution
Inequality
Labour market failure
Labour market flexibility
Maastricht Treaty

Marginal revenue product
Market structure
Model
Monopolistic competition
Monopoly
Monopsony
Non-pecuniary advantages
Occupational immobility
Oligopoly
Perfect competition
Segmented labour markets
Social Charter
Supply of labour
Supply side
Trade union
Trade union
Transfer earnings
Unit labour cost
Wage bargaining
Wage determination

OCR Module 2885 Transport economics

Competitive behaviour
Contestability
Cost benefit analysis
Deregulation
Direct control
Efficiency
Fixed costs
Franchise monopoly
Franchise
Freight transport
Imperfect information
Integrated transport policy
Investment
Maastricht Treaty
Market structure
Monopolistic competition
Monopoly
Monopsony
Natural monopoly

Negative externality
Non-pecuniary advantages
Oligopoly
Perfect competition
Private sector
Privatisation
Pollution
Resource allocation
Road pricing
Royal Commission on Environmental
Pollution
Segmented labour markets
Social benefits
Social costs
Supply side policies
Transport modes
Transport operations
Variable costs

OCR Module 2886 Economics of development

Absolute advantage
Balanced growth
Capital accumulation
Colonialism
Comparative advantage
Culture
Currency stabilisation
Debt Problem
Developed countries
Developing countries
Dual economy
Economic development
Exchange rate fluctuations
Export promotion
Factor endowment
Financial markets
Foreign debt management
Foreign direct investment
Formal economy
Gains from trade
Globalisation
Harrod-Domar model
Human development index
Lewis' model
IMF
Import substitution
Industrialisation
Inequality
Informal economy
International capital flows
International Monetary Fund
Low income countries
Middle income countries
Migration

Multinationals
National income statistics
Newly industrialised countries
NGOs
Non-governmental organisations
Non-material progress
Patterns of trade
Population change
Population control
Poverty
Price stability
Primary sector
Quaternary sector
Rostow's model
Savings ratio
Secondary sector
Sectoral change
Stabilisation policy
State planning
Structural adjustment
Structural change
Terms of trade
Tertiary sector
Trade agreements
Trade liberalisation
Transitional economies
Transnational corporation
Unbalanced growth
Urban economy
Underemployment
Unemployment
World Bank
World Trade Organisation

OCR Module 2887 The UK economy

Absolute advantage
Comparative advantage
Competitiveness
Balance of payments
Bank of England
Broad money
Budget
Budget (the)
Budget deficit
Budget surplus
Credit creation multiplier
Deciles
Direct controls
Direct tax
Distribution of income
Economic growth
Economic performance
Equity
Exchange rates
Exchange rate policy
Exchange Equalisation Account
Export promotion
Fiscal policy
Foreign direct investment
Globalisation
Government expenditure
Government borrowing
Hot money
Import substitution
Import controls
Income distribution
Income tax
Indirect tax
Inflation
Interest rates

IMF
International Monetary Fund
Liquidity preference
Lorenz curve
Loanable funds theory
M0
M4
Marshall-Lerner condition
Minimum wage
Monetary policy
Money supply
Narrow money
Phillips curve
Policy conflicts
Policy instruments
Productivity
PSNCR
Productivity
Public borrowing
Quantity theory of money
Quotas
Real GDP
Relocation of labour
Retraining
Supply side policies
Standard of living
Trade agreements
Trade liberalisation
Treasury (the)
Unemployment
VAT
Value added tax
Wealth
World Bank
World Trade Organisation

OCR Module 2888 Economics in a European context

Allocative efficiency
Centrally planned economies
Competitive markets
Convergence
Convergence criteria
Copenhagen criteria
Customs union
Economic efficiency
Economic integration
Economic union
EU enlargement
Euro-zone
Financial sector reform
Free movement of people
Free trade areas

Government intervention
Gradualism
Integration
International trade
Liberalisation
Maastricht Treaty
Macro-economic performance
Macro-economic stabilisation
Market failure
Market structures
Non-tariff barriers
Optimal currency area
Privatisation
Productive efficiency
Protectionism

OCR revision lists

SYNOPTIC ASSESSMENT

From September 2000, all A level specifications will include the new phrase: 'synoptic assessment'. This means an examination that tests a candidate's understanding of the subject as a whole; how different subject areas relate to each other. In all subjects, this exam must take place at the end of the course, and must comprise 20% of the total marks for the A level. The government believes that this will be the toughest test within an A level.

To succeed with synoptic questions, candidates need to think in an integrated manner. In economics, this might mean understanding the impact of a change in demand on individual firms or a whole industry; or how changes in the labour market might affect the rate of inflation; or how changes in exchange rate policy affect firms and individuals; or the impact of new technologies on firms and on the rate of economic growth. This should not be a great problem for economics students, as teachers have been used to emphasising the links between different topics. Nevertheless, the following section has been devised to help synoptic revision.

Synoptic revision

Synoptic revision means bringing together the different parts of the subject. Examiners will test this by creating situations which demand an integrated solution. For example, increasing international trade both within and beyond the EU means that for most countries, both exports and imports are rising steadily. Questions may explore the impact of this on firms, individuals and the economy as a whole.

Candidates need to make connections between the theme and the ideas they have encountered during the course. They will need quickly to survey the likely implications of the growth in trade. A spider diagram is shown below, in which the first arrow shows the areas of impact. Second stage arrows then show how the analysis may be developed.

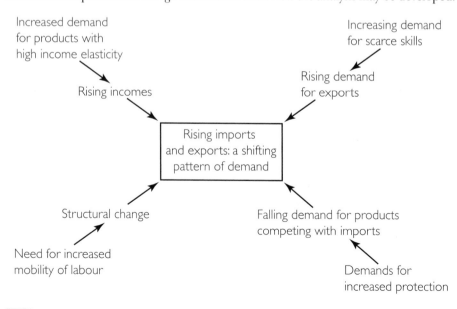

The first diagram defines the theory and the real world factors which relate to the general theme. Next, candidates can look at a more specific question, organising their thoughts in a more focussed way. This could be helped by creating a hierarchy of ideas like the one shown in the second diagram. Final completion of the process involves looking at how the different elements relate to each other. This is also shown in the second figure. The dotted lines represent connections. For example, you may be asked to examine the impact of reducing trade barriers on the EU as a whole and the UK in particular.

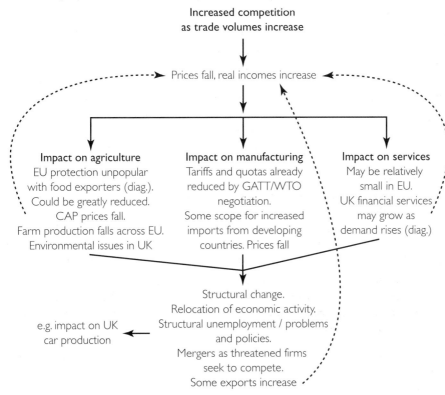

Having looked carefully at these diagrams relating to international trade, try out the other themes listed below. We recommend completing one per day in the lead-up to a synoptic exam.

Further themes for synoptic assessment thought maps

1 Market failure and government intervention
2 How fiscal and monetary policy are used
3 The impact of the UK joining the Euro
4 The factors which affect competitiveness
5 The impact of the single market on firms and individuals
6 The consequences of rapid growth
7 How inflation and unemployment have changed over time
8 The likely consequences of recession
9 The role of supply side policies.

EXAMINERS' TERMS

INTRODUCTION

The following entries should help explain what examiners mean by the words they use in exam questions. It is important to remember, though, that the words are only half the story. The other key factor is the mark allocation. This not only gives an indication of the length of answer required, but also the depth. The higher the mark allocation, the more likely it is that the examiner is looking for the skills of analysis and, especially, evaluation – and the more likely that the exam question will be marked on the basis of levels of response.

Account for: provide reasons for, exploring the causes.

Analyse: to break a topic down into its component parts. This should help to identify the causes and effects of the issue and to explain the process whereby the causes bring about the effects. This encourages more depth of study. It implies a writing style that uses continuous prose in fully developed paragraphs. Bear in mind the word 'why?' when analysing. Do not ignore opportunities to use diagrams which help to explain what happens.

Assess: weigh up and thereby *evaluate* two or more options or arguments.

Assumptions: (see *state your assumptions*)

Comment: draw conclusions from the evidence, possibly in the form of a stated opinion. For example, in the first part of a question you might be required to *analyse* the causes of a specific instance of market failure; part b) might ask you to comment on the likely consequences. You might reach a conclusion about the likelihood of under-consumption, then state your opinion about the probable loss of welfare involved. It may be helpful to comment upon any further information needed.

Consider: another term inviting you to weigh up options or arguments in the form of continuous paragraphs of writing.

Compare: explore the similarities and the differences in two situations.

Critically analyse means to look in depth at an issue (*analyse*) from the perspective of a critic. In other words the examiner is encouraging you not to take the issue at face value; instead you should be questioning the assumptions or evidence involved. However, it is important to remember that film 'critics' may write a favourable review. You, too, should look at the strengths as well as the weaknesses involved.

Debate: put both sides of the case as forcefully as you can, then criticise each side from the perspective of the other. Take, for example, the essay title 'Debate the issue of whether the UK should join EMU'. You should put forward the views both for and against, then tackle the arguments of those in favour from the point of view of opponents (and vice versa). You may decide, in the end, to 'vote' or abstain, as in a real debate.

Decide which: make a choice between the options, supported by your reasoning.

Define: explain the meaning of the term as precisely as you can; giving an example can help, but is not a substitute for explanation.

Discuss: put forward both sides of a case before coming to a conclusion. Discussion would require continuous writing and would be likely to be marked on a levels of response basis, with a high proportion of marks awarded for evaluation.

Discuss critically: a little different from '*discuss*', though the examiner appears to be hinting that there may be a reason to be sceptical of the theory or question under discussion. Therefore you should look carefully for weaknesses in the logic.

Distinguish between: (as in 'distinguish between revenue and profit'). Here, you should explain each of the two terms and then look for the point of difference between them: 'the difference is that costs have been deducted from revenue to find profit'.

Evaluate: this vital term means weighing up evidence in order to reach a judgement. In the context of an essay, you will have to present that evidence (explaining the significance of each part of it) before reaching a conclusion. As the term invites your judgement, do be willing to state your opinion within the conclusion, e.g. 'In my view ...'. It can be helpful to keep in mind the phrase 'to what extent ...?'.

Examine means to look in detail at the argument, evidence or theory presented. It requires continuous writing and should be rounded off with a conclusion.

Explain: expand upon in order to show your understanding of the term or theory being tested. The depth of explanation required will be indicated by the mark allocation. Giving a well-chosen example will often gain a mark.

Give: this means list, as in 'Give two possible reasons for reducing interest rates.' There is no requirement to explain the points you make.

How might: this phrase suggests a need to explain a process, as in 'How might a firm choose between two investment options?' You must explain the process with care, then consider the mark allocation before deciding whether a conclusion is required. If five marks are available, no conclusion would be necessary; with 25 marks, however, you would be wise to evaluate your answer.

Identify: to name one or more examples of the topic being examined. Usually this would require no more than a list, with one mark awarded per point made.

Justify your answer: present an argument in favour of the views you are expressing, for example: 'Should the Post Office be privatised? Justify your answer.' Although the question appears to be expecting a yes or no at the outset, it is better to wait until the end to state your opinion, because you will have given the matter enough thought to be able to justify your decision.

Levels of response: a way of marking answers based upon different academic skills rather than the quantity of knowledge shown. This is the way in which most high-mark questions are examined. If 10 marks are available for 'Explain the impact of higher interest rates upon firms', a levels of response marking scheme would put a ceiling on the number of marks available for listing points. Therefore you are better off writing a full explanation of two or three points.

List: briefly state (same as *give*).

Mark allocation: the number of marks on offer for each part of a question.

Outline: provide a description of an event, theory or method. The length and the level of detail will be governed by the mark allocation.

Show your workings: this phrase is used often with numerical questions, but should never be ignored. In the pressure of the exam room, almost every candidate will slip up somewhere in a complex calculation. If there are 10 marks on offer for the answer '£24 800', the candidate who gives the answer '£248 000' with no workings will get 0, while a candidate with the same answer will get 9 marks if the workings show where the single slip was made. The secret with numerical questions is not to get 10 out of 10 one time and 0 the next. It is better to get 8 or 9 marks every time.

Sketch a diagram: this suggests a quick drawing on the ordinary exam writing paper. To convey any meaning, the sketch will need properly labelled axes and lines and a clear title. Where possible the diagram should be drawn in a way which matches precisely the points being made. For example if in the situation being described, demand is inelastic, the line should have a steep slope.

State: means the same as *give*.

State and explain: this should be tackled exactly in this way, i.e. *give* a reason (in perhaps 4–8 words) then explain it (in perhaps 4–8 lines).

State your assumptions: distinguish clearly between the changes you are analysing and other possible changes which might affect the situation. For example, if you are explaining the effect on exports of the use of new technologies and you are assuming that exchange rates will stay the same, say so.

Suggest means to put forward an idea. If few marks are allocated, this might require no more than a list of points. The word is used more commonly, though, in the context of higher-mark case study or essay questions. In this case it would require a full explanation and justification for the suggestions made.

To what extent: this commonly used examining phrase requires you to reach a judgement about the degree to which a statement, theory or evidence is true. It is likely that the levels of response marking scheme will reward evaluation especially heavily. So focus on relatively few themes, deal with each in depth and then make a judgement about 'to what extent ...'.

What do you understand by? (or **What is meant by?**): explain the meaning of the term or phrase given. An example may be helpful, but is not a substitute for explanation.

Why might: this phrase invites you to suggest possible explanations for why a firm or individual may have chosen a course of action. Any answer will be accepted as long as it is not too far-fetched; but remember that examiners want to reward your economics understanding, so try to draw from relevant theories.

Newcastle-under-Lyme College
Staffordshire